Where Credit Is Due

Bringing Equity to Credit and Housing after the Market Meltdown

Edited by
Christy Rogers and
john a. powell

UNIVERSITY PRESS OF AMERICA, ® INC.
Lanham • Boulder • New York • Toronto • Plymouth, UK

**Copyright © 2013 by
University Press of America,® Inc.**
4501 Forbes Boulevard
Suite 200
Lanham, Maryland 20706
UPA Acquisitions Department (301) 459-3366

10 Thornbury Road
Plymouth PL6 7PP
United Kingdom

Library of Congress Control Number: 2011929794
ISBN: 978-0-7618-5606-1 (paperback : alk. paper)
eISBN: 978-0-7618-5607-8

Contents

Acknowledgments

The work published in this book was made possible through the generous support of the W.K. Kellogg Foundation.

Chapter 3, *Subprime Lending, Foreclosure and Race: An Introduction to the Role of Securitization in Residential Mortgage Finance*, is reprinted with permission of the *Cardozo Law Review*, where an original version of this article originally appeared in April of 2007: Christopher L. Peterson, *Predatory Structured Finance*, 28 Cardozo Law Review 2185 (2007).

Chapter 14, *Give Credit Where Credit Is Due: Overhauling the CRA*, appears with acknowledgment of the generous support from the Ford Foundation and the Furman Center for Real Estate and Urban Policy at NYU, which has made this article and Mark Willis's ongoing work on CRA possible. (The opinions expressed in this chapter are Willis's own.)

Chapter 16, *The Housing and Credit Crisis Revisited: Looking Back and Moving Forward,* is reprinted with permission of *Cleveland State Law Review*, where an original version of the article appeared in 2009: john powell and Jason Reece, *The Future of Fair Housing and Fair Credit: From Crisis to Opportunity*, Cleveland State Law Review, Volume 57, Number 2 (2009).

Introduction

Gail C. Christopher, DN

Structural racism can be viewed as a system of hierarchy that dispenses opportunity in inequitable ways, assuring privilege and power for whites and disadvantage and limitation for people of color. There is, perhaps, no more powerful illustration of contemporary structural racism than the exponential growth of unfair and unequal credit and lending practices that served as kindling for what became the fire—the subprime mortgage crisis. But, like most consequences of structural racism in America today, the subprime mortgage crisis and its devastating effects on global and local economies are seldom, if ever, framed as manifestations of structural racism. This book is a seminal contribution because it does offer this critically-needed analysis. It has the potential to help move readers and policy makers beyond denial of the multifaceted, racially-based drivers of financial practices, policies and our economy.

Denial can be viewed as a refusal or inability to face a painful reality. The unfinished business of racial stratification and subsequent racialization of American society is a painful reality that our nation seems unable to face. Overcoming denial, from a psychological perspective, requires movement through multiple phases of understanding. The first phase is simple—awareness and acceptance of fact. The next phases are not as straightforward. We must accept the facts, and then examine consequences and their implications. Ultimately, we must experience the feelings that drive choices and patterns on conscious and unconscious levels. The facts are clear about disproportionate targeting, impact and consequences of the subprime mortgage crisis in communities of color. Borrowers of color were more than 30 percent more likely to receive a higher-rate loan than white borrowers, even after accounting for differences in credit risk. A disproportionately high number of foreclosures caused families of color with children to be evicted.

In addition to helping readers and policy makers move beyond the facts of the racialized subprime mortgage crisis, this thorough analysis will enable readers to move through the subsequent two phases of the denial continuum. The chapters in this book address the consequences and implications of the racialized subprime mortgage travesty. Unfair practices, incentives, predatory lending patterns and exploitation were fertilized by historically entrenched exclusionary policies. They took root and grew unimpeded in racially segregated, under-resourced neighborhoods across this nation. Dwindling family assets and reversals in fragile emergent opportunity structures for social and economic progress are among the painful consequences. But as any effective therapist knows, you can move through denial's hallmark phases—facts, consequences, and implications—and still not be motivated to change. America has been stuck in this "place" for far too long. The last stage of denial is to confront the feelings that actually mobilize or paralyze. Reading these brilliantly researched and eloquently written chapters will move readers of conscience and good will to confront feelings of anger, shock, and frustration. Hopefully readers will be moved to a state of determination to undo these persistent dynamics of racialized economic policy. Failure to do so presents a threat to the future of this entire nation. Fear of the worst economic outcomes might motivate the will to change. Better yet, love and caring for the children who will bear the burden of this financial crisis for generations to come could inspire needed corrective action. In just a few short years, by 2013, most of the children in the United States will be children of color.

The mission of the W.K. Kellogg Foundation is to support children, families, and communities as they strengthen and create conditions that propel vulnerable children to achieve success as individuals and as contributors to the larger community and society. Persistent residential segregation by race and the consequences of limited education, employment, health and life opportunities have been exacerbated by the subprime mortgage crisis. Conditions for vulnerable children are appreciably worse now than before this economic meltdown. Addressing the racialized nuances of the subprime mortgage crisis is a prerequisite to improve outcomes for vulnerable children in this country. *Where Credit is Due: Bringing Equity to Credit and Housing After the Market Meltdown* is a timely and critically needed resource for this important work.

Chapter One

Overview

Christy Rogers

Many of us are still reeling from the fallout of the subprime lending and fore-closure debacle, and the resulting global economic instability. Whether we, or someone we cared about, lost a home, watched retirement savings sink, suffered from state and local budget cuts, or lost a job, the foreclosure crisis and the recession have in some way touched us all. Unfortunately, as we turn to recovery from the foreclosure crisis and the recession, some important triggers of—and lessons from—the crisis are being lost. These triggers include a history of racial discrimination in lending, racial segregation in housing, dual (i.e. separate and unequal) credit markets, and a loss of consumer protections. And the lessons we are learning from the crisis can be misleading if we do not consider the incentives for subprime lending and the ultimate outcomes of the crisis. Rather than a failed attempt at homeownership by "bad borrowers," the facts show that unregulated mortgage brokers often targeted low-income borrowers in communities of color with unsustainable loans, largely to attract bonuses and feed a securitization regime so poorly understood and regulated that it ultimately destabilized the global economy.

Broadly speaking, the federal response has largely triaged the economic damage wrought by the crisis without yet addressing its underlying causes. Unfortunately, as University of California-Riverside economist Gary Dymski notes, the debate among economists on the subprime lending crisis has "largely occurred with virtually no attention to racial discrimination and redlining, nor to predatory lending." It is therefore unsurprising, albeit disappointing, that the debate around economic stabilization and recovery has the same blind spots. "In an ironic twist," Dymski writes within these pages (Chapter 2), "it is as if the subprime crisis itself . . . has disappeared while hiding in plain sight."[1] Policy resources have focused on salvaging the existing monopolistic banking

1

landscape, while resources to extend credit to underserved populations and stabilize neighborhoods have been much smaller in scope.

From our perspective, the federal lack of focus on a fundamental cause of the crisis—predatory or unsustainable credit "alternatives" and the racially and geographically demarcated lines along which they are distributed—is an analytic and strategic mistake. The Financial Crisis Inquiry Commission is considering twenty-two areas of interest, not one of which is the history of racial segregation in credit markets, redlining, predatory lending targeted to communities of color, or the like.[2]

Meanwhile, entire neighborhoods and even entire communities, like post-Big 3 Detroit, Michigan, and post-Katrina New Orleans, Louisiana, stand on the edge of a complete unraveling of homeownership and asset-building opportunity, of continuing economic marginalization and deterioration, and erosion of fair housing opportunities. Extraordinary people are coming together in these communities to dream of a new future and a new way of working, saving, borrowing, and supporting collaborative and participatory neighborhood planning. However, they feel undercut by the lack of federal enforcement of existing fair housing and fair credit laws, the saturation and complexity of predatory financial tools, and the lack or limited scale of alternative financial institutions such as mission-driven credit unions.

In the fall of 2007, the Kirwan Institute launched a comprehensive research initiative on the emerging subprime lending and foreclosure crisis and its impact on communities of color across the nation. In October 2008, a month after the failure of Lehman Brothers, Kirwan held a national conference to explore the roots of the crisis and to better arm advocates and policymakers with effective, strategic responses. In early 2009, we proposed a follow-up initiative that deepened our understanding of the crisis and focused on identifying key federal reforms and advocacy needs. We also wanted to better understand how the foreclosure and credit crisis was unfolding across the country, and how communities were responding. Thanks to a timely grant from the W.K. Kellogg Foundation, we pursued this work in the latter half of 2009. Our research and policy initiative included conversations with twenty-five diverse advisory board members, fourteen in-depth commissioned works and eleven short thought pieces by leading academics and practitioners, and an in-person look at the fair housing and fair credit landscape in distinctly different regions across the country. *Where Credit is Due: Bringing Equity to Credit and Housing After the Market Meltdown,* a collection of the longer commissioned works, provides a helpful framework for those challenged with addressing today's housing and credit markets in the wake of the subprime lending crisis, layered with a racial equity lens.

SUMMARY FINDINGS AND RECOMMENDATIONS

First, regional contexts and local relationships matter. A major focus of our initiative was to better understand the local consequences of the subprime lending and foreclosure crisis, the prospects for fair housing and fair credit in different markets across the United States, and their implications for federal policy.

Several convenings with advocacy partners revealed that the delivery of fair credit and fair housing, even in this age of globalization (and in a world of de-personalized, web-based services), is often about local relationships, particular places, and their histories. People at every meeting noted distrust, racism, shameful histories of exclusion, and the withdrawal of relationship banking as negatively affecting mainstream financial inclusion. People who use alternative financial services were often driven to them by immediate need and convenience, coupled with the historical memory of unfair treatment, inflexibility and remoteness of mainstream financial institutions. Further, each region will have different paths to fair credit and fair housing, dependent on local political will, the strength of the local economy, the local presence (or lack of) fair housing and fair credit choices, the presence and cooperation of diverse advocacy groups, and the face-to-face relationships that characterize (or used to characterize) relationship banking and the housing search.

While communities' priorities for achieving fair credit differed, what the convenings did have in common was the expression of a readiness to make radical change. People were ready to try something truly new and aggressive— from demanding a more inclusive community development process (Seattle, Washington), to challenging the lack of fair housing support and protection from federal agencies (Austin, Texas), to alternative banking and credit institutions (everywhere), to alternative homeownership models (Detroit, Michigan). Unfortunately, opportunities to act were limited by local organizations' thin resources.

Recommendations:

- Recognize that the paths to fair credit and fair housing will differ according to regional context and local history. Take local impediments to fair housing and fair credit—racially discriminatory history, proliferation of predatory credit, resistance to mainstream institutions—seriously.
- Understand the differences among local economies, community infrastructures, and marginalized populations.
- Assist local and regional fair housing and community reinvestment activists in their efforts to organize, mobilize, and lobby.

- Promote local, multi-partner pilot projects that are mission-driven to affirmatively promote fair credit (like the National League of Cities' "Bank On Cities" initiative).
- Connect fair housing, fair lending, community reinvestment, civil rights and other advocacy groups (financial reform, faith-based, labor, etc.) at the national, state, and local levels to promote *comprehensive* consumer protection, fair credit and fair housing reform. Reverse the "silo" approach. We found that cross-sector connection was most needed at the state and local levels.

Second, local efforts should be supported by a federal platform of consumer protections, and a federal commitment to affirmatively promote fair credit and fair housing for all our citizens. Each convening, while reflecting local priorities, resources, resistance points, and targets, demonstrated that we have suffered a systemic failure. This failure is reflected by a lack of meaningful credit and neighborhood choices for people of color; a basic lack of jobs, income, and wealth for marginalized people and communities; and a lack of consumer protections. As dedicated as they are, local groups cannot go at it alone, particularly when the deck is stacked against them.

Federal agencies must step up enforcement of existing fair credit, fair lending, and fair housing laws and they must provide robust consumer protection and education. Federal agencies must also do their part to affirmatively further fair housing through all their relevant programs and entities, encouraging the affirmative provision of sustainable credit where predatory alternatives predominate. People should be able to make and implement meaningful choices regarding fair financial options and fair housing. For this to happen, they must have a range of options, and only an *affirmative commitment* to fair housing and fair credit will make these options materialize. This affirmative duty should be measurable—goals should be set, data should be assessed, and policies that are not working should be corrected.

Recommendations:

- Promote regulatory reform of the product, rather than the institution. For example: we should regulate mortgages, full stop; currently, we regulate some of the institutions that originate them, but not others.
- Rework and "re-brand" the Community Reinvestment Act (CRA) into an updated, comprehensive tool to promote the provision of sustainable credit products to the people and neighborhoods that most need them.
- Recognize and enforce the duty to affirmatively further fair housing in relevant federal agencies and programs including stimulus programs, the U.S.

Department of Housing and Urban Development (HUD), the successors to Fannie Mae and Freddie Mac, and community development and foreclosure mitigation programs.

- Press for better and more comprehensive data (race, gender, and geography) for all federal spending programs, including stimulus funding. Expand the Home Mortgage Disclosure Act (HMDA) data reporting requirements to include loan term information, such as borrower interest rates, credit scores, loan reset periods, balloon payments, Adjustable Rate Mortgage (ARM) margins and indices, and loan product underwriting.
- Enact a comprehensive, nationwide plan to protect renters from foreclosure.

Third, we must compellingly communicate what a fair and just twenty-first century economic system looks like, and what kind of financial system can support it, as Manuel Pastor, Rhonda Ortiz, and Vanessa Carter explain in Chapter 15, "Breaking the Bank/(Re)Making the Bank." We must not focus solely on how to "fix" the mortgage system or salvage individual homes (although mortgage lending regulation and foreclosure relief is important), but also focus on the wider set of conditions that allowed for systemic failure. The subprime lending and foreclosure fiasco (and the concomitant worldwide economic volatility) is a manifestation of global inequality and unfair access to banking and financial services, not an isolated anomaly or the fault of a handful of fraudulent lenders and borrowers. As Pastor, Ortiz and Carter write:

> Our point is simple. While we do need a new policy package, such advocacy also needs to be embedded in a broader social movement for financial justice. The focus should not simply be on foreclosure relief, but on a new financial frame that has at its heart the restoration of opportunity for all.

Unfortunately, social justice advocates often lack the data we need, lose the messaging war, and fail to connect advocates across domains to work together for change. For example, financial reform was sometimes erroneously framed as separate from (and even in competition with) political advocacy around jobs, education, and health care, rather than as a related outcome of unfair access to opportunity. In addition, the crisis has complex roots and disengaging terminology ("collateral debt obligations," "cram-down," etc.), which can be difficult to connect to everyday, on-the-ground realities.

Recommendations:

- Contribute to a national communications effort around the importance of adequate consumer protections against financial predation, the provision of

sustainable financial alternatives, and the danger of excluding a majority of American workers from a solid financial future.
• Explore the potential for fundamental changes to regulation and financial incentives. Current incentives are perverse—they promote credit products inherently more likely to fail or result in punitive fees to those least able to manage them.
• Support the national networks of fair housing, community reinvestment, fair lending and financial reform movements to increase their advocacy effectiveness. Promote connections among these groups as well.

Unfortunately, this crisis is not new, nor is it over. People of color have been excluded from wealth-building opportunities via homeownership continuously throughout our history: First, from the outright denial of credit and residential racial discrimination of the 1930s to the 1960s; second, from the federally-sponsored urban renewal programs of the 1960s and 1970s that disrupted and scattered urban minority residents and businesses; and lastly, from the subprime lending and foreclosure crisis of the 2000s that has cost communities of color up to a quarter of a trillion dollars in home equity. Loan modification disparities may be the aftershock of the subprime earthquake, further entrenching the disparate loss of home ownership and equity-building opportunities for people of color. Policies must be re-structured to encourage healthy, sustainable and fair credit and housing markets, and to better protect consumers.

HOW DID WE GET HERE? A BRIEF HISTORY OF THE SUBPRIME LENDING AND FORECLOSURE CRISIS

The need to analyze and act at the global, national, and local scales is evidenced by the macro-economic transformations of finance and banking, the growth of inequality, US deregulation and lack of consumer protections, and the local landscapes of segregation and inequality that resulted in separate and unequal credit markets. This section briefly summarizes each of these developments, drawing largely on our previous research on the roots of the crisis and a commissioned work for this initiative by Gary Dymski, "Understanding the Subprime Crisis: Institutional Evolution and Theoretical Views."

The Landscape of Inequality

Over half a century ago, a vast expansion of homeownership, led by New Deal legislation, was limited largely to all-white neighborhoods in suburban, new housing stock—underwriting criteria devalued or refused to insure integrated, minority, or old housing stock neighborhoods.[3] These racially discriminatory federal guidelines were then absorbed into private market practices. Refusing to extend credit to low-income communities of color became known as "redlining" due to the red lines drawn on property maps that indicated "hazardous" (no loan) areas. Although *de jure* racial segregation in lending is no longer legal, the patterns and practices of discrimination in housing markets have persisted into the twenty-first century.[4] With little residential or commercial lending from mainstream banking institutions for decades, isolated communities of color have suffered from high-cost credit institutions that have little competition: payday lenders, rent-to-own, check cashing, and most recently, subprime home loans. Without competitive credit institutions, families lack information about options, making them primary targets for subprime lending.

Present-day subprime mortgage brokers targeted these communities not out of personal racial animosity, but because these neighborhoods were starved of prime credit entirely, or because families were "equity rich but cash poor," with paid-off homes but unmet credit needs (such as college tuition or medical expenses), a condition that drove subprime refinancing growth.[5] Termed "reverse redlining," the targeting of credit-starved neighborhoods is and was possible because prior redlining had isolated these communities from mainstream banking and lending. Rick Cohen reports in Chapter 4 that in Newark, New Jersey's North Ward and Ironbound neighborhoods, "Immigrant groups were targeted by mortgage brokers peddling high cost mortgages to families that could have qualified for conventional financing." Because less than half of immigrants use formal banking institutions, they are easy targets for high-cost mortgage products:

> The payday lenders, pawn shops, and rent-to-own stores that specialize in immigrant neighborhoods do not help customers build credit histories and generally escape the oversight and regulation of consumer regulatory entities, or, as weak as the protection might be, the Community Reinvestment Act scrutiny by the Comptroller of the Currency or state banking departments of conventional bank lenders.

Federal Reserve studies in 2004, 2005 and 2006 found disparities in the rate that minorities (and those living in neighborhoods with significant minority concentrations) received subprime loans.[6] Subprime loans had a distinct geography even down to specific loan terms, such as prepayment penalties. Rural and minority neighborhoods were more likely to receive prepayment penalties, even after controlling for a set of underwriting factors.[7] This geography of exploitation may partly explain why borrowers of color were more than 30%

more likely to receive a higher-rate loan than white borrowers, even after accounting for differences in risk.[8] In Chapter 5, "Subprime Lending, Mortgage Foreclosures and Race: How Far Have We Come and How Far Have We To Go?" The Reinvestment Fund found that neighborhoods in Philadelphia, Pennsylvania, and Baltimore, Maryland, which had the greatest concentrations of people of color, received the highest percentages of subprime loans.[9]

GLOBALIZATION, BANKING AND FINANCE INNOVATION, AND DEREGULATION

Globally, the worldwide appetite for securitized debt, including mortgage debt, fed the mortgage crisis. Securitization is the process by which public and private agencies buy home mortgages, deposit large amounts of them in pools, and then sell participation in the pools to investors on Wall Street. A securitized mortgage note is actually held by a special purpose vehicle (SPV), a business entity with the sole purpose of holding the pool of mortgages. The SPV hires a servicer to collect and distribute payments of principal and interest. Securitization provided a way for capital markets to finance—and capture some of the profits from—large-scale mortgage lending. Modern securitization began in 1970, with the issuance of the first publicly traded mortgage backed security by the Government National Mortgage Association (Ginnie Mae). In Chapter 3, "Subprime Lending, Foreclosure and Race: An Introduction to the Role of Securitization in Residential Mortgage Finance," legal scholar and securitization expert Chris Peterson observes that:

> With these new pass-through investment vehicles, investors could hold a share of large (and diversified) numbers of mortgages insured by the government in the case of Ginnie Mae, or guaranteed by the large stable government sponsored enterprises (GSEs) in the case of Freddie Mac and Fannie Mae (who also began securitizing shortly thereafter). Because the agencies now guaranteed the principal and interest income of their securities even when mortgagors defaulted, investors saw the securities as a low-risk investment even without the assurances of a rating organization, such as Standard and Poor's or Moody's.

The private sector's ability to securitize separately from GSEs grew after 1975, when rating organizations began rating the securities. Subprime lending and securitization became popular quickly on Wall Street, and capital flowed heavily into the securitized mortgage markets. Loans were packaged and sold as quickly as they were originated, and new loans were secured with funding from previous sales.

This system required standardizing mortgage underwriting and origination on a large scale (which resulted in automated underwriting and the parallel decline of relationship banking), and the institutional underwriting/guaranteeing of credit debt. As Dymski notes, soaring subprime lending took place at a time of global financial market integration and US financial and economic dominance: "The transition from the old housing-finance system to the new was accomplished at a time when the United States was both the principal global source of reserve currency and a preferred safe haven. In addition, it occurred while the United States had huge current-account deficits, which have necessitated systematic capital-account inflows" (Dymski, 7).

The critical shift that securitization facilitated was from lenders issuing mortgages in order to hold them to maturity, to lenders (or more likely, unregulated brokers) issuing mortgages in order to sell them to investors or underwriters in the secondary mortgage market (an "originate and distribute" model). With the fees raised from the sale, the lenders or brokers would issue new mortgages, and on and on. Standardization and a deep secondary market also allowed smaller non-bank, non-thrift lenders to originate mortgage debt (Dymski, 7).

Unfortunately, these new lenders, including independent mortgage brokers, were not subject to the same regulations and oversight as banks were, such as complying with the Community Reinvestment Act. Despite erroneous claims that CRA fostered ill-advised lending, in the peak years of the housing bubble (2005 and 2006), only 6% of subprime loans were extended by CRA-covered lenders in their communities to lower income borrowers or neighborhoods. In fact, the CRA helped banks develop expertise on extending sustainable non-traditional loans. As Mark Willis, former head of community development for JP Morgan Chase, reflects in "Give Credit Where Credit is Due: Overhauling the CRA:"

> CRA has helped banks better understand the needs of their communities and correct misperceptions as to market risks and opportunities. Products and services tailored to the needs of the community have emerged and banks have found ways to serve the communities in safe and sound ways. Another positive result was the establishment within many of the larger banks of dedicated units that became proficient at structuring complex, affordable-housing or community-economic-development deals involving multiple sources of subsidies and players."

Unfortunately, CRA loans were often "outcompeted" by the alternative products that emerged from standardization, modernization, and critically, changes in federal legislation. Three pieces of legislation are largely credited for setting the stage for a rise in subprime and predatory lending: The Depository Institutions Deregulation and Monetary Control Act of 1980 (DIDMCA),

The Alternative Mortgage Transaction Parity Act of 1982 (AMTPA), and the 1986 Tax Reform Act. DIDMCA effectively eliminated states' interest rate ceilings on home mortgages where the lender has a first lien. Two years after DIDMCA, the Alternative Mortgage Transaction Parity Act (AMTPA) was passed. AMTPA preempted state statutes that regulated alternative mortgage transactions, such as those with balloon payments, variable rates, and negative amortization. Subprime lending did not grow significantly, however, until after the Tax Reform Act of 1986 (TRA86). Under TRA86, taxpayers could no longer deduct interest from consumer loans, but could deduct interest on loans secured by the taxpayer's principal (and one other) residence.

Under these conditions, subprime lending grew 900% from 1993–1999, while other mortgage lending activity actually declined (Dymski, 12, citing HUD 2000). Mortgage brokers themselves created some of the "demand" for subprime mortgages—a *Wall Street Journal* article in 2007 reported that in 2005, 55% of people with subprime mortgages had credit scores high enough to qualify for conventional loans; in 2006, this figure rose to 61% (Dymski, 16). Meanwhile, no federal regulatory agency was explicitly tasked with consumer protection as a mandate, and those that could have intervened in systemic risky behavior failed to do so.

Income and Wealth Polarization and the Banking Response

The growth of unfair and unequal credit grew up alongside not only the banking and finance modernization of the late 20th century, but a four-decade widening of income and wealth inequality[10] that has created a relatively small group of extremely affluent people who are offered the best and most robust financial services, and a huge (and growing) group of unbanked and underbanked families with intermittent or low-income jobs and few assets. In short, many more people in the United States saw their incomes stagnating or declining while costs continued to rise, and their demands for credit grew. In fact, "[l]ending to lower-income customers has expanded faster than lending to middle- and upper-income customers" (Dymski, 14). Dymski reviewed data from Survey of Consumer Finances and found that low-income households have had surging levels of debt without proportionate increases in asset levels from 1992–2004. This pattern has racialized contours: more than half of all African American households and over four in ten Latino households are either unbanked or underbanked (Dymski, 11, citing FDIC December 2009 study). These are the primary clients for alternative services, such as check cashing, money orders, money remittances, and payday loans. People use payday lending in part to get away from insufficient fund fees at big banks and to avoid high late fees for rent, credit card, and utility payments

(Dymski, 13, citing Blair 2005). The majority of payday loan customers are banked (payday clients must have a checking account), but earning under $50,000; African Americans and military families are overrepresented.

These families are increasingly unable to meet expensive education, health care, and housing costs, and thus are increasingly in need of credit. When we led a discussion in Detroit around the future of fair housing and fair credit, the work group identified *unemployment* as the major barrier to sustainable credit, touching on the wider structural barriers to opportunity, such as a basic lack of employment opportunities and income. In fact, the FDIC's recent study on unbanked and underbanked[11] households reported that "[n]ot having enough money to feel they need an account is the most common reason why unbanked households are not participating in the mainstream financial system."[12] The study also reveals that people of color are far more likely to be unbanked and underbanked: for example, African Americans are seven times more likely to be unbanked than whites.[13]

The new model that banks have developed to serve lower-income and lower-wealth customers depends largely on fees. Mortgage companies first shifted from interest- to fee-based income by originating loans to sell, not hold; banks then followed suit with other products (Dymski, 8). Much media and congressional attention was focused on debit and credit card fees. A little-covered but enormous global profit maker for non-bank institutions is the remittance market. Remittances (funds that workers send back to their families in their country of origin) are the largest interactions between immigrants and the financial sector, yet most of the transactions are through non-bank entities that charge high fees. In any instance, the shift to a fee structure actually *worsens* the financial outlook for most families. From the subprime mortgage prepayment penalties to credit card fees to insufficient funds fees to remittance fees, the individuals shouldering the punitive fees are those least able to bear the burden.

WHERE ARE WE NOW? THE VIEW FROM THE GROUND

A major focus of our research and policy advocacy initiative was to better understand the local consequences of the subprime lending and foreclosure crisis and the prospects for fair housing and fair credit in different markets across the United States, and their implications for federal policy. We commissioned several authors to explore local manifestations of the crisis, and held advocacy convenings around the country to better understand the different regional perspectives on the barriers and solutions to fair credit and fair housing in the wake of the crisis.

In his commissioned work, Mark Ireland documents the threat to largely unprotected renters in Minneapolis, Minnesota who must find new homes and new schools for their children when they face eviction from landlord foreclosure. Ireland's original research showed that rental properties comprised 61% of all the foreclosures that occurred in North Minneapolis in 2006–2007; Ireland also found that households with children were disproportionately affected. Almost 40% of foreclosed addresses had children in the Minneapolis public schools, and 60% of the school children were African American. Looking at lending patterns, Ireland found that subprime lenders did a disproportionate amount of lending in North Minneapolis and that prime lenders did disproportionately little lending. While the latter finding may seem obvious, it in fact points to the lack of choices for residents in these neighborhoods and the importance of an affirmative extension of sustainable credit options into neighborhoods currently overrun with non-prime and often predatory options. Looking at the status of the properties post-foreclosure, Ireland made alarming findings: 83% of the foreclosed properties had, on average, eight 911 calls post-Sheriff's Sale. A vast majority of the calls occurred when the property was under control of either the mortgage loan servicing company or the person who bought the property from the servicing company. Clearly, the foreclosed properties pose a significant safety hazard to the neighborhood. Ireland concludes with a call for a comprehensive, nationwide plan to protect renters facing foreclosure.

Hannah Thomas' work in Chapter 9 considers the consequences of foreclosure to individuals and families, starting with the immediate loss of the home and the stress associated with home loss, moving beyond that into "asset stripping" or raiding cash savings and retirement accounts to try to stay in the home. (See Thomas, "An Ethnographic View of Impact: Asset Stripping for People of Color.") Thomas found that foreclosure usually began with some combination of unaffordable mortgage, *plus* loss of a job, divorce, or other economic hardship. That is, people were keeping current with payments until some sort of financial shock. Usually the subsequent asset stripping resulted in a draining of savings, but only temporarily held off foreclosure (or sale of the property at a loss). In her sample, 47% of homeowners depleted their 401Ks; the vast majority depleted their savings to try and save the home. Thomas writes that many black and Hispanic families were in fact now worse off than if they had not tried for homeownership with subprime loans. Foreclosure results in a negative impact on credit scores (which can, in turn, impact insurance rates, the ability to rent an apartment or get a new loan, and even get a job), the need to move and change kids' schools, and stress. Having drained their own personal savings, retirement funds, or children's college funds to try and salvage the home—only to have to sell at a loss or go into foreclosure—people are now unable to finance their own retirement, their kids' college expenses, etc. As Thomas writes, this results in a negatively impacted *future*—a net loss for social mobility:

> These stories represent an unknown, but likely important percentage of homeowners who are currently in foreclosure in Boston's communities of color. They represent families who were slowly working towards middle-class status—college education for themselves with 401K plans, college aspirations for their children, and growing levels of homeownership. The reality is that as this foreclosure crisis worsens, more of these families who had been gaining some social mobility will be losing their financial footing, sliding back into a financially precarious situation.

Thomas suggests that public policy must incentivize prime mortgage originators to extend credit to communities of color, and address the lack of trust that people have with mainstream banks. She also suggests that mortgage originators take into account *asset vulnerability* of borrowers, and that we think of ways to collectivize risk, such as community resource pools that people can draw on when they encounter financial emergencies.

In Chapter 6, "Subprime Lending in the City of Cleveland and Cuyahoga County," Jeff Dillman argues that the underlying assumptions driving policy decisions over the last thirty years is that the market does a better job than government on evaluating risk, offering alternative products, and regulating itself. As the subprime lending crisis has shown, the market did a poor job on all fronts. In fact, Dillman points out that the incentives in the subprime market were perverse: people less likely to be able to sustain a loan were given products inherently more likely to default. Further, the premiums paid to unregulated brokers were based on both interest rates (which incentivized brokers to put people into higher rates than they qualified for) and loan principal (which incentivized brokers to encourage financing up to 100% of the home loan and/or financing other loans like credit card balances into the home loan), making the mortgage product even more risky. Lastly, the fact that the loans were sold or securitized immediately after origination decreased any investment the mortgage originator had in the sustainability of the loan. In a revealing examination of the data, Dillman showed that in Cleveland, Ohio, increased subprime lending existed alongside a continued disparity in denial rates (access to credit) and high-cost loans (terms of credit). In a similar study that looked at metropolitan areas across the United States, Wyly et. al. found that those places with the highest loan denial rate had the highest shares of high-cost subprime lending (Wyly et. al. 2008: 9). The authors concluded that subprime credit does not actually reduce the problems of unequal denial and exclusion; it in fact exists alongside continuing market segregation (Wyly et. al. 2008: 20).[14]

Dillman's paper suggests that either we have to counter the narrative that defends the market as the best allocator of benefits and burdens, or we have to structure the market in such ways that we incentivize integration, accessible housing, and reduced discrimination—again, incentivizing the *affirmative* provision of fair credit and fair housing in a deregulated market.

In Chapter 8, Deyanira Del Rio shows how the current mortgage and foreclosure crises have affected immigrant communities, with a focus on New York City, New York. Her work identifies barriers to fair lending among immigrant communities and describes specific abusive practices leveled at low-income and undocumented immigrant homebuyers. Del Rio finds that non-citizen and undocumented immigrants face increasingly formidable obstacles to securing mortgages and housing on fair terms, including the recent decline in Individual Taxpayer Identification Number lending, the charged political debate around immigration reform, and the absence of explicit federal fair housing protections prohibiting discrimination based on citizenship or immigration status. Ensuring equitable access to mortgage and housing markets among immigrants—who represent the fastest-growing segment of the US population—will be critical to stabilizing the national housing market and ensuring future housing demand.

Del Rio recommends the following: amending fair housing and fair lending laws—including the federal Fair Housing Act—to explicitly prohibit discrimination against non-citizens and undocumented immigrants; pressing regulated financial institutions to provide equitable banking and credit access in immigrant communities; evaluating the extent to which banks meet the credit needs of immigrant communities in Community Reinvestment Act examinations; and examining banks and lenders for possible discrimination against foreign-born individuals.

Advocacy Convenings with Partners in Seattle, Austin, Detroit, and New Orleans

A series of four open convenings with partners in Seattle, Detroit, Austin, and New Orleans solicited residents' views on the impact of the crisis and the future of fair credit and fair housing in their community in order to prioritize top barriers and solutions to fair credit, neighborhood revitalization, and opportunity-based housing in the wake of the crisis. The geographic differences in the responses were striking.

In terms of barriers to sustainable credit, Seattle participants pointed to the profits banks stood to make on fee-based transactions and the aggressive marketing of financial products with confusing and complex "fine print." Austin residents foregrounded the lack of access to information and education on financial products, particularly for immigrants. Detroiters were overwhelmed by job loss in the face of the Big 3 automaker implosion and the lack of financial options for people. New Orleans residents noted that regional financial health was seasonal and dependent on a badly damaged tourist economy, and that people were steered to the seemingly ubiquitous subprime and high-cost products. Therefore, communities' priorities for achieving fair credit differed: Seattle prioritized legal enforcement of existing consumer protection laws; Austin wanted a "community intermediary" to better serve borrowers; Detroit looked to alternative models of credit mapped to their community needs; and New Orleans advocated for higher wages, especially in the tourism industry. The discussions revealed that the delivery of fair credit is about local relationships, particular places, and their histories—people at every meeting noted distrust, racism, shameful histories of exclusion, and the withdrawal of relationship banking as negatively affecting mainstream financial inclusion. Beyond issues of trust and access, people mentioned the punitive fee structure of mainstream banks. In other words, people who use alternative financial services were often driven to them by either lack of options or bad treatment from mainstream institutions.

The discussion around neighborhood revitalization tended to involve a shared set of concerns regarding the neighborhood planning process: specifically, who was involved in the process, how the city managed the process, how accountable elected and administrative officials were to residents, and how to address racism and exclusion. Interestingly, despite these shared concerns over process, the paths to inclusive revitalization differed in each place. Seattle called for stakeholder involvement early in the process, Austin prioritized an integrated vision for planning and development, Detroit pressed for resident education, and New Orleans voted for leadership change. Barriers to opportunity-based housing (affordable housing in high-opportunity neighborhoods) included traditional barriers to affirmatively furthering fair housing: discrimination and "NIMBY"-ism, a lack of inclusionary developments, and the high cost of development in high-opportunity neighborhoods. However, the cities again differed in their priorities for addressing the problem. Seattle called for more deliberate siting of affordable housing, Austin proposed aggressive legal action against the city and state for its failures to affirmatively further fair housing, Detroit called for an entirely new "toolbox" of financial and development strategies, and New Orleans advocated for a public education campaign around affordable housing and how it could benefit many of New Orleans' workers. The discussions around neighborhood revitalization and fair housing opportunity identified a set of similar challenges, but different paths to move ahead. Housing opportunity, like access to fair credit, is dependent on local planning and implementation.

While each convening reflected local priorities, resources, and resistance points, taken together they demonstrate that we have suffered a systemic failure. This failure is often reflected by a lack of meaningful credit and neighborhood choices, a basic lack of income, wealth, assets and savings, and a lack of consumer protections, particularly for marginalized communities and people of color. Each region will have different paths to fair credit and fair housing—indeed, the provision of fair housing and fair credit is still largely a *local* affair, dependent on local political will, the strength of the local economy, the presence and cooperation of diverse advocacy groups, and the face-to-face relationships that characterize (or used to characterize) relationship banking and the housing search. However, these local efforts must be supported by a federal platform of consumer protection and a commitment to affirmatively promote fair credit and fair housing for all our citizens.

Emerging from all convenings was a common readiness to make change. People are ready to try something new—from demanding a more inclusive community development process (Seattle), to challenging the lack of fair housing support and protection from federal agencies (Austin), to alternative banking and credit institutions (everywhere), to alternative homeownership models (Detroit).

Big-Picture Challenges and Solutions from Strategists in Washington, DC and Oakland, California

Two additional policy and advocacy strategy sessions, co-hosted with partner organizations in Washington, DC and Oakland, California provided a unique insight into the challenges shared by the fair lending, fair housing, community reinvestment, research, and civil rights advocacy groups on both coasts. These challenges are discussed below.

First, we do not have complete and publicly available data on mortgage loan performance, mortgage delivery channels, borrower demographics, loan modifications, and credit scores that would enable better research, policy design, and policy advocacy. Even the Federal Reserve does not have full access to loan performance data. There is no nationally standardized, publicly available foreclosure data. We do not have data on the quality and sustainability of loan modifications, nor do we know who falls out (and why) between the temporary and permanent loan modification programs. The Treasury Department should be tracking how its grantees and recipients are using their funds to affirmatively further fair housing. Treasury is reporting some data on the Home Affordable Modification Program (HAMP), but the data is aggregated and cannot be used for detailed analysis. Fannie Mae is currently collecting data as an agent of the Treasury, another reason to focus on the new organization and mandate of the successor to the GSEs.

Second, the speed of the crisis has not allowed time for relationship-building among economic justice, social justice, fair lending, civil rights, and fair housing movements. These relationships are becoming better nurtured in Washington, DC (our convening being an example), but are often absent at the state level. The question of state-level advocacy relationship building was key in California.

Third, we are losing the messaging war. The narrative of this crisis as a failure of individual responsibility and/or an overreaching government (i.e., erroneously blaming the CRA for the crisis) is only growing. This issue is framed as separate from (or even in competition with) political advocacy around jobs, education, and health care, rather than as a related outcome of unfair access to opportunity. The crisis has complex roots and disengaging terminology ("collateral debt obligations," "cram-down," etc.), which can be difficult to connect to everyday, on-the-ground realities. We face an extraordinarily well-funded financial industry that has deep pockets to pay for effective lobbying. At the Oakland convening, the need for a very well funded communications and lobbying campaign around fair financial options and consumer protection was identified as an important need.

FEDERAL POLICY: CRA, THE SUCCESSORS TO FANNIE AND FREDDIE, AND THE AFFIRMATIVE OBLIGATION TO FURTHER FAIR HOUSING

Strategists suggested that we take a different approach to regulation—to regulate financial *products* universally, not the channel/institution. For example, non-regulated, independent mortgage brokers issued the lion's share of subprime mortgages. People also underscored the need for better data from all "players," and suggested the penalization of servicers who do not comply with data requirements. There was a call to support real property databases held by county recorders (currently undermined by MERS), and a need for a policy and advocacy crisis "database" or "repository" that provides data, analysis, case studies, etc. to advocates and policymakers quickly.

The Federal Policy Landscape

Experts agree that despite its successes, the CRA is oriented towards outdated models of banking and community development (see Chapter 14, Willis, "Give Credit Where Credit is Due: Overhauling the CRA"), and is in danger of being further attacked, ignored or ineffectively reformed—despite the fact that the CRA was *not* responsible for irresponsible lending. A new affirmative obligation to offer fair and sustainable credit must respond to the global,

consolidated, and internet-based nature of modern banking. All financial institutions should be covered by this new obligation, and this obligation should
be enforced by one regulator with a consumer protection mandate. Attendees
at our Washington, DC policy convening suggested linking CRA incentives
to "carrots," like getting government business, as well as to "sticks" like the
threat of a merger denial. People also suggested rewarding CDFI and community development lending, and rewarding loan quality, not quantity. Another
goal was to make fair housing an explicit obligation in any future housing-
and neighborhood-focused recovery program or funding stream (like HAMP,
NSP, etc.).

Ira Goldstein, Kennan Gross, and Dan Urevick-Ackelsberg analyzed the
Neighborhood Stabilization Program (NSP) in Chapter 10, "Affirmatively
Furthering Fair Housing: A Critical Component of the Neighborhood Stabilization Program." The authors argue that rather than remediating a few
houses in racially and socioeconomically isolated neighborhoods (which is
what the current program design encourages), NSP funds should be used to
affirmatively further fair housing. Goldstein, Gross and Urevick-Ackelsberg
provide the following guidance: NSP recipients must (1) consciously and purposefully administer their programs, taking account of the racial composition
of where funds are being obligated; (2) view NSP as one of several federal
programs available to recipients, all of which have obligations to affirmatively further fair housing; (3) as regulations allow, administer NSP and other
related federal programs as if there are both place-based and people-based
components; and (4) utilize objective market data to design an implementation strategy.

Jillian Olinger's research in Chapter 11 on government-sponsored enterprise (GSE) performance highlights a critical lesson of the subprime lending
and foreclosure crisis: getting families into sustainable homeownership is
about much more than just "turning on the spigot" of credit (see "Fannie, Freddie, and the Future of Fair Housing"). Access to credit is important, but increasingly important are the terms of that credit. This includes attention to the
financial terms of the credit instrument (interest rate adjustments, pre-payment
fees, etc.) and to the neighborhoods that people can access with their credit.
Olinger's research also highlights that access to credit is not the only critical
factor for homeownership—human capital and mobility matter too. Simply
put, issuing unregulated mortgages in bulk does not necessarily move people
into sustainable homeownership options in neighborhoods of their choice.
Only careful regulation of financial products and an affirmative commitment
to healthy neighborhoods together can advance fair housing opportunity.

Indeed, the mandate to affirmatively further fair housing goes beyond the
'usual suspects' of fair housing advocacy. Henry Korman argues that fair

housing data must become part of the reporting structures of housing over-sight agencies, including the Securities and Exchange Commission (SEC), in Chapter 13, "Furthering Fair Housing, The Housing Finance System, and the Government Sponsored Enterprises." According to Korman, the extent of SEC involvement in securities transactions that affect housing means that "it is an 'agency having regulatory or supervisory authority over financial institutions' engaged in activities related to housing, thus requiring the SEC to act 'in a manner affirmatively to further the purposes of' Title VIII of the Civil Rights Act." Korman goes on to show that in light of the disproportion-ate impact of subprime lending and foreclosures on people and communities of color, and in light of the evidence that family housing syndicated with Low Income Housing Tax Credit (LIHTC) is often located in segregated, high poverty locations, that the SEC must become part of any reinvigorated fair lending strategy. In addition, all relevant regulatory agencies must assess the civil rights effect of the characteristics used for bundling mortgages and credit.

Providing a different perspective on the future of the GSEs, Thomas Stan-ton (in Chapter 12, "Fannie Mae and Freddie Mac: How Can We Improve Their Support of the Mortgage Market?") argues that the GSEs should not again become private organizations with special government backing. Rec-ognizing that the mortgage market will need substantial government support in the short term, Stanton suggests that Fannie Mae and Freddie Mac could become government corporations, i.e., government agencies. Support for the mortgage market might include funding new mortgages with lower bor-rowing costs, including prudent affordable housing loans, providing help for troubled mortgage borrowers, improving consumer protection for borrowers, and supporting other government housing programs and especially the Fed-eral Housing Administration (FHA).

WHAT SHOULD WE DO FROM HERE?
PRINCIPLES FOR FAIR CREDIT AND
FAIR HOUSING REFORM

This crisis has had global roots and global consequences, yet the impact of the crisis on the social justice landscape and how activists are responding on a global scale is little understood. Our observation is that unlike the interna-tional conversations on climate change, which attracted the activism of many US- and globally-based NGOs and interest groups, the conversation around the credit system was largely closed to advocates. Unfortunately, advocates did not demand a place at the table. We must do better.

We must have a national-level conversation around broad themes that have sometimes been submerged in the particulars of the subprime crisis and the policy response. These themes should include, what is a fair economic system and how does a financial system best support it? This question has not been adequately considered since the deregulation period. As Dymski notes: "After all, since US banking-regulation legislation was first passed in 1980, the broader question of how to adapt a financial regulatory apparatus designed for a regulated banking system to the emerging deregulated environment has itself still not been answered" (Dymski, 21). As we've seen from this crisis, policy both set the market 'free' by preempting state regulation of subprime lending, interest rates, etc., and failed to protect consumers by failing to adequately regulate institutions and by failing to hold consumer protection as a priority. This combination allowed for the algal bloom of unsustainable subprime mortgages targeted to communities least able to bear their high cost and the ultimate foreclosure crisis.

The way in which fair access to credit is understood matters with respect to policy design and implementation. Fair credit does not necessarily mean that everyone is offered the same product or service; nor does it mean a return to the way things were prior to the crisis. Fair *does* mean attention to why there are systemic differences in access to credit (Dymski, 9). It means that people, places and economies should be approached with an understanding of their situations and histories. We need to affirmatively recruit marginalized people and communities into healthy credit options, not only stabilize whites' access to credit.

Because unequal and segregated credit emerged hand-in-hand with racially segregated housing markets, the provision of fair credit and fair housing opportunity must be pursued together. These tools of community and asset exclusion reinforced each other—people of color were denied credit and could not build and pass on intergenerational wealth. They must be understood and unwound together. Most household wealth in the US is (or was) in home equity. Without the ability to buy a home in a stable or appreciating neighborhood, people are barred from this means of wealth accumulation. And without sustainable credit, people will not be able to stay in their homes and build up assets. We still need anti-discrimination laws and policies, but they must be complemented with an affirmative duty to further fair credit and fair housing. This affirmative duty should be measurable—goals should be set, data should be assessed, and policies that are not working should be corrected.

The following pages detail how the consequences of our unfair credit and housing markets and our lack of consumer protections have been devastating. Community stability, social mobility, family health, and individuals' ability to retire, invest, pay for medical bills, and send kids to college are all at risk.

Nothing short of our collective future is at risk, and nothing short of a long-term, multi-faceted effort to affirmatively promote integration into opportunity for all of our people is required.

NOTES

1. Gary Dymski, "Understanding the Subprime Crisis: Institutional Evolution and Theoretical Views."

2. http://www.fcic.gov/about.

3. john a. powell and Kathleen M. Graham, "Urban Fragmentation as a Barrier to Equal Opportunity." Chapter 7 of *Rights at Risk: Equality in an Age of Terrorism, eds.* Dianne M. Piché, William L. Taylor, and Robin A. Reed. Washington, D.C.: Citizens' Commission on Civil Rights (2002).

4. For overviews of various challenges in housing policy, see Galster, G. (1998). "Residential segregation in American cities: A contrary review." *Population Research and Policy Review* 7(2): 93–112; Galster, G. and E. Godfrey (2005). "By Words and Deeds: Racial Steering by Real Estate Agents in the US in 2000." *Journal of the American Planning Association* 71(3): 251–268; powell, j. (2003). "Opportunity-Based Housing." *Journal of Affordable Housing and Community Development Law* 12: 188; Roisman, F. W. (1997–1998). "Mandates Unsatisfied: The Low Income Housing Tax Credit Program and the Civil Rights Laws." *University of Miami Law Review* (52): 1011–1050; Turner, M. A., S. L. Ross, et al. (2002*). Discrimination In Metropolitan Housing Markets: National Results From Phase I HDS 2000*, U.S. Department of Housing and Urban Development; Yinger, J. (1998). "Housing Discrimination is Still Worth Worrying About." *Housing Policy Debate* 9(4): 893–927. For an overview of structural racism, see "A Report to the U.N. Committee for the Elimination of Racial Discrimination on the occasion of its review of the Periodic Report of the United States of America" (February 2008). http://www2.ohchr.org/english/bodies/cerd/docs/ngos/usa/USHRN2.doc.

5. Michael A. Stegman, Allison Freeman, and Jong-Gyu Paik, "The Portfolios and Wealth of Low-Income Homeowners and Renters: Findings from an Evaluation of Self-Help Ventures Fund's Community Advantage Program." Community Development Working Paper 2007–02, Federal Reserve Bank of San Francisco (2007), p. 29–30.

6. Ibid.

7. John Farris and Christopher A. Richardson, "The Geography of Subprime Mortgage Prepayment Penalty Patterns." *Housing Policy Debate* 15 (3): 2004. See also Paul S. Calem, Kevin Gillen, and Susan Wachter, "The Neighborhood Distribution of Subprime Mortgage Lending." *Journal of Real Estate Finance and Economics* 29:4, 393–410 (2004).

8. Debbie Gruenstein Bocian, Keith S. Ernst and Wei Li, "Unfair Lending: The Effect of Race and Ethnicity on the Price of Subprime Mortgages." Center for Responsible Lending, 2006. Accessed at http://www.responsiblelending.org/mortgage-lending/research-analysis/rr011–Unfair_Lending-0506.pdf.

9. Ira Goldstein (The Reinvestment Fund) and Dan Urevick-Ackelsberg, "Subprime Lending, Mortgage Foreclosures and Race: How Far Have We Come and How Far Have We to Go?" Paper commissioned for the Kirwan Institute for the Study of Race and Ethnicity at The Ohio State University for its National Convening on Subprime Lending, Foreclosure and Race, October 2–3, 2008.

10. The Children's Defense Fund notes: "On average [over the last 30 years], the income of the top 20 percent of households was about 15 times greater than that of the households in the bottom 20 percent—the widest gap on record based on an analysis of U.S. Census Bureau figures." Children's Defense Fund, *The State of America's Children* 2005 (page 4). Back in 2002, economist Paul Krugman reported that 1 percent of families receive about 16% of total pretax income, while median family income has risen only about 0.5% a year—an increase mostly due to wives working longer hours. Krugman argued that this astonishing concentration of wealth at the top is why the U.S. has more poverty and lower life expectancy than any other major advanced nation. (Paul Krugman, Op-Ed column in *The New York Times*, "For Richer." 10/20/2002.) See also James Lardner and David A. Smith, editors, *Inequality Matters: The Growing Economic Divide in America and Its Poisonous Consequences*. New York: The Free Press (2005).

11. Underbanked households have a checking or savings account but rely on alternative financial services ("AFS") such as non-bank money orders and non-bank check cashing, pawn shops, payday loans, rent-to-own agreements ("RTOs"), and refund anticipation loans ("RALs"). The study reported that the two most frequently used AFS products are non-bank money orders and check cashing. *FDIC National Survey of Unbanked and Underbanked Households.* December 2009. Executive Summary, page 5. http://www.fdic.gov/householdsurvey/Executive_Summary.pdf.

12. *FDIC National Survey of Unbanked and Underbanked Households.* December 2009. Executive Summary, page 4. http://www.fdic.gov/householdsurvey/Executive_Summary.pdf.

13. Minorities more likely to be unbanked include blacks (an estimated 21.7% of black households are unbanked), Hispanics (19.3%), and American Indian/Alaskans (15.6%). Racial groups less likely to be unbanked are Asians (3.5%) and whites (3.3%). Ibid, page 3.

14. Wyly, E. K., M. Moos, et al. (2008), "Subprime Mortgage Segmentation in the American Urban System." *Tijdschrift voor Economische en Sociale Geografie* 99(1): 3–23.

Chapter Two

Understanding the Subprime Crisis

Institutional Evolution and Theoretical Views

Gary A. Dymski

The subprime crisis has been at the center of the US and global news cycle for two years. Its emergence in 2007 triggered a parade of dramatic consequences: the collapse of two Bear Stearns structured investment funds in May 2007; the freezing of US money markets in August and September 2007; the run on, and collapse of, Northern Rock Trust in England in late September 2007; the failure of Bear Stearns in May 2008; the failure of Lehman Brothers in September 2008, along with the "receivership" of FNMA and FHLMC and the takeovers of Washington Mutual and of Wachovia; the passage of the $700 billion Troubled Asset Relief Program in October 2008; and the passage of the American Relief and Recovery Act in February 2009.

These months of dramatic action were so momentous that political commentary and debate focused on how to use fiscal and financial-regulatory policies to fix the global and national economies. What began with the exploitation of minority borrowers in marginalized neighborhoods has evolved into a threat to the commanding heights of global finance. So by this time, every talking economic theorist, political hopeful, and think-tank analyst with a closet global model has put forth their own diagnosis of what is broken and what needs fixing.

In an ironic twist, it is as if the subprime crisis itself—represented by numerous households, a disproportionate number of whom are African American and Latino, who have been issued mortgage loans with exploitative and unsustainable terms-has disappeared while hiding in plain sight. Indeed, minority borrowers' profligacy and banks' legal mandate (such as it is) to meet the credit needs of lower-income (and hence heavily-minority) portions of their market areas have been mentioned frequently as among the root causes of the subprime debacle. Meanwhile, in neighborhood after dusty neighborhood, subprime loans turn into abandonments, foreclosures, and bank repossessions.

New clusters of speculative homebuyers scoop up heavily discounted homes whose former owners are thrown onto the kindness of their relatives or neighbors, or onto the streets.

Our task in this chapter is to provide some needed balance by undertaking an analysis of the economics of the subprime crisis. Our first task is to review the institutional economic dynamics of the subprime crisis. Section 2 analyzes the shifts in banking strategy, in financial markets, and in macroeconomic and microeconomic conditions that transformed financial exclusion in the US and made subprime loans into viable credit instruments. Next, Section 3 shows how subprime lending emerged as one category of predatory lending. It describes the explosion of predatory lending of all kinds in the 1990s and early 2000s, and the wildfire spread of subprime loans in the mid-2000s.

Sections 4 and 5 analyze economists' understandings of this unfolding situation. Section 4 examines economists' views of subprime lending, in the context of their views of US financial exclusion more broadly—credit-market redlining, discrimination, and predatory lending. Two contemporary approaches to credit markets are featured: the efficient-market and asymmetric-information views. Section 5 reviews economists' unfolding understandings of the subprime crisis per se, paying special attention to the links between economists' views and policy responses to the subprime crisis.

THE INSTITUTIONAL ORIGINS OF THE SUBPRIME CRISIS: BANKING TRANSFORMED THE END OF US-COORDINATED MACROECONOMIC STABILITY AND THE CRISIS OF US BANKING AND HOUSING FINANCE

In the United States, regulations and laws put into effect in the Depression created a segmented financial system. This segmentation included geographic divisions among banks, a legacy of this nation's settlement by frontier expansion. Functional divisions were strengthened in response to the Great Crash. Private commercial banks collected household savings and made loans to businesses; mortgage companies and savings and loan associations emerged to collect savings and meet mortgage demands.[1]

The banks and financial firms operating in these regulated markets deployed conservative rules about lending and borrowing. For one thing, their hands were tied by extensive rules governing the markets they could serve, the products they could sell, and the prices they could offer on those products; for another, the stable macroeconomic milieu of the immediate post-War period assured stable cash-flows from "following the rules."

These arrangements began gradually breaking down in the 1960s. Money-center banks developed more aggressive growth strategies and challenged regulatory restrictions on their sources of funds. Financial markets grew in function and complexity, outside of the close purview of government regulators. Larger firms increasingly obtained credit directly in these markets. Banks were forced to seek out new borrowers. This led larger banks to engage in extensive cross-border lending from the mid-1970s onward.

Macroeconomic instability, which plagued the US economy in the 1970s, worsened by 1979. Several years of high inflation, high interest rates, and recession afflicted the US (and for that matter, much of the global) economy. The high interest rates led depositors to pull their money out of the banks; these rates plus global recession led first to systemic defaults on banks' overseas loans, and then to the US savings-and-loan crisis.

Under this combined pressure, the US banking structure first cracked and then crumbled. The extensive government regulations that segmented financial product markets, limited banks' geographic expansion, and governed many financial-market prices were eliminated in the 1980s and 1990s. An extensive wave of bank mergers was launched within the US banking system. The remarkably balkanized US banking system was gradually reconfigured as a system of hierarchically-organized regional banks (Corestates, Wachovia, and First Union, Bay Bank and First Boston, BancOne and Keybank, and so on). Over the course of time, this system of competing "super-regional banks" eventually consolidated into a set of four nationally-dominant mega-banks.[2]

The Strategic Repositioning of Banking

For a time, it appeared that technological change, recurrent overseas-lending crises, and the increasing ease of entry into financial activities would doom both traditional banks and the large money-center banks whose operations overlapped investment-banking and broker-dealer activities. However, banks have been remaking themselves strategically. The old idea of bank behavior—holding to term a portfolio of short-term and long-term loans made to members of a well-defined customer base—has been retired. New models are emerging, including, but not limited to, the "originate and distribute" approach, which underlay the subprime crisis.

The remaking of banking has proceeded differently in distinct segments of financial and banking markets. One part of this remaking involved the spreading scope of activities permitted to banks. Recently, much attention has been given to the impact of the Gramm-Bliley Act of 1999, which eliminated the 'investment-banking'/'commercial-banking' distinction that had been in place since the Glass-Steagall Act. In truth, the permitted scope of banking activities has been expanding continuously since the 1980 federal banking deregulation act.[3] Banks organized to take advantage of mass-marketing opportunities have been able to expand into new loan products, new financial services, eventually including insurance and brokerage services.

A second key to this remaking has been the expansion of processes and institutional means for emitting, underwriting, and selling or buying financial securities on a wholesale, not retail, basis.

A pioneer here was the money-market mutual fund (MMMF), first created by Merrill Lynch in 1972. The MMMF permitted small savers—those previously able to put aside $5,000–$10,000 in a time deposit—to collectively purchase larger-scale financial assets (for example, negotiable certificates of deposit, which are denominated in units of $100,000 or more) without sacrificing access to liquidity. A further development was the mutual fund, which permitted small-scale savers to bundle together their savings so as to hold a portfolio far more diversified than any one saver could have afforded.

As deregulation proceeded, bank holding companies were able to undertake ever more of these activities. So banks could compete to offer services based on wholesale-to-retail linkages to customers they had previously lost to MMMFs and other non-bank intermediaries. Some of these services were attractive to the larger non-financial firms whose borrowing-and-cash-flow business began to escape banks' balance sheets in the 1970s. Banks and non-banks have also renewed their provision of financial services to non-financial firms in this category by offering non-traditional forms of insurance—lines of credit, loan guarantees, and derivatives.

Indeed, a fierce competition over the emission, distribution, and underwriting of large-scale equity and debt issues broke out in the 1980s among banking mega firms, investment banks, and broker-dealers. Another competition arose over derivatives. This competition resulted in one global mega-crisis—the 1998 collapse of the Long-Term Capital Investment hedge fund. This crisis was certainly a warning sign about potentially adverse consequences of hyper-competition in lightly regulated financial markets. It should be kept in mind, however, that the global financial system has been experiencing severe crises regularly—the 1982 Latin American crisis, the 1994–5 Mexican "Tequila" crisis, the 1997 Asian financial crisis, etc. On each occasion, no lasting damage was done, so it appeared to policy-makers that after-the-fact regulatory adjustments would suffice to insure that market instruments could continue to evolve without causing permanent damage.

In competing for shares of emerging markets in financial services, banks developed capabilities that proved useful in serving their existing customer bases. In particular, banks evolved new processes for the creation and marketing of securities, and an ever-expanding set of mechanisms for transforming, underwriting, and off-loading risk. The key means of offloading risk was an expanding set of secondary markets. Loans were not sold directly onto these markets; they were first bundled together and divided into promised payment streams—often by maturity and risk classes. So, in the markets they took the appearance of pure payment streams, divorced from the specific circumstances of borrowers' time and place.

Lenders initiating these mechanisms, in turn, were able to reduce their lending-related risk. For one thing, measurement of default risk was standardized. The use of FICO scores to measure borrowers' financial fragility provided the most well-known means of standardization, but there were others too. For another thing, securitized loans sold into the market did not appear on lenders' balance sheets. And furthermore, banks' liquidity risk, rooted in maturity mismatches, was reduced as they sold loans off into the securities marketplace. Banks did not have to pre-commit to obtaining short-term borrowed funds for the loans they had made and then sold off to be managed by other intermediaries. The question of whether off-balance-sheet risks originated by banks were ultimately banks' responsibility would emerge as a central challenge in the subprime crisis of 2007–08. Another crisis-related challenge would involve the adequacy of liquidity to support banks on- and off-balance-sheet loan portfolios. But initially, 'out of sight, out of mind' was the applicable principle. Consequently, banks began to market new loan instruments that took advantage of the possibilities opened up by securitization.

In short, sophisticated information technologies, the growing number of liquid resale and derivatives markets, and the plethora of modern-day media outlets, taken together, permitted banks to enter credit markets ever more deeply. And they were able to extend the range of credit instruments they offered, apparently without parallel increases in their institutional riskiness. Later it would become clear that banks' individual decisions to increase expected profits by expanding into securitization and into more loan markets were taken without considering the impact on the effect of heightened liquidity and default risk in the overall credit markets. That is, spillover effects were ignored. But in the late 1980s and 1990s, it seemed that a brave new world of finance was in creation.

THE REINVENTION OF CONSUMER BANKING

Taking advantage of their new risk-management and information-technology tools, banks re-engineered consumer banking. Large banks in the United States have taken the lead in creating standardized, mass-market financial products that meet the needs of large numbers of households, often conveniently located in geographic proximity to one another in prosperous residential areas.[4] They cross-sell services and aim at nurturing brand loyalty and "one-size-fits- all" services for the customers of their "upscale retail banking" activities. In the United States, many mergers have been undertaken with the aim of extending merging banks' marketing reach and the captive audiences their deposit-market instruments create. This shift, of course, has occurred even as technological change and income-wealth polarization has created growing numbers of sophisticated, financially independent, upper-income households.

But while the search in consumer banking is for more customers, not all customers are incorporated in the same way. Cross-subsidies within banking markets have been radically restricted. No longer do blue-chip borrowers, for example, implicitly support loans for mom-and-pop customers. Blue-chips have too many market options to be forced to absorb such subsidies. Instead, cross-subsidies are provided only across-markets (and within customer classes), to customers whose business is sought for multiple financial products.

Potential customers who lack the potential to be stable, multi-product consumers of bank services are not discarded. They are offered restrictive sets of services for which they must pay full price or bear the risks. The packaging and delivery of core banking activities—facilitating purchase-and-sale transactions, receiving income, making payments, storing value, and financial saving—is a new focal point, even for banks that are deeply involved in investment-banking, securities, insurance, and other activities. Bank cards, check-cashing, and money-order services are increasingly being marketed to lower-income households not by independent suppliers or informal markets, but by subsidiaries of multinational banks. Because these households often are cash-short but have access to income flows (if more unstable and lower-level income flows than more prosperous households), they are targeted for short-term loans in a wide range of forms, including payday loans. And because these lower-income households lack competitive alternatives in many cases, the financial products they buy often have built-in substantial margins for the lenders.

The Reinvention of Housing Finance

Housing expenditures have been extremely volatile over the business cycle during the post-war period, but surprisingly, the mid-1980s savings and loans collapse had little effect on housing finance.[5] The reason was that US housing finance was already in the midst of a transformation from an intermediary-based to a securities-market-based system. Previously, lenders held mortgages to maturity, and consequently were exposed (as noted above) to default and liquidity risks. In the new system, lenders made mortgages to sell them. Commercial banks interested in expanding their share of consumer-banking markets provided the mechanisms for implementing securitization. The process of originating, servicing, and holding mortgages was split into its constituent parts, with each part priced and performed separately.

A successful securities-based system housing finance required the com-modification of risky mortgage assets. This required two steps. The first was the standardization of the instruments being bundled and sold, which required the adoption of standardized mortgage eligibility criteria. These criteria made 'relationship' lending unnecessary, and allowed both a new array of non-bank, non-thrift lenders to originate mortgage debt, and a new array of institutions to hold it. The second was the separation of loan-making from risk-bearing. The willingness of wealth-holding institutions to take on securitized mortgaged debt was accomplished by insuring the ready availability of government and private underwriting of mortgage debt. Two federally-chartered agencies, the Federal National Mortgage Association (FNMA) and the Federal Home Loan Mortgage Corporation (FHLMC), have long provided a secondary market for qualifying mortgages. A third agency, the Government National Mortgage Association (GNMA or Ginnie Mae), provides a secondary market for FHA, VA, and FmHA mortgages. These agencies have continued to underwrite most mortgage credit; further, these agencies hold a significant share of US mortgage debt.

Until the last several years, most of the mortgage debt since the mid-1980s has involved conforming conventional loans, which are bundled and underwritten by these agencies, and then either held in agency portfolios or sold off. These agencies have accommodated the larger flow demand for securitized mortgages by increasing their proportion of pass-through securities. Pass-through securities are claims on mortgage debt, which are underwritten by one of these agencies—that is, the buyer of a share in such a security has a claim on mortgage cash-flows. The activities of these agencies are supplemented by several private mortgage insurers that underwrite "non-conforming" loans, "jumbo" loans larger than are allowed under FNMA. The current limit of $417,000 for FNMA has led in the last several years to more mortgage paper moving into the "jumbo" loan category. In sum, the reconfiguration of US housing finance did not require the invention of new institutions. Instead, it required an expansion in the scope of participation in the secondary mortgage-debt market. The divorce of risk-bearing from loan-absorption was so complete that thrifts were able to maintain a large share of originations even as they lost deposit share.

The Discounting and Offloading of Perceived Risks

The shifts in banking-firm practices and activities described here also shifted the locus of risks within the US financial system. These shifts occurred both at the macro and at the micro level.

Macro-risk arose because mortgage securitization depended on a resilient demand for mortgage-backed securities; and this depended on the United States' unique position within the global Neoliberal regime. The transition from the old housing-finance system to the new was accomplished at a time when the United States was both the principal global source of reserve currency and a preferred safe haven. In addition, it occurred while the United States had huge current-account deficits, which have necessitated systematic capital-account inflows. Mortgage-backed securities, like Treasury securities, responded to the needs of offshore investors. Government-agency underwritten securities denominated in the world's reserve currency, an attractive option at a time of recurrent global financial disorganization.

How about micro-risks? Given that risks, once created in a borrower-lender relationship, must be borne, one might wonder about the impact of the securitization of mortgage debt on risk-bearing. The new epoch of securitization was accompanied through ambiguity regarding both types of risk. The various types of insurance available for mortgages reduce default risk, but *only* if the third-party insurer accepts an implicit promise to pay. Both FNMA and the private-market insurers have insisted consistently that they bear limited liability. The market, however, has tended to treat their participation as akin to a de-facto government guarantee, based on an implicit "too-big-to-fail" premise. Liquidity risk, in turn, was initially associated with most mortgage-based securities, since these were issued on a fixed-rate basis. Buyers of these securities typically reduced this risk through maturity matching; but some residual liquidity risk remained. Adjustable-rate mortgages (ARMs) are well suited for eliminating liquidity risk, but ARMs initially were not good prospects for securitization because of the computability problems their uncertain terms caused for actuarial-sound calculations of price. This constraint was eventually relaxed as the market for securities grew and as computability capacity—and markets for hedging interest-rate risks—increased in number.

From the perspective of banking strategy, this transformation of the mortgage market had profound implications. For one thing, competing savings and loan institutions virtually disappeared, opening up a new field of competition. At the same time, however, that field was populated by a new category of financial institution—the mortgage company. Mortgage companies did not make loans to keep them on their books, as had the thrifts; they made loans only to sell them. Banks followed suit, initially in the mortgage market. They began to systematically sell off mortgages to offload risk, and in so doing, the basis of their income-earning activities shifted from interest to fee-based income.

INSTITUTIONAL ORIGINS OF THE SUBPRIME CRISIS:
FINANCIAL EXCLUSION TRANSFORMED

Financial Exclusion before the 1990s:
Redlining, Discrimination, and the Unbanked

Racial inequality in access to credit and to banking services has existed as long as racial inequality itself, which is to say, from the founding of the Americas. Until the subprime era dawned in the 1990s, racial inequality in credit and banking took three primary forms:

- Redlining—the systematic denial of home mortgages to urban areas with high proportions of minority residents, regardless of these areas' economic characteristics (and of the economic characteristics of potential borrowers);
- Racial discrimination—the existence of systematically higher denial rates for home-mortgage credit to minority applicants, despite these applicants' underlying creditworthiness;
- Unbanked areas and people—the tendency of banks and savings and loans to avoid opening branches or to close branches in areas with concentrations of minority borrowers; and as a consequence of both lenders' discrimination against minority individuals and of lenders' paucity of branches in minority areas, there is a disproportionate number of unbanked individuals among minorities.

There is not enough space here to enter into a full-fledged discussion of racial discrimination and redlining in credit markets, but some summary comments are appropriate. First, what has been especially egregious about redlining and discrimination in credit markets is that banks and non-bank lenders have disregarded the actual economic circumstances of individuals and areas—racial bias has clouded market processes and led to arbitrarily unfair credit denial. The critique of these practices accepts the idea that borrowers and areas with economically different characteristics *should* be treated differently in the market. In effect, the problem is that black and white loan applicants with similar levels of repayment risk are not treated equally in credit applications. Either they are more likely to be denied credit, or are offered less advantageous terms and conditions when credit is offered.

Any accusation of racial discrimination or redlining invariably gives rise to controversy over lenders' intent and over the nature of fair and equal treatment in the credit market. On one extreme are cases in which meritorious applicants are denied credit. In such cases, investigations may uncover racial perpetrators (racist loan agents or assessors), or racially-biased evaluations that are not justified by any business purpose. Such discrimination is clearly irrational. Chicago economist Gary Becker's 1971 study of racial discrimination views this sort of behavior as the dominant instance; he predicts that because it is irrational (non-racist lenders will make more good loans than racists), market forces will cause discrimination to disappear.

Things are not always so clear, however. Economists have suggested that discrimination may be rational in some cases. Specifically, it is rational when it is costly to acquire information about borrowers' 'true' levels of credit-worthiness, and lenders can use race or characteristics correlated with race to make valid predictions about borrowers' ability to repay debt and their probability of default.[6] In such a situation, two individuals of different races with the same financial background may be treated differently because the lender augments this information with generalized information based on the differential experience of racial populations, not on individuals. Of course, this differential population experience may have arisen due to racially-biased evaluations and racial perpetrators. So on one side, those who are subject to such rational discrimination can ask why they should be victimized; on the other side, those who use race (or proxies for race) to make credit decisions may ask why they should not use all relevant data to avoid undue risks.

Needless to say, these ambiguities have led to debates among policy-makers and economists over what constitutes unfair treatment in credit and banking markets. These debates were far from resolved when new forms of predatory lending, including subprime loans, arose. It should also be noted that the determination of fairness requires not just an assessment of whether two populations' creditworthiness differs systematically, but whether it is fair and just that such systematic differences have arisen. When systematic differences by race (or by some other criteria) are deemed unjust, then some sort of affirmative action or redistribution of resources follows as a logical response. In any event, controversy has not abated over the extent to which racial redlining and discrimination have generated unfair outcomes, and over what should be done about it. Indeed, the controversy over whether subprime lending represents exploitative or opportunity-enhancing behavior by banks can be understood as an extension of this older argument.

Beyond controversies over access to housing credit, the other outstand-ing problem faced by minority communities involved access to bank ac-counts and to the financial services—checking, secure savings for financial balances, and so on—that banks offer through their branch offices. This was partly due to banks' reluctance to maintain branch offices in lower-income and high-minority communities.[7] It also had to do with banks' redivision of their customer bases, discussed above. And since minority communities have disproportionate numbers of lower-income customers, banks' pull-back of branches created bank-branch deserts in the midst of many urban areas.

The result was that even while many minorities increased their income levels and professional status, the number of unbanked households remained persistently large. Studies of the under-banked population have come up with widely varying estimates. A November 1999 survey found that 28% of all individuals and 20% of all households in the US were unbanked (General Accounting Office 2002). A 2001 study found 30% of all US households to be either unbanked or underbanked (Katkov 2002). Underbanked households consist of those with low-balance checking accounts or savings accounts that are seldom used. This total is ethnically diverse—more than 50% white, and 27% black, with Latinos accounting for 16%. These numbers indicate that minorities are far more likely to be unbanked or underbanked than other Americans. There has been ambiguous evidence about whether the number of unbanked and underbanked households has risen systematically since 2000 (see Aizcorbe *et al* 2003).[8]

The FDIC weighed in with a December 2009 report that attempts to provide definitive numbers. This study, which reports on the results of a January 2009 survey of 47,000 households, indicates that 7.7% of all US households are unbanked. However, only 3.3% of whites and 3.5% of Asians are unbanked, whereas 21.7% of African Americans, 19.3% of Latino/Hispanic households, and 15.6% of Native Americans are unbanked. Meanwhile, 17.9% of all US households are underbanked. Here too, the underbanked are far more likely to be minority. Some 7.2% of Asians and 14.9% of whites are underbanked. But the figure for African Americans is 31.7%; for Native Americans, 28.9%; and for Latinos/Hispanics, 24.0%. So, over half of all African American households, and over 4 in 10 Latino/Hispanic and Native American households, are either unbanked or underbanked.

For those outside the banking system, the core alternative financial services are check cashing, money orders, money remittances, and payday loans. According to Katkov (2002), the majority of these firms' revenues are generated by the unbanked and underbanked. He estimates that 68% of money transfers are from the underbanked, while 52% of payday loans are made to unbanked people. The FDIC (2009) study provides rich data supporting the idea that the unbanked and underbanked arrange for their financial services in various ways, with convenience being a key factor.

THE EMERGENCE OF PREDATORY LENDING

Since the mid-1990s, new forms of discriminatory credit have emerged, referred to collectively as "predatory" lending. Predatory loans are collateralized loans, usually based on the income or home-equity of the borrower.

These loans are significantly costlier or entail higher fees or otherwise entail more onerous terms (such as trigger clauses for non-payment) than for loans made to other customers in other areas, on the basis of similar collateral.

Staten and Yezer (2004) point out that there is no commonly accepted definition of predatory lending. Nonetheless, attention has focused on two types of predatory loan: the subprime mortgage and the payday loan. Engel and McCoy (2002) suggest that three categories of mortgage loan be differentiated: prime, legitimate subprime, and predatory. They define predatory mortgage loans as those involving any of five characteristics: "(1) loans structured to result in seriously disproportionate net harm to borrowers, (2) harmful rent seeking, (3) loans involving fraud or deceptive practices, (4) other forms of lack of transparency in loans that are not actionable as fraud, and (5) loans that require borrowers to waive meaningful legal redress." (P. 1260).

A payday loan, by contrast, is a loan that provides a percentage of the cash due to an employee from an employer; when payday comes, the lender receives the paycheck. The difference between the amount lent and the amount received constitutes the return for the lender (plus any fees charged). These loans often lead to excessive rates of household and firm non-payment, and thus to foreclosures and personal financial distress. Payday loans often, but not always, involve excessively high interest rates.

Adding fees or increasing rates generates substantially higher effective repayment rates and increases the prospect of non-payment, putting borrower collateral at risk. One or both types of loans are usually supplied by non-banks (and sometimes banks). Predatory lending often involves aggressive telemarketing, phone-phishing, and other methods based on demographic targeting—especially, the targeting of minority households that have traditionally been denied access to credit.[9]

Predatory lending began growing frenetically by the mid-1990s. Long before most reporters were aware of them, subprime loan practices were heavily impacting lower-income and minority neighborhoods, especially elderly, low-income, and minority borrowers. For example, Canner *et al.* (1999, page 709) found that in 1998, subprime and manufactured housing lenders accounted for 34 percent of all home purchase mortgage applications and 14 percent of originations. These lenders' impact on low-income and minority individuals was even more pronounced. According to Canner *et al.*, in 1998, subprime and manufactured housing lenders made a fifth of all mortgages extended to lower-income and Latino borrowers, and a third of all those made to African American borrowers. Subprime lending grew 900 percent in the period 1993–99, even while other mortgage lending activity actually declined (US Department of Housing and Urban Development 2000). A nationwide study of 2000 HMDA data by Bradford (2002) found that African Americans were, on average, more than twice as likely as whites to receive subprime loans, and Latinos more than 40%-220% more likely.[10]

Available evidence suggests that lower income and minority borrowers are being targeted by these specialized—and often predatory—lenders. Community-reinvestment advocates and consumers are challenging business practices that sometimes victimize borrowers. As evidence of the aggressive business practices pursued in this market, Ameriquest Mortgage Company of Orange, California was forced to settle a consumer protection lawsuit for $325 million in January 2006. Tellingly, this was second in dollar value, in US history, only to Household Finance Corporation's $484 million settlement in 2002 (after its sale to HSBC). The *Washington Post* story summarizing the settlement gives some indication of the practices that have plagued this industry:

> Under the agreement, Ameriquest loan officers will be required to tell borrowers such things as what a loan's interest rate will be, how much it could rise and whether the loan includes a prepayment penalty. Loan officers who do not make that disclosure will be subject to discipline. The company would also be forbidden from giving sales agents financial incentives for pushing consumers into higher-interest loans or prepayment penalties. (Downey 2006)

Meanwhile, the payday loan—the practice of advancing workers a portion of the money they stand to earn from their paychecks—was becoming common in check-cashing stores. As with subprime loans, financing is often provided by large bank holding companies. This form of credit is also spreading very fast, as is the infrastructure of lenders disbursing it. Payday lenders were unheard of 15 years ago. But several years ago, Sheila Bair (2005) estimated there were 22,000 store locations offering payday loans, with a market volume of $40 billion, in the 37 states that allowed this practice. Her study found that the average 2005 fee for a $100–payday check was $18; the average fee per transaction was $37; and the average store location was taking in approximately $200,000 annually in payday loan fees.

The payday loan industry grew rapidly in the 2000s—Bair estimates an increase of 46% in the number of payday-loan locations between 2001 and 2005, and a 70% increase in fees. This rapid growth can be explained by the interaction of two factors: banks' increasingly high not-sufficient-funds (NSF) fees—the fees that banks charge customers who cannot cover all payments for which they have written checks, and the increasingly high late fees charged for rent, credit-card, and utility payments. About $22 billion in NSF fees and $57 billion in late fees were collected in 2003 (Bair 2005).

Interestingly, the customers for these loans are not the unbanked. Payday-loan customers must have checking accounts. Some 29% earn less than

$25,000 a year, and 52% earn $25–$50,000 annually. African Americans and military families are overrepresented, with 41% owning homes. There is recurrent use; most customers use payday loans 7–12 times per year.[11]

Why Predatory Lending and Low-Income Financial Markets Grew

Why have predatory loan markets—and more broadly, financial instruments targeting those that previously would not have been provided with credit—grown so much?[12] The convergence of several forces operating at two different levels of financial-market processes explains what has happened. The first level involved the emergence of the demand for, and supply of, non-traditional (and predatory) financial services, including expanded lending.

Demand for services among lower-income households has grown tremendously. As noted above, the number of un- and under-banked people is sizable. The increasing polarization of US income and wealth has meant that more people—and thus potential customers—are in the bottom rungs of the distribution. Those on the lower end of the income distribution have significantly fewer assets than those in the upper end; this increases their riskiness as borrowers and implies they will need to access credit markets (Wolff and Zacharias 2009). Further, lower-income households in the US typically have much more volatile incomes than do other households (Gosselin 2004). Hence they have a recurring need for credit as a way of closing their income-expenditure gaps. Newly published research, using an all-in measure of the distribution of income and wealth, finds that the racial gaps in these measures of material well-being have not changed substantially over the past 40 years (Masterson, Zacharias, and Wolff 2009).

We now turn to the supply side of these markets. Probably the key factor is the emergence of a new consumer-banking business model for lower-income households. The idea is to generate profits from a combination of fees and interest. Fee-based income can be generated by providing transaction services and access to credit. Providing access to credit to lower-income households, as to others, generates fees from their credit contracts. These households' higher risks are offset interest from credit contracts. Higher risks are offset by having fees paid up-front, by imposing penalty fees for contract termination, and by making loans whenever possible on the basis of attachable assets. Targeting customers who have been largely neglected by formal-sector firms comprises another part of this business model. Of particular interest would be potential customers with relatively low incomes who have either relatively stable incomes or the prospect of higher future earnings, and who own equity in non-financial assets. Focusing on overlooked customers means that firms can exercise some market power—these customers can be charged higher fees and rates than if they were being offered accounts by mainstream financial institutions.

This model readily explains the initial growth of the subprime mortgage-loan market. During the long history of racial segregation in US cities, most minorities lived in segregated areas though some of these residents were able to purchase homes. These minority-majority areas of US cities sometimes have been gentrified, but more often have stagnated. The incomes of resident homeowners in these areas are generally modest; and often, because of spatial jobs-residential mismatches, family member of these homeowners have had trouble finding stable employment. This customer profile explains why sub-prime mortgages first emerged in such neighborhoods as second mortgages on homes whose primary mortgage loans have been partly or even fully paid down. The logic of the payday loan industry is very similar—next month's paycheck serves as a guarantee against loss for this new form of lending.

Consequently, lending to lower-income customers has expanded faster than lending to middle- and upper-income customers. Data from the Survey of Consumer Finances (taken every three years) show that households in the two lowest-income quintiles have had surging levels of debt, not paralleled by proportionate increases in asset levels from 1992 to 2004. Furthermore, the financial-obligation ratios of both homeowner and renter households rose steadily from 1990 until 2008, with those of renters consistently higher than those of homeowners.

Apart from credit operations, transactions and money-transfer operations serving lower-income customers also exploded in recent years. A key factor here was the explosive growth of global remittances. In 2003, cross-border remittances originating in the United States totaled $39 billion, 31.4% of the global total (Orozco 2004). But banks had only a minor share of remittance fees. There were 40 million transmissions of money from the United States to Mexico in 2003; the four highest-volume banks—Citibank, Wells Fargo, Harris Bank, and Bank of America—accounted for only $1.2 million (3%). Banks would like more of this market: in the late 1990s, fees were as much as 15% of a typical transfer; by 2004, fees remained high, but had fallen con-siderably to 7.5% (Orozco 2004). Megabanks and niche banks alike began competing for this market by cutting costs and creating more appropriate accounts and convenient locations. Banks have not succeeded thus far in capturing much of either migrant workers' or new immigrants' bank account or remittance business.

Another element pushing banks toward lower-income customers has been the creation of bank and payroll cards. The evolution of card technology has permitted the emergence of new, card-based payment media. Employers have increasingly used smart, reloadable cards to pay their workers, including migrant workers. Products for card-based purchases and money transfers have also developed rapidly.[13] A 2005 study (US Comptroller of the Currency 2005) estimated that 20% of unbanked US households were using smart payroll cards by 2004—up from 0% in 1998. Fees are $1.50–$5.00 per month for consumers; retailers pay a fee of about 1% to the card company as well. In the United States, retail automated clearinghouse transactions grew 15% to 19% annually from 1979 to 2000; debit card transactions grew 42% annually from 1995 to 2000 (Gerdes and Walton II 2002).

Significant growth in lending to lower-income—and riskier—customers also depended on another set of institutional developments—the emergence of secondary markets for this debt. The premise of the securitization that transformed housing finance in the United States in the 1980s, as noted above, was standardization. FNMA and FHLMC created mortgage-backed securities by accepting only "plain vanilla" loans. This term meant both that mortgage terms and conditions were standardized and that credit risks were shared by lenders and homeowners (via down-payment and loan/income standards). In effect, mortgage securitization in the 1980s involved the homogenization of risk, providing privileges to low-risk borrowers and minimizing the consequences of loan default when it did occur.

However, mortgage securitization was gradually transformed in the 1990s. Technologies of securitization and risk-pooling developed in parallel with the growth of pools of finance—such as hedge and private-equity funds-seeking above-market rates of return. The creation of "jumbo" mortgages underwritten by non-governmental entities in the 1980s suggested that private markets could assemble and sell housing-based securities. With increasing risk tolerance and increases in computability—and with fees to be made—private markets developed methods for bundling and pricing mortgages with heterogeneous terms and risk characteristics. As noted, most subprime mortgagees in the 1990s had collateral at stake. So while subprime borrowers' longer-term payment prospects were often doubtful, the combination of high fees, high penalties, and pledged collateral made these loans profitable.

The supply of both financial services to lower-income households and market mechanisms for securitizing these households' debt was expanded by the increasing interpenetration among major banking corporations, finance companies, and subprime lenders. On one hand, large lenders bought up lenders in the late 1990s, and rationalized what had been a chaotic set of loan originators (Quinn 1998). Wall Street investment banks channeled an increasing amount of funds to subprime lenders (an average of $80 billion annually in 1998 and 1999); and Wall Street insurers backed the mortgage-backed securities that subprime lenders sold off into the markets (Henriques and

Bergman 2000). Some bank holding companies purchased subprime lenders. Citicorp acquired Associates First Capital Corporation, which was then under investigation by the Federal Trade Commission and the Justice Department.[14] Associates First represented a step toward Citicorp's goal of establishing its Citifinancial subsidiary as the nation's largest consumer finance company (Oppel and McGeehan 2000).[15] This consumer-lending subsidiary quickly proved valuable in stabilizing Citicorp's earnings. (Sapsford, Cohen, *et al.* 2004, *Business Week* 2002).

Subprime Lending and the Housing Bubble

As we have seen, then, the 1990s saw a new appreciation for the revenue potential of lower-income financial markets and the creation of new housing-finance markets. What the creation of the subprime loan did, more fundamentally, was to significantly widen the pipeline for distributing risk. Subprime lenders at one end of this pipeline made mortgage loans; at its other end, these securities could be sold worldwide. While mortgage-backed securities built from "plain vanilla" mortgages attracted risk-averse buyers, the structured investment vehicles (SIVs) into which subprime mortgages were made created higher-risk, higher-return options.[16]

In the 2000s, these options were adapted for new purposes, in effect widening the pipeline for originating risk. The demand for residential real estate began to take off in the late 1990s; by the early 2000s, a housing bubble gripped the US. In some areas, the housing-price boom blossomed into a mania. Homeowners wanted bigger houses and those who weren't yet home-owners wanted to get into the housing market, even at premium prices. The stagnation of household incomes—and, it should be said, the clear bias of housing policy toward home-ownership, rather than renting—fed potential buyers' sense of desperation. The fact that many potential home buyers had neither the income nor savings to support "plain vanilla mortgages"—which prescribed that no more than 30% of income spent on housing, and 20% down on any mortgage loan—fed a feeling of desperation, of "now or never," especially in markets experiencing the fastest price appreciation.

Lenders' and brokers' successful experience in creating loans for borrowers with very risky parameters suggested the required solution: to create loans tailored to the special risks of those whose income and down-payment profiles had not kept pace with many cities' white-hot housing markets. Since housing prices were rocketing upward, buyers could be given loans for amounts more than 80% of their new homes' prices; or they could be given two loans, one for the 80% that had typically been financed, the remainder for most or even all of the down-payment. To get potential buyers "into" a home, a below-market "teaser" rate could be charged for the first two years (typically) of the borrowers' primary mortgage. Any gap between market and "teaser" rates could be amortized, and the entire mortgage refinanced at a risk-adjusted market rate after the "teaser" rate expired. In "hot" markets, buyers increasingly had to resort to loans with "teaser" or adjustable rates (Wray 2007, p. 9.). But as housing euphoria grew, both lender and borrower alike anticipated that housing-price appreciation would permit refinancing on a sounder basis before the 24–month window closed.

The rising housing-price/income ratio explains some but not all of the growing demand for subprime mortgage loans. Mortgage brokers manufactured some of it themselves. A survey of 2005 and 2006 experience found that 55% and 61% of those acquiring subprime mortgages, respectively, had credit scores high enough to obtain conventional loans (Brooks and Simon 2007). This study also found that the mortgage brokers selling these claims earned fees far higher than conventional mortgages would have netted. Subprime loans remained concentrated in minority areas; these loans' excessive use when not warranted by underlying credit scores especially disadvantaged minority loan applicants (Wyly, Moos, *et al.* 2008).

On the supply side of the housing-finance market, funds were plentiful. The US current-account balance stayed negative: so savings continued to flow into US asset markets. The market for mortgage-backed securities had always attracted foreign investors. Now, many UK and European banks, and even some Asian banks, acquired subprime paper (Mollenkamp, Taylor and McDonald 2007). A strong dollar and low nominal interest rates negated liquidity risk.

Banks' strategic shifts toward fee-based income and the increasing interpenetration among financial firms led to what one insider described as "… fierce competition for these loans. … They were a major source of revenues and perceived profits for both the investors and the investment banks." Another participant in these markets observed, "The easiest way to grab market share was by paying more than your competitors." (Anderson and Bajaj 2007).

Collateralized Debt Obligations, Market Interpenetration, and Financial Crisis

Section 3 describes the widening of the subprime pipeline at the point of origination, as subprime (or semi-subprime) loans were used to make loans in the broader housing market. This same pipeline was widened in another dimension as well. Specifically, the notion of estimating and insuring against the risk of a set of loans with heterogeneous risk and other characteristics, then bundling and selling these loans off as securities, spread far beyond the boundaries of the mortgage market. The market's appetite for risk suggested to bankers, especially at large institutions, that a new era of lending had arisen in which banks "originated" credit with the intention of "distributing" it to numerous holders.

The premise was that the holders of credit risk could increase their returns via de-facto portfolio diversification—taking advantage of the lack of complete correlation in the risk-return profiles of the different kinds of credit included in the SIVs they held. In addition to mortgage credit, many types of credit were securitized and included in SIVs—bridge loans for leveraged buyouts, real-estate acquisition loans, construction finance, credit-card receivables, and so on. The relative transparency associated with "plain vanilla" pass-through mortgage-backed securities was replaced by SIVs' opacity. Banks geared up to supply loans to the securitization pipeline could move diverse types of debt off their balance sheets—with fees to be made each step of the way.

SIVs found ready funding in the money markets. High profit rates left many corporations awash in funds. The prospect of sustained low nominal interest rates—linked, as noted above, to the US capital-account surplus—made it seem quite natural to fund SIVs with commercial paper. Indeed, "asset-backed commercial paper" became commonplace. The United State's low nominal interest rates weakened any concerns about liquidity risk. And various means of insuring against SIVs' credit risk were found; indeed, credit risk derivatives were often used to shift risks onto third parties (*The Economist 2007a*). SIVs seemed a sure-fire way to generate interest-margin-based income with minimal equity investment. As the *Wall Street Journal* put it, SIVs "boomed because they allowed banks to reap profits from investments in newfangled securities, but without setting aside capital to mitigate the risk" (Mollenkamp, Solomon, Sidel, and Bauerlein 2007).

By the mid-2000s, subprime loans and SIVs were growing explosively. In the period from 2001–03, mortgage originations totaled $9.04 trillion, of which 8.4% were subprime loans; and 55% of subprime originations, or $418 billion, were securitized. In the 2004–06 period, total mortgage originations were the same in nominal terms, $9.02 trillion. However, 19.6% of all originations consisted of subprime loans, of which 78.8%—some $1,391 billion—were securitized.[17] SIVs became a $400 billion industry. By the mid-2000s, megabanks the world over were heavily invested in SIVs and US mortgage paper, much of it subprime. These investments interlinked these firms' balance sheets as any one lender's loans—and the guarantees that lender had arranged—might be distributed via financial instruments held across the globe.

The subprime crisis built momentum, beginning in 2007, through a series of interconnected events that had a domino effect over a large geographic area. Some 80 subprime mortgage companies failed in the first seven months of 2007. The big credit-ratings agencies came under pressure to overhaul their methods of assessing default risk in the US subprime market (Pittman 2007). As they did so, banking firms in the United States and abroad were affected. On June 20, 2007, Bear, Stearns was forced to shut down two subprime funds it operated for its investors (Kelly, Ng, and Reilly 2007). Six weeks later, American Home Mortgage closed its doors (Dash 2007). Meanwhile, Countrywide Financial, which had originated about one-sixth of recent US mortgage loans, descended more and more visibly into crisis (Hagerty and Richardson *2007*).

In August, Deutschebank bailed out the German bank IKB and other banks when it could no longer access the money markets to finance Rhineland Funding, an offshore vehicle containing $17.5 billion of collateralized debt obligations, including some US subprime mortgages (*The Economist 2*007b). Some of the largest banks, such as Goldman Sachs, added fuel to the crisis by continuing to package and sell securities backed by subprime mortgages, even while reducing their exposure to subprime debt on their own balance sheets (Anderson and Bajaj 2007). By September 2007, between 16% and 24% of the subprime securities packaged by global banks in 2006 were at least 60 days in arrears—a total of $73.7 billion in these securities alone. By December 2007, 15 percent of the $6 billion in new originations Goldman had made in the first nine months of 2007 were already delinquent by more than 60 days.

In 2008, the situation became successively grimmer. Numerous homes went into foreclosure. Many of these had been marketed to the formerly racially-excluded and built in close proximity to areas historically subject to mortgage-market redlining. That is, even when subprime lending had expanded beyond the inner city in the bubble period, racial dividing lines in urban land use had remained in place. So when the crisis hit, it had a disproportionate impact on minority and lower-income neighborhoods (California Reinvestment Committee *et al* 2008); minority households, the most likely to be targeted by subprime lenders, were also most likely to live in neighborhoods in which subprime-based foreclosure cycles would cause terrible losses (Housing and Economic Rights Advocates and California Reinvestment Coalition 2007).

Additionally, short-term credit for subprime paper and SIVs dried up. Consequently, ever more global banks, in the United States and abroad, were forced to take subprime paper back onto their balance sheets, declaring losses in the tens of billions. These banks had to seek out capital injections even while drastically tightening credit supply.

This narrative will not further pursue institutional developments—the Troubled Asset Relief Program (TARP), governmental confusion about how to confront the bank insolvency problem, the distribution of bailout funds between megabanks and smaller banks, and so on. Suffice it to say that subsequent events have provided little reassurance that a normal state of affairs in banking and credit markets has been restored. At best, the megabanks that led the way into the subprime crisis have mostly paid back their TARP funds, and raised new capital in the markets. But their lending remains anemic at best; it isn't clear whether the "originate-and- distribute" model of lending can be re-initiated amidst far greater market suspicion about credit risk and about the solvency of banks emitting this paper. Smaller banks have, in the meantime, been more and more distressed as economic conditions in their market areas deteriorate. The year 2009 brought the highest number of bank failures (148 through December 28) since 1992; 30 banks failed in 2008. Foreclosure rates finally leveled off, but the number of homeowners in arrears and of bank-owned ("REO" or real-estate owned) homes hit new peaks.

Economists' Understandings of Financial Exclusion, Predatory Lending, and High-Risk Securitization

The final two sections of this chapter turn from the unfolding history of the subprime crisis to economic theory. The next section examines how economists understand the subprime crisis, and how this informs their proposed policy responses to this crisis. This section prepares the way for that discussion by examining how economists understand subprime lending; this, in turn, requires examining economists' understanding of credit-market redlining and discrimination.

There are two approaches to explaining credit-market behavior. The first is the "efficient market" approach often identified with "freshwater" economists; the second is the asymmetric-information approach linked with "saltwater" economists. We focus on these two "mainstream" approaches to economics because these views have been the most prominent in national media coverage. Some key perspectives of "heterodox" economic approaches are discussed briefly in section 4.

Redlining, Discrimination, Predatory Lending and Efficient Markets

Most economists have what Schumpeter (1954) called an analytical pre-commitment to the idea that businesses and households who depend on market processes to achieve their material ends (whether survival or riches) look after their own self-interest. While agreeing to use this distinctive lens for seeing the world, economists disagree on how to implement their analyses. Are interests formed at the individual level alone, or do they reflect class positions in production, or racial/ethnic and gender divisions? Do some players within the economy wield significant social power? Do nonlinear relations affect market dynamics?

Broadly speaking, at this level of generality, economists can be divided into two groups: one group prefers to generate models under the assumption that conditions for reaching socially optimal outcomes—equilibria—through decentralized market processes do exist. This section pursues this logic; the next section explores the idea that because of asymmetric information, market outcomes can systematically generate socially suboptimal outcomes.

The idea is that this provides a secure benchmark for what *should* happen. The conditions in question include the notion that social and market power (the ability of monopoly buyers or sellers to determine prices) is unimportant, and that all participants in markets must accept market prices. Another key assumption is that the distribution of information is relatively unimportant. Some market participants may have more information than others, but because those with information advantages will use them in ways that will be reflected in prices it doesn't matter much. This means that all agents, whether or not they have informational advantages, can use price signals to guide their behavior. So informational advantages are eventually 'arbitraged away.' Agents cannot sustain whatever positions of market power they may temporarily acquire. In the end, left to the inexorable logic of competition and self-interest, the price mechanism is fair. We might say, more precisely, that it is fairer than any alternative method of allocating scarce resources among competing ends. Efforts by government to reallocate or regulate resources, in particular, will distort the price signals that market participants are sending to one another, thus leading to socially-sub-optimal outcomes—if with the best of intentions.

So if markets are so perfect, why have activists and analysts alleged that race-based redlining and discrimination exist in credit markets? Recall that these phenomena may be traced in part to racial *perpetrators*—suppliers of credit whose unwillingness to make market transactions with minorities will lead to their leaving "money on the table." As noted, such racially-biased lenders should either be eliminated or forced to change their practices by market competition with unbiased lenders. A second possibility is cost barriers to making full and complete assessments of each potential borrower. Suppose there is unequally distributed information about each loan applicant's creditworthiness. If it is costly to extract this information, and—as noted above—if creditworthiness is correlated with factors that are correlated with race, then individual or area race can be used rationally to determine who will and will not get credit, all things equal.[18]

Since racial inequality in access to credit remained relatively constant over time, but econometric tests for lender bias did not universally sway expert opinion, the second possibility regarding cost barriers has been regarded as more convincing. Indeed, the cost argument goes further. Suppose first that the riskiness of the various sets of borrowers differs along several directions (probability of default, likelihood of early termination of mortgage contract, and so on). Then it may be difficult to price this risk accurately using simple credit contracts. Next, supposing that risk can be appropriately priced; there is a question of funding this risk. And since mortgage finance has moved away from intermediary-held loans toward market-sold contracts, this means finding wealth-holders willing and able to provide the required finance, which means having contracts that can be assessed and priced differentially. This in turn requires mechanisms for bundling, pricing, and distributing risk in the market. But as we have seen, this is precisely what the emerging market nexus in housing finance provided.

This approach suggests that subprime and alt-A loans—and for that matter, payday loans—should be priced differently from "plain vanilla" loans, both for those demanding mortgage credit and for those supplying it. The fact that subprime borrowers face stiffer penalties and higher rates is simply the market's response to their circumstances.

A knife's-edge problem arises when it comes to regulating these new lending instruments.[19] On one side, if one suspects that lenders are using their market power (and/or borrowers' isolation within credit markets) to extract unfair contractual terms from borrowers, the solution is to permit more lenders to supply credit to these customers. This implies regulating less so that more providers of finance are induced (by the temporarily high profit markets) to serve these previously excluded credit customers. On the other side, insofar as one suspects that lenders providing these new loan products may be prone to excessive risk-taking, and/or may exploit the naïve or desperate, then prudent regulation of these new credit markets should be put into place. This would simply parallel the long-established regulations for formal-sector banks. Another dimension of government involvement also comes into play, however: explicit or implicit subsidies or guarantees of privileged activities. In the financial arena, these subsidies especially involve guarantees against failure, the exact extent of which are fuzzy for both regulators and market participants.[20]

This knife's-edge problem has not been resolved since predatory lending first arose in the 1990s. This is hardly surprising. After all, since US banking-deregulation legislation was first passed in 1980, the broader question of how to adapt a financial regulatory apparatus designed for a regulated banking system to the emerging deregulated environment has itself still not been answered.

In this perspective, innovations such as subprime lending and securitization promise to improve credit allocation and to expand access to capital. For example, Fender and Mitchell (2005, page 2) argue that structured finance overcomes "adverse selection and segmentation," while Partnoy and Skeel (2007) discuss how "financial engineering [can be used] to complete markets." They write: "Because synthetic CDOs ... essentially create new instruments, instead of using assets already on bank balance sheets ... complete markets by providing new financial instruments at lower prices." (11–12) On the side of borrowers, more complete markets provide a wider range of contractual choice.[21] As Barth *et al.* (2008) put it:

> Those individuals choosing adjustable-rate mortgages typically receive an initial interest rate that is lower than one with a fixed-rate mortgage, but then face the prospect of higher rates if market interest rates rise. At the same time, the development and wide use of credit scores for individual borrowers and credit ratings for individual issuances of mortgage-backed securities provided more information for both lenders and borrowers to better assess and price risk. (4)

In this framework, these developments will clearly lead to more socially optimal equilibria: subprime and Alt-A mortgages expand credit-market choice and permit more efficient financial risk sharing. Austan Goolsbee, while he was principal economic advisor to candidate Barack Obama, articulated precisely this view of the potentially positive social and economic impacts of subprime lending in an op-ed article in the *New York Times*.[22]

Redlining, Discrimination, Predatory Lending and Asymmetric Information

The efficient-markets view of markets set out in section 4.1 has a strong hold on economists' imagination: economists who regard themselves as "mainstream" find it difficult to disagree with the notion that except in special circumstances, unconstrained market processes generate higher levels of economic welfare than alternative non-market arrangements. Thus, allocation through markets is normally preferable to other methods of resource allocation.[23] This said, many economists who define themselves as mainstream believe that market processes, left to themselves, can systematically generate sub-optimal outcomes. This potential for sub-optimality arises analytically because of one or more deviations from the conditions required to achieve a unique, optimal equilibrium.

Much recent work in the contemporary fields of development, labor economics, and monetary economics builds on one crucial deviation from these conditions—asymmetric information in credit or labor markets. To see what this deviation is and why it matters, suppose first that some agents in the economy have more resources (wealth) than others, so that some agents will either hire others to work for them, lend money to other agents, or both.[24] And suppose that those doing the hiring and the lending have perfect information about those being hired and/or those receiving credit—specifically, about their competence and about the level of effort they will put forth if hired or provided with credit. If credit markets open under perfect information, lenders can maximize expected return and minimize the probability of default by lending only to borrowers who are the most capable and who will use the funds they receive most efficiently.

Now, narrowing our focus to credit markets, suppose that loan applicants know their own capabilities and their own efficiency in using loans if they are selected as borrowers (that is, each knows her own type and effort level), but lenders do not. Suppose lenders have set a loan rate sufficiently low that loan applicants' demand for credit exceeds the loans the lender is able or willing to make. Anyone who needs credit will line up in this market—the capable and the incapable, the efficient and the inefficient. If market signals work, lenders could simply increase the loan rate, inducing some loan applicants to drop out of the market; at some point, loan supply would equal loan demand. But there is no reason to think that the quality of the applicant pool will remain the same as the price of credit rises. To the contrary, more capable and more efficient applicants are likely to have more options, so the quality of the applicant pool is likely to deteriorate. This means that lenders must find other devices than the price mechanism to sort the more capable and more efficient applicants from the rest. Regarding efficiency (effort level), lenders can closely monitor borrowers, and/or make future borrowing contingent on current performance. Regarding capability (applicant type), lenders can search out signals about loan applicants' type, so as to screen in the more capable and to screen out the less capable.

The implications of the addition of asymmetric information, then, are profound. Mathematically, markets so affected no longer have one optimal market equilibrium, but many equilibria. So the analysts of these markets must sort out what information lenders (in this case) are using, how they are using it, and in turn how loan applicants are reacting to lenders' sorting procedures. While the tools of game theory can help sort out the analytical possibilities, a satisfactory analysis of any such economic situation *must* consider what political institutions and societal characteristics in a given situation may affect the behavior of lenders or borrowers (or both).[25]

This brings us back to redlining and discrimination. In Stiglitz' most in-fluential article on credit rationing, he and co-author Andrew Weiss use "red lining" as an example of how lenders can differentiate among "observation-ally distinguishable" borrowers by type (Stiglitz and Weiss 1981). If the racial composition of an area is correlated with borrower creditworthiness, then banks can sort by area race as a low-cost means of sorting loan applica-tions by credit risk. Asymmetric information theory also readily explains why lenders might "rationally" use individual applicants' race to sort by credit risk. This is not fair for several reasons, but lenders make decisions based on what is profitable, not what is fair.[26]

Predatory lending can, in turn, be understood by imagining that lenders screen loan applicants, about whose creditworthiness they lack information, not into two categories (creditworthy or not), but into three or more categories. Some customers may qualify for loans in a primary credit market; others, for loans in a credit market for riskier customers; others, in a credit market for even riskier customers; and so on. An alternative possibility is that one set of lenders makes "qualify/not qualify" decisions in a primary market; those loan applicants ra-tioned out of this market then turn to a second set of lenders, and then perhaps to a third and fourth set. [27] Those receiving loans far down the riskiness scale will have stiff terms and conditions that can be interpreted as predatory.

As a purely logical exercise, then, the asymmetric-information approach can provide a plausible explanation for redlining, "rational" discrimination, and predatory lending. The theorist need not pursue the matter further; in-deed, Stiglitz and Weiss did not in the 1981 article in which they described "red lining;" indeed, they did not even mention "race" as the "observationally distinguishable" characteristic in question.

What this approach *does* do differently than the efficient-markets ap-proach, however, is to open the door to further investigations about the links between market outcomes and broader social dynamics. After all, the "red lining" explanation relies on, even while not elaborating on, correlations between area or individual race and socio-economic variables. The door is opened to analyses of how this market fits into this broader socio-economic matrix. Efficient-market approaches want to keep this door closed, so as to isolate how markets can most faithfully serve as vehicles for maximizing in-dividual and firm "welfare," given the distribution of wealth, talents, and so on. This is why, when market malfunctions occur, suspicion centers on how it might be that government interference may have prevented the market from being properly isolated so as to do its allotted work.

Thus, whereas the efficient-markets approach puts into analytical focus only the specific market mechanisms relevant to any analysis, the asym-metric-information approach puts into play the broader interplay of market, regulation, and social context. Indeed, since his 1981 article with Weiss was published, Stiglitz has realized the potential inherent in this framework for conducting critical, political-economic analysis of real-world problems and crises. He has not revisited—and thus not revised—his analysis of neighborhood redlining as a "rational" outcome. But he has written profound critiques of financial globalization, focusing especially on how East Asian economic growth, which relied in part on government-led credit allocation, collapsed into crisis once these markets were opened to speculative credit flows.[28]

This opening to the analysis of the broader social context, in turn, opens the way for dialogue with other social scientists, including non-mainstream ("heterodox") economists. This dialogue is facilitated by the fact that some of the most important ideas of heterodox economists are readily translated into the conceptual categories of asymmetric-information theory. For example, power is a key concept in radical political economy. There are multiple ways of defining power, to be sure. One way is to observe that because those on the "short side" of the market can choose among customers or applicants, whereas those on the "long side" cannot, the former have power over the latter.[29] So in the credit-rationing case, lenders have power over loan applicants.

Post Keynesians, by contrast, prioritize the impact of uncertainty on economic outcomes. Reliable, statistically knowable information does not exist for some of the most important decisions that agents must make in markets.[30] In such situations, they tend to base their decisions on what other agents think they know. Their degree of confidence in their own assessment is very fragile—an adverse shock can destroy confidence and lead agents to violently shift their stance in markets. Clearly, socio-economic divides (race, gender, etc.) among loan applicants in the context of missing information can cause lenders—their eyes very much on one another's decision-making—to make different sorts of decision for different applicant groups (who gets credit, who gets offered a subprime versus a prime loan, etc.).

The relevance of these "heterodox" ideas about how power and uncertainty can come into play in market dynamics, biasing outcomes and accentuating or prolonging breakdowns in formerly stable market arrangements, is obvious. Clearly there is much to be gained from combining, when possible, analytical methods from mainstream and heterodox economists alike, especially in contemplating phenomena as socially complex as predatory lending and financial crises.

WHAT DOES ECONOMIC THEORY TEACH US ABOUT THE SUBPRIME CRISIS?

The subprime crisis and subsequent financial collapse and recession have generated a huge outpouring of writing by economist and economic commentators about its causes and possible policy solutions. This final section of the chapter undertakes an abbreviated tour through this commentary. This tour is undertaken so as to make the point that what economic theory (which is to say, economists) "teaches" us about the subprime crisis and policy responses to it has little to do with the institutional background of subprime lending and the subprime crisis, and instead focuses on debates and issues internal to economics. A number of influential economists describe subprime borrowers as their theoretical priors imagine these borrowers are, with little regard for their actual circumstances. Further, economists are all but silent on some of the most crucial institutional dimensions of the subprime crisis, such as the shifting strategies of banks, in large part because contemporary economic theory has abstracted from most institutional features of real economies.

This inattention to some of the core political-economic causes and implications of the subprime crisis is not surprising, in light of the fact that many economists have characterized subprime lending per se as welfare improving and not exploitative. It does mean that efforts to construct policy responses to the subprime crisis that touch the individuals and communities victimized by predatory lending are unlikely to emerge from any consensus reached by economists.

Economists' Views about Why the Subprime Crisis Occurred

The first thing to be said about economists' reactions to the subprime crisis, when its first manifestations appeared in 2007, is that economists have had ample opportunities to react to financial crisis in the past quarter-century. Debates about financial instability and financial regulation have encompassed the US savings-and-loan and Latin American debt crises in the 1980s, and over the Mexican "Tequila," Asian, and Russian/Long Term Capital Management financial crises in the 1990s, to mention only the most prominent. These earlier crises—as serious and devastating as they have been for many nations throughout the world—have not threatened the viability of the US financial system per se, nor the prosperity of the US macro economy per se. They have been, in effect, controlled explosions, and as such have provided ammunition for participants in the recurrent battles between those with "freshwater" and "saltwater" views.

Given this history of neoliberal-era financial crises, and given the view of many economists that subprime lending had enhanced opportunity for borrowers, many economists initially downplayed the subprime crisis. For example, economists affiliated with both the Brookings Institution and the American Enterprise Institute (AEI)—respectively, Downs (2007) and Calomiris (2007)—registered their skepticism that this meltdown would have profound effects on either the economy as a whole or on the housing and housing-finance markets. Some commentators did stake out the opposite view: Dean Baker was writing numerous papers arguing that the housing bubble was there in full sight (see, for example, Baker 2006); and Henry Kaufman (2007) wrote an op-ed column in the *Wall Street Journal* that warned of "our risky new financial markets."[31]

But while Kaufman, nicknamed "Dr. Doom," had been regarded as the most influential analyst of US finance in the 1980s, his 2007 commentary received little attention in the press or in the blogosphere, as Yves Smith pointed out in an August 16, 2007 post to his "naked capitalism" blog. Perhaps more in line with the general view of market analysts was the opinion expressed by AEI's Alex Pollock (2007) that the subprime crisis is only the latest example of a long history of boom-bust cycles in financial markets. That is, history repeats itself, and yet people with access to financial markets learn nothing from it. This suggests that it is useless and even counterproductive to intervene to offset losses. Allen Meltzer expressed this view clearly in the pages of *The Wall Street Journal*, writing (a month before Kaufman's article appeared), "Capitalism without failure is like religion without sin. The answer to excessive risk-taking is 'let 'em fail.' ... Bailouts encourage excessive risk-taking; failures encourage prudent risk taking." (Meltzer 2007).

Two *New York Times* columnists weighed in on the other side of the equation, emphasizing the social as well as economic dimensions of the emerging crisis. Bob Herbert (2007) reminded readers of the roots of subprime lending in racial exclusion and in unfair, inadequately regulated lending practices. Krugman (2007a, 2007b, 2007c) also continually emphasized the culpability and bad faith shown by lenders, and the need to focus on wronged homeowners as well as a dangerously insolvent banking system. He wrote (2007c):

> There are, in fact, three distinct concerns associated with the rising tide of foreclosures in America. One is financial stability: as banks and other institutions take huge losses on their mortgage-related investments, the financial system as a whole is getting wobbly. Another is human suffering: hundreds of thousands, and probably millions, of American families will lose their homes. Finally, there's injustice: the subprime boom involved predatory lending—high-interest loans foisted on borrowers who qualified for lower rates—on an epic scale.

As the situation worsened, economists' attention focused more on understanding what specifically had gone wrong in *this* crisis. In a financial crisis rooted in bad debt, this means finding the sector responsible, blaming it, and proposing reforms. In the savings-and-loan (S&L) crisis of the 1980s, the last US crisis of comparable magnitude, proposed reforms included tightening regulation, eliminating or selling off weak institutions, and providing government support while asset prices recovered. In resolving that crisis, all those steps were taken. The debate over who to blame and what to do differed from the S&L-era debate in three ways, which unfolded sequentially in 2007 and 2008: first, the list of potential wrong-doers or duped innocents included mortgagees; second, virtually every US megabank was at risk of insolvency; third, the viability of global financial markets was uncertain; fourth, a global recession resulted from (or at least coincided with) the deepening crisis.

The deepening of the crisis in real time—played out against the political drama of the 2008 presidential-succession campaign—had two important effects. First, analysts' and policy-makers' attention was diffused, not concentrated. The solution of the situation of subprime borrowers—duped innocents, manipulative speculators, exploited minorities, in some combination—fell from view in policy discussion, replaced by a debate over megabank bailouts, which in turn was replaced by a debate over economic-recovery strategies. Second, the multiplying dysfunctions of the US economy shifted the ground of the policy conversation: it was not possible to sustain a technocratic discussion about how to resolve a serious but contained problem. Instead, analysts asked for solutions over ever-expanding portions of the an increasingly troubled economy. Trying to connect the dots on the cause of, and solutions for, this expanding set of crises forced experts and observers alike to draw on their underlying philosophies of government and market. And these philosophies, of course, differ markedly from one person to the next. This makes impossible the fragile fiction often required when those with partisan differences must solve significant political problems—the notion that 'as sensible people, we all agree (or agree to disagree) on most things, and can thus resolve our bottom-line differences regarding this *one issue*.'

For many economists, the notion that 'we all believe in market efficiency, in the end' provides this solidaristic fiction; it was called on, for example, in resolving the S&L crisis.[32] However, differences among efficient-market economists that appear subtle in controlled contexts of that sort widened into distinct visions of the relationship between government and the market. In one vision, the subprime crisis occurred because market forces had been undermined.

For example, writing about FNMA and FHLMC, Wallison and Calomiris (2008) point out the "inherent conflict between their government mission and their private ownership." (1) Calomiris was more specific in an article written a month later; the subprime crisis arose because of "...agency problems in asset management. In the current debacle, as in previous real estate-related financial shocks, government financial subsidies for bearing risk seem to have been key triggering factors, along with accommodative monetary policy." (Calomiris 2008: 1) In October 2009, Calomiris articulated a view of financial crises at odds with the "hardy perennial" story articulated by Pollock: he argued that banking crises generally occurred due to "risk-inviting rules" established by banking systems' regulators (Calomiris 2009a). In the same month, he argued against the notion that global banks that had become "too big to fail" were problematic: instead, he argued they are growth-enhancing and efficiency-creating (Calomiris 2009b).

Wallison's recent writings have also emphasized the idea that government interference in banking markets—in effect, too much regulation—is the underlying cause of the crisis. Wallison is among those who have asserted that the Community Reinvestment Act forced banks into making home loans to borrowers whose incomes were 80% or less of median income and encouraged banks to buy subprime loans (Wallison 2009a). He has also argued that FNMA and FHLMC engaged in purchases of excessively risky subprime loans because they enjoyed the umbrella of federal protection, if only implicitly (Wallison 2008). More recently, Wallison has argued that Congress has worsened the moral-hazard problem by using the Federal Housing Agency to take on more unsustainable subprime loans, burdening taxpayers ever more (Wallison 2009b). It should be said that the charge that the CRA caused the subprime crisis has no basis in fact. The CRA predates the creation of subprime loans by almost two decades; and most subprime loans were made by lenders not covered under the CRA (Center for Responsible Lending 2008). Those involved in advocating for and monitoring the CRA took an adverse view to predatory lending (including subprime mortgages) since it emerged, and recommended that the CRA ratings of banks that engaged in predatory lending be penalized (Engel and McCoy 2007). Wallison's interpretation of what the CRA requires is miscast.[33] What *is* clear, however, is that Wallison sees a pattern of ever-more-governmental interference in bank credit allocation, which in his view only leads the US banking system deeper into crisis.

But other analysts who take an efficient-markets view of subprime lending did not blame government subsidies. Instead, they emphasized inadequate regulation, which provided incentives for undue risk-taking. Quigley (2008), for example, wrote:

> One does not need to invoke the menace of unscrupulous and imprudent lenders or of equally predatory borrowers to explain the rapid collapse of the mortgage market as house price increases slowed in 2006, before ultimately declining. There were certainly enough unscrupulous lenders and predatory borrowers in the market, but the incentives faced by decent people—mortgagors and mortgagees—made their behavior much less sensitive to the underlying risks. ... How, you may wonder, could contracts with such poor incentives have evolved? To some extent, that remains a mystery. But to a large extent, the system worked just fine, as long as property values were rising and interest

rates falling—so that bad loans made at teaser rates could be refinanced after a couple of years at even lower rates. (2–3)

Quigley opens up two possibilities here beyond the "perverse government policies" narrative that Calomiris pursues: first, unscrupulous players could exploit the unwary and naive in under-regulated markets; second, people can be systematically fooled when caught in an asset bubble. These two possibilities have been explored by Morris (2008) and Shiller (2008), respectively. Neither possibility challenges the idea that market participants are rational; but each shows that letting market behavior loose without oversight can lead to disasters. Analysts like Shiller and Quigley insist that prudential regulation can improve outcomes, without generating governmental "control of markets."

Understanding the Links between Economists' Views and Economic Theory

The reader might note that Quigley's response to Calomiris does not directly address the issue of whether the CRA can plausibly be linked to the subprime crisis. Direct refutations of this link have generally not been economists.[34] Instead, Quigley defends the need for government policy in broad terms. This has been characteristic of pro-government-regulation economists' responses to subprime-related charges made by anti-regulation economists.

This leads to an important point regarding this entire policy and theoretical debate. With the exception of some writing by some heterodox economists, and by economists at modestly-ranked departments, this entire debate among economists about subprime lending and the subprime crisis has largely occurred with virtually no attention to racial discrimination and redlining, or to predatory lending.[35] These terms do not receive even a mention in any of the texts referred to above. This list can now be multiplied a hundred-fold. Many economic theorists have proposed new wrinkles in their economic models, and sometimes entirely new models, attempting to capture some of the dynamics of the unfolding financial and banking crisis. But in this vast outpouring, there has been no mention of financial exclusion, predatory lending, or racial inequality and exploitation. To introduce such issues into models that other economists will judge, in the first place, by whether they are equilibrium models as close to the efficient-markets norm as possible, would disqualify their authors from having a chance to influence the modeling conventions (and to capture the resulting storm of citations) of post-crisis models of borrowing and lending. Analysis of incentives, asset bubbles, and government/market interaction is sufficient to formulate hypotheses about "what went wrong."

Nor is financial economics' blind spot restricted to racial inequality and exploitation in credit markets per se. Economists who study the institutional transformation of financial practices and structures, for example, have entirely ignored the implications of this transformation for racial inequality and financial exclusion. In effect, economists have been so uninterested in racial inequality as a core topic of theoretical inquiry—and so skeptical of any efforts to show that racial inequality matters empirically—that they are blind to its critical role in the current financial crisis.

Economists are far more likely to debate issues that other economists— especially prestigious ones—are debating. This has been demonstrated very dramatically in the past several months. The notion that economics itself as a discipline should be indicted (or transformed) for not foreseeing the financial crisis has been circulating informally in think tanks and university departments for some time. But then Paul Krugman did some finger pointing in a September 2009 article in the *New York Times* Sunday magazine. Krugman criticized the profession both for not generating models that anticipated the financial crisis, and for its failure to broadly embrace the need for large-scale fiscal stimulus efforts in the wake of that crisis. His broadside evoked furious responses from members of the profession.[36] It is safe to say that few economists' core convictions that their models remain valuable on analytical and practical grounds have been shaken; even Krugman's critique doesn't suggest that sociologists' or historians' models of economic markets should be given equal weight. To the contrary, he wants economics models that allow for the "possibility of the kind of collapse that happened last year." (Krugman 2009).

In essence, debate in economics about the subprime crisis followed the same trajectory as has the broader policy debate: efforts at understanding the subprime crisis have been quickly swamped by those aimed at the subsequent collapse and recession. Further, just as ideas about how best to intervene in the real-world crisis differ because of conflicting political ideologies, points of view in economics differ because of deep differences regarding how market behavior should be modeled. And as in the world of politics, the depth and persistence of the current problems of the American political economy have heightened polemics within the dismal science.

Policy Alternatives and Economic Theory: Getting Beyond Efficient Markets

This chapter has presented, first of all, a political economy of the emergence of the subprime crisis. This crisis has to be seen in the context of several interwoven trajectories—the crisis and remaking of the US banking system from the 1980s onward, the history of financial exclusion and racial inequality in financial services, and the evolution of financial markets and of banking strategy. Next, this chapter has presented a summary of how economics has understood subprime lending—including its precedents, racial redlining and credit-market discrimination—and the subprime crisis.

The political economy story is dramatic. Before the 1990s, banks' reluctance had led to credit starvation in minority and lower-income neighborhoods. From the mid-1990s on, cities were awash with credit. Banks set up or contracted with intermediaries to make and securitize huge volumes of subprime and payday loans. The same lender might make exploitative loans in some portions of a city, while making prime loans elsewhere. Lenders, banks, and markets came to regard aggressive and even expectationally unsustainable terms and conditions for a subset of their borrowers as normal business practices. These practices soon migrated from inner-city areas to the broader markets; and then the crisis came.

This crisis, which has devastated financial firms' balance sheets, promises to shift the United States into yet a new lending regime—one in which banks' search for safety may lead to renewed financial exclusion. We can expect that financial firms, in the wake of the subprime crisis, will more insistently search for those loan customers that have sufficient wealth and income that loans made to them will be virtually default-free. But there are fewer (apparently) default-proof customers in a general population that also has an increasing proportion of lower-income households, and a skyrocketing share of households with damaged credit and/or foreclosures on their records. So the likelihood in market after market is that potential borrowers will break into two prototypical groups: one group whose assets and position are secure, and which both national and overseas lenders will regard as 'good risks' with whom they want long-term, sustained relationships; and a second group, whose wealth levels are so low that contracts are written with the hope of extracting sufficient returns in the short run to compensate for what will inevitably be (for most) longer-term insolvency problems. These new lines of financial exclusion will not be racially neutral: to the contrary, they will deepen the historical patterns of racial wealth differentials.

Despite this dramatic prospect, we have seen that economists have had very little to say about either subprime lending or the links between the subprime crisis and the historical patterns of financial exclusion and racial inequality in the United States. Subprime lending has been defined here in the context of the long tradition of treating minorities and the socially excluded, both at the individual and the community levels, differently than other customers. Some economists understand that if problems exist, market competition will eventually take care of them; so markets should be left free to do their magic. Other economists are less sold on free markets per se: they acknowledge that while banks and other lenders may have their reasons—profit maximization—for engaging in exclusion or predatory lending. They feel that justice is not served, but often are blocked from objecting more strongly because of their deep-seated belief in market efficiency: if the market is working as well as it can, how can one object?

There are still other economists than those featured in this paper, economists who embrace the importance of institutional history, who understand that power imbalances and exploitation are fundamental features of real-world economic dynamics. These economists regard efficiency as a concept that necessarily involves a social evaluation of market outcomes, as well as the individual-welfare assessment (the Pareto criterion) that is taught in graduate microeconomics courses. Some of these economists anticipated the dynamics that occurred (Galbraith 2009). And they may have hoped that the subprime crisis, unraveling as it did both the financial structure and the prosperity of the American people, would have already led to a deeper reconsideration of both how the economy should be organized and how economics should be done. Such hopes have not come to pass, at least not yet. Policy debate among economists, who are mostly blind to racial inequality, passed swiftly right over problems of predatory lending and onto questions of whether megabanks should be saved and how the macro economy could be most efficiently stabilized.

It is not clear at this writing whether the economic storm has passed or merely paused. We do know that banks' historical—if contested—legacy of denying equal credit-market access led to the creation of new instruments of financial exploitation that, once generalized and transported into a raging home-purchase market, led the banking system and the US economy to the edge of a very high cliff. We do not know whether we are floating or still falling—whether the conditions are in place for renewed growth. It does not seem that the megabanks that provided the high-octane fuel for subprime lending are yet prepared to lend; so the economy—an economy populated by millions who have lost wealth, homes, businesses, and stability—must get along without them, unless, that is, banks' role and obligations to the broader economy are redefined. For while the destruction of billions of dollars' worth of bank equity may have been some kind of retribution for banks' failure to turn away from historical patterns of exclusion and injustice, we know that most banks—especially the largest—have dodged a bullet. And while bankers ponder how to preserve their bonuses, and economists wonder what wrinkles to insert into their formal models, the American people are confronting the same unanswered question that was posed at the beginning of this crisis: how to build a socially-functional banking system which helps people meet their financial needs and which protects and expands their wealth, free of exploitation and exclusion.

BIBLIOGRAPHY

Aizcorbe, Ana, Arthur B. Kennickell and Kevin B. Moore, "Recent changes in U.S. family finances: evidence from the 1998 and 2001 Survey of Consumer Finances," *Federal Reserve Bulletin*, January 2003, 1–32.

Anderson, Jenny and Vikas Bajaj, 'Wary of Risk, Bankers Sold Shaky Debt,' *New York Times*, December 6, 2007, p. A1.

Arrow, Kenneth J., "Models of job discrimination," in A. Pascal, Editor, *Racial Discrimination in Economic Life*, D.C. Heath, Lexington, MA, 1972.

Ashton, Philip. "An Appetite for Yield: The Anatomy of the Subprime Mortgage Crisis," *Environment and Planning A* 41(6), 2008, pp. 1420–41.

Bair, Sheila, *Low-Cost Payday Loans: Obstacles and Opportunities*. Isenberg School of Management, University of Massachusetts, Amherst. June 2005.

Baker, Dean, "The Menace of an Unchecked Housing Bubble," *Economists' Voice* 3(4), March 2006.

Barth, James R., Tong Li, T. Phumiwasana, and Glenn Yago, "A Short History of the Sub-Prime Mortgage Market Meltdown." *GH Bank Housing Journal*. Los Angeles, Milken Institute, 2008.

Bowles, Samuel, and Herbert Gintis, "Walrasian Economics in Retrospect," *Quarterly Journal of Economics* 115(4), November 2000, pp. 1411–1439.

Bradford, Calvin, *Risk or Race? Racial Disparities and the Subprime Refinance Market*. Washington, DC: Center for Community Change, 2002.

Brooks, Rick and Ruth Simon, "As Housing Boomed, Industry Pushed Loans to a Broader Market," *Wall Street Journal*, December 3, 2007, A1.

Business Week, "The Besieged Banker: Bill Harrison must Prove J.P. Morgan Chase wasn't a Star-Crossed Merger," April 22, 2002.

California Reinvestment Coalition, *Inequities in California's Subprime Mortgage Market*, San Francisco: California Research Coalition, November 2002.

California Reinvestment Coalition, Community Reinvestment Association of North Carolina, Empire Justice Center, Massachusetts Affordable Housing Alliance, Neighborhood Economic Development Advocacy Project, Ohio Fair Lending Coalition and Woodstock Institute, *Paying More for the American Dream: The Subprime Shakeout and Its Impact on Lower-Income and Minority Communities*. San Francisco: California Reinvestment Coalition, 2008.

Calomiris, C.W., "Not (yet) a 'Minsky moment,'" American Enterprise Institute website, accessed at http://www.aei.org/docLib/20071010_Not(Yet)AMinskyMoment.pdf, December 11, 2007.

Calomiris, Charles W., "The Subprime Turmoil: What's Old, What's New, and What's Next," working paper, American Enterprise Institute October 1, 2008.

Calomiris, Charles, "Banking Crises and the Rules of the Game," NBER Working Paper 15403. Cambridge, MA: National Bureau of Economic Research, October 2009 (2009a).

Calomiris, Charles, "In the World of Banks, Bigger Can Be Better," *Wall Street Journal*, October 20, 2009. (2009b).

Calomiris, Charles W., Charles M. Kahn and Stanley D. Longhofer, "Housing-Finance Intervention and Private Incentives: Helping Minorities and the Poor," *Journal of Money, Credit and Banking* 26(3, Part 2), August 1994, pp. 634–74.

Canner, Glenn B., Wayne Passmore and Elizabeth Laderman, "The Role of Specialized Lenders in Extending Mortgages to Lower-Income and Minority Homebuyers." *Federal Reserve Bulletin*, November 1999, pp. 709–723.

Center for Responsible Lending, "CRA is not to Blame for the Mortgage Meltdown," CRL Issue Brief, October 3, 2008. Accessed at http://www.responsiblelending. org/mortgage-lending/policy-legislation/congress/cra-not-to-blame-for-crisis.pdf on December 28, 2009.

Cochrane, John H., "How did Paul Krugman get it so Wrong?" accessed on January 2, 2010 at http://modeledbehavior.com/2009/09/11/john-cochrane-responds-to-paul-krugman-full-text/.

Dash, Eric, "American Home Mortgage says it will Close," *New York Times*, August 3, 2007.

Downey, Kirstin, "Mortgage Lender Settles Lawsuit: Ameriquest Will Pay $325 Million," *Washington Post*, January 24, 2006, p. D01.

Downs, A., "Credit crisis: the sky is not falling," Policy Brief #164, Economic Studies, The Brookings Institution, October 31, 2007.

Dymski, Gary A., *The Bank Merger Wave*. Armonk, NY: M.E. Sharpe, Inc. 1999.

Dymski, Gary A., "Racial Exclusion and the Political Economy of the Subprime Crisis," *Historical Materialism* 17(2), 2009, pp. 149–179.

Dymski, Gary A., "Afterword: Mortgage Markets and the Urban Problematic in the Global Transition," *International Journal on Urban and Regional Research,* 33:2, special issue on sociology & geography of mortgage markets, June 2009, Pp. 427–42.

Dymski, Gary A., "U.S. Housing as Capital Accumulation: The Contradictory Transformation of American Housing Finance, Households and Communities," in *Housing Finance Futures: Housing Policies, Gender Inequality and Financial Globalization on the Pacific Rim*. Ed. by Gary Dymski and Dorene Isenberg. Armonk, NY: M.E. Sharpe, 2002.

Dymski, Gary A., "Discrimination in the Credit and Housing Markets: Findings and Challenges," in *Handbook on the Economics of Discrimination*, Ed. by William Rodgers. Cheltenham, UK: Edward Elgar, 2006, pp. 215–259.

Dymski, Gary A. and John M. Veitch, "Financial Transformation and the Metropolis: Booms, Busts and Banking in Los Angeles," *Environment and Planning A*. 28(7), July 1996, pp. 1233–1260.

Engel, Kathleen, and Patricia A. McCoy, "The CRA Implications of Predatory Lending," *Fordham Urban Law Journal*, 29(4), April 2002, pp. 1571–1606.

Federal Deposit Insurance Corporation, *FDIC Survey of Unbanked and Underbanked Households*. Washington, DC: Federal Deposit Insurance Corporation, December 2009.

Fender, Ingo, and Janet Mitchell, "Risk, Complexity, and the Use of Ratings in Structured Finance," working paper, Bank for International Settlements and National Bank of Belgium, March 2005.

Galbraith, James K., "Who Are These Economists, Anyway?" *Theory and Action*, Fall 2009, 85–98.

General Accounting Office 2002, *Electronic Transfers: Use by Federal Payment Recipients has Increased but Obstacles to Greater Participation Remain*, Report to the Subcommittee on Oversight and Investigations, Committee on Financial Services, U.S. House of Representatives. Report Number GAO-02–913. Washington, DC: General Accounting Office, September.

Gerardi, Kristopher, Harvey S. Rosen, Paul Willen, "Do Households Benefit from Financial Deregulation and Innovation? The Case of the Mortgage Market," *National Bureau of Economic Research Working Paper 12967*, Cambridge MA: National Bureau of Economic Research, March 2007.

Gerdes, Geoffrey R., and Jack K. Walton II, "The use of checks and other noncash payment instruments in the United States," *Federal Reserve Bulletin*, Board of Governors of the Federal Reserve System (U.S.), August 2002, pp. 360–374.

Goolsbee, Austan, "'Irresponsible' Mortgages Have Opened Doors to Many of the Excluded," *New York Times,* March 29, 2007, P. C3.

Gordon, Robert, "Did Liberals Cause the Sub-Prime Crisis?" *The American Prospect* (web version), April 7, 2008, accessed at http://www.prospect.org/cs/articles?article=did_liberals_cause_the_subprime_crisis.

Gosselin, Peter, "The Poor Have More Things Today—Including Wild Income Swings," *Los Angeles Times*, December 12, 2004.

Hagerty, J.R., and K. Richardson, "Countrywide shows even prime loans are beginning to sour," Wall Street Journal, *July 25, 2007, C1.*

Henriques, Diana B., and Lowell Bergman, "Profiting From Fine Print With Wall Street's Help," *Wall Street Journal*, March 15, 2000.

Herbert, Bob, "A Swarm of Swindlers," *New York Times*, November 20, 2007.

Hogarth, Jeanne, Christoslav Anguelov, and Jinhook Lee, "Who has a Bank Account? Exploring Changes over Time, 1989–2001," *Journal of Family and Economic Issues* 26(1), March 2005, pp. 7–30.

Housing and Economic Rights Advocates and California Reinvestment Coalition, "Foreclosed: The Burden of Homeownership Loss on City of Oakland and Alameda County Residents," San Francisco: California Reinvestment Coalition, December 2007.

Hunter, William C. and Mary Beth Walker. "The Cultural Affinity Hypothesis and Mortgage Lending Decisions." Journal of Real Estate Finance and Economics 13 (July 1996), 57–70.

Joint HUD-Treasury Task Force on Predatory Lending, Curbing Predatory Home Mortgage Lending. Washington, DC: U.S. Department of Housing and Urban Development (HUD), June 2000.

Katkov, Neil, *ATMs: Self-Service for the Unbanked.* October. Tokyo: Celent Communications, 2002.

Kaufman, H., "Our risky new financial markets," *Wall Street Journal, August 15, 2007.*

Kelly, Kate, Serena Ng and David Reilly, "Two Big Funds At Bear Stearns Face Shutdown As Rescue Plan Falters Amid Subprime Woes, Merrill Asserts Claims," *Wall Street Journal*, June 20, 2007, p. A1.

Keynes, John Maynard, "The General Theory of Employment," *Quarterly Journal of Economics* 51(2), February 1937, pp. 209–223.

Krugman, Paul, "Very Scary Things," *New York Times,* August 10, 2007. (2007a).

Krugman, Paul, "Gone Baby Gone," *New York Times,* October 22, 2007. (2007b).

Krugman, Paul, "Henry Paulson's Priorities," *New York Times*, December 10. (2007c).

Krugman, Paul, *"How did economists get it so wrong?" New York Times,* September 6, 2009.

Litan, Robert E., and George G. Kaufman, editors, *Assessing Bank Reform: FDICIA One Year Later.* Washington, DC: Brookings Institution, 1993.

Masterson, Thomas, Ajit Zacharias, and Edward N. Wolff, "Long-Term Trends in the Levy Institute Measure of Economic Well-Being (LIMEW), United States, 1959–2004," Economics Working Paper 556, Annandale-on-Hudson, NY: The Levy Economics Institute, 2009.

McCoy, Patricia and Elvin Wyly, "Special Issue on Market Failures and. Predatory Lending," *Housing Policy Debate* 15(3), 2004.

Meltzer, Allen, "Let 'Em Fail," *Wall Street Journal*, July 21, 2007: A6.

Mollenkamp, Carrick, "Retiring First Union Chairman Cuts Deal for $1.8 Million a Year plus his Pension," *Wall Street Journal*, November 15, 2000, p. A10.

Mollenkamp, Carrick, Edward Taylor and Ian McDonald, "How the Subprime Mess Ensnared German bank; IKB gets a Bailout," *Wall Street Journal*, August 10, 2007, page A1.

Mollenkamp, Carrick, Deborah Solomon, Robin Sidel and Valerie Bauerlein 2007, "How London Created a Snarl in Global Markets," *Wall Street Journal*, October 18: A1.

Morris, Charles, *Trillion-Dollar Meltdown.* Jackson, TN: PublicAffairs, 2008.

Mulligan, Casey B., "Is Macroeconomics Off Track?" *The Economists' Voice*, November 2009.

Oppel, Richard A., Jr., "Citigroup to pay up to $20 Million in deceptive-lending case," New York Times, September 7, 2001.

Oppel, Richard, and Patrick McGeehan, "Citigroup Announces Changes to Guard Against Abusive Loan Practices," *New York Times*, November 8, 2000.

Orozco, Manuel, *The Remittance Marketplace: Prices, Policy and Financial Institutions.* Washington, DC: Pew Hispanic Center, June 2004.

Pittman, Mark, "Moody's, S&P Understate Subprime Risk, Study Says (Update2)," *Bloomberg News Service*, May 3, 2007.

Partnoy, Frank, and David A. Skeel, Jr., "The promise and perils of credit derivatives," *University of Cincinnati Law Review* 75(2), Spring 2007, 1027.

Pollard, Jane, "Banking at the margins: a geography of financial exclusion in Los Angeles," *Environment and Planning A* 28(7), July 1996, pp. 1209–1232.

Pollock, Alex, "Subprime Bust Expands," *The American—a magazine of ideas*. Accessed at american.com, http://american.com/archive/2007/august-0807/subprime-bust-expands, December 11, 2007.

Punch, Linda, "Beckoning The Unbanked," *Credit Card Management* 17(7), October 2004, pp. 28.

Quigley, J.M. (2008) Compensation and incentives in the mortgage business. *Economists' Voice*, October.

Quinn, Lawrence Richter, "The buying up of subprime," *Mortgage Banking*, April 1, 1998. http://www.lexisnexis.com/.

Sapsford, Jathon, Laurie P. Cohen, and Monica Langley, "High Finance: J.P. Morgan Chase to Buy Bank One," *Wall Street Journal,* January 15, 2004, pp. A1.

Schumpeter, Joseph A., *History of Economic Analysis*. Oxford: Oxford University Press, 1954.

Seidman, Ellen, "No, Larry, CRA Didn't Cause the Sub-Prime Mess," April 15, 2008, accessed at http://www.newamerica.net/blog/asset-building/2008/no-larry-cra-didn-t-cause-sub-prime-mess-3210.

Shiller, Robert J. *The Subprime Solution*. Princeton: Princeton University Press, 2008.

Siconolfi, Michael, "Did Authorities Miss a Chance To Ease Crunch?" *Wall Street Journal*, December 10, 2007, C1.

Sinkey, Jr., Joseph F. 1981, *Problem and Failed Institutions in the Commercial Banking Industry.* Greenwich, Connecticut: JAI Press, Inc.

Squires, Gregory D., editor, *From Redlining to Reinvestment*. Philadelphia: Temple University Press, 1993.

Staten, Michael E. and Anthony M. Yezer 2004, "Introduction to the Special Issue," "Special Issue: 'subprime Lending: Empirical Studies,'" *Journal of Real Estate Finance and Economics* 29:4: 359–63.

Staten, M.E., and A.M. Yezer, "Introduction to the special issue," "Special Issue: 'subprime Lending: Empirical Studies,'" Journal of real estate finance and economics Vol. 29:4, 2004, 359–63.

Stiglitz, Joseph E., "The Causes and Consequences of the Dependence of Quality on Price," Journal of Economic Literature 25(1), March 1987, pp. 1–48.

Stiglitz, Joseph E., "Information and the Change in the Paradigm in Economics," Nobel Prize Lecture, December 8, 2001.

Stiglitz, Joseph E., *Globalization and its Discontents*. New York: W.W. Norton, 2003.

Stiglitz, Joseph E., and Andrew Weiss, "Credit Rationing in Markets with Incomplete Information," *American Economic Review* 71(3), June 1981, pp. 393–410.

The Economist, "At the Risky End of Finance," August 21, 2007, pp. 80–82 (2007a).

The Economist, "Sold Down the River Rhine," August 11, 2007, p. 66 (2007b).

Tully, Shawn, "Wall Street's Money Machine Breaks Down: The Subprime Mortgage Crisis Keeps Getting Worse-and Claiming More Victims," *Fortune*, November 12, 2007.

US Comptroller of the Currency, "Payroll Cards: An Innovative Product for Reaching the Unbanked and Underbanked," *Community Development Insights*. Washington, DC: Community Affairs Department, Comptroller of the Currency, June 2005.

US Department of Housing and Urban Development, Unequal Burden: Income and Racial Disparities in Subprime Lending in America. Washington, DC: Department of Housing and Urban Development, April 2000.

Vandenberg, Paul, "Adapting to the Financial Landscape: Evidence from Small Firms in Nairobi," *World Development,* 31(11), 2003, pp. 1829–1843.

Wallison, Peter J., "Cause and Effect: Government Policies and the Financial Crisis," *AEI OUTLOOK Series.* Washington, DC: American Enterprise Institute, November 2008.

Wallison, Peter J., "The True Origins of This Financial Crisis," American Spectator, February 2009. (2009a).

Wallison, Peter J., "Barney Frank, Predatory Lender," *Wall Street Journal,* October 15, 2009. (2009b).

Wallison, P.J., and C. W. Calomiris (2008), The last trillion-dollar commitment, the destruction of Fannie Mae and Freddie Mac. *Financial Services Outlook,* Washington, DC, American Enterprise Institute for Public Policy Research, September.

Wolff, Edward N., and Ajit Zacharias, 2009. "Household Wealth and the Measurement of Economic Well-Being in the United States," *Journal of Economic Inequality* 7(2), June 2009, pp. 83–115.

Wray, L. Randall, "Lessons from the Subprime Meltdown," Working paper no. 522, Levy Economics Institute of Bard College, December 2007.

Wyly, Elvin, Markus Moos, Holly Foxcroft, and Emmanuel Kabahizi, "Subprime Mortgage Segmentation in the American Urban System," *Tijdschrift voor Economische en Sociale Geografie*, 99(1), February 2008, pp. 3–23.

NOTES

1. The historical material presented in this section is drawn from the author's writings over a number of years, especially Dymski (1999) and Dymski (2009). The material on discrimination and redlining in section 3 draws heavily on Dymski (2006). Those interested in further documentation or references are urged go get in touch with the author.

2. This evolution was significantly advanced during the subprime crisis: Wells Fargo used its purchase of Wachovia to establish an East Coast branch network; JP Morgan-Chase's purchase of Washington Mutual gave it a West Coast market presence.

3. The formal name of this 1980 federal law is the Depository Institutions Deregulation and Monetary Control Act of 1980.

4. US banks have taken the lead in formulating the elements of "upscale retail banking" for several reasons. First, liquid investment alternatives for non-elite households (such as money-market mutual funds, equity-based mutual funds, and so on) were pioneered in the US. Second, the large number of US commercial banks and savings institutions, and the low level of market concentration in US consumer banking markets (by international standards) created the possibility for more gains from innovations in the mix, marketing, and delivery of consumer banking products.

Third, banking deregulation in the US occurred somewhat earlier in time than in other nations. Fourth, the continual suburban expansion of middle- and upper-income households in the US continually creates new market-entry possibilities for banks positioned to meet the particular needs of these households.

5. See Dymski (2002).

6. Arrow (1972) first suggested this idea in an essay on labor market discrimination. Stiglitz and Weiss (1981) points out that banks might rationally redline minority neighborhoods if race is a signal of higher risk.

7. For empirical studies of bank-branch locational inequality in Los Angeles, see Dymski and Veitch (1996) and Pollard (1996). These authors show that banks have systematically closed branches in inner-core areas, while opening branches in emerging suburban areas. These inner-core branches often were established in earlier days when these neighborhoods were not majority-minority, and/or had belonged to merged banks no longer in operation.

8. According to the Federal Reserve's triennial Survey of Consumer Finances, the share of households without a current account fell from 15% in 1989 to 10.5% in 1998, and then rose slightly to 11% in 2001. A very different interpretation of these same data was offered by Hogarth *et al.* (2005), who assert: "Results indicate that holding socioeconomic characteristics as well as households' need for an account, abilities to manage the account, access to accounts, and previous experiences constant, account ownership increased over time, with the biggest gains between 1995 and 1998. Increases over time were experienced across the spectrum of income, net worth, education, race, and age characteristics." (7).

9. A November 2001 study of California cities by the California Reinvestment Committee (CRC), using a borrower survey instrument, found that a third of subprime borrowers were solicited by loan marketers, and that minorities and the elderly are targeted in these marketing efforts. These loans often have onerous terms and conditions; in the CRC study, three in five respondents have punitive repayment penalty provisions, while 70 percent saw their terms worsen at closing. Other common abuses include high upfront fees and costly lump-sum credit insurance.

10. Also see United States HUD (2000) and the extensive statistics in ACORN (2000). The Department of Housing and Urban Development, together with the Treasury Department, published a study that discusses the core issues raised by subprime lending and reports on the results of several public forums and task forces (Joint HUD-Treasury Task Force, 2000). The findings reported in the text have also been largely supported in the academic research that is beginning to emerge on predatory lending. Most of the initial empirical academic studies are collected in two journals' special issues: volume 29, number 4 of the *Journal of Real Estate Finance and Economics*, published in 2004, with an introductory essay by guest editors Staten and Yezer (2004); and volume 15, number 3 of *Housing Policy Debate*, with an overview essay by McCoy and Wyly (2004).

11. The 2009 FDIC study shows that unbanked and underbanked households are far more likely than others to use payday loans and other informal-market loan products.

12. Community reinvestment advocates tend to use the term "predatory lending" in describing payday and subprime lending. This term would be challenged by analysts hypothesizing that serving the needs of lower income and riskier borrowers requires higher rates and tighter terms and conditions than more creditworthy customers will be charged. See section 4 below.

13. Visa and Mastercard have used data from these new card markets, which has helped them develop better credit-risk assessment methods for lower-income customers (Punch 2004).

14. In another case, First Union Bancorp bought the Money Store in June 1998. First Union subsequently closed this unit in mid-2000 in the wake of massive losses (Mollenkamp 2000). In 2003, HSBC bought Household International, parent of Household Finance Company, after the latter settled on charges that it had engaged in predatory lending.

15. Fair-lending advocates resisted this development. For example, Martin Eakes of the Durham (NC) Self-Help Credit Union commented, "Those of us who have worked on the community level ... believe that Associates is a rogue company and may alone account for 20 percent of all abusive home loans in the nation." (Oppel 2001).

16. The first SIVs were created for Citigroup in 1988 and 1989 (Mollenkamp, Solomon, *et al.* 2007).

17. These data, from the Mortgage Market Statistical Annual, appear as Table 1 of Wray 2007, p. 30.

18. One approach here is to suppose that lenders may have 'cultural affinity' with loan applicants of their own race. In this event, informational barriers will be higher whenever lenders and loan applicants are drawn from different racial/ethnic groups. Thus, if most bankers are white, non-white applicants will be at a disadvantage. See, in particular, Calomiris *et al.* (1994) and Hunter and Walker (1996).

19. A "knife's edge" problem in economics arises when a precise balance between two offsetting forces is needed to sustain an equilibrium.

20. The author of this text was writing his dissertation in the economic studies section of the Brookings Institution in the mid-1980s, a time during which debate about the causes of, and solutions to, the savings-and-loan crisis occurred on a nearly-daily basis. The many experts and regulators who came to Brookings to discuss this topic, at that time, were all agreed that while no explicit federal guarantees underlay the mortgage-backed securities market, at the end of the day the federal government would guarantee against these securities' failure. At the crux of the matter were FNMA and FHLMC; as we have seen, their underwriting permitted the take-off of the mortgage-backed securities market. These two agencies were nominally independent, and not part of the federal budget; but they were carrying out a crucial social/political/economic function- that is, facilitating the flow of mortgages in the US economy. The semi-public/semi-private ambiguity about FNMA and FHLMC has been problematic and unresolved since that time. It remains unresolved at this writing.

21. Ashton (2008) also explores the notion that subprime lending represents market completion.

22. Goolsbee (2007). Goolsbee's arguments were based largely on Gerardi, Rosen, and Willen (2007).

23. Economists "outside the mainstream" generally would disagree with this "in principle" statement, on the basis that power, social conflict, historical oppression, or other factors underlie the distribution of economic resources; so to suppose that even apparently neutral market allocations can be fair or non-exploitative is to write history out of economic analysis. Entire libraries have been written on the divides within economics and between economics and other social sciences (and the consequences of these divides); recently, the author of this paper wrote an article reflecting on this problem in analyses of urban issues (Dymski 2009).

24. The argument that follows is based on Stiglitz (1987).

25. An example of relevant political institutions would be the state-owned banks that helped guide East Asian growth in the 1980s and early 1990s; an example of societal characteristics would be the social cohesion among rural women in South Asia, which facilitated the creation of the Grameen Bank lending model. Joseph Stiglitz, one of the principle contributors to this approach, terms it "information economics;" he argues that the implications are so fundamental as to constitute a paradigm change in economics (Stiglitz 2001).

26. There are two problems with using race as a signal of loan-applicant 'type.' First, signals should ideally be emitted purposely by applicants; the classic example involves candidates for post-secondary teaching posts, who emit signals of their capability by earning advanced degrees in their fields. Race is not 'earned,' but is socially defined fails this test. Second, racial inequality varies systematically in all the factor markets—labor, credit, and capital. So it will always be feasible for a lender (say) to justify loan denial based on a minority applicant's greater vulnerability in the labor market—and vice versa. This sets up a trap: members of groups that are easily typed and consistently disadvantaged across all factor markets will be unable to systematically overcome their disadvantaged status in any one factor market.

27. As Vandenberg (2003) points out, borrowers in financial markets are not passive but are active: they will do what they must to find credit, the question being at what price, and on what terms, and with what security and risk they will find it.

28. See, for example, Stiglitz (2003).

29. See, for example, Bowles and Gintis (2000).

30. Keynes put it this way in a famous passage: "By 'uncertain' knowledge, let me explain, I do not mean merely to distinguish what is known for certain from what is only probable. The game of roulette is not subject, in this sense, to uncertainty. ... the expectation of life is only slightly uncertain.... The sense in which I am using the term is that in which the prospect of a European war is uncertain, or the price of copper and the rate of interest twenty years hence, or the obsolescence of a new invention, or the position of private wealth owners in the social system in 1970. About these matters there is no scientific basis on which to form any calculable probability whatever. We simply do not know." (Keynes 1937, pp. 213–214).

31. There is some irony in this juxtaposition, as Charles Calomiris is the Henry Kaufman Professor of Financial Institutions at Columbia University.

32. See Litan and Kaufman (1993), which memorializes an ex-post discussion among key policy-makers involved in the thrift crisis.

33. It should be noted that Peter Wallison was not uniquely associated with this view of the CRA.

34. See, for example, Gordon (2008) and Seidman (2008).

35. For a summary of some of these writings, see Galbraith (2009). Other social scientists, of course, have done extensive research on the links between racial inequalities and subprime lending; see the work cited in footnotes 9 and 23 above.

36. On the profession's failure to predict the financial crisis, see Cochrane (2009); on Krugman's recommended fiscal policy, see Mulligan (2009).

Chapter Three

Subprime Lending, Foreclosure and Race

An Introduction to the Role of Securitization in Residential Mortgage Finance

Christopher L. Peterson

In recent years, Wall Street financiers opened up a new frontier of home mortgage lending to Americans of relatively modest means with minimal down payments and through exotic, untested financial products.[1] Capital markets largely funded this new breed of aggressive subprime mortgage finance through "securitization"—the process of bundling assets, such as mortgage loans, into large pools and then reselling those assets as securities to investors.[2] Financiers justified this new private "subprime" home mortgage market to leaders and to the American people with a promise of new opportunities for home ownership.[3] Today, the course of events has proven this promise to be, at least for the time being, empty.[4] Millions of Americans borrowed money against their homes and now cannot afford to repay. Current estimates suggest that over six million mortgages—nearly 13% of all American residential loans—will end in foreclosure by 2012.[5] After years of frenzied investment in risky home mortgages sold to investors outside the traditional public secondary market channels, the American financial markets are now facing financial upheaval and the prospect of structural change of a magnitude not seen since the Great Depression.

This chapter attempts to provide a short, accessible introduction to the evolution and structure of the American home mortgage lending industry, with particular emphasis on how securitization of subprime home mortgages led to the current foreclosure crisis. Initially, Part I of this summary briefly describes the early American mortgage lending market before and after Franklin Roosevelt's "New Deal." Next, Part II of this chapter summarizes the evolution and operation of subprime mortgage securitization. Part III concludes with observations on how securitization encouraged poor underwriting practices and predatory loan terms.

THE EARLY SECONDARY
RESIDENTIAL MORTGAGE MARKET

Simple Origins: Two Party Mortgage Finance

The earliest American home mortgage lending institutions were small co-operative groups of neighbors and friends called building societies. Modeled after similar British institutions formed in the late eighteenth century, American building societies first appeared in 1831.[6] In the first building societies, members of the group agreed to make a weekly contribution to a common building fund.[7] In return, the society paid for the construction of a home for each member of the group, one family at a time.[8] All members were obliged to continue making contributions until every member obtained a home, at which time the society terminated.[9] Throughout the nineteenth century, building societies became more popular, eventually shedding their terminal nature, employing professional management, and taking savings deposits instead of mutual contributions.[10] By the late nineteenth century, US building societies were more commonly referred to as "building and loans," a label which later morphed into "savings and loans," and eventually into today's term "thrifts."[11] Commercial banks generally refused to make mortgages, eschewing the liquidity and risk problems of this type of credit.[12] However, in the mid-to-late-1800s, mutual savings banks,[13] private mortgage lending firms, and some insurance companies joined building and loans in making home mortgages.[14]

Despite these sources of credit, by the beginning of the twentieth century, consumers hoping to own a home had quite limited financing options. Most mortgages required a large down payment of around 40 percent of the home purchase price.[15] Moreover, early twentieth century mortgage loans had terms typically averaging between three and six years.[16] These short repayment durations necessitated high monthly payments, often followed by a large balloon payment of the remaining balance, due at the end of the loan term.[17] Relatively few families could overcome these financial hurdles. Moreover, lenders had both formal and informal policies that discriminated against minorities and women. As a result, none but the most affluent men of European ancestry had reliable and widespread access to home finance.[18]

Early home mortgage lenders themselves had limited options in acquiring the capital to make home mortgage loans. By far, the most common mortgage lenders were individual non-professional landowners who usually accepted a mortgage along with partial payment in connection with the sale of property.[19] Building societies only had the funds they could gather in deposits from their local community and had little opportunity to assign their loans.[20]

Insurance companies made mortgage loans out of the funds gathered from insurance premiums and then held those loans in their portfolio.[21]

The earliest efforts to form a secondary market came out of private mortgage companies, which, by the 1880s, were making mortgage loans around the country through local agents.[22] Some of these companies raised funds by issuing bonds to East Coast and European investors.[23] Called "mortgage-backed bonds," these loans included a promise to pay a fixed amount, and also security agreements where the mortgage company pledged its loans as collateral for the bond.[24] Foreshadowing some of the problems in today's market, this system proved extremely unstable. Because distant and uninformed investors bore the ultimate risk on individual home mortgages, lenders and their local agents had an incentive to use inflated appraisals and fraudulent origination practices to generate up-front profits.[25] When recessions in the 1890s produced widespread consumer defaults, all of these mortgage companies folded and their investors took horrendous losses.[26] Thus, with the exception of a few fitful experiments, early American mortgage loans were two party transactions with lenders holding their own notes, collecting payments, and foreclosing on defaulting borrowers when necessary.

The Government as Assignee: Three Party Mortgage Finance After the Great Depression

The defining event shaping the secondary mortgage market in the twentieth century was the Great Depression. When millions of people lost their jobs in the early 1930s, prices for goods, services, and land all dramatically declined.[27] Agricultural prices were so low, family farmers could not profit from selling their crops.[28] Demand for goods and the investment capital from the stock market both dried up, forcing manufacturers to lay off workers.[29] In the mortgage lending market, lenders were forced to call in their loans as *half* of all single-family mortgages fell into default.[30] In foreclosure, real estate prices were so low, lenders could not recoup their investment by selling seized homes.[31] Because lenders were understandably reluctant to continue making uncollectible loans, the mortgage finance and housing construction industries ground to a halt.[32]

Throughout the 1930s, the federal government took a series of steps to restart and expand these industries. This Depression-era legislation established an infrastructure for mortgage lending which, in addition to helping establish the American middle class, is crucial for understanding the playing field within which today's predatory lenders operate. First, during the Hoover administration, Congress created the twelve regional Federal Home Loan Banks (FHLBs).[33] Analogous to the federal-reserve banks, the FHLBs loaned money to thrifts, which in turn lent these funds to consumers.[34] Although started with government capital, the FHLBs gradually accumulated private funds and eventually became wholly owned by their member thrifts. The FHLBs gave thrifts a reliable and inexpensive source of funds to supplement consumer deposits, which allowed thrifts to develop into the most significant source of home mortgage credit in the mid-twentieth century.

Nevertheless, at the beginning of the Roosevelt administration, lenders were still reluctant to re-enter the market. FDR backed three important legislative initiatives, all of which pushed the federal government further into residential mortgage lending.[35] First, in 1933, Congress created the Home Owners Loan Corporation (HOLC). HOLC used taxpayer funds to buy mortgages owed by financially distressed families.[36] HOLC then refinanced these borrowers into more affordable government loans with longer terms.[37] Second, in 1934, Congress created the Federal Housing Administration (FHA), tasking it with offering government guaranteed insurance to home mortgage lenders.[38] For loans that met FHA's underwriting criteria, the government agreed to pay mortgage lenders the difference between the price fetched by a repossessed home and its outstanding loan balance.[39] In effect, this insurance protected the lender from the borrower's credit risk and from downward movement in realty prices. FHA's insurance facilitated mortgage loans with much longer durations, down payments of only 20 percent of the home value, and more affordable monthly installments.[40] With loan terms of up to thirty years, families could now purchase a home over the duration of an adult's working life. FHA's underwriting guidelines also created industry standards which encouraged cautious and professional behavior in loan origination.[41] Finally, in 1938, Congress created the Federal National Mortgage Association (FNMA), now more popularly known as "Fannie Mae."[42] Fannie Mae's function was to act as an assignee by purchasing FHA's "nonconventional" insured loans.[43] Not only was a qualifying mortgage guaranteed, but the lender, if it chose, could assign the loan to Fannie Mae for cash, quickly recouping its investment plus a premium.[44] This secondary market outlet alleviated fears of illiquidity, inducing many mortgage loan companies, insurance companies, and even commercial banks back into the consumer home loan business.

Collectively, these government initiatives (along with millions of cheap automobiles cranked out by the post-World War II industrial base) facilitated migration of the nesting white middle class to rapidly expanding suburbs surrounding American cities.[45] In effect, the Depression-era legislation created what Douglas Diamond and Michael Lea have described as two housing finance "circuits."[46] Thrifts and the twelve regional Federal Home Loan Banks constituted the first circuit. The second circuit included mortgage loan companies, insurance companies, and banks—all of whom relied on FHA insurance (as well as analogous Veterans Administration insurance offered after World War II)[47] and assigned their loans to Fannie Mae. While the thrift circuit was the larger of the two until the 1980s, the Fannie Mae circuit proved more influential in determining today's secondary market structure.[48]

What both circuits shared, and continue to share, is a unifying theme of federal government sponsorship.[49] In the thrift circuit, even after member thrifts became the sole owners of the regional Federal Home Loan Banks, the federal government still "backstopped" them with authorization to borrow from the US Treasury.[50] In the second home finance circuit, the government purchased and held consumer borrowers' promissory notes.[51] Both circuits are best conceptualized as a three-party model: borrower, lender, and the government as a guarantor or assignee. Moreover, as discussed further in Part IV, the fact that a federal agency was the most important assignee of home mortgages exerted significant influence on the mortgage loan assignment laws that now govern trafficking in predatory loans.

The Government as Issuer: The Innovation of Public Residential Mortgage Securities

In the post-war years, the two circuits provided historically unprecedented levels of secured credit to Americans. The larger thrift circuit focused primarily on conventional mortgages that were either uninsured or underwritten with private mortgage insurance.[52] The second circuit became increasingly reliant on mortgage companies that focused on nonconventional FHA-and-VA-insured loans, which were then assigned to Fannie Mae. By the 1960s, growth in the Fannie Mae circuit was limited by the policy objectives of government insurance programs. The federal government directed its mortgage insurance programs with policy objectives in mind, such as "increasing military housing, national defense housing, urban renewal housing, nursing homes, mobile home parks, and housing for the elderly, among others."[53] Many mortgage bankers wanted to penetrate into the conventional market dominated by the thrifts, but lacked the reliable and inexpensive capital necessary to do so.[54] The result was pressure on the federal government to provide a source of liquidity for conventional loans made by non-depository mortgage lenders.

Once again, the federal government responded by facilitating the development of new home mortgage finance infrastructure. In 1968, Congress partitioned Fannie Mae into two separate organizations. The first organization retained the original function, but operated under a new name: The Government National Mortgage Association.[55] "Ginnie Mae," as it became known, continued to purchase nonconventional FHA- and VA-insured mortgages.[56]

The second organization kept the old name, but received a new mission. Fannie Mae became a private federally chartered corporation whose primary function would be to purchase conventional home mortgages from private lenders.[57] At this point, Fannie Mae still held home mortgages in its own portfolio, and in turn borrowed money in its own name to finance its operations. The hope was that this new private incarnation of Fannie Mae would provide a reliable low-cost source of funds for lenders wishing to offer conventional, non-government insured mortgages. In 1970, Congress created "Freddie Mac" to serve a similar role as Fannie Mae.[58]

A short time later, a fundamentally new method of obtaining funds for mortgage loans developed: securitization. Rather than holding mortgages themselves, both Ginnie Mae and then Freddie Mac began issuing mortgage-backed securities that "passed through" interest income to investors.[59] The agencies would purchase home mortgages, deposit large numbers of them in "pools," and sell participations in the pools to investors on Wall Street. With these new pass-through investment vehicles, investors could hold a share of large (and diversified) numbers of mortgages insured by the government in the case of Ginnie Mae, or guaranteed by the large stable government sponsored enterprises (GSEs) in the case of Freddie Mac and Fannie Mae (who also began securitizing shortly thereafter).[60] Because the agencies now guaranteed the principal and interest income of their securities even when mortgagors defaulted, investors saw the securities as a low-risk investment even without the assurances of a rating organization, such as Standard and Poor's or Moody's.[61] Investors could buy and easily resell their investments in order to best suit their portfolios and investment strategies.[62] These mortgage-backed securities had stability and liquidity, which generated greater spreads over comparable term treasury obligations than securities of similar risk.[63] Securitization of mortgage loans by the GSEs allowed the larger capital markets to directly invest in American home ownership at a lower cost than the older depository lending model of business.[64]

PRIVATE LABEL SECURITIZATION

The Evolution of Private Securitization

Like the GSEs, purely private institutions saw the potential benefits of pooling home mortgages into mortgage-backed securities and soon began attempting to channel capital into home mortgage lending in similar ways.[65] In the early 1970s, the baby boom generation was just reaching the age and means necessary to buy homes.[66] Private financiers wanted to mobilize capital to serve this enormous potential demand for credit.[67] Moreover, because the

GSEs invested in mortgages with specific middle class oriented policy objectives in mind, they would not purchase unusually large ("jumbo") mortgages, mortgages with variable interest rates (ARMs), home equity loans, or—most importantly for our purposes—subprime mortgages.[68] Unmet demand in these market segments left enticing (and large) niches for private investors.[69]

In 1977, Bank of America and Salomon Brothers (with some limited cooperation from Freddie Mac) moved to take advantage of these potential markets by issuing a security where outstanding loans were held in trust, with investors as beneficiaries.[70] The trust itself was entirely passive—it had no employees or assets aside from the home mortgages themselves.[71] Participations in these trusts are generally recognized as the first mortgage-backed securities issued by the private sector—now called "private label" mortgage-backed securities.[72]

Initially, investment in these "securitized" mortgages suffered from legal and pricing problems stemming in part from the novelty of the new method of finance.[73] For instance, some large public investment funds were effectively precluded from investing in mortgage-backed securities by laws meant to prevent purchases of undiversified or risky investments.[74] The New York State Retirement System, for example, could not invest in mortgages of less than a million dollars on the theory that the risks from smaller individual consumer home mortgages were too great.[75] Also, investors and brokers alike had difficulty comparing the present value of bundles of thirty-year home mortgages. Since few investors were willing to keep their money tied up for thirty years, they needed a relatively reliable method for predicting what actual yields would be, so investors could compare those yields to yields of other potential investments. Without such a method, mortgage-backed securities suffered from liquidity problems and were accordingly artificially undervalued.[76] Eventually, the market, along with some help from Congress in the mid-1980s,[77] succeeded in developing financial tools to overcome these hurdles. For purposes of this Article, three key innovations facilitated growth in private label home mortgage-backed securities.

The first crucial innovation facilitating securitization was the development of pricing models that could estimate the present value of the right to receive a portion of the revenue from a pool of loans. Because mortgage-backed securities issued by the government-sponsored enterprises held an implicit federal guarantee, investors felt comfortable in using the face value of those securities to make investment decisions. But in the private mortgage-backed securities market, there were no comparable assurances for investors. They had to carefully consider the possibility that securities would not pay out as promised when deciding whether or not to invest. When private label mortgage-backed securities first evolved, there was great uncertainty on how to go about making these judgments.[78] Initially, investment brokers used general-ized rules of thumb to estimate value.[79] But, these estimations quickly gave way when mathematical models backed with empirical data became avail-able.[80] First, academics and investment analysts came up with satisfactory pricing models.[81] Some of the early pricing models relied on public records of FHA mortgage histories. As mortgage-backed securities became more complex, Wall Street spent millions of dollars refining these models and gen-erally researching ways to estimate the value of pools of home mortgages.[82] Ultimately, investment analysts and academics succeeded in creating models which gave investors sufficient confidence to create tradeable securities.[83]

A second innovation was the development of risk- and term-partitioned securities.[84] Early home mortgage-backed securities would simply transfer, or "pass through" consumer payments on each loan in the pool to inves-tors.[85] Each investor received income from the investment as if they owned a small piece of each loan in the pool of mortgages. This created two key disadvantages for investors. First, investors could not specify ahead of time when they would be paid. For investors who had certain financial obligations, the long and uncertain return horizon on pass-through mortgage securities was a serious drawback. Taking an insurance company as an example, if it stored customers' premiums in mortgage-backed securities, it would run the risk that the company might need to liquefy its participations in unfavorable market conditions in order to pay out insurance claims or satisfy state insur-ance regulatory reserve requirements. Similarly, if many borrowers in a pool of mortgages were to pay off their loans early (perhaps because declining interest rates induced refinancing), investors would not only get a smaller re-turn than hoped for (because less interest would have accrued on the prepaid mortgages), but they would also get their money back sooner than expected. This development would force the insurance company to search for new in-vestment options that often carry transaction costs that cut into their marginal return on assets. Furthermore, pass-through mortgage-backed securities of-fered only one equally shared credit risk to each investor. Different investors have widely varying tolerances of risk. Some choose aggressive higher-risk/higher return investment strategies, while others choose to play it safe. Pass-through mortgage-backed securities issued from a large pool of mortgages offered each of these investors only one potential investment: ownership of the income streams as paid by loans in the pool.

Partitioned securities were a response to these problems.[86] Instead of directly passing through loan payments to investors, the income created by loans in the pool was divided into different income streams suited to the time and risk prefer-ences of investors.[87] Thus, investment bankers learned to tailor securities to the needs of different investors, making investment in mortgage-backed securities desirable to a broader range of potential investors.[88] Partitioned mortgage securities divide the income of mortgage pools into different "tranches" or "strips," each of which can be purchased by investors.[89]

By way of illustration, one security might entitle an investor to receive all the interest income—an "interest-only tranche"—from a pool of mortgages, while another security might entitle investors to receive all payment toward loan principle—a "principle-only tranche."[90] Because borrowers tend to refinance when interest rates go down, an investor who expects interest rates to drop will prefer to invest in a principle-only tranche over an interest-only tranche, since the investor is likely to quickly recoup her investment as borrowers pay their mortgages off in full.[91] An interest-only tranche would be less desirable because interest income would suffer as borrowers prepay and the outstanding number of loans within the pool generating interest declines.[92] Thus, by offering a variety of separate investment vehicles, security tranches allow investors to take strong market positions on expected movement in prepayment and interest rates.[93]

Mortgage pool trustees also learned to tailor tranches to appeal to investors that prefer investing at a variety of maturation levels.[94] For instance, insurance companies often know beforehand when the window will close on customer claims against a given insurance policy. These insurance companies may be particularly interested in a mortgage-backed security tranche with maturation dates designed to coincide with the closing of the insurance company's policy liability window.[95] Similarly, stripped mortgage-backed securities with short term maturations allow banks to invest in securities that match their short term deposit liabilities.[96] Investors sometimes call issuing of these investment vehicles "time tranching" in comparison to "credit tranching," which is based upon investment risk.[97] Collectively, different types of tranching allowed mortgage pool trustees to attract a wider variety of investors to their securities than would have been possible using "pass through" vehicles.

A final development facilitating a private label home mortgage securitization market was the introduction of rating agencies and credit enhancements. Most investors were willing to purchase government-agency-issued mortgage-backed securities purely on the strength of agency reputations and assurances.[98] But investors in private label mortgage-backed securities needed some additional assurance on whether private mortgage tranches would actually pay out as promised. For this information, investors turned to rating agencies.[99] Today, the three national rating agencies, Standard and Poor's, Moody's, and Fitch Investment Company, assist investors by collecting information and research on the risk posed by various investments.[100] After doing due diligence, ratings agencies issue a credit rating on each tranche, signaling to potential investors the likelihood that a particular instrument will pay interest and principle according to its terms.[101] In order to receive investment grade credit ratings on some tranches of the mortgage pool, credit rating agencies usually require the issuer to augment the reliability of those tranches through "credit enhancements."[102] Credit enhancements are contractual arrangements that increase the likelihood that a particular participation in the pool of loans will pay out according to its terms.[103]

Some analysts classify two basic types of credit enhancement: internal and external.[104] Internal credit enhancements manipulate the characteristics of the loan pool to make on-time repayment of some tranches more likely. Senior/subordinated credit structures, for example, enhance the credit risk of senior tranches by allocating losses to subordinate or junior tranches first.[105] Thus, senior tranche investors can expect on-time payment unless pool losses are so severe that junior tranches become saturated.[106] Another internal credit enhancement is commonly known as a "turbo structure."[107] Here investors purchase a promised payout on a tranche that is less than the aggregate assets of the underlying mortgages.[108] A turbo structure is secured by more collateral than would be necessary to pay on time if none of the underlying mortgages underperform.[109] If the mortgages perform well, then the turbo tranches are retired early. If the mortgages underperform, the turbo tranche still pays off on time so long as the losses do not exceed the level of over-collateralization.[110] A final internal credit enhancement is a simple cash collateral account.[111] Here the security issuer funds a cash account which is held in trust for the benefit of investors who collect any tranche payout deficit out of the cash account. After all the enhanced tranches pay out, any remaining cash in the account is returned to the issuer.[112]

Conversely, external credit enhancement relies on some third party who is willing to guarantee some or all of the loan pool's returns.[113] External credit enhancement can take the form of insurance, letters of credit, or contractual guarantees.[114] External credit enhancement will usually cover tranche losses up to a written dollar amount for the duration of the life of the pool.[115] One limitation of this strategy is that, other things being equal, the credit rating given to the mortgage-backed securities will only be as high as the third party enhancer's credit rating.[116] Nevertheless, the potential rewards from home mortgage securitization were such that many companies, including some with outstanding credit ratings, were willing to insure or guarantee senior tranches.[117]

Securitization in Action: A Typical Contemporary Home Mortgage Securitization Conduit

These developments in the private label home mortgage-backed securities market facilitated a rapid increase in securitization.[118] Expanding far beyond home mortgages, Wall Street has securitized credit card debt, automobile loans, commercial loans, equipment leases, and loans to developing countries.[119] Indeed, receivables from virtually any income-producing asset have been securitized,[120] including physician and hospital accounts,[121] oil exploration,[122] lawsuit settlement proceeds,[123] entire business ventures,[124] or even baseball stadiums.[125] One firm famously led the way in intellectual property securitization by issuing "Bowie Bonds," with future royalties expected from pop-musician David Bowie's music portfolio.[126] More important for our purposes, throughout the 1990s Wall Street investment banking firms created a host of complex and innovative financial conduits that funneled vast amounts of money through modestly capitalized consumer financial services companies into home mortgage loans.[127] Much of this new credit was extended to borrowers with problematic credit histories (or borrowers with good credit histories who were nevertheless treated like borrowers with problematic credit histories). Although there is substantial variety in actual securitization conduits,[128] Figure 3.1 provides a graphic depiction that attempts to sum-

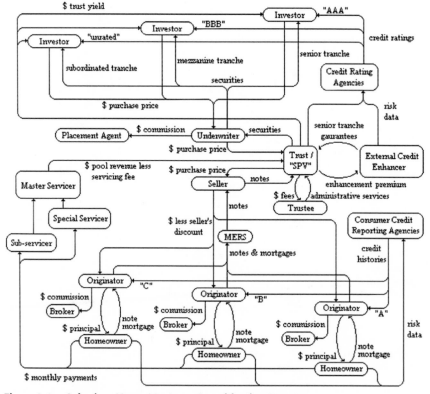

Figure 3.1. Subprime Home Mortgage Securitization Structure.

marize the flow of capital and information in a typical contemporary private label securitization of subprime home mortgage loans.

Initially, a mortgage broker identifies a potential borrower through a variety of marketing approaches including direct mail, telemarketing, door-to-door solicitation, and television or radio advertising. The originator and broker together identify a loan which may or may not be suitable to the borrower's needs. The home mortgage will consolidate the borrower's other unsecured debts, refinance a pre-existing home mortgage, or possibly fund the purchase price of a home. In determining the interest rate and other pricing variables, the broker and the originator rely on one or more consumer credit reporting agencies that compile databases of information about past credit performance, currently outstanding debt, prior civil judgments, and bankruptcies. Consumers are given a credit score, often based on the statistical models of Fair Issacson & Co., a firm that specializes in evaluating consumer repayment. Then, the borrower formally applies for the loan. At closing, which typically takes place a week or two later, the borrower signs all the necessary paperwork binding herself to a loan which may or may not have the terms originally described. Some brokers fund the loan directly using their own funds or a warehouse line of credit, while other brokers act as an agent using the originator's capital to fund the loan.[129] In any case, the originator establishes its right to payment by giving public notice of the mortgage through recording it with a county recorder's office.[130] Then, in a typical conduit, the originator will quickly transfer the loan to a subsidiary of an investment-banking firm.[131]This subsidiary, which is alternatively called the securitization sponsor, or seller, then transfers the loan and hundreds of others like it into a pool of loans.[132] This pool of loans will become its own business entity, called a special purpose vehicle (SPV).[133] The SPV can be a corporation, partnership, or limited liability company, but most often is a trust.[134] Aside from the mortgages, the SPV has no other assets, employees, or function beyond the act of owning the loans. Under the agreement transferring the loans into the pool, the SPV agrees to sell pieces of itself to investors.[135] In a typical transaction, an underwriter purchases all the "securities"—here meaning derivative income streams drawn from payments on the underlying mortgages—issued by the pool.[136] Usually employing one or more placement agents who work on commission, the underwriter then sells securities to a variety of investors with different portfolio needs. In designing the SPV and its investment tranches, the seller typically works closely with a credit rating agency that will rate the credit risk of each tranche.[137] The credit rating agency investigates the credit risk of the underlying mortgages as well as the risks posed from pooling the mortgages together.[138] Inquiry as to the former, known as "mortgage risk," focuses above all upon borrower net equity over time—which is to say, the risk that foreclosure on a defaulting mortgage will not recoup invested funds.[139] Evaluation of "pool risk" looks at factors such as the size of the loan pool and the geographic diversity of underlying mortgages.[140] Credit ratings on each tranche are essential, since they obviate the need for each individual investor to do due diligence on the underlying mortgages in the pool.[141] The rating agency will typically require some form of credit enhancement on some tranches to assign them higher investment ratings. Often this enhancement will take the form of a third-party guarantee from an insurance company on losses from mortgage defaults and prepayments.

The seller also arranges to sell the rights to service the loan pool to a company which will correspond with consumers, receive monthly payments, monitor collateral, and when necessary, foreclose on homes.[142] Sometimes the originator retains servicing rights, which has the advantage of maintaining a business relationship with homeowners.[143] But often servicing is done by a company specializing in this activity.[144] Increasingly, pooling and servicing agreements allow for several different servicing companies with different debt collection roles. A master servicer may have management responsibility for the entire loan pool. Similar to a subcontractor in construction, the master servicer may subcontract to sub-servicers with a loan type or geographic specialty.[145] The pooling and servicing agreement may also allow for a special servicer that focuses exclusively on loans that fall into default or have some other characteristics making repayment unlikely.[146] Some servicing agreements require servicers to purchase subordinated tranches issued from the mortgage pool in order to preserve the incentive to aggressively collect on the loans.[147] Servicing rights also change hands often—several times a year for some loans.[148] If, for instance, a servicing company is not meeting collection goals or is charging the trust too much, the trustee may contract with a new servicer.

In many securitization deals, sellers and trustees agree to hire a document custodian to keep track of the mountains of paperwork on loans in the pool.[149] A related role is commonly played by a unique company called Mortgage Electronic Registration System, Inc. (MERS, Inc.).[150] MERS, Inc. is a corporation registered in Delaware and headquartered in the Virginia suburbs of Washington, D.C.[151] With the cooperation of the Mortgage Bankers Association of America and several leading mortgage banking firms, MERS, Inc. developed and maintains a national computer networked database known as the MERS. Originators and secondary market players pay membership dues and per-transaction fees to MERS, Inc. in exchange for the right to use and access MERS records. The system itself electronically tracks ownership and servicing rights of mortgages.[152] Currently, more than half of all home mortgage loans originated in the United States are registered on the MERS system.[153]

In addition to keeping track of ownership and servicing rights, MERS has attempted to take on a different, more aggressive, legal role. When closing on a home mortgage, participating originators now often list MERS as the "mortgagee of record" on the paper mortgage.[154] The mortgage is then recorded with the county property recorder's office under MERS, Inc.'s name, rather than the originator's name—even though MERS does not solicit, fund, service, or ever actually own the loan. MERS then purports to remain the mortgagee of record for the duration of the loan, even after the originator or a subsequent assignee transfers the loan into an SPV for securitization. MERS justifies its role by explaining that it is acting as a "nominee" for the parties.[155]

The parties obtain two principal benefits from attempting to use MERS as a "mortgagee of record in nominee capacity." First, under state secured credit laws, when a mortgage is assigned, the assignee must record the assignment with the county recording office, or risk losing priority vis-à-vis other creditors, buyers, or lienors.[156] Most counties charge a fee to record the assignment, and use these fees to cover the cost of maintaining the real property records. Some counties also use recording fees to fund their court systems, legal aid organizations, or schools. In this respect, MERS' role in acting as a mortgagee of record in nominee capacity is simply a tax evasion tool. By paying MERS a fee, the parties to a securitization lower their operating costs.[157] The second advantage MERS offers its customers comes later when homeowners fall behind on their monthly payments. In addition to its document custodial role, and its tax evasive role, MERS also frequently attempts to bring home foreclosure proceedings in its own name.[158] This eliminates the need for the trust—which actually owns the loan—to foreclose in its own name, or to reassign the loan to a servicer or the originator to bring the foreclosure.[159]

Altogether, these businesses created an extremely powerful and lucrative device for marshaling capital into home mortgage loans. Securitization appeared to decrease the information costs for investors interested in investing in home mortgages. By pooling mortgages together and relying on a rating agency to assess the securities funded by the pool, investors thought they had a relatively reliable prediction of expected returns, without investigating each individual originator and each individual loan.[160] Also, securitization allowed loan originators to make great profit from origination fees by leveraging limited access to capital into many loans. Even lenders with modest capital could quickly assign their loans into a securitization conduit, and use the proceeds of the sale to make a new round of loans.[161] These characteristics led to an unprecedented increase in consumer access to purchase money mortgages, home equity lines of credit, and especially cash-out refinancing—many of which are today in serious arrears.

Conclusion: Observations on the Role of
Securitization in the Subprime Foreclosure Crisis

The secondary market for privately securitized home mortgages helped facilitate the subprime mortgage crisis in at least three significant ways. First, securitization allowed small lenders and brokers with minimal reputational capital to churn out vast mortgage loan volume with little or no accountability.[162] Because securitizing originators quickly assigned their loans, their own capital was only invested in any given loan for a short period of time. Once a loan was sold, the originator could use the proceeds of the sale to find a new consumer for another loan, and so on. In effect, securitization allowed Wall Street capital to transform relatively small businesses into multi-million dollar institutions with a tremendous impact on the lives of entire communities. The difficulty of monitoring loan brokers for poor underwriting and consumer protection law violations, the complexity of measuring risk in pool securities, the incentive of Wall Street investment bankers to push through deals to generate fees, commissions and revenue, all led to a system-wide culture of emphasizing loan quantity over credit quality.

Second, an outdated legal and regulatory system failed to provide an incentive against poor underwriting and abusive practices. Federal and state consumer protection laws were written before the evolution of privately securitized mortgages. As a result, many of the key consumer protection laws, such as the Truth in Lending Act, the Fair Debt Collection Practices Act, and the Federal Trade Commission's Holder in Due Course notice rule presume antiquated business practices, and were thus ill-suited to regulate the subprime market. Take the definition of the term "creditor" in the Truth in Lending Act as a simple example. The statute defines a creditor as "the person to whom the debt arising from the consumer credit transaction is initially payable on the face of the evidence of indebtedness."[163] This definition is important since the private cause of action creating the possibility of liability under the act extends only to "any creditor who fails to comply" with the Act's requirements.[164] While this definition resonates with the notion of a lender as we commonly think of it, this notion is increasingly discordant with reality. In the vast majority of subprime home mortgage loans, a mortgage loan broker conducts most of the actual tasks associated with origination of the loan, including, and especially, face-to-face communication with the borrower.[165] Because brokers usually do not fund the loan, they are not the party to whom the loan is initially payable. Because the statute presupposes a unitary notion of a single individual or business that solicits, documents, and funds a loan, the most basic term defining the scope of the act does not reflect the simple reality of typical business practices. The absurd result is that the federal statute, which purports to promote useful and accurate disclosure of credit prices, does not govern the business or individual that actually *speaks* to a mortgage applicant. Rather, liability for the statute is confined to errors in the complex paperwork, which many consumers have difficulty reading, and which are typically ignored in hurried loan closings long after borrowers arrive at a decision on which broker and/or lender to use. Far from an extraordinary example, the inapplicability of the Truth in Lending Act to mortgage brokers is similar to basic exemptions for securitization participants from liability in virtually every federal statute. In the end, our finance technology outpaced our consumer protection law, in effect deregulating the most vulnerable segment of the mortgage market.

Third, securitization made enforcement of the consumer protection law that did apply to structured finance deals much more expensive for consumers. Discovery, negotiation, loan modification, settlement, and litigation in general are all more difficult for consumers with securitized loans than for loans funded by the traditional publically sponsored secondary market. Unlike traditional financial institutions that originated and serviced loans themselves, in structured finance deals the many different companies and investors involved have differing incentives. Forty years ago a borrower might need to serve only one party; today, bringing a full range of predatory lending claims and defenses can require litigating against ten or more different businesses. This is a daunting task indeed, since at the outset, the consumer will almost always have no knowledge of the name, address or other contact information for many of these firms. Indeed, counsel for the foreclosing party probably does not know which businesses were involved in performing the various functions associated with the loan. Phone calls to the loan's servicer are frequently ignored, subject to excruciating delays, or typically only reach unknowledgeable staff, who themselves lack information on the larger business relationships. For their part, securitization trustees are not in the business of counseling the thousands of mortgagors pooled in each of the many real estate trusts they oversee. Policy makers must not underestimate the staggering difficulty of reconstructing the facts involved in only one loan.[166] Securitization creates an opaque business structure that consumers have great difficulty forgathering.

With the recent seizure of Fannie Mae and Freddie Mac by the federal government, and the scarcity of investors willing to risk their assets in private mortgage-backed securities, the future of American home finance is uncertain. One suspects that governance minimalists will attempt to use the inability of the Fannie Mae and Freddie Mac to adjust to the housing depreciation caused by private subprime securitization as a pretext for dismantling the federal secondary mortgage market infrastructure that has served our nation well since the Great Depression. Irrespective of how the home mortgage market of tomorrow will be funded, it is clear that a comprehensive overhaul of the nation's consumer finance law and regulation is the *sine qua non* of any meaningful new housing policy.

NOTES

1. Dan Immergluck, Credit to the Community: community Reinvestment and Fair Lending Policy in the United States 40 (2004).

2. The finance industry does not have a universally agreed upon definition of the terms "securitization" or "structured finance." *See* Henry A. Davis, *The Definition of Structured Finance: Results from a Survey*, 11 J. of Structured Fin., Fall 2005, at 5. However, for purposes of this article "securitization" will refer to the process of pooling assets, such as mortgage loans, and then reselling them to investors. Andrew Davidson et al., Securitization: Structuring and Investment Analysis 3 (2003). "Structured finance," in turn, refers to the process by which securitized assets are made more desirable to investors, such as by dividing the income into securities with different credit risks and maturation dates, or by isolating the assets from the risk that the originator of the assets will declare bankruptcy. *Id.* In practice, the notions of securitizing and structuring are often used interchangeably. *See, e.g.*, Steven L. Schwarcz, Structured Finance: A Guide to the Principles of Asset Securitization (Adam D. Ford ed., 3d. ed. 2002 & Supp 2005); James A Rosenthal & Juan M. Ocampo, Securitization of Credit: Inside the New Technology of Finance 3–5 (1988) ("Credit securitization is the carefully structured process whereby loans and other receivables are packaged, underwritten, and sold in the form of securities (instruments called asset-backed securities).").

3. Richard A. Oppel, Jr. & Patrick McGeehan, *Lenders Try to Fend Off Laws on Subprime Loans*, N.Y. Times, April 4, 2001, C1.

4. Center for Responsible Lending, Subprime Lending: A Net Drain on Homeownership 2 (2007), *available at* http://www.responsiblelending.org/issues/mortgage/research/subprime-lending-is-a-drain-on-home-ownership.html.

5. *Foreclosures to Affect 6.5 Mln by 2012*, Reuters News Service, Apr. 22, 2008.

6. M. Manfred Fabritius & William Borges, Saving the Savings & Loan: The U.S. Thrift Industry and the Texas Experience 1950–1988, at 12 (1989); Michael J. Lea, *Innovation and the Cost of Mortgage Credit: A Historical Perspective*, 7 Housing Pol'y Debate 147, 154 (1996).

7. Mark Boleat, The Building Society Industry 3 (1982).

8. Rhoda James, Cosmo Graham & Mary Seneviratne, *Building Societies, Customer Complaints, and the Ombudsman*, 23 Anglo-Am. L. Rev. 214, 214–15 (1994).

9. Boleat, *supra* note 7, at 3; *Benefit Building Societies*, 29 L. Mag & L. Rev. Q.J. Juris. 3d sev 323, 324–25 (1870). *See also* Benefit Building Societies, 14 L. Rev. & Q.J. Brit. & Foreign Juris. 1 (1851) (discussing legal foundations of mid-nineteenth century building societies).

10. Lea, *supra* note 6, at 155.

11. *Id.* at 156. Of course today's thrifts bear little resemblance to their nineteenth century forebears. Contemporary thrifts are often indistinguishable from banks and engage in a virtually unlimited range of business and consumer financial services. For more thorough treatment of this commercial evolution, see generally Boleat, *supra* note 7; Fabritius & Borges, *supra* note 6.

12. Immergluck, *supra* note 1, at 33.

13. Some state legislatures chartered mutual savings banks which had some characteristics of building and loans and some characteristics of traditional commercial banks. Thomas B. Marvell, The Federal Home Loan Bank Board 4 (1969). The primary focus of the first savings banks was to take small deposits to encourage thrift in working class communities. Immergluck, *supra* note 1, at 34–35. By the late 1800s, they had also become an important source of mortgage finance. Lea, *supra* note 6, at 156.

14. Lea, *supra* note 6, at 156.

15. Kenneth A. Snowden, *Mortgage Rates and American Capital Market Development in the Late Nineteenth Century*, 47 J. Econ. Hist. 671, 675 (1987).

16. *See* D. M. Frederiksen, *Mortgage Banking in America*, 2 J. Pol. Econ 203, 206 (1894); Snowden, *supra* note 15, at 675.

17. Office of Federal Housing Enterprise Oversight, Report to Congress: Celebrating 10 Years of Excellence 1993–2003, at 11 (June 2003), [hereinafter OFHEO Report to Congress].

18. Christopher L. Peterson, Taming the Sharks: Towards a Cure for the High-Cost Credit Market 81 (2004) (discussing origins of American credit discrimination).

19. Frederiksen, *supra* note 16, at 209 (mortgages taken by local and non-local individuals constituted 73 percent of American residential mortgages recorded between 1879 and 1890).

20. Building society loans constituted about seven percent of recorded mortgages. *Id.* We should expect that few businesses would be willing to take building society loan assignments since these potential assignees would have a debilitating comparative disadvantage in evaluating the likelihood of default.

21. Insurance company loans constituted about 5 percent of recorded mortgages. *Id.*

22. *Id.* at 210–13; Lea, *supra* note 6, at 156. Some of these companies specialized in lending to settlers taking advantage of the homestead laws. Fredericksen, *supra* note 16, at 213.

23. Frederiksen, *supra* note 16, at 207; Lea, *supra* note 6, at 156–58.

24. *See* WM. Colebrooke, A Treatise on the Law of Collateral Securities as Applied to negotiable, Quasi-Negotiable and Non-Negotiable in Action 250–57 (1883); Fredericksen, *supra* note 16, at 210; Lea, *supra* note 6, at 156–58. Often ownership of the mortgages was held in a trust, not dissimilar to today's special purpose vehicles. Fredericksen, *supra* note 16, at 210.

25. Lea, *supra* note 6, at 158. Much like today's mortgage brokers, some mortgage loan company agents in the 1880s received up-front commissions which amounted to around as much as an interest rate point over the life of the loan. Fredericksen, *supra* note 16, at 206. Loan agents cashed in on land speculation as settlers in the Dakotas, Nebraska, Kansas and other territories made claims to land, borrowed money, and

defaulted without making any improvements or establishing successful homesteads. *Id.* at 213.

26. Fredericksen, *supra* note 16, at 213; Christine A. Pavel, Securitization: The Analysis and Development of the Loan-Based/Asset- Backed Securities Market 56 n.2 (1989).

27. Edwin F. Gay, *The Great Depression*, 10 Foreign Affairs 529, 530 (1932); Ben S. Bernake, *Macroeconomics of the Great Depression: A Comparative* Approach, in Essays on the Great Depression 5, 6 (Ben S. Bernake, ed., 2000).

28. Ben S. Bernake, *Nonmonetary Effects of the Financial Crisis in the Propagation of the Great Depression,* 73 Am. Econ. Rev. 257, 260 (1983); Howard Zinn, A People's History of the United States: 1492–Present 378–80 (1995).

29. Arthur E. Wilmarth, Jr., *Did Universal Banks Play a Significant role in the U.S. Economy's Boom-and-Bust Cycle of 1921–33? A Preliminary Assessment,* 4 Current Dev. In Monetary & Fin. L. 559, 582 (2006).

30. OFHEO Report to Congress, *supra* note 17, at 11.

31. Marvell, *supra* note 13, at 19.

32. Gay, *supra* note 27, at 533.

33. Immergluck, *supra* note 1, at 36.

34. Marvell, *supra* note 13, at 20–21.

35. *See* Franklin D. Roosevelt, A Message Asking for Legislation to Save Small Home Mortgages from Foreclosure (Apr. 13, 1933), *in* 2 The Public Papers and Addresses of Franklin D. Roosevelt, at 135 (1938) (illustrating FDR's vision for government leadership in mortgage lending markets).

36. Although HOLC's refinanced mortgages were initially funded by taxpayers, homeowners eventually paid back all the money used by the agency. Marvell, *supra* note 13, at 24. HOLC was created as a temporary agency to help the country out of the depression. It stopped refinancing loans in 1936 and was altogether out of business by the early 1950s. *Id.* at 25.

37. Steven A. Ramirez, *The Law and Macroeconomics of the New Deal at 70,* 62 Md. L. Rev. 515, 560 (2003). In about two years HOLC refinanced over a million loans amounting to approximately ten percent of the country's outstanding residential non-farm mortgages. Kenneth T. Jackson, *Race, Ethnicity, and Real Estate Appraisal: The Home Owners Loan Corporation and the Federal Housing Administration,* 6 J. Urb. Hist. 419, 421 (1980). Conversely, HOLC also used overtly racist underwriting and appraisal practices, such as rating minority neighborhoods much more unfavorably than white neighborhoods. Michael H. Schill & Susan M. Wachter, *The Spatial Bias of Federal Housing Law and Policy: Concentrated Poverty in Urban America,* 143 U. Pa. L. Rev. 1285, 1309 (1995). This federal leadership set a dangerous discriminatory precedent which far outlived the agency itself. Peter P. Swire, *The Persistent Problem of Lending Discrimination: A Law and Economic Analysis,* 73 Tex. L. Rev. 787, 799–802 (1995).

38. Robin Paul Malloy, *The Secondary Mortgage Market—A Catalyst for Change in Real Estate Transactions,* 39 SW. L.J. 991, 992 (1986); Immergluck, *supra* note 1, at 38.

39. Malloy, *supra* note 38, at 992. *See also* Quintin Johnstone, *Private Mortgage Insurance*, 39 Wake Forest L. Rev. 783, 785–87, 823–825 (2004) (describing operation of mortgage insurance).

40. Immergulck, *supra* note 1, at 38.

41. FHA did not, however, encourage equal treatment of all groups. Like HOLC, FHA not only tolerated, but also encouraged exclusion of ethnic minorities. Immergluck, *supra* note 1, at 93–95.

42. Malloy, *supra* note 38, at 993.

43. *Id.* at 993. Residential mortgages are still usually divided into two categories: "conventional" and "nonconventional" loans. Anand K. Bhattacharya, Frank J. Fabozzi & S. Esther Chang, *Overview of the Mortgage Market, in* The Handbook of Mortgage Backed Securities 3, 3 (Frank J. Fabozzi ed., 5th ed. 2001). In a conventional loan, if the borrower defaults and the loan becomes uncollectible, then the lender or the lender's assignee suffers the loss. *Id.* In contrast, nonconventional loans are insured by the federal government. *Id.* Such insurance is still provided by the FHA, the VA or the Rural Development Administration (RDA). *Id.* The Reconstruction Finance Corporation (RFC) actually preceded Fannie Mae in purchasing FHA insured loans. However, like HOLC, it was another temporary agency which disbanded in 1948. Malloy, *supra* note 38, at 993.

44. Malloy, *supra* note 38, at 992–93.

45. Kenneth T. Jackson, Crabgrass Frontier: The Suburbanization of the United States 195, 200 (1985). Excluded yet again were many white working class families, families headed by single women, and families of color, all of whom tended to lack the credit profile Fannie Mae and the thrifts required to participate in this new "prime" home mortgage lending market. Swire, *supra* note 37, at 798–99.

46. Douglas B. Diamond, Jr. & Michael J. Lea, *The Decline of Special Circuits in Developed Country Housing Finance*, 3 Housing Pol'y Debate 747, 756–57 (1992).

47. Malloy, *supra* note 38, at 992.

48. Diamond & Lea, *supra* note 46, at 56–61.

49. *See* Federal National Mortgage Association, *Federal National Association Background, in* 1 Real Estate Securities Regulation Sourcebook 1087, 1087–88 (1975) (providing a characterization of different levels of government sponsorship in quasi-governmental agencies). Dan Immergluck has explained that:

> In both circuits, the public sector has seeded, nurtured, and been largely responsible for the size and functioning of mortgage markets now and in the foreseeable future. Without federal involvement, we would today have far fewer home owners or potential home owners. Thus, the size of the home lending market today and for the foreseeable future rests on a federally initiated, supported, and sponsored infrastructure.

Immergluck, *supra* note 1, at 40.

50. *Id.*

51. Sivesind explains, "Since low-risk FHA-VA loans could be sold to investors across the country, the programs facilitated the early development of an integrated, national mortgage market at little direct cost to the government." Charles M. Sivesind,

Mortgage-Backed Securities: The Revolution in Real Estate Finance, in Housing and the New Financial Markets 311, 312–13 (Richard L. Florida ed., 1986).

52. Diamond & Lea, *supra* note 46, at 56–61. *See also supra* note 43 (explaining origin of the term "conventional" in mortgage lending).

53. Immergluck, *supra* note 1, at 39 (citing Kerry Vandell, *FHA Restructuring Proposals: Alternatives and Implications*, 6 Housing Pol'y Debate 299, 311 (1995)).

54. Richard S. Landau, *The Evolution of Mortgage Backed Securities, in* The Secondary Mortgage Market: A Handbook of Techniques and Critical Issues in Contemporary Mortgage Finance 135, 135–36 (Jess Lederman ed., 1987).

55. Sivesind, *supra* note 51, at 317.

56. *Id.*

57. *Id.* at 315–16.

58. *Id.* at 318–19.

59. Schwarcz, *Structured Finance, supra* note 105, at 609. *See also* Linda Lowell, *Mortgage Pass-Through Securities, in* The Handbook of Mortgage-Backed Securities 25, 26 (Frank J. Fabozzi ed., 5th ed. 2001) ("Pass-through securities are created when mortgages are pooled together and undivided interests or participations in the pool are sold.").

60. Richard S. Landau, *The Evolution of Mortgage-Backed Securities, in* The Secondary Mortgage Market: A Handbook of Strategies, Techniques and Critical Issues in Contemporary Mortgage Finance 135, 135 (Jess Lederman ed., 1987).

61. Although Ginnie Mae securities are guaranteed by the full faith and credit of the U.S. government, Fannie Mae and Freddie Mac securities are not. Nevertheless, many investors have traditionally regarded the two GSEs as "too big to fail,"—the view that there is an implicit government guarantee of agency securities, if not an actual one. Richard Scott Carnell, *Handling the Failure of a Government-Sponsored Enterprise*, 80 Wash. L. Rev. 565, 630–31 (2005). Whether investors are correct in this view is a matter of growing debate. *See id.* at 596; Benton E. Gup, *Are Fannie Mae and Freddie Mac Too Big to Fail?, in,* Policies and Practices in Government Bailouts 285, 310 (Benton E. Gup, ed., 2003).

62. Sivesind, *supra* note 51, at 313.

63. Loan pools insured by Fannie Mae and Freddie Mac must meet relatively strict underwriting guidelines and must be originated on standardized forms designated by the agencies. Anand K. Bhattacharya et al., *Overview of the Mortgage Market, in* The Handbook of Mortgage-Backed Securities 3, 22 (Frank J. Fabozzi ed., 5th ed. 2001). These procedures help homogenize the risk from different loans with agency loan pools, in turn alleviating the concerns of all but the most risk averse investors.

64. Joseph C. Shenker & Anthony J. Colletta, *Asset Securitization: Evolution, Current Issues and New Frontiers*, 69 Tex. L. Rev. 1369 (1991) at 1383.

65. Sivesind, *supra* note 51, at 320.

66. Lewis S. Ranieri, *The Origins of Securitization, Sources of Its Growth, and Its Future Potential, in* A Primer on Securitization 31, 31 (Leon T. Kendall & Michael J. Fishman, eds., 1996).

67. *Id.*, at 31–32.

68. Meir Kohn, Financial Institutions and Markets 623–24 (1994).

69. Claire A. Hill, *Securitization: A Low-Cost Sweetener for Lemons*, 74 Wa. U. L.Q. 1061, 1121 (1996). One result of these trends was that thrifts began to more aggressively use their home mortgage portfolios as security for long term bond issues. Ranieri, *supra* note 66, at 32. These bonds, sometimes called mortgage-backed bonds, are different from mortgage-backed securities. Shenker & Colletta, *supra* note 64, at 1380–81. Income from the underlying mortgages in mortgage-backed bonds is not passed through to bond investors. *Id.* Rather the mortgages simply serve as collateral subject to foreclosure in the event of default on the bond. *Id.* The principal disadvantage of this financing structure is that the bond must be overcollateralized to cover the costs of foreclosure in the event of default on the bond. Ranieri, *supra* note 66, at 32. This creates a pocket of swamped resources in comparison to pass-through mortgage-backed securities. Much older than mortgage-backed securities, mortgage-backed bonds date at least as far back as the late nineteenth century mortgage companies that were wiped out in the recessions of the 1890s. Shenker & Colletta, *supra* note 64, at 1380–81; Lea, *supra* note 6, at 158.

70. Ranieri, *supra* note 66, at 33–34; Sivesind, *supra* note 51, at 321.

71. Ranieri, *supra* note 66, at 32–33.

72. Richard A. Brown & Susan E. Burnhouse, *Implications of the Supply-Side Revolution in Consumer Lending*, 24 St. Louis U. Pub. L. Rev. 363, 392 (2005). Private label mortgage-backed securities are also sometimes called non-agency securities in contrast to the older "agency" securitized mortgage loans issued by the GSEs. ANDREW DAVIDSON ET AL., SECURITIZATION: STRUCTURING AND INVESTMENT ANALYSIS 288–89 (2003). Some commentators also refer to private label mortgage-backed securities as "nonconforming," since they do not meet the underwriting standards of the GSEs. *Id.*

73. Ranieri, *supra* note 66, at 36.

74. *Id.*, at 33.

75. *Id.*

76. Shenker & Colletta, *supra* note 64, at 1380.

77. Following lobbying efforts of investment bankers, Congress passed legislation to clear out the legal obstacles to private securitization of home mortgages. Ranieri, *supra* note 66, at 37. The most important legal development was passage of the Secondary Mortgage Market Enhancement Act of 1984 (SMMEA) in which Congress preempted a variety of state laws that inhibited private home mortgage securitization, including state retirement fund laws which prevented public pension funds from investing in private home mortgage securities. Pub. L. No. 98–440, § 106(a), 98 Stat. 1689, 1691–92 (1984) (codified at 15 U.S.C. §77r-1). SMMEA also preempted state blue sky laws to allow securitizers to avoid registering under state securities laws to the same extent that securities issued by Fannie Mae, Freddie Mac, or Ginnie Mae were exempt. *Id.* § 106(c), 98 Stat. at 1689 (codified at 15 U.S.C. § 77r-1(c)). In addition to preempting state laws, SMMEA authorized delayed delivery of home mortgage-backed securities in order to facilitate forward trading. *Id.* § 102–04, 98 Stat. at 1690–91 (codified at 15 U.S.C. §§ 78g(g), 78h(a), 78k(d)(1)). And, it permitted national banks, federal credit unions, and federal savings and loans associations to invest in privately issued home mortgage-backed securities. *Id.* § 105, 98 Stat. at

1691 (codified at 12 U.S.C. §§ 24, 1757). *See* Shenker & Colletta, *supra* note 64, at 1386 (summarizing key SMMEA provisions).

78. Ranieri, *supra* note 66, at 35–36.

79. *Id.,* at 35.

80. *See* Davidson, et al., *supra* note 72, at 131–180 (introducing mortgage-backed security price modeling).

81. Ranieri, *supra* note 66, at 35–36.

82. Joel W. Brown & William M. Wadden IV, *Mortgage Credit Analysis, in* The Handbook of Mortgage-Backed Securities 315, 315 (Frank J. Fabozzi, ed., 5th ed., 2001). Early pricing models often relied on data collected on actual performance of FHA loans, giving a limited empirical foundation to pricing models. Lowell, *supra* note 59, at 39–40.

83. Kurt Eggert, *Held Up in Due Course: Predatory Lending, Securitization, and the Holder in Due Course Doctrine*, 35 Creighton L. Rev. 503, 537 (2002); Ranieri, *supra* note 66, at 35.

84. Brown & Burnhouse, *supra* note 72, at 392.

85. Pavel, *supra* note 26, at 4.

86. Lowell, *supra* note 59, at 25.

87. Leon T. Kendall, *Securitization: A New Era in American Finance, in* A Primer on Securitization 1, 8–9 (Leon T. Kendall & Michael J. Fishman eds., 1996).

88. *Id.*

89. Eggert, *Predatory Lending, supra* note 83, at 540. "Tranche" is French for "slice." Larousse French-English/English-French Dictionary 922–23 (Faye Carney ed., 1993).

90. Eggert, *Predatory Lending, supra* note 83, at 540.

91. Lakhbir Hayre et al., *Stripped Mortgage-Backed Securities, in,* The Handbook of Mortgage Backed Securities 151, 151 (Frank J. Fabozzi ed., 2001).

92. Eggert, *Predatory Lending, supra* note 83, at 540.

93. Hayre et al., *supra* note 91, at 151.

94. Ranieri, *supra* note 66, at 36–37.

95. Hayre et al., *supra* note 91, at 155.

96. Mortgage Research Group, Lehman Brothers Inc., *Collateralized Mortgage Obligations, in,* The Handbook of Mortgage Backed Securities 169, 169–170 (Frank J. Fabozzi ed., 2001).

97. Brown & Wadden, *supra* note 82, at 315.

98. Ranieri, *supra* note 66, at 36.

99. Davidson et al., *supra* note 72, at 24–25.

100. *See, e.g.*, Neil D. Baron, *The Role of Rating Agencies in the Securitization Process, in* A Primer on Securitization 81, 81–83 (Leon T. Kendall & Michael J. Fishman eds., 1996).

101. *Id.* Investment credit ratings do not assess whether an investment will be profitable, but merely whether an instrument will pay according to its terms. *Id.* For instance, if an investor invests in mortgage-backed securities, and interest rates subsequently rise, then the investor will be stuck with a relatively low rate of return. Credit ratings do not address this sort of investment risk. *Id.*

102. Daniel Singer, *Securitization Basics*, *in* Accessing Capital Markets Through Securitization 13, 17 (Frank J. Fabozzi ed., 2001).

103. Davidson et al., *supra* note 72, at 24–25.

104. *See* Singer, *supra* note 102, at 17–8; Frank J. Fabozzi et al., *Nonagency CMOs*, *in* The Handbook of Mortgage Backed Securities 267, 268 (Frank J. Fabozzi ed., 5th ed. 2001); Lina Hsu & Cyrus Mohebbi, *Credit Enhancement in ABS Structures*, *in* Accessing Capital Markets Through Securitization 35, 35–38 (Frank J. Fabozzi ed., 2001); Davidson et al., *supra* note 72, at 25.

105. Singer, *supra* note 102, at 18. This form of internal credit enhancement relies on the participation of investors that specialize in subordinated tranche investment. Schwarcz explains, "[t]he originator . . . allocates certain repayment risks to these investors, who are in the business of assessing and accepting such risks and who consequently are willing to accept a higher level of risk than the average investor." *Steven L. Schwarcz, The Alchemy of Asset Securitization*, 1 Stan. J. L. Bus. & Fin. 133, 143 (1994). One hopes he is correct. Another possibility is that residual tranche investors are making uninformed investment decisions. *See Wayne Passmore & Roger W. Sparks, Automated Underwriting and the Profitability of Mortgage Securitization, 28 REAL ESTATE ECON. 285, 285–86 (2000).* Still another possibility is that residual tranche investors are managers of servicing or origination companies that derive sufficient short term profit from fees excluded from the pooling and servicing agreement. These fees might be sufficiently profitable that managers would accept poor performance on longer term securities.

106. Hsu & Mohebbi, *supra* note 104, at 37.

107. *Id.* at 38.

108. *Id.*

109. *Id.*

110. *Id.*

111. Singer, *supra* note 102, at 18.

112. *Id.*

113. Fabozzi et al., *supra* note 104, at 268; Hsu & Mohebbi, *supra* note 104, at 35. *See also* Robert D. Aicher et al., *Credit Enhancement: Letters of Credit, Guaranties, Insurance, and Swaps (The Clash of Cultures)*, 59 Bus. Law. 897 (2004) (comparing litigation advantages of different forms of third party external credit enhancement).

114. Aicher, *supra* note 113, at 898.

115. Fabozzi et al., *supra* note 104, at 268.

116. Hsu & Mohebbi, *supra* note 104, at 36.

117. *Id.*; Fabozzi et al., *supra* note 104, at 268.

118. Between 1994 and 1998 alone, outstanding U.S. private label mortgage-backed securities doubled from approximately 200 billion to 400 billion. *See* Davidson et al., *supra* note 72, at 288.

119. Kendall, *supra* note 87, at 7.

120. Suzanne Woolley & Stan Crock, *You Can Securitize Virtually Everything*, Bus. Wk., July 20, 1992, at 78.

121. *See* Charles E. Harrell & Mark D. Folk, *Financing American Health Security: The Securitization of Healthcare Receivables*, 50 Bus. Law. 47 (1994); Gregory R.

Salathe, *Reducing Health Care Costs through Hospital Accounts Receivable Securitization*, 80 Va. L. Rev. 549 (1994).

122. *See generally* Charles E. Harrell et al., *Securitization of Oil, Gas, and Other Natural Resource Assets: Emerging Financing Techniques*, 52 Bus. Law. 885 (1997).

123. *See generally* Walter Henry Clay McKay, *Reaping the Tobacco Settlement Windfall: The Viability of Future Settlement Payment Securitization as an Option for State Legislatures*, 52 Ala. L. Rev. 705 (2001).

124. *See generally* Claire A. Hill, *Whole Business Securitizations in Emerging Markets*, 12 Duke J. Comp & Int'l L. 521 (2002); Vinod Kothari, *Whole Business Securitization: Secured Lending Repackaged: A Comment on Hill*, 12 Duke J. Comp. & Int'l L. 537 (2002).

125. Cynthia A. Baker & J. Paul Forrester, *Home Run! A Case Study of Financing the New Stadium for the St. Louis Cardinals*, 10(2) J. Structured Fin. 69 (2004).

126. Sam Adler, *David Bowie $55 Million Haul: Using a Musician's Assets to Structure a Bond Offering*, 13 Ent. L. & Fin. 1 (1997); Lisa M. Fairfax, *When You Wish Upon a Star: Explaining the Cautious Growth of Royalty-Backed Securitization*, 1999 Colum. Bus. L. Rev. 441, 442; Jennifer Burke Sylva, *Bowie Bonds Sold for Far More than a Song: The Securitization of Intellectual Property as a Super-Charged Vehicle for High Technology Financing*, 15 Santa Clara Computer & High Tech L.J. 195 (1999). *See also* Jay H. Eisbruck, *Blockbuster or Flop? The History and Evolution of Film Receivables Securitization, 1995–2005*, 11 J. Structured Fin. 11 (2005); Andrew E. Katz, *Financial Alchemy Turns Intellectual Property Into Cash: Securitization of Trademarks, Copyrights, and Other Intellectual Property Assets*, 8 J. Structured and Project Fin. 59 (2003).

127. SECURITIZATION OF FINANCIAL ASSETS § 3.02[D] (Jason H.P. Kravitt ed., 2002 & Supp.).

128. Schwarcz goes so far as to say they are "limited only by the creativity of the professionals involved." Schwarcz, *Alchemy of Asset Securitization, supra* note 105, at 138. While this may go too far, it is certainly well beyond the scope of this article to classify all of them. This exposition of securitization conduits is necessarily a generalization.

129. There are a variety of methods lenders and brokers use to initially fund home mortgage loans. Professor Eggert explains, "[m]ortgage brokers may originate the loans in their own names in three ways: (1) by using 'table funding' provided by the pre-arranged buyer of the loan; (2) by access to a warehouse line of credit; or (3) by supplying the broker's own funds." Eggert, *Predatory Lending, supra* note 83, at 538 (citations omitted).

130. Unrecorded mortgage loans may become uncollectible if a subsequent creditor lends against the same residence or if the residence is sold without permission from the mortgagee. *See* Lynn M. LoPucki & Elizabeth Warren, Secured Credit: A Systems Approach 337–352 (5th ed. 2005) (providing introduction to the mortgage recording system). Typically, when a mortgage lender assigns one if its loans, the assignee must re-record its mortgage (and pay another fee) with the county recording office or risk losing its priority vis-à-vis other creditors or purchasers. *Id.*

131. Eggert, *Predatory Lending, supra* note 83, at 538.

132. Sometimes the loan will be held in an SPV that is a wholly-owned subsidiary of the originator or the underwriter while awaiting assignment into an independent SPV that will issue securities. *See, e.g.*, Schwarcz, *Alchemy of Asset Securitization, supra* note 105 , at 142 (describing advantages of "two tier" securitization conduit structures).

133. Shenker & Colletta, *supra* note 64, at 1377–78. Some commentators use the equivalent term special purpose entity, or "SPE."

134. Hill, *supra* note 69, at 1067 n.25, 1098 n.162.

135. Eggert, *supra* note 83, at 539 n.156.

136. Although the term "securities" is commonly used to describe investors' participations interests in asset pools, the actual legal rights may or may not be securities for purposes of federal and state securities laws. Hill, *supra* note 69, at 1067–68; Shenker & Colletta, *supra* note 64, at 1378–79.

137. A Kirkland and Ellis partner specializing in securitization colorfully summarizes this process:

> "Obtaining rating agency approval is no mean feat. The rating agencies are thorough and cautious, and they can be idiosyncratic. Rating agency bashing is a popular sport in asset-backed circles, but it must be admitted that the rating agencies have a difficult assignment. They are provided with reams of data and documents and are put under a lot of time pressure. It is reasonable to assume that at any given time the average rating agency analyst has more deals than fingers. Even the best intentioned analyst may have so many deals ahead of yours that delay is inevitable."

Kenneth P. Morrison, *Observations on Effecting Your First Asset-Backed Securities Offering, in* Accessing Capital Markets Through Securitization 41, 44–45 (Frank J. Fabozzi ed., 2001).

138. Michael F. Molesky, *An Overview of Mortgage Credit Risks from a Rating Agency Perspective, in* The Secondary Mortgage Market: A Handbook of Strategies, Techniques, and Critical Issues in Contemporary Mortgage Finance 317, 318, 324 (Jess Lederman ed., 1987); Georgette C. Poindexter, *Subordinated Rolling Equity: Analyzing Real Estate Loan Default in the Era of Securitization*, 50 Emory L.J. 519, 544 (2001).

139. Molesky, *supra* note 138, at 318. Net equity is defined as "the market value of the home less the outstanding balance of the mortgage less the selling costs." *Id.*

140. Larger loan pools are less likely to vary from credit rating agency pricing models, which are based on loan performance data from extremely large populations. *See* Molesky, *supra* note 138, at 334. Geographic diversity of homes securing the loan pool protects investors from severe losses due to regional economic downturns. Anthony B. Sanders, *Commercial Mortgage-Backed Securities, in* The Handbook of Mortgage Backed Securities 661, 667 (Frank J. Fabozzi ed., 5th ed. 2001).

141. *See* Eggert, *Predatory Lending, supra* note 83, at 540; Morrison, *supra* note 137, at 45; Schwarcz, *Alchemy of Asset Securitization, supra* note 105, at 136.

142. R.K. Arnold, *Is There Life on MERS*, 11 Prop and Prob. 32, 34 (July/August 1997).

143. Elizabeth Renuart, *An Overview of the Predatory Mortgage Lending Process*, 15 Housing Pol'y Debate 467, 473 (2004).

144. Arnold, *supra* note 142, at 34; Eggert, *Predatory Lending, supra* note 83, at 544.

145. Securitization of Financial Assets, *supra* note 127, at § 16.05[A][6].

146. Poindexter, *supra* note 138, at 537–38; Eggert, *Predatory Lending, supra* note 83, at 544.

147. Richard Levine & Phoebe J. Moreo, *An Investor's Guide to B Pieces*, *in*,Trends in Commercial Mortgage-Backed Securities 172, 180 (Frank J. Fobozzi ed., 1998).

148. Arnold, *supra* note 142, at 35.

149. Poindexter, *supra* note 138, at 539.

150. In the past few years MERS registration has grown very rapidly. At the beginning of 2001 MERS had registered 3.5 million mortgages in its system—"less than five percent of all the outstanding mortgages in America." Dale A. Whitman, *Chinese Mortgage Law: An American Perspective*, 15 Colum. J. Asian L. 35, 61 (2001). But, by September of 2002, this figure rose to ten million. *MERS registers 10 Million Loans*, Inside MERS (MERS Inc.), Nov.-Dec. 2002, at 1. In November of 2003 MERS registered its 20 millionth loan—a growth rate in loans registered of almost 200% per year. *MERS Registers 20 Million Loans*, Inside MERS (MERS Inc.), Jan.-Feb. 2004, at 1. The MERS website proclaims that the corporation's "mission" is to "register every mortgage loan in the United States." MERS, About MERS, available at http://www.mersinc.org/about/index.aspx (last visited June 9, 2004).

151. Arnold, *supra* note 142, at 33.

152. MERS, Inc. does not currently handle notes as an agent for holders. Whitman, *supra* note 150, at 61.

153. R.K. Arnold, *Viewpoint*, Inside MERS (MERS Inc.), May-June 2004, at 1.

154. Alternatively, the originator may close in its own name and then record an assignment to MERS. Phyllis K. Slesinger & Daniel McLaughlin, *Mortgage Electronic Registration System*, 31 Idaho. L. Rev. 805, 806–7 (1995).

155. Slesinger and McLaughlin attempt to explain:

Consistent with mortgage participations where a lead participant holds legal title on behalf of the other participants, and with secondary market transactions where mortgage servicers hold legal title on behalf of their investors, MERS will serve as mortgagee of record in a nominee capacity only. After registration, all subsequent interests will be established electronically.

Slesinger & McLaughlin, *supra* note 165, at 806–7.

156. Arnold, *supra* note 142, at 35–36.

157. Whitman, *supra* note 150, at 61.

158. Baxter Dunaway, 2 Law of Distressed Real Estate § 24:20 (2003).

159. Arnold, *supra* note 142, at 35. (asserting "foreclosures can be done in the name of MERS without the need to reassign the mortgage."). There remain significant unsettled legal issues regarding MERS' authority to foreclose. Some courts have dismissed foreclosure suits brought by MERS, insisting that the actual owner of the loan must bring the foreclosure. *See* Mortgage Electronic Registration Systems, Inc.

v Dewinter, Case No. 16–2004–CA-002440–XXXX-MA, Division CV-H, Fourth Judicial Circuit, Florida (2005).

160. Hill, *supra* note 69, at 1086–87.

161. Eggert, *Predatory Lending, supra* note 83, at 546.

162. Eggert, supra note 83, at 546; Kathleen C. Engel & Patricia A. McCoy, *Predatory Lending: What Does Wall Street Have to Do with It?* 15 Housing Pol'y Debate 715 (2004); Diana B. Henriques with Lowell Bergman, *Mortgaged Lives: A Special Report: Profiting From Fine Print With Wall Street's Help*, N.Y. Times, March 15, 2000. at A1; Bobbi Murray, *Wall Street's Soiled Hands*, The Nation, July 15, 2002.

163. 15 U.S.C. § 1602(f).

164. 15 U.S.C. § 1640(a).

165. Many mortgage market insiders have begun to discard terms "lender" and "broker" instead using "mortgage-makers". *See, e.g.*, Jesse Eisinger, *Long and Short: Mortgage Market Begins to See Cracks as Subprime-Loan Problems Emerge,*Wall St. j., Aug. 30, 2006, at C1 ("The worry has been that in the rush to gain customers during the housing boom, mortgage-makers lowered their lending standards. During the boom times, investment banks overlooked these concerns because they had no problem finding buyers for their mortgage and debt products.").

166. Bobbi Murray, *supra* note 162. Reprinted with permission of the *Cardozo Law Review*, where an original version of this article originally appeared in April of 2007: Christopher L. Peterson, *Predatory Structured Finance*, 28 Cardozo Law Review 2185 (2007).

Chapter Four

A Structural Racism Lens on Subprime Foreclosures and Vacant Properties

Rick Cohen

As seen by critics, structural racism is fundamentally word games and semantics; substitute "low-income" for "race" and there is no difference in the analysis or policy recommendations. As seen by ideological supporters who actually don't grasp the meaning of the word "structural," the lens is turned to questions of "racist attitudes" rather than persistent disparate outcomes.

In 2008, exchanges in the pages of the *Chronicle of Philanthropy* concerning a conservative theorist's odd critique of structural racism ended up with the example of the subprime lending crisis as the example debated. A response to the *Chronicle*'s conservative columnist cited the subprime mortgage foreclosure issue as one that exemplifies outcomes that could be defined as evidence of structural racism.[1] The columnist countered that the subprime issue and the suggested policy responses were racially neutral, not induced by racial animus, and equally likely to have been generated from an analysis of the subprime crisis through a low-income rather than structural racism lens.[2]

The persistent, disparate racial impacts of the subprime-lending crisis actually offer, unfortunately, an excellent example of how structural racism operates. Contrary to the perspectives of those who focus on searching for discriminatory intent as the sine qua non, in some cases the subprime process draws on policies that were justified over the years as advancing the interests of racial and ethnic minorities in the housing market. Subprime lending was touted as making homeownership available to African Americans and Latinos who had been denied home mortgages due to the pernicious policy of bank (and insurance) redlining. Financing obtainable using limited documentation was meant to vault families into homeownership from which they would have been excluded had they encountered conventional mortgage underwriting standards. The home equity loans that homeowners sought through subprime lenders ostensibly gave older homeowners access to cash they could use for needed expenditures without, in theory, risking the security of their homes. Even subtracting from the analysis the concept of outright "predatory" lending, the results of the subprime lending crisis still end up with persistently disparate racial and ethnic outcomes that may not be effectively solved by default policy responses.

The subprime crisis carries the seeds of structural racism not from discriminatory intent, but from ostensibly racially benign or supposedly ameliorative policies and programs. This is a difficult message for the nation to hear. The pushback has been strong. For example, the financial sector has fed the press numerous stories of working class African American and Latino home purchasers who purchased much too expensive "McMansions" by misrepresenting their incomes and assets.

A less obvious pushback is the feeling among some observers that the problem of subprime foreclosures is not an inner-city phenomenon, but a suburban ring issue; families obtaining financing for home purchases in the suburbs and discovering that the costs of their mortgages exploded faster than the sizes of their take-home pay. While there is some truth to a phenomenon of suburban subprime foreclosures, involving financing often provided by developers and their affiliated mortgage brokers to fast-track suburban tract sales,[3] frequently that suburban subprime dynamic also contains its own structural racism component.

In the rapidly gentrifying, increasingly white metropolitan Washington DC, the subprime foreclosure phenomenon is being seen in suburban jurisdictions that are majority-minority (such as Prince Georges County, Maryland), or in suburban pockets where minority population growth has been concentrated over the past few years (Latino and Asian pockets in Fairfax and Prince William counties in Virginia and Montgomery County, Maryland).[4] Some of the burgeoning numbers of subprime foreclosures in suburban Cuyahoga County are actually in the inner-ring suburbs that abut Cleveland, Ohio in largely low-income minority neighborhoods.[5]

Nonetheless, the mechanisms of denial stymie action at the local, state, and national levels, or shape actions in a way that may perpetuate rather than remedy the underlying conditions that have nurtured the disparate racial impacts of the subprime foreclosure problem. This brief analysis suggests some fruitful areas for understanding the concrete manifestations of the disparate racial and ethnic impacts of the subprime crisis as they emerged during the initial tsunami of subprime mortgage foreclosures in 2007 and 2008.

AGGREGATION CONDITIONS

The subprime mortgage crisis did not sneak up on this nation and take it by surprise. The problem was festering in a financial system that was predicated on each player in the system—lenders, brokers, servicers—taking whatever they could get through fees and profits and passing along the problem to someone else, with a "not-my-responsibility" attitude. Even now, with the subprime wave crashing through inner-city (and suburban) communities for the past few years, solutions are still hard to come by and implement. The players who created this crisis are barely budging from hard-line positions, resistant to making changes unless incentivized through federal government tax credits[6] or federal bailouts, such as the much-ballyhooed Bear Stearns bailout or the government's approval of the Bank of America acquisition of Countrywide.

Communities with burgeoning vacancies discover lenders and servicers freer with lip service than action in restructuring mortgages or donating properties for rehabilitation and restoration. While some nonprofit organizations with credibility, such as Neighborhood Reinvestment (NeighborWorks America) and the Housing Preservation Fund, participated in President George W. Bush's Hope Now coalition of lenders and servicers who promised to help homeowners at risk, the program was designed in a way to assist a relatively small slice of homeowners,[7] and the actual assistance has been flimsy and inconsequential in most cases.

Legislation to deal with the problem of actual foreclosures and subsequent vacant and abandoned properties was passed by Congress, with financing structured in ways that make it difficult to imagine how deals will actually work. Little or nothing is being done to correct the more fundamental problems of how the nation's financial institutions and their fundamental lending and down-payment policies combined to create this problem in the first place, and solutions being crafted for the nation's two largest GSEs may actually perpetuate some problems, while giving Fannie Mae and Freddie Mac latitudes to buy more expensive mortgages for luxury homes as the payoff for purportedly helping out in the subprime crisis.

Overall, the subprime mortgage foreclosure crisis has generated numerous analytical reports of high quality. But the sense is one of analysis by paralysis. Notwithstanding an abundance of excellent statistical data and interpretative analysis, effective remedial action has been hard to find. The noteworthy efforts of community-based nonprofits such as the East Side Organizing Project in Cleveland, Ohio; the Community Development Law Center in Indianapolis, Indiana; and others stand out against a backdrop of how little is actually occurring to counter the negative effects of the subprime crisis, much less attack the underlying structural elements that gave rise to the subprime mortgage crisis in the first place.

More than two million homeowners were in danger of losing their homes by the end of 2009 due to "exploding" adjustable rate mortgages, and perhaps a similar number were at risk between 2009 and 2010 due to another form of subprimes, "Alt-A" mortgages. Some 500,000 vacant, foreclosed properties dotted inner-city neighborhoods in 2008. The massive scale of the subprime crisis makes the prospects for organizing and action hard to conceive. Dwarfing the scale and cost of the Savings and Loan crisis of the 1980s, the subprime crisis needs a federal commitment in the billions to slow down a train wreck for America's moderate and lower income homeowners.

But, given the complexity and multiple moving parts of the subprime crisis, it is possible to disaggregate the problem through a lens of the disparate impacts of the crisis on racial and ethnic minorities in a way that should enable advocates to conceptualize interventions and actions specific to populations and geographies particularly hard hit by the crisis—and not likely to be well served by the generic solutions emerging at the moment from municipal, state, and federal policy makers.

DISPARATE IMPACTS

Several organizations have generated statistics on the broadly disparate impact of the subprime mortgage foreclosure crisis on racial and ethnic populations. Like the underlying problems of bank and insurance redlining and the subsequent revelations about predatory lending, the subprime problem has had significantly disproportionate impacts on African Americans and Latinos.

According to the findings in *Foreclosed: State of the Dream 2008*, released by United for a Fair Economy (UFE), people of color are more than three times as likely as whites to have had subprime mortgages, and high-cost loans accounted for 55% of loans to African Americans, but only 17% of loans to whites.[8] Like many other sources, the UFE study noted that the subprime crisis has already chipped away at minority homeownership rates. Minority homeownership was responsible for the bulk of the increase in homeownership rates in the past decade, but much of that has already been lost due to foreclosures.

The UFE report confirmed the findings of the Center for Responsible Lending, which concluded that African American borrowers were substantially more likely than similarly situated white borrowers to receive higher rate subprime loans with onerous prepayment penalties.[9] The nonprofit researchers' analyses are supported by federal government data: an underreported HUD study noted that "even when controlling for differentials in available household, loan, and property characteristics, blacks and Hispanics (particularly non-white Hispanics) have significantly higher interest rates than comparable white households. For African Americans, this differential is 21–to-42 basis points, while for non-white Hispanics, the range is 13–to-15 basis points."[10] While the HUD authors take pains to suggest that this outcome is unrelated to discriminatory policies, the disparate outcomes are clear.

The racially disparate nature of the subprime dynamic has actually been known for some time, but not particularly publicized until the spike in delinquencies and foreclosures in 2006 and 2007. For example, Consumers Union examined cities in Texas in 2002, and reached a clear statistically justified conclusion: "…race matters. The race/ethnicity of borrowers is a powerful factor in the penetration of subprime lending in Texas communities. Our study shows that subprime loans are concentrated in geographical areas with a higher concentration of minority residents. Even after accounting for other factors, the likelihood of getting a subprime loan increases for minority borrowers, especially black borrowers. Among higher-income borrowers, the distinction between subprime lending to whites and subprime lending to minorities is stark."[11]

Sometimes aggregate statistics hide the human dimensions of the problem, but the mainstream press has covered this issue, noting the implications of the subprime mortgage crisis undermining and reversing asset wealth gains and neighborhood stabilization accomplishments in minority communities.

Citing Federal Reserve statistics that "About 46% of Hispanics and 55% of blacks who took out purchase mortgages in 2005 got higher-cost loans, compared with about 17% of whites and Asians," *USA Today* reported on African American and Latino homeowners with exploding first and second mortgage ARMs. They were facing foreclosures because they had not understood—and had not had appropriate information and counseling about—the risks and costs of adjustable rate mortgages, or had had to seek unconventional financing because of their lack of sufficient documentation.[12] The *USA Today* article started with Chicago, Illinois, for good reason: in a study of 2005 mortgage lending by seven lenders (including Countrywide and Washington Mutual) in New York City, New York; Los Angeles, California; Boston, Massachusetts; Chicago, Illinois; Charlotte, North Carolina; and Rochester, New York, Chicago topped the list with the highest disparity between African Americans and whites receiving high cost home loans (and Boston showed the highest disparity between Latinos and whites).[13]

Local studies across the nation demonstrate that in inner-city neighborhoods, the subprime foreclosure crisis is being felt most significantly in minority neighborhoods by people-of-color homeowners. In New York City, the majority of loans in minority neighborhoods such as Bushwick and East New York were subprime.[14] In Atlanta, Georgia, the Pittsburg and Sylvan Hills neighborhoods have been epicenters of the subprime crisis. It is important to remember that this problem is not simply a phenomenon of large cities.

Small cities have been ravaged, particularly small cities with significant if not majority populations of people of color: Natchez, Mississippi; Lawrence, Massachusetts; El Paso and McAllen, Texas; and many others.

What is striking about many of the cities where subprime problems are concentrated, the resources deployed to address these problems are in short supply. At the municipal level, places such as Newark, New Jersey; Indianapolis, Indiana; and Atlanta face municipal budgets with deficits in the millions, leading authorities to plunder federal programs such as Community Development Block Grants (CDBG) and HOME Investment Partnerships Program (HOME) to pay for general expenditures, and taxpayers to launch, as in Indianapolis, real estate tax revolts that exacerbate the revenue problems. In smaller communities, the size of subsidy programs is too small to make a dent on acquiring and rehabilitating foreclosed properties, and unlike these larger cities, the small and mid-sized communities lack the presence of large foundations such as the John D. and Catherine T. MacArthur Foundation (in Chicago), the Kresge Foundation (Detroit, Michigan), the Lilly Endowment (Indianapolis), and others that might put some philanthropic dollars toward building capacity for tackling this problem.

VACANT FORECLOSED PROPERTIES

In some cities, two years of subprime mortgage foreclosures have undone two decades of community development work. Certainly, in areas such as the East Side neighborhood in St. Paul, Minnesota, the reversal has been stunning, with vacant property rates reaching levels as high as they were when community development organizations were motivated to take on the abandonment issue in the 1980s and before.

But in many cities, the subprime mortgage foreclosure problem constitutes simply one more layer of vacant properties on top of a rash of vacancies that already existed. For example, in Indianapolis, community organizers note that the impact of the subprime mortgage foreclosure process was difficult to discern because of the wave of vacancies that already existed. The same certainly holds true for cities such as Detroit and Buffalo, New York, among others. Detroit may be the consistent leader in the nation for subprime foreclosures, but it occurs against a backdrop of thirty years of decreasing housing demand.

Nationally, housing vacancies have been increasing steadily since the 1990s, with a significant increase between 2000 and 2004—largely before the spike in subprime mortgage foreclosures. For some communities such as Phoenix, Arizona and Las Vegas, Nevada, local authorities anticipate that future job growth will result in purchasers and renters absorbing housing that has become vacant due to subprime foreclosures. But, as "weak market" housing expert Alan Mallach noted in Congressional testimony, "Officials cannot make that assumption in Dayton, (Ohio), Flint, (Michigan) or Buffalo. Properties there will have to be held longer, maintained longer, and ultimately either demolished or rehabilitated before they can be put back to productive use."[15]

Due to weak markets in many instances, the vacant units are simply sitting unused and unmarketed, a problem only exacerbated by the subprime crisis. For example, a 2003 survey of vacant units in Marion County in Indianapolis revealed 7,900 vacant properties containing 9,000 vacant units. Of these vacant properties, 21% were vacant and boarded and another 57% vacant without either boarding up or evidence of being on the market; only 22% were vacant and for sale.[16] The city of Buffalo, as of 2008, had 20,000 vacant residential properties, a dynamic which local organizers note was only exacerbated by, hardly caused by, the subprime crisis.[17] A report on burgeoning vacancies in Buffalo, noting an increase of 2,300 vacant and undeliverable addresses reported by the US Postal Service (a great indicator of true vacancies and abandonment) between the fall of 2006 and the fall of 2007, did not even mention subprime foreclosures as a significant contributing factor.[18]

In largely minority communities, immigrant communities, and declining manufacturing economies, the subprime mortgage foreclosure crisis deepened a housing market abyss that primarily impacts lower income families. Despite the fact that families cannot obtain affordable rental housing or access financing for purchasing new homes (due to tightening credit markets), the policy response is going to be, by virtue of weak housing market demand, demolitions rather than acquisition, rehab, and redevelopment of vacant properties. For these communities, the subprime crisis is the culmination of a perfect storm—concentrated poverty plus long-term job losses topped by the exploding ARMs of subprime loans.

IMMIGRANTS

The subprime mortgage foreclosure crisis has had devastating effects on immigrant populations. In Newark's North Ward and Ironbound neighborhoods, for example, immigrant groups were targeted by mortgage brokers peddling high cost mortgages to families that could have qualified for conventional financing. Lawrence, Massachusetts, is majority Latino and the virtual epicenter of the subprime foreclosure crisis in that state, though Framingham, Waltham, Boston, and other cities are well represented by immigrant purchasers. Nonetheless, the largest majority-Latino city in Massachusetts reveals stunning foreclosure statistics: In 2008, Lawrence was first in the state in the number of projected foreclosures per 1,000 residential properties at 40.18; by this ratio, Boston's foreclosure rate didn't even make the state's top 20 cities. Lawrence was long known as the state's "arson capital," but through the beneficial impacts of immigration, it developed a thriving housing market in the 1990s. The disproportionate impact of subprime mortgages on Latinos will take its toll on entire communities, like Lawrence, in addition to displacing individual homeowners.

To convince families to take on financing clearly to their detriment, frequently the lenders recruited mortgage brokers from immigrant groups to sell to their own. For example, the *Washington Post* reported on numerous cases in the Virginia suburbs where many Afghan immigrants have moved, noting cases of Afghan brokers persuading Afghan purchasers to take the subprime deals. The Spanish-language press in New York City has reported on cases of subprime mortgages where homebuyers were lured with the promise of minimal documentation to qualify. In Massachusetts, struggling Brazilians, who account for three out of every ten homes sold to immigrants in that state, appear to have been sold subprime deals by brokers who themselves were immigrants.

No surprise, but undocumented immigrants have been particularly victimized. They were pitched "NINJA" loans ("no income, no jobs, or assets"), but the subprime crisis swept up documented, as well as undocumented homebuyers. An underlying problem is that less than half of immigrants use formal banking institutions for their regular financial services, making them easy prey for purveyors of exotic, high cost mortgage products. The payday lenders, pawn shops, and rent-to-own stores that specialize in immigrant neighborhoods do not help customers build credit histories, and generally escape the oversight and regulation of consumer regulatory entities or, as weak as the protection might be, the Community Reinvestment Act scrutiny by the Comptroller of the Currency or state banking departments of conventional bank lenders.

As a rapidly growing component of the US population, Latinos have been significant users of subprime mortgages in all of their forms: ARMs, Option ARMs, Alt-A mortgages, and more. Nationally, in the early 1990s, one-fifth of home purchase mortgages for Latino purchasers were subprime compared to one-tenth for non-Latino whites, and in some metropolitan areas such as Hartford, Connecticut, and San Antonio, Texas, the proportion of subprime loans for Latino buyers reached 30 percent or more, though some data suggest that about half of Hispanic homeowners have subprime loans. Some conventional lenders, such as Bank of America and Citibank, that made efforts to reach undocumented immigrants with loans and banking service have had their confidence rewarded as ITIN mortgages (for applicants with "individual taxpayer identification numbers") has shown infinitesimal delinquency and foreclosure rates. But unlike the subprime shark brokers, banks offering ITIN mortgages ask for substantial income and credit evidence to ascertain that borrowers will be able to keep up with mortgage payments.

RENTAL

Coverage of the subprime mortgage foreclosure crisis leads to a narrative that involves homeownership. The public is not aware that a significant number of delinquent and foreclosed properties are not single-family properties, but two-family or three-family residential properties, or more. In some instances, these properties include an owner-occupant in one of the units, but frequently they were purchased and owned by investors who lost their properties in foreclosures. Several commentators describe renters as the collateral victims of the subprime mortgage foreclosure crisis.

In Newark and other communities in Essex County, New Jersey, the vacant foreclosed properties that could not be resold at foreclosure auctions include many vinyl-clad so-called "Bayonne boxes," built by speculators and now virtually unmarketable. The Boston Redevelopment Authority, for example, acquired a set of foreclosed properties in the Hendry Street area of Dorchester Bay, all of them traditional "triple-deckers," with at least two of the units in these buildings having been rentals before the subprime foreclosure.

Perhaps one in five subprime-foreclosed units is renter-occupied.[19] Anecdotal and statistical evidence from around the nation suggests higher levels of renters affected by subprime foreclosures: In some zip codes in Kansas City, Missouri, half of owners facing foreclosures do not live in those properties, or at least are registered at other addresses;[20] in Hennepin County (Minneapolis), Minnesota, where the bulk of the state's subprime foreclosures are concentrated, a significant number are renter-occupied with tenants scrambling to find advice on their rights.[21]

For as lousy as the system is toward homeowners with tanking mortgages, for renters, the situation is pure laissez faire economics:

• Typically, when a foreclosure is started, tenants are not notified. They may not even be aware of a foreclosure in process until well after the process is underway. When an owner walks away from a property prior to foreclosure, or sometimes even after the foreclosure has proceeded, tenants find themselves occupying properties with no one responsible for maintenance, utilities, and upkeep. Community organizations in Newark, for example, reported instances of tenants coming to city hall asking for instructions on how to pay water and sewerage bills in the absence of departed property owners.

- When a property goes into foreclosure, the tenant effectively has just about no rights and often can be evicted virtually on the spot. In most cities, tenants have few protections in small 2– and 3–unit buildings anyhow, but with foreclosures, they are simply put out into the street with little or no notice. In theory, little prevents a bank or a new owner acquiring a property at a foreclosure auction from simply evicting the tenants, except in very limited circumstances, although energetic Legal Services attorneys have been aggressively achieving protections for tenants in some foreclosures by banks and by secondary market institutions.[22]
- A tenant's lease affords the renting family little or no protection. The bank or servicer that acquires the property in a foreclosure proceeding is not obligated to honor the landlord's lease with the tenant. Perhaps a tenant might be able to initiate legal action against the now-departed landlord for damages of some sort, but that usually doesn't mean that they have any ability to retain their positions as occupants of the foreclosed property.

Amazingly, due to geometrically increasing rental-housing costs in many markets, many moderate-income renters took to subprime-financed home-ownership as a cheaper alternative, only to lose their properties to exploding ARMs and other exotic financing products. Add to those displaced families the evicted tenant occupants of foreclosed properties, and the result is further pressure on already overheated rental markets. In the terms of investors, the "fundamentals of the rental market" will improve, with higher rent levels and lower rental vacancies, due to the pressure of families displaced due to subprime foreclosures,[23] with rental markets tightening further in already high cost areas such as New York City; Seattle, Washington; and San Francisco, California.[24]

The reality is that for much of the short-term response to the subprime crisis, the solution is to take foreclosed properties and make them available as scattered-site rental units or lease-purchase (rent-to-own) properties. But because of a consistent bias against renters as less committed to their neighborhoods than homeowners, most city governments are militantly against adding to the rental inventory,[25] much less subsidizing rental units with public funds such as HOME or CDBG funds that would trigger affordability restrictions.

It would be a serious error to ignore the racial and ethnic dimension of this problem. As the Joint Center's studies show, racial/ethnic minorities account for nearly half of all renters, with Latinos accounting for nearly half of the increase in rental numbers (while the number of white renters dropped) between 1995 and 2005. Immigrant households were 1/6 of all renter households, and 80% of all immigrant families were renters.[26]

It isn't news that the gap between families qualified for rental subsidies and the number of available Section 8 vouchers and other affordability mechanisms is huge and widening. In combination with ever-decreasing public housing inventories, perhaps one-fourth of eligible households are able to obtain rental subsidies. While much of the public attention focuses on the homeownership dimension of the subprime foreclosure problem, the structural dimension of a large class of unprotected renters who simply lose their units in the process, without barely a scintilla of legal protection, much less resources offered in emerging federal legislation, suggests a policy issue that merits significant attention.

This situation is exacerbated by the scattered-site nature of the subprime foreclosed properties: the acquisition and rehabilitation of these properties, even if used for short-term lease-purchase developments, adds to the management costs of the nonprofit or for-profit owners. Most won't touch scattered-site rental or lease-purchase projects (other than the occasional scattered-site specialist such as the Cleveland Housing Network, and even CHN has had to get help with its scattered-site tax credit projects). The result is a housing stock and market that requires, at least temporarily, a rental solution, but the system of typical incentives for developers as well as local public attitudes militates against rental. The losers are lower-income minority householders who could qualify for rentals or lease-purchase units if there was political will and the public subsidy.

OLDER HOMEOWNERS

In the public's view, the subprime crisis is a home purchase crisis—families purchased homes with mortgages that they couldn't afford and should have known better (the blame-the-victim perspective that banks are using to defend their actions and that opponents of federal programs are citing in their opposition to "bail-outs"), or that they failed to understand, and in many cases may not have been able to understand, the exploding and ultimately punitive terms of their mortgages. But a significant number of victims of the subprime crisis are losing homes that were not purchased in the past few years, but homes they have lived in much longer.

A sizable portion of the subprime victims have been families who refinanced existing mortgages in order to realize some of the built-up equity as cash. These "home equity" loans attracted subprime lenders to stable or stabilizing inner-city neighborhoods where longer term, often older homeowners might be attracted to the prospect of tapping the built-up equity in their homes for home improvements or consumer expenditures. For moderate-income families, these "cash-out" loans offered quick access to cash that the homeowners might not have ever been able to tap in theory. A HUD study of subprime loans from ten years ago revealed that half of subprime loans in African American neighborhoods were refinance loans, compared to less than one-tenth in white neighborhoods. Other studies comparing neighborhoods by race and income in various cities revealed that these refinance loans were disproportionately marketed to African American neighborhoods,[27] including starkly disparate statistics from Boston, where in 2003 more than 25% of refinance loans were provided to African American borrowers, 19% to Hispanic borrowers, and only 5.6% to white borrowers; all were subprime loans.[28]

As of 2004, the share of subprime loans that were refinance loans varied from more than 10% in the Pacific states region to more than one-fourth in the Southwest. MSAs with typically high rates of subprime refinance loans were in North and South Carolina, Georgia, Alabama, and Mississippi in the Southeast, and Louisiana, Arkansas, Texas, and New Mexico in the Southwest.[29] According to the Center for Responsible Lending, a majority of subprime loans do not go for home purchases, and only one-fourth actually go to first-time homebuyers.[30] The effect has been to take stable neighborhoods in places like Detroit and undermine them by aiming at older homeowners, frequently householders in their 50s and 60s. Unlike potentially more geographically mobile younger homeowners, these home equity victims confront a disruptive uprooting against which they have little or no recourse.

The resulting problem is one that disproportionately affects older homeowners in inner-city neighborhoods and undermines the progress of communities that had made significant strides toward stable housing market dynamics. "Equity rich" but cash poor older homeowners have been attractive targets for subprime lenders and brokers. But it isn't simply a matter of refinancing. Older homeowners typically hold subprime mortgages: in 2001, more than half of the mortgages of homeowners 45 and older were subprime, compared to 12% for homeowners 35 or less.[31] Is this a problem clearly related to disparate racial outcomes? Subsequent studies from the AARP reached that conclusion: "Older borrowers who were widowed, female, black, and less educated held a significantly greater percentage of subprime loans than older borrowers who were married, male, non-black, and more educated."[32]

SUBSIDIES

From the very beginning of considerations to bring foreclosed properties back into productive use, the resource picture has been focused on federal subsidies, such as additions to the Community Development Block Grant and reprogramming of various tax credit programs, like the New Markets Tax Credit and the Low Income Housing Credit.

In Columbus, Ohio, an affiliate of Enterprise Community Partners (formerly the Enterprise Foundation) has been acquiring and rehabilitating foreclosed properties financed by a mix of public subsidies, including New Markets Tax Credit (NMTC) plus a combination of local subsidies; in suburban Newark an aggressive and creative nonprofit called HANDS structured a bulk acquisition of some 40 properties from one major subprime lender; and in the Twin Cities area, the Greater Minneapolis Metropolitan Housing Corporation has been drawing on a privately capitalized fund to acquire, rehab, and resell foreclosed properties. Much of what is contemplated is predicated on private financing, including program-related investments and other kinds of social investments from philanthropic grant makers.

But on the ground, local governments are looking toward solutions that do not trigger the use of CDBG or HOME subsidies for a very obvious reason: these subsidies come with mandatory affordability and resale restrictions, meaning that the re-occupants of these formerly restored units might be lower income. Even more frightening to some local officials is that the properties might be converted to rental or some form of social ownership such as community land trusts, limited equity cooperatives, or other forms of shared equity ownership.

The opportunity, if it can be called such, of the collapse of the financial markets' predatory approach to affordable homeownership is that for communities with huge swaths of foreclosed properties, conversion to shared-equity approaches might now be feasible. A spokesperson for the NeighborWorks America "Multi-Family Initiative" suggested that the foreclosure crisis might be a spark for local governments and the nonprofit sector to take up the challenge of the Ford Foundation's George McCarthy to make 10–to-25% of the housing of major cities permanently affordable.[33]

Despite lip service, there is often little in various plans that would mandate long-term affordability as an element of the solution to this crisis. Anecdotal reports from activists in Indianapolis and Richmond, Virginia, for example, suggest that local authorities are generally resistant to any solutions other than restriction-free homeownership. Few of the actual proposals for a response to the challenge of 500,000 vacant, foreclosed properties by the end of 2008 actually broached the concept of long-term affordability. Generally, affordability is dictated by the market; since the housing markets in some of these cities are weak, the subsequent sales of reclaimed subprime-foreclosed properties will be affordable simply because market conditions don't support higher sales prices. Influential organizations such as the free-market oriented

Initiative for a Competitive Inner City (ICIC) have issued policy proposals that omit long-term affordability controls and alternatives to fee-simple homeownership.[34]

The reality is that unless the federal government intervenes to mandate that lenders and servicers turn over properties to localities and nonprofits, the total development costs for foreclosed properties will result in units outside of the affordability range of moderate and even many middle-income purchasers. Certainly, in expensive markets such as Los Angeles and Boston, many properties that reach foreclosure auctions still end up selling at huge costs. But even in weaker and less robust sectors of these markets, the combination of acquisition, rehab, holding, and disposition costs add up to total development costs that need subsidies if they are going to be marketed for moderate and lower income households.

For example, if a nonprofit were to want to do a "bulk acquisition" of the 46 *Real Estate Owned (REO)* properties owned by Countrywide in Indianapolis, Countrywide was marketing the properties for an acquisition price of $3,168,590, or $68,882 per property as of the writing of this article.[35] This is in Indianapolis, where the market tanked before the subprime foreclosure crisis, yet Countrywide persists in asking for substantial pre-rehab acquisition prices (with the comic turn of ending each asking price with $900, like gasoline prices that always end in 99 cents). Perhaps Countrywide might have been willing to offer a discount to a nonprofit with the economic wherewithal to make a bid for the properties, but Countrywide's REO units are scattered throughout the city, so managing and securing the scattered site properties present additional costs to the acquiring entity. While some properties might be in reasonably good physical condition, it is a rule of thumb that upon foreclosure, properties are subject to vandalism (disappearing copper pipes, etc.), suggesting that more than moderate rehabs are in order. And with slow markets and tight mortgage financing, the time that a nonprofit would have to hold and manage the properties before ultimate disposition is potentially long. As a rule of thumb, assuming that the lenders and servicers continue to show little or no willingness to budge on prices except under political duress, the total development costs on subprime foreclosed properties will be two to three times the listed acquisition prices—and to make those affordable, even in weak markets, it will take deep subsidies.

A significant contrast is the proposal from Enterprise Community Partners (ECP) and the Center for American Progress calling for the creation of the "Great American Dream Neighborhood Stabilization" Fund (GARDNS), which explicitly builds in deed restrictions and "soft seconds" to maintain the affordability of reclaimed units for a period of time, or suggests that redeveloped housing go into community land trusts (where affordability is guaranteed by deed riders with covenants on the land).[36] But government openness to social responses to the subprime foreclosure problem is scattered at best, notwithstanding lip service to the contrary. The result is that people in the housing market who could be helped by the restoration of foreclosed properties through shared equity mechanisms will largely lose out due to ideological barriers from private lenders and government officials.

STRUCTURAL SOLUTIONS

It is striking that the battles over how to restructure and save homeowners in their homes, requiring lenders and servicers to restructure the terms of their loans (sacrificing loan principal and shaving interest rates), will be fought out in Congress and the bankruptcy courts. Any solution will be too late for the millions of homeowners currently at risk due to exploding ARMs and other current forms of subprime loans (the success of HOPE NOW and other counseling will be minimal until the lenders and servicers are compelled to accept changes in loan terms, not simply modifications in payment schedules). The beneficiaries will be the homeowners at risk in the next phase of subprime foreclosures, the Alt-A loans, which will begin coming due in large numbers in 2009 and particularly in 2010 and 2011. Oddly enough, the Alt-A borrowers tend to be higher income and less minority than families holding 2–28 or 3–27 ARMs. In essence, the public's halting response to the subprime crisis of today, with a significant minority component, will benefit the next wave of subprime borrowers, with a smaller racial and ethnic minority profile.

Partly, the structural racism response to the subprime solution has been to push for faster and more aggressive responses due to the clearly disparate racial impacts and outcomes of delinquencies and foreclosures, undoing decades of slow but discernable progress in improving housing and neighborhood conditions for African American and Latino families. But what is needed is not simply speed, but solutions that get at the racial underpinnings of aspects of the problem, including potentially these:

- Social housing solutions: Some of the prospective responses to the problem require thinking differently about ownership. Fee simple homeownership for lower-income households that lack the resource wherewithal to withstand the financial shocks of job losses and other factors simply means that these homeowners lose everything. Social housing solutions—limited equity cooperatives, community land trusts, etc.—controlled by community-based organizations have to be considered unless our society is basically satisfied with a constant churning of minority families and neighborhoods as the miner's canary of the nation's economic problems.

- Community-based organizations: The hidden story of the subprime crisis is that for the most part community-based nonprofits have not been at fault. In fact, the housing developed and financed by community development corporations, community land trusts, and others, have shown minimal evidence of subprime problems.[37] Unlike fee-driven builders and brokers, community development corporations, for all of their financial limitations, basically put home purchasers into conventional loans, supplemented by pre- and post-purchase counseling. The results are obvious and suggest future policy directions.
- Community banking: Unless there is some new study about to be released suggesting contrary information, the nation's minority-owned African American and Latino banks have been solid performers on home mortgage and home equity loans, in contrast to the heinous performance of lenders such as Countrywide, Washington Mutual, Deutschebank, etc. For both minority-owned banks and community development financial institutions (CDFIs), there are roles to be played in crafting community-level responses. CDFI portfolios have faced challenges as a result of the economic downturn, but have nonetheless outperformed the portfolios of commercial lenders, despite the CDFIs' typical investment focuses in low- and moderate-income neighborhoods. They need infusions of additional capital to increase their liquidity if they are to be able to play the roles they might in responding to the subprime crisis.
- Federal subsidies through municipalities: An odd dynamic in the debates on Capitol Hill has been a presumption that providing money to municipal governments will end up with waste and inefficiency compared to funneling federal resources through state governments. The supposed rationality of state allocations, given that most state legislatures are dominated by suburban and sometimes rural jurisdictions, seems to perpetuate the notion that localities with minority populations governed by African American and Latino mayors and city councils cannot govern themselves and craft locally specific solutions.
- Social investment: National legislation to respond to the prospect of 500,000 vacant REO properties anticipates a mix of grants and loans, the lending frequently of a relatively short-term nature. Given market conditions and total development costs, responding to the glut of vacant, foreclosed properties in American cities requires financing not predicated on a lot of lending. Given acquisition, holding, and rehab costs, the projects cannot sustain much lending, not to mention short-term lending. This is an opportunity for major, tax-endowed institutions (for example, foundations sitting on well above a half-trillion dollars in assets) to make equity investments in local funds, controlled by local entities, to acquire and rehab foreclosed properties.

- Minority homeownership: Beyond social housing solutions, the nation must eschew responses that simply turn prospective minority homeowners into a future class of victims in the next, unimaginable but assured wave of structural racism in the housing market. Already, proposals are emerging that seem to replicate the problems of the current subprime crisis, albeit under different terminology, all but guaranteeing a future reprise of this dynamic. A response to the specific challenges of increasing minority homeownership is called for.
- Speculation: Federal programs should not reward speculators and "house-flippers" who specialize in acquiring and quickly remarketing foreclosed properties with tax incentives and subsidies simply because they take fore-closed properties out of the bank-owned REO inventories. In response to the subprime problem, Congress has, in some instances, unwittingly been supporting, reviving, and undergirding the worst of speculators (who in some cities, market themselves with flyers saying "we buy ugly houses"). Those speculators' actions may, for legislators' purposes, result in the temporary reuse of foreclosed properties, but overall serve to further un-dermine neighborhood community development. As banks and servicers bring foreclosed properties to auction, these speculators always end up first in line to pick up properties before community-based nonprofits can even get there, stripping the properties of whatever they can, and then flipping the properties before walking. Targeting these speculators whose targets are generally minority neighborhoods is worth considering.
- Municipal tools: As anyone dealing with the foreclosed property problem at the local level can attest, acquiring subprime foreclosed properties is nightmarish. There are multiple lenders, servicers, and investors, all say-ing that the decision-making responsibility lies with someone else, almost none willing to budget on prices. On any block, the number of foreclosures is matched by a multiplicity of lenders and servicers. In the absence of, or perhaps even with federal action, localities should be able to use their pow-ers of eminent domain and redevelopment to acquire foreclosed properties in particularly hard-hit minority neighborhoods, compensating lenders and servicers not for the mortgage price, but for the actual (often nonexistent) market value. In this way, municipalities and their nonprofit partners could then gain control of blocs of properties with the potential of taking decisive actions to return properties to productive uses. While there are initiatives by national nonprofit community development intermediaries, such as the Local Initiatives Support Corporation, Enterprise Community Partners, NeighborWorks America, and the Housing Partnership Network, to lever-age a pool of foundation capital for a national acquisition fund, much of the acquisition challenge will still require municipalities to make maximum use of the tools at their disposal locally.

- Litigation: The disparate racial outcomes of the subprime crisis ought to be a reason for localities and nonprofits to consider litigation against lenders and servicers. Municipalities such as Cleveland and Baltimore have litigated against the subprime lenders, and the press has suggested that these suits have not achieved anything positive. That is entirely wrong. In Cleveland, the lenders are coming to the table to negotiate bulk dispositions with community organizations and the city government, in part because of the effect of the litigation. The litigation brought the lenders to the table for negotiations. Because of the demonstrable disparate racial outcomes of the subprime crisis, litigation strategies could result in community-specific progress with certain lenders and servicers.

This is a very brief recounting of only some of the disparate racial outcomes of the subprime crisis and some potential solutions that could be considered that build on a structural racism analysis. Since this piece was written, the nation has generated responses in the form of the Neighborhood Stabilization Program that was refunded and expanded in the federal stimulus program, the American Recovery and Reinvestment Act of 2009. NSP and ARRA add new resources to the subprime equation, but they do not address the structural racism underpinnings that led to the subprime mortgage crisis. To remove the racial and ethnic dimension of the subprime crisis and imagine that this is simply a housing-markets problem looking for a housing-finance correction or solution, is to miss the potential power of a structural racism approach.

NOTES

1. Aaron Dorfman and Nikki Jagpal, "Foundations and 'Structural Racism': Take Another Look*,"* *The Chronicle of Philanthropy* (May 29, 2008).

2. "Philanthropy and Racism," *The Chronicle of Philanthropy* (June 12, 2008).

3. The Brooking Institution's Christopher B. Leinberger highlights "starter home" tracts such as the 132–unit Windy Ridge development outside of Charlotte, North Carolina, with 81 foreclosures, in "The Next Slum?," *The Atlantic* (March 2008).

4. Prince Georges has the highest rate of foreclosures of any county in Maryland and Prince William County had the most foreclosure filings in the metro Washington area in early 2008, cf. Jonathan Mummolo and Bill Brubaker, "As Foreclosed Homes Empty, Crime Arrives," *Washington Post* (April 27, 2008).

5. Erik Eckholm, "Foreclosures Force Suburbs to Fight Blight," *New York Times* (March 23, 2007).

6. A bipartisan legislative package in Congress in early 2008 included $6 billion in tax credits (actually an extension of the carryback allowance period from two to four years, so that builders who had profitable years and paid taxes in 2004 could

apply those profits to 2009 and 2010, essentially a tax refund for taxes already paid) for the construction industry, cf. Cynthia Tucker, "Our Opinions: Subprime senators: Senate shoots down most ideas that would aid homeowners rather than builders and bankers," *Atlanta Journal Constitution* (April 7, 2008); on Capitol Hill, the tax credit for home builders was seen as a legislative attempt to purchase the cooperation of the home builder lobby.

7. Despite the promises of President Bush and Treasury Secretary Paulson, the Hope Now coalition has been unable to provide assistance to most homeowners who have called the Hope Now hotline. Although the original notion was that lenders and servicers would restructure mortgages for the narrow slice of homeowners who qualified for Hope Now assistance, in nearly all cases, the most that was done for homeowners was to restructure their mortgage payment schedules, not reducing principal or interest levels. Cf. Lynnley Browning, "Distressed Owners Are Frustrated by Aid Group," *New York Times* (April 2, 2008). None of this should have been surprising; the Hope Now coalition of lenders and servicers emerged from the Financial Services Roundtable, a lender/servicer trade association, and the executive director of Hope Now is a former subprime mortgage lender. Supposedly, only about 4% of callers ever even get to speak to a Hope Now counselor. The Center for Responsible Lending's analysis of the Hope Now plan suggests that even if the participating lenders were to live up to their rhetoric, due to the plan's provisions regarding who qualifies for help, only 3% of subprime loan recipients are likely to receive assistance in the form of restructured loans, cf. *Voluntary Loan ModificationsFall Far Short: Foreclosure Crisis Will Continue Unabated Without Court-Supervised* Modifications (January 30, 2008).

8. United for a Fair Economy, *Foreclosed: State of the Dream* http://www.faireconomy.org/files/StateOfDream_01_16_08_Web.pdf.

9. Center for Responsible Lending, *Unfair Lending: The Effect of Race and Ethnicity on the Price of Subprime Mortgages* at http://www.responsiblelending.org/mortgage-lending/research-analysis/unfair-lending-the-effect-of-race-and-ethnicity-on-the-price-of-subprime-mortgages.html.

10. Boehm et. al., *Mortgage Pricing Differentials Across Hispanic, Black, and White Households: Evidence from the American Housing Survey* at http://www.huduser.org/publications/homeown/hisp_homeown5.html.

11. Minority Subprime Borrowers (Consumers Union, October 2002); an earlier study of Texas cities by Calvin Bradford for the Center for Community Change (*Risk or Race? Racial Disparities and the Subprime Refinance Market*) generated much higher racial impaction numbers than the Consumers Union study of the same geography, but Bradford's analysis excluded FHA and VA loans from the base against which subprime loans were calculated.

12. Sue Kirchhoff and Judy Keen, "Minorities Hit Hard by Rising Costs of Subprime Loans," in *USA Today* (April 25, 2007).

13. Celeste Busk, "Minorities Getting Lion's Share of Subprime Loans," *Chicago Sun-Times* (March 16, 2007).

14. Ford Fessenden, "Subprime Mortgages Concentrated in City's Minority Neighborhoods," *New York Times* (October 15, 2007).

15. Testimony Of Alan Mallach, FAICP To The Domestic Policy Subcommittee Of The House Oversight And Government Reform Committee, May 21, 2008.

16. City of Indianapolis, Vacant Housing Initiative: Report Prepared for the Abandoned House Work Group Meeting December 2nd, 2003.

17. News release from Congressman Brian Higgins (May 8, 2008), "Hails Passage of Legislation Echoing Provisions Called for In Higgins Legislation."

18. Michael Clarke and Anthony Armstrong, *Vacancy and Abandonment in Buffalo, NY* (Local Initiatives Support Corporation).

19. The Joint Center for Housing Studies counts one-in-five foreclosure actions in 2007 involving 1– to 4–unit rental properties with non-resident owners (*America's Rental Housing—The Key to a Balanced National Policy* (Joint Center for Housing Studies, 2008)), but that misses the renters in 2–, 3–, and 4–unit properties with one unit owner-occupied. The tenant vulnerability to the subprime foreclosure crisis may be seriously understated.

20. Paul Wenske, "Renters Caught in Subprime Mortgage Crunch," *Kansas City Star* (May 26, 2008).

21. Steve Brandt and Warren Wolfe, 'Wave of foreclosures hits renters," *Star Tribune* (October 29, 2007).

22. Tenants with Section 8 vouchers get some additional protection due to the federal laws that might permit their leases to survive a foreclosure, and in some states and the District of Columbia, the courts are beginning in some instances, particularly where there are rent-control ordinances, as meriting some protections.

23. "US rental market gains seen after subprime debacle," *Reuters* (May 29, 2008).

24. Matt Woolsey, "Market looks good for landlords: More Americans are renting as foreclosures and risky lending roil the housing market," *Forbes.com* (2008).

25. The City of Cleveland appears to be a noteworthy exception, working with Neighborhood Progress, Inc. and the Cleveland Housing Network to acquire foreclosed properties for lease-purchase rehab and management, a specialty of the Network and suitable to Cleveland's weak homeownership market.

26. *America's Rental Housing—The Key to a Balanced National Policy* (Joint Center for Housing Studies, 2008).

27. Cf. Dennis E. Gale, *Subprime And Predatory Mortgage Refinancing: Information Technology, Credit Scoring And Vulnerable Borrowers* (Institute of Business and Economic Research, Fisher Center for Real Estate and Urban Economics, May 2001) for a review of the HUD study and others documenting the subprime refinance trends prior to 2000.

28. Jim Campen, *Borrowing Trouble: Subprime Lending in Greater Boston 2000–2003* (January 2005), Table 2; Campen's 2008 study, *Changing Patterns: Mortgage Lending to Traditionally Underserved Borrowers & Neighborhoods in Boston, Greater Boston and Massachusetts, 2006* (February 2008) demonstrates that this pattern of racially disparate refinance lending continues.

29. Allan Fishbein and Patrick Woodall, *Subprime Cities: Patterns of Geographic Disparity in Subprime Lending* (Consumer Federation of America, 2005).

30. *Subprime Lending is A Net Drain on Homeownership* (Center for Responsible Lending, CRL Issue Paper No. 14, March 27, 2007).

31. Neal Walters and Sharon Hermanson, *Subprime Mortgage Lending and Older Borrowers* (AARP, March 2001).

32. Neal Walters and Sharon Hermanson, *Older Subprime Refinance Mortgage Borrowers* (AARP, July 2002).

33. Don Akchin, "Shared-Equity Ownership: Has Its Time Come?" *Neighbor-Works Bright Ideas* (Fall 2007), p. 21.

34. *Foreclosures and the Inner City: The Current Mortgage Crisis and Its Inner City Implications* (Initiative for a Competitive Inner City, 2008).

35. Calculations based on the advertised asking price, which Countrywide described as "bargains," of some 70 Countrywide REO listings, for Indianapolis, information accessed on March 7, 2008.

36. David Abramowitz, *Addressing Foreclosures: A Great American Dream Neighborhood Stabilization Plan* (Center for American Progress, January 31, 2008), p. 10.

37. Rick Cohen, "How Foundations Can Heal the Housing Crisis", the *Chronicle of Philanthropy* (June 12, 2008); Rick Cohen, "Nonprofits Stand Out in Subprime Crisis", in the *Philanthropy Journal* (April 21, 2008); Rick Cohen, "Nonprofits and the Subprime Meltdown", in the *Nonprofit Quarterly (Cohen Report)* (April 15, 2008); Rick Cohen, "Foreclosed, but not Forewarned: Subprime Mess Will Put Pressure on Charities", in the *NonProfit Times* (February 1, 2008).

Chapter Five

Subprime Lending, Mortgage Foreclosure and Race

How Far Have We Come and How Far Have We to Go?

Ira Goldstein and Dan Urevick-Ackelsberg

For most of the twentieth century, lending discrimination occurred primarily through the denial of credit to minority group members and to the neighborhoods in which they lived. Redlining is a place-based practice in which lenders denied mortgage credit to neighborhoods with substantial numbers of minorities—typically African Americans and Latinos. Together with the differential treatment of minority and white applicants, a people-based practice, mortgage credit discrimination accelerated segregation and neighborhood decline. For many years, the private market and federal government, (through the explicit practices of the Federal Housing Administration) operated under laws and policies that permitted (and many argue, promoted) redlining and racial segregation.[1]

After the passage of a number of historically significant federal laws in the 1960s and 1970s, especially the Fair Housing Act (Title VIII of the Civil Rights Act of 1968) and the Equal Credit Opportunity Act of 1974 (ECOA), federal law and policy outlawed lending discrimination, and started to require data collection among federally-regulated lending institutions. However, early enforcement of federal fair lending laws was anemic as evidenced by the limited number of legal actions filed, most of which were by private actors.[2] Data collection on lending institutions did not begin in earnest amongst regulators until petitions were made to the financial regulatory agencies by the National Urban League in 1971. Failing to adequately respond to the National Urban League's earlier demands, as well as requests from the US Department of Housing and Urban Development (HUD) and the Department of Justice, the Urban League filed suits against the financial regulators in 1976. The settlement of those suits had the regulators agreeing to a set of changes (both examination and data reporting) designed to meet the civil rights aspect of their duties.[3]

With the passage of the Home Mortgage Disclosure Act in 1975, and the Community Reinvestment Act in 1977, came a large body of research by academics, regulators and advocacy groups (both community-based and industry). Much of that research showed a relationship between the racial composition of an area and the extent to which mortgage credit was extended (and later, as the reporting requirements of HMDA changed, the differential rates of denial between white and minority applicants).[4] Using the early HMDA data, research throughout the 1980s examined the flow of capital into minority communities and consistently found lending disparities. While early HMDA studies were frequently critiqued because they lacked complete empirical control for the level of effective demand, study after study found that race and ethnicity had negative effects on credit flows.[5] Shlay and Goldstein (1993) reviewed 23 post-1980 through 1991 studies that examined the effect of the presence of African Americans (18 studies), Hispanics (8 studies) or minorities generally (5 studies) in an area. Every study found a negative relationship between the presence of these groups in neighborhoods and the amount of conventional mortgage credit that flowed into them. These studies all had their limitations, but they did serve to document what many community development and civil rights advocates had complained of: that minority group members and minority communities were not receiving a sufficiency of mortgage credit to thrive.

Nineteen eighty-eight marked the twentieth anniversary of the federal FHAct and the year of its most significant amendments. Not only did Congress amend the law to include protections for families with children (i.e., familial status) and persons with disabilities (i.e., handicap status), they also gave HUD significant enforcement powers going beyond mere attempts to settle cases (i.e., the authority granted in 1968). HUD was given authority to prosecute cases of discrimination, and to obtain monetary and injunctive relief for persons found to have been victims of a discriminatory housing practice. Additionally, Congress gave the secretary of HUD the authority to file complaints alleging discriminatory housing practices on his own initiative (Section 810 of the Fair Housing Act).[6]

Concomitant with the wave of HMDA-based research was a remarkably influential series of articles published in 1988 by the *Atlanta Journal-Constitution* written by Bill Dedman. Using a variety of quantitative and qualitative sources of data, Dedman's Pulitzer Prize-winning series shined a very bright light on racial disparities in home mortgage lending in Atlanta, Georgia.

Prompted by the public attention to Dedman's series and a recently expanded FHAct, Justice commenced inquiries into the lending practices of 64 institutions. The responses from those institutions lead to Justice's more focused investigation and ultimate charge (in 1992) of racial discrimination

---

The Fair Housing Act
Title VIII of the Civil Rights Act of 1968, as amended

Section 804: [42 U.S.C. 3604] Discrimination in sale or rental of housing and other prohibited practices.

(a) To refuse to sell or rent after the making of a bona fide offer, or to refuse to negotiate for the sale or rental of, or otherwise make unavailable or deny, a dwelling to any person because of race, color, religion, sex, familial status, or national origin.

Section 805: [42 U.S.C. 3605] Discrimination in Residential Real Estate-Related Transactions

(a)   In General.—It shall be unlawful for any person or other entity whose business includes engaging in residential real estate-related transactions to discriminate against any person in making available such a transaction, or in the terms or conditions of such a transaction, because of race, color, religion, sex, handicap, familial status, or national origin.

(b)   Definition.—As used in this section, the term "residential real estate-related transaction" means any of the following:

(1)   the making or purchasing of loans or providing other financial assistance—

a.   for purchasing, constructing, improving, repairing, or maintaining a dwelling; or

b.   secured by residential real estate.

Figure 5.1.

under the FHAct and ECOA, in the seminal case—the United States v. Decatur Federal Savings and Loan Association (Ritter, 1996). Decatur was the first case where Justice charged a *pattern or practice*[7] of racial discrimination in lending. Justice alleged, among other things, that Decatur marketed its loans primarily to white consumers, excluded African American areas from its lending footprint, and refused to offer loan products that were especially desirable to African American communities (such as FHA and VA loans). Justice also alleged that Decatur employed only a small number of African Americans in key lending positions, provided assistance to white applicants that was denied to African American applicants, and denied equally qualified African Americans loans more frequently than their white counterparts. In a consent decree with Justice, Decatur agreed to a number of remedial measures including, but not limited to: affirmative advertising practices; practices designed to equate the mortgage production levels of loan officers in minority and white areas; appointment of a review underwriter and a review appraiser to ensure equal treatment of applicants and applicants' properties; train staff in the relevant fair housing laws and Decatur's obligations under the consent decree; deposit $1 million into a fund to compensate aggrieved persons; and submit reports of activities and compliance to Justice.[8]

While Justice began to prosecute cases, other groups began to use federally mandated data from lending institutions to investigate whether racial discrimination—not just disparities in credit flows--appeared to exist. Most notable among those studies was the Federal Reserve Bank of Boston's 1992 study using HMDA data augmented with a variety of traditional underwriting variables obtained from lenders (absent from all other studies to-date); this study showed that racial discrimination existed in the Boston, Massachusetts metropolitan lending market. The authors of this study reported that controlling for relevant financial risk factors, African Americans were rejected for loans 56% more often than whites. While the results of this study lead to a "…wholesale media and social science assault…on the study's credibility…" (Goering and Wienk, p. 15), the study's main findings confirmed the observed racial disparity (c.f., Carr and Megbolugbe, 1993).

Throughout the decade of the 1990s, the common view of what lending discrimination entailed shifted from classic differential treatment leading to the denial of credit and redlining as exemplified in *Decatur*. In 1999, HUD released a study conducted by the Urban Institute using paired mortgage application testing that found persistent discrimination against minorities, not just in the rates in which they were rejected, but in the terms of their loans (price discrimination). And using data from the American Housing Survey, HUD found considerable rates of unexplained differences in pricing between white homeowners and their African American and Latino counterparts. Thus, the paradigm was shifting away from a denial of credit to one in which credit was extended, but under different terms.[9] HUD's examination of 1998 HMDA data demonstrated that loans from subprime lenders (a relatively recent market phenomena) were five times more likely to be made in African American neighborhoods than in white neighborhoods. Additionally, homeowners in high-income African American neighborhoods were twice as likely to receive loans from subprime lenders as residents in low-income white neighborhoods. HUD then examined lending in five cities: Atlanta, Georgia, Philadelphia, Pennsylvania, New York, New York, Chicago, Illinois and Baltimore, Maryland. They found that African Americans received disproportionate shares of loans from subprime lenders in all five cities. Calem, et al. (2002) examined HMDA data in Philadelphia and Chicago to determine the equality in the likelihood of whether African Americans and whites received loans from subprime lenders; they also examined the impact of the racial composition of the area in which a collateral property was located. They found that over and above area and individual credit risk factors, minority group members and residents of minority communities received more loans from subprime lenders than they should have. The one exception to the pattern was refinance loans in Philadelphia. This exception was, according to the authors, possibly related to the active CRA lending in several minority communities in Philadelphia.

Both the research and Justice's involvement in fair lending cases evolved along with the shifting paradigm of what lending discrimination in the twenty-first century meant. From classic redlining in Decatur, Justice pursued cases alleging price discrimination, and eventually, to 'reverse redlining' and practices that could be described as *predatory lending*. Predatory lending was gaining recognition as an evolving type of lending discrimination and was acknowledged as such in academic literature,[10] private lawsuits,[11] and also by the state[12] and federal governments. This body of cases sent a signal to the lending industry of the vigor and parameters of the US government's interpretation of the FHAct.

This evolution is generally understood to trace its roots to a set of legislative changes and associated changes in the financial sector. Specifically, three pieces of legislation—the Depository Institutions Deregulation and Monetary Control Act of 1980 (DIDMCA), the Alternative Mortgage Transaction Parity Act of 1982 (AMTPA) and the 1986 Tax Reform Act—are generally credited with setting the stage for a rise in subprime mortgage lending and that set of transactions commonly referred to as "predatory lending."[13] Moreover, the rise of the process of securitizing subprime loans created a seemingly limitless well of funds looking to find a home in the first-lien (i.e., purchase money and refinances of existing loan(s) into the first position) mortgage market. HUD reported that subprime lending, which totaled $20 billion nationwide in 1993, increased to $150 billion in 1998. Subprime volume reportedly increased to $625 billion in 2005 (Goldstein, 2007; Gramlich, 2007) and to between $600 billion and $634 billion by 2006.[14] Alt-A lending volume increased from $60 billion in 2001 to $400 billion in 2006 (Coleman, et al., 2008; Zandi, 2009).

Starting with 2004 HMDA data reports, lenders included information concerning whether the loan made was at a rate at least 300 basis points higher than the relevant Treasury yield for a comparable maturity-commonly denoting a subprime loan. And in 2004, 2005 and 2006, the Federal Reserve analyzed HMDA data and found disparities in the rate that minorities, and those living in neighborhoods with significant minority concentrations, receive subprime loans. For example, in 2004 the Federal Reserve partnered with the Credit Research Center of Georgetown University to examine additional risk factors that could explain why HMDA consistently showed that minorities were more likely to receive subprime loans. After controlling for a number of risk factors, disparities between whites and African Americans and whites and Latinos were reduced, but remained statistically significant.[15]

A number of scholars and industry/advocacy groups examined HMDA (and augmented HMDA) data and similarly found disparities in the rate minority group members and residents of minority communities received subprime loans. For example, the Center for Responsible Lending combined HMDA data with borrower information from a loan servicer, including FICO scores, presence of private-mortgage insurance, and loan-to-value ratios. They found that even after taking these data into account, African American borrowers were more likely to receive subprime purchase and refinance loans. The disparities were especially great amongst the subset of borrowers who have prepayment penalties. Latino borrowers purchasing homes were 29–to–142% more likely to receive a higher rate loan than whites. (Differences with refinances were not statistically significant at a 95% confidence interval). At TRF, we examined HMDA data in a number of areas, including Baltimore, Philadelphia, Newark, New Jersey and Washington, D.C. To varying degrees, but in all locations, residents of minority neighborhoods were more likely to receive subprime loans than residents of comparable white areas.

Targeting of minorities for subprime lending is not only a case of encouraging a group of people to pay more for their mortgage, but also exposing them to a greater risk of losing their home. It is axiomatic that a subprime loan is more likely to default than a prime loan, and that more defaults lead to more foreclosures.[16] In Chicago, Atlanta, and in the state of New Jersey, researchers have all noted that increased subprime lending-consistently higher in minority communities-leads to higher numbers of foreclosures. Other research suggests that those resultant foreclosures adversely impact surrounding property values (Immergluck and Smith, 2006), and accelerate racial transition from white to African American (Lauria and Baxter, 1999).

THE REGULATORY AND LAW
ENFORCEMENT ENVIRONMENTS

Despite an increased awareness of lending discrimination and the pitfalls of subprime lending, there appears to be an inverse relationship between the rise of subprime lending and HUD's and Justice's record of targeting abusive lending and lending discrimination. After appearing to take steps towards targeting the subprime lending industry in a small number of actions, federal fair lending cases have slowed. Early in the Bush Administration, Justice announced that it will no longer pursue disparate impact cases, a useful theory for some of the more complex predatory lending cases, and their filing of fair housing/fair lending cases slowed to a trickle by 2008.[17]

HUD significantly reduced the number of FHAct cases it charged per year (of which lending cases are only a subset) from 88 in fiscal year 2001 to 31 in fiscal year 2007 (National Fair Housing Alliance, 2008). HUD's administrative process for adjudicating housing/lending discrimination complaints that it investigated and deemed a violation of the FHAct declined so much, that it no longer had administrative law judges on staff to hear cases that HUD charged, nor did it elect to send the cases to federal district court. HUD's history of filing Secretary-initiated lending cases is scant, and owing to the complexity of systemic lending discrimination cases and HUD's shortage of internal specialists to conduct the complex and oftentimes statistical investigations, these cases languished without resolution.[18] While Congress saw fit to entrust the responsibility for enforcing the FHAct with HUD because of the institutional knowledge and experience in the housing market, the custodians of that responsibility allowed the administrative process to wither through much of the decade beginning in 2000.

Excerpts from: "Long Road to Justice; the Civil Rights Division at 50"

The results of these efforts were remarkable in such a short period of time. Due in part to the Division's work and its general impact on the banking profession, the availability of loans to minorities expanded dramatically. At the same time, however, the Division has done little over the past 10 years to require conventional lenders to penetrate the African American and Latino homeownership markets nationwide. It has failed to challenge the discriminatory predatory practices–such as steering blacks and Latinos to subprime loans and lenders when they could qualify for conventional loans–that affect the lending market so dramatically today...

The general criticisms of politicization, anemic enforcement, and a disregard of mission further affect housing discrimination enforcement, as they do with regards to other civil rights issues...

The number of enforcement cases brought by the Division–both "pattern or practice" and HUD election cases–has dropped significantly in recent years; and that decrease is most evident in cases alleging racial discrimination...
Unfortunately, as with many other sections of the civil rights Division in recent years, many qualified attorneys have left and/or been pushed out by the admnistration...

Leadership Conference on Civil Rights Education Fund, pp 23-24.

Figure 5.2.

Several state officials and private actors attempted to fill the void. For example, the attorney general of the State of Massachusetts targeted abusive lending, including recent cases against Fremont Mortgage and Countrywide. The City of Baltimore sued Wells Fargo, alleging race discrimination in lending and the resultant foreclosures. However, for multiple reasons, state prosecutions and private lawsuits are no substitute for federal action.

First, the impact of a state or city lawsuit against a lender is generally smaller and has less reach than federal prosecutions. Second, attorneys general do not have the same jurisdiction to prosecute banks as that of the federal government. For example, after targeting national banks, former New York Attorney General Eliot Spitzer was sued by the Office of the Comptroller of the Currency (OCC) OCC, which argued successfully that the attorney general did not have the power to regulate national banks, and that those banks were not subject to increasingly stringent state anti-predatory lending laws. In sum, the early (post-1988 FHAct amendments) history of Justice teaches us that to have systemic influence on the industry, federal regulation and prosecution must be active. [See Figure 5.3]

SUBPRIME LENDING, FORECLOSURES AND RACE

The failure of subprime lenders post-1990 is no secret. High-volume national lenders have been failing (or acquired and closed) since the 1990s, based, at least in part, on the poor quality of their loans and the drying up of the capital they needed to extend loans; United Companies Lending Corporation, The Money Store, Equicredit, Option One, Ameriquest, New Century, to name a few. In the early to mid 2000s, we observed threats to the continued viability (and later the ultimate demise) of lenders that did a mix of prime, Alt-A and subprime loans (e.g., Countrywide). Meanwhile, FHA loans, which lost significant market share to subprime loans over the years, have rebounded considerably. In both Pennsylvania and Maryland, more FHA loans were made in the first half of calendar year 2008 than in all of 2005.[19] FHA is reclaiming a part of the mortgage market formerly captured by the nation's subprime lenders. The critical question for FHA is whether the lenders originating FHA loans can claim market share and at the same time maintain strong, responsible underwriting- and loss-mitigation techniques.

There is evidence that a group of "risky lenders" clustered their lending in lower income and minority communities (California Reinvestment Coalition, et al., 2008). High-risk subprime lenders, defined by their authors as lenders that went out of business in the recent collapse of the subprime lending industry, originated significantly disparate shares of their loans in minority communities. The implication of this work is that the disparate share of risky loans in

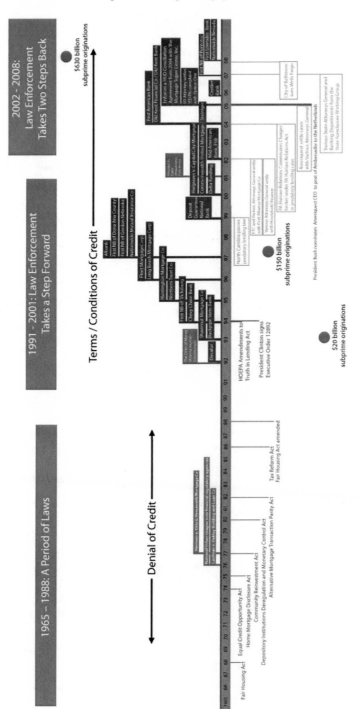

Figure 5.3.

minority areas will likely go into foreclosure at elevated rates, and thus the resultant damage will be magnified (and for the people, of any race or ethnic origin, who reside in those communities). In *Lost Values*, Goldstein examined 1998 loans that reached foreclosure in Philadelphia and found that three of the top five lenders with loans in foreclosure were out of business. However, even the proportion of 'risky lenders'—subprime lenders that have gone out of business during the credit crunch—appear concentrated in minority communities.

Research has shown that minority group members and residents of minority communities are more likely to receive subprime loans. When those subprime loans reach delinquency faster and more frequently than prime loans, and those delinquencies lead to increased levels of foreclosures, they are felt unevenly by various communities. The "market corrections" that put these lenders out of business do not help the borrowers or communities within which their bad loans were originated. The market may have corrected, but the risky loans, which caused them to fail, are still in the hands of many homeowners, portending even more foreclosures. It is from this framework that we examine subprime lending, delinquencies and foreclosures in two cities—Baltimore and Philadelphia—and the differing levels of impact they have on communities and people of color.

The link between race and predatory lending is less well established; most research linking the two establishes the relationship between race and subprime lending. Equating the two, however, is imprecise. Predatory lending is a term that became part of the public dialogue in the mid-to-late 1990s. A bright-line definition of the term still eludes us. But in general, people define predatory loans as including one or more of the following characteristics: (1) a set of loan terms, costs and conditions under which the loan was made that are neither commensurate with the true risk of the borrower, nor are they such that the borrower could likely maintain them over the life of the loan (e.g., interest rates and fees, single premium credit life insurance, pre-payment penalties); (2) the borrower was targeted for a given loan product because of some characteristic that makes them uniquely vulnerable to that disadvantageous loan (e.g., borrowers who have a documented history of borrowing from finance companies would thus be willing to take out expensive loans); (3) there is a vast imbalance in information and experience between the borrower and lender that the lender can exploit. Typically, the loans that are considered predatory are subprime, but not all subprime loans are predatory.[20] Goldstein (2007) went beyond the association of race and subprime lending to include characteristics of transactions emblematic of predatory lending (i.e., rapid refinancing of loans, loans exceeding the likely value of the property, smaller second-position loans refinanced into a large first-position loan). This research found a positive relationship between the racial composition of an area and the prevalence of predatory lending, but that relationship was far from perfect.

Philadelphia

As in communities across the country, minority group members in Philadelphia (and the communities in which they live) received significantly greater portions of subprime lending than their white counterparts. These differentially high levels of subprime lending lead to elevated levels of delinquencies, resulting in concentrations of foreclosures.

HMDA data for Philadelphia show how uneven subprime lending in Philadelphia is amongst different races and ethnicities. In 2006, non-Hispanic whites and Asian Americans received subprime loans 24.6% and 16.1% of the time, respectively. Hispanics and African Americans received subprime loans 47.8% and 58.5% of the time, respectively.

Neighborhoods with greater concentrations of minority group members also received greater proportions of subprime loans than mostly white neighborhoods. In 2006, Philadelphia neighborhoods with less than 10% minorities, and those with 10% to 19.9% minorities, received subprime loans 29.6% and 22.7% of the time, respectively. Neighborhoods with 20% to 49.9% minorities received subprime loans 31.7% of the time. And, those neighborhoods with the greatest concentration of minorities, with 50% to 79.9% minorities and 80% to 100% minorities, received the highest percentages of subprime loans at 41.8% and 57.7%, respectively. [See Figure 5.4]

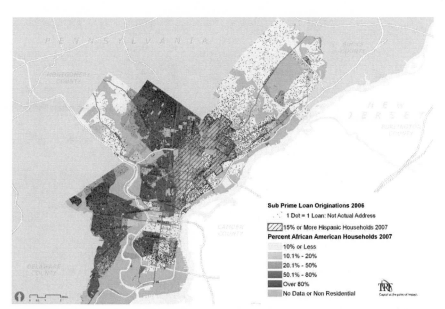

Figure 5.4. Racial/Ethnic Composition and Subprime Loan Originations in Philadelphia (2006).

Data on lending are reported for Census tracts; data on delinquency at the level of the zip code. These two geographies cannot be precisely matched. However, when we break down Philadelphia zip codes by the racial composition of the residents within those zip codes, we observe that the greater percentage of a zip code that is populated by minority group members, the greater the percentages of loans that are not current (specifically, in delinquency or foreclosure). The median zip code in Philadelphia had 26.7% of its subprime loans in a non-current status. Eight of the nine zip codes with at least 80% African Americans, and seven out of eight zip codes with 50% to 79.9% African Americans, had a greater percentage of loans in a non-current status than the median. [See Figure 5.5]

If a neighborhood has a disproportionate number of subprime loans, and those subprime loans reach delinquency at a greater rate than in other neighborhoods, the negative effects of the subprime lending are magnified. Given those rates of delinquency, we see communities with greater minority concentrations are now harder hit by foreclosures than predominantly white neighborhoods.

Assuming a lag time from originations to foreclosures, elevated levels of foreclosures in Philadelphia directly track the rise in subprime lending—a finding similar to that reported by TRF in its report to the secretary of banking for the Commonwealth of Pennsylvania in 2005. While subprime lending

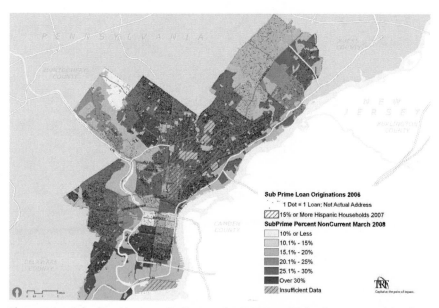

Figure 5.5.   Subprime Mortgage Delinquencies (2008) and Subprime Loan Originations in Philadelphia (2006).

has only recently made a dramatic entry into the national consciousness, in Philadelphia (and across Pennsylvania) homeowners have been struggling with the ramifications of it for some time. In 1995, Philadelphia had 2,347 foreclosures. By 2002, the number increased to 6,200. Foreclosures trended down over the next few years, but never fell below 5,000. And in 2006 and 2007, foreclosures began to rise again. By 2007, foreclosures were almost identical to 2002 levels. And based on the first six months of 2008, we predict there will be roughly 8,000 foreclosures in the city this year, easily the most in Philadelphia history, and a 340% increase from 1995.

After studying subprime lending and subprime delinquencies and their relationship to race, the next logical step is to examine whether these fore-closures disproportionately affect minority communities. TRF's research on foreclosure typically traces back from the entity filing the foreclosure against the borrower to the lender that originated the loan now subject to foreclosure. Moreover, we attached the property subject of the foreclosure to its precise geographic location. Much like research on redlining and its after-effects, ex-amining a foreclosure in relation to the characteristics of the neighborhood in which it occurs provides insight into how different communities are affected by, and potentially targeted by, different loan products.[21]

TRF placed 23,342 foreclosures from 2000 to 2003, and 21,906 foreclo-sures from 2004 to 2007, at their street address and examined the percentage of African Americans who live in those neighborhoods. We then created an expected share of foreclosures for groupings of neighborhoods, based on the percentage of the city's owner-occupied housing units in those neighborhoods.

With greater levels of subprime lending, and increased levels of those sub-prime loans going into delinquency, it is of little surprise that foreclosures in Philadelphia are disproportionately located in African American neighbor-hoods. For 2000 to 2003 foreclosures, we use 2000 Census data to examine the racial composition of a neighborhood, and what share of Philadelphia's owner-occupied housing stock that neighborhood holds. Over these four years, mostly white neighborhoods (with less than 10% African American household-ers) accounted for 42.2% of Philadelphia's owner-occupied housing, but only 23.4% of foreclosures, or approximately 55% of the foreclosures that would be expected given their share of the city's housing stock. Conversely, mostly African American neighborhoods (with more than 80% African American householders) accounted for 29.6% of Philadelphia's housing stock, but 38.7% of foreclosures, or 131% of the expected number of foreclosures. Neighbor-hoods with 20.1% to 50%, and 50.1% to 80%, African Americans bore an even greater burden of foreclosures, with 147% and 149% of their expected share. Neighborhoods with 10.1% to 20% African American households had just slightly more (105%) foreclosures than expected. [See Figure 5.6]

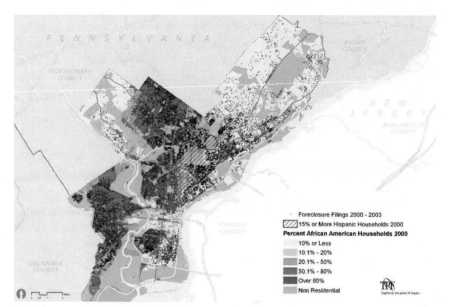

Figure 5.6. Racial/Ethnic Composition and Mortgage Foreclosures in Philadelphia (2000–2003).

Foreclosures from 2004 to 2007 tell a similar story. Neighborhoods with less than 10% African Americans had only 53% of the number of foreclosures that would be expected given the share of the city's owner-occupied housing stock. Neighborhoods with 10.1% to 20% African Americans had somewhat less foreclosures than expected (91% of expected foreclosures). However, neighborhoods with 20.1% to 50% African Americans (132% of expected foreclosures), 50.1% to 80% African Americans (152% of expected foreclosures) and greater than 80% African Americans (134% of expected foreclosures) experienced greater foreclosures than their share of owner-occupied housing would suggest. [See Figure 5.7]

Baltimore

Within the city of Baltimore, both minority group members and the neighborhoods where they live are more likely to receive subprime loans than white borrowers and borrowers in predominantly white areas. In 2006, for example, 26.5% of all purchase and refinance loans for non-Hispanic whites were subprime. For Latinos and African Americans, this figure climbed to 51.1% and 60.7%, respectively. Echoing calls of redlining and reverse redlining, Baltimore neighborhoods with larger concentrations of minority group members have more subprime lending than predominantly white neighborhoods. Subprime loan originations constituted 26.7% of all loans in neighborhoods with less than 10% minorities, and 24% of loans in neighborhoods with 10%

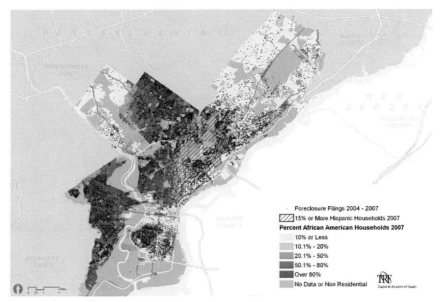

Figure 5.7. Racial/Ethnic Composition and Mortgage Foreclosures in Philadelphia (2004–2007).

to 19.9% minorities. For neighborhoods with 20% to 49.9% minorities, and 50% to 79.9% minorities, subprime lending increased to 40.8% and 49.3%. respectively. For neighborhoods that have at least 80% minority group members, this figure increases to 61.2%. [See Figure 5.8]

While it is impossible to detail how many of these loans specifically will reach foreclosure, as in Philadelphia, we can examine how subprime loans are performing in 2008 in zip codes with high percentages of minority group members. With a smaller number of zip codes to examine in Baltimore than Philadelphia, the relationship between the percentage of a zip code that is comprised by minority group members and the percentage of subprime loans in a non-current status is similar—although not quite as strong.

The median zip code in Baltimore had 24.4% of its loans in a non-current status. Three out of four zip codes with at least 80% African Americans had levels of non-currency above the median. Four out of eight zips with 50% to 79.9% African Americans, two out of five zips with 20% to 49.9% African Americans, and one out of two zips with 10% to 19.9% African Americans had levels of subprime non-currency above the city median. The single zip code with less than 10% African Americans had almost one-third the percentage of loans in a non-currency status than any other zip code in Baltimore. [See Figure 5.9]

As in Philadelphia, high levels of foreclosures are not a new phenomenon in Baltimore. While foreclosures increased significantly from 2006 to 2007, those numbers are actually smaller than any single year from 2000 to 2003.

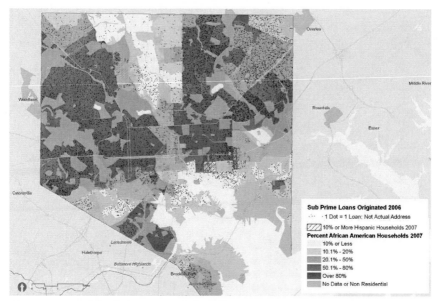

Figure 5.8. Racial/Ethnic Composition and Subprime Loan Originations in Baltimore (2006).

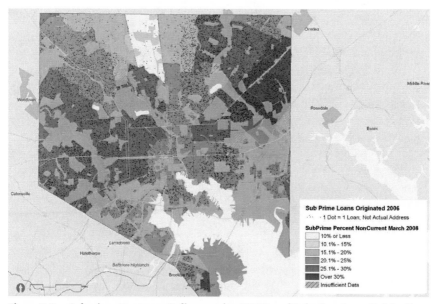

Figure 5.9. Subprime Mortgage Delinquencies (2008) and Subprime Loan Originations in Baltimore (2006).

And, as in Philadelphia, neighborhoods with greater numbers of African Americans receive a disproportionate number of foreclosures. TRF placed 19,750 foreclosures from 2000 to 2003, and 14,253 foreclosures from 2004 to 2007, at their street address, and examined the percentage of African Americans that live in those neighborhoods. We then created an expected share of foreclosures for groupings of neighborhoods, based on the percentage of owner-occupied housing units in those neighborhoods.

Examining 2000 to 2003 foreclosures versus 2000 demographic data, neighborhoods with less than 10% African American householders, and neighborhoods with 10.1% to 20% African American householders, had 46% and 77% of their expected numbers of foreclosures respectively. Neighborhoods with 20.1% to 50%, 50.1% to 80%, and more than 80% African American householders had more foreclosures than expected, at 110%, 118% and 125%, respectively. [See Figure 5.10]

TRF's examination of foreclosure filings from 2004 to 2007 against 2007 demographic data reveals the same pattern. Neighborhoods with 10% or less, 10.1% to 20%, and 20.1% to 50% African American householders had 41%, 57% and 96% of their expected share of Baltimore foreclosures respectively. Neighborhoods with 50.1% to 80% and greater than 80% African American householders had 113% and 132% of their expected number of foreclosures respectively. [See Figure 5.11]

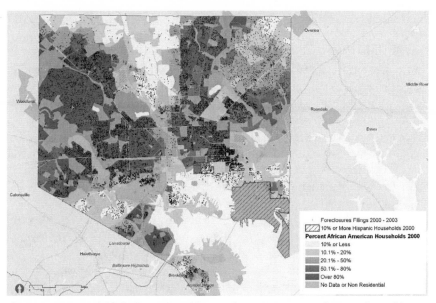

Figure 5.10. Racial/Ethnic Composition and Mortgage Foreclosures in Baltimore (2000–2003).

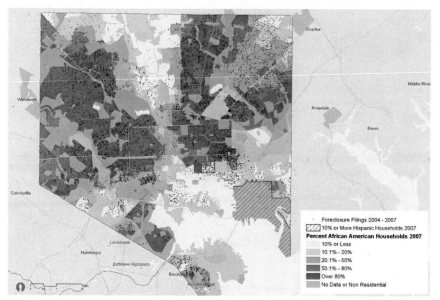

Figure 5.11. Racial/Ethnic Composition and Mortgage Foreclosures in Philadelphia (2004–2007).

CONCLUSIONS

The federal government is now taking unprecedented steps to deal with the impact of the real estate and mortgage market meltdown. It is hard to know now the true need for all of these actions or the future consequences (intended and unintended). What we do know is that our difficulties result, at least in part, from deregulation coupled with a lack of federal law enforcement. We also know that without the tangible risk of the occasional prosecution, market actors will do that which maximizes their individual gain. This problem—amounting to more than $1 trillion—came about because our current approach to market regulation allowed for the privatization of gain and socialization of risk and loss.

An evaluation of the existing research shows that the phenomenon of subprime lending and the resultant foreclosures have had an adverse and disproportionate effect on minority group members and residents (of any race or ethnicity) of predominantly minority communities. While an individual's race or the racial composition of the community may not have been a conscious decision-making factor in how someone came to get a given loan, in the end, one's racial or ethnic identity and the history associated with the racial composition of their neighborhood relates to the harm they now feel from the problems in our real estate and mortgage markets. There is general agreement that some significant civil rights ground appears to have been gained in the dozen years after the 1988 amendments to the FHAct, but much of that progress was lost between 2000 and 2008.

Assuming the will to do so, it will likely take years to fix the administrative structure and law enforcement processes at HUD and Justice. In the interim, except for those people who will be protected by the few pro-active state attorneys general and private fair housing attorneys and organizations, peoples' rights will be lost on claims they may have had under the FHAct and ECOA.[22] After taking a step forward with the FHAct in 1988, we seem to have taken two back. In our mad rush to try and figure out how to repair the housing and mortgage sectors, we must not lose sight of the human beings behind the SIVs, CDOs, ARMs and MBSs, and that a disproportionate share of them were the casualties of a system that operated in a discriminatory fashion. It will not be enough to change the mechanics of the financial regulatory structure. HUD and Justice must reinvigorate their pursuit of their core civil rights missions.

BIBLIOGRAPHY

Apgar, William C. and Allegra Calder. "The Dual Mortgage Market: the persistence of discrimination in mortgage lending." Joint Center for Housing Studies at Harvard University, Working Paper W05–11, 2005. Retrieved from: http://www.jchs. harvard.edu/publications/finance/w05–11.pdf.

Avery, Robert B., Kenneth P. Brevoort, and Glenn B. Canner. "Higher-Priced Home Lending and the 2005 HMDA Data." Federal Reserve Bulletin, 92 (September 8), 123–166, 2006.

Avery, Robert B., Kenneth P. Brevoort, and Glenn B. Canner. The 2006 HMDA Data. Federal Reserve Bulletin, 93 (December 21), 73–109, 2007

Avery, Robert B., Glenn B. Canner and Robert E. Cook. "New Information Reported under HMDA and Its Application in Fair Lending Enforcement." Federal Reserve Bulletin, 91 (Summer), 344–394, 2005.

Benston, George J. Mortgage Redlining Research: a review and critical analysis. In The Regulation of Financial Institutions. Conference series no. 21 (October), 143–95. Federal Reserve Bank of Boston, 1979.

Bocian, Debbie G., Keith S. Ernst and Wei Li. "Unfair Lending: The effect of race and ethnicity on the price of subprime mortgages." Center for Responsible Lending, 2006. Available at: http://www.responsiblelending.org/pdfs/rr011–Unfair_Lending-0506.pdf.

Bocian, Debbie G. and Richard Zhai. "Borrowers in Higher Minority Areas More Likely to Receive Prepayment Penalties on Subprime Loans." Center for Responsible Lending, 2005. Available at: http://www.responsiblelending.org/mortgage-lending/research-analysis/rr004–PPP_Minority_Neighborhoods-0105.pdf.

Calem, Paul S., Kevin Gillen, and Susan Wachter. "The Neighborhood Distribution of Subprime Mortgage Lending." University of Pennsylvania Institute for Law and Economic Research, Research Paper 03–39, 2003.

California Reinvestment Coalition, Community Reinvestment Association of North Carolina, Empire Justice Center, Massachusetts Affordable Housing Alliance, Neighborhood Economic Development Advocacy Project, Ohio Fair Lending Coalition, Woodstock Institute. "Paying more for the American Dream; a subprime shakeout and its impact on lower-income and minority communities," 2008. Retrieved from: http://www.woodstockinst.org/publications/research-reports/.

Carr, James H. and Lopa Kolluri. "Predatory Lending: An Overview. Housing Policy Debate, Fannie Mae Foundation." 2001.

Carr, James H. and Isaac F. Megbolugbe. The Federal Reserve Bank of Boston Study on Mortgage Lending Revisited. Housing Policy Debate, 4, 2, 277–313, 1993.

Coleman IV, Major, Michael LaCour-Little and Kerry D. Vandell. "Subprime Lending and the Housing Bubble: Tail wags dog." 2008. Retrieved from: http://www.merage.uci.edu/ResearchAndCenters/CRE/Resources/Documents/%5B420%5DSubprime_Lending_and_the_Housing_Bubble.pdf.

Dedman, Bill. "The Color of Money; Home Mortgage Lending Practices Discriminate Against Blacks." the *Atlanta Journal* / the *Atlanta Constitution*, 1988. Retrieved from: www.powerreporting.com/color/color_of_money.pdf.

Engel, Kathy and Patricia McCoy. "A Tale of Three Markets: The Law and Economics of Predatory Lending." Texas Law Review, 80, 6, 1255–1381, 2002.

Ernst, Keith, Deborah N. Goldstein, and Christopher A. Richardson. "Legal and Economic Inducements to Predatory Lending.: In Squires, 103–132, 2004.

Galster, George. "Research on Discrimination in Housing and Mortgage Markets: assessment and future directions." Housing Policy Debate, 3, 2, 639–683, 1992.

Goldstein, Deborah. "Understanding Predatory Lending: moving towards a common definition and workable solutions." Joint Center for Housing Studies of Harvard University, Working Paper 99–11, 1999.

Goldstein, Ira J. "Lost Values: A Study of Predatory Lending in Philadelphia." The Reinvestment Fund, 2007.

Goering, John and Ron Wienk (eds). "Mortgage Lending, Racial Discrimination and Federal Policy." Washington, DC: Urban Institute Press, 1996

Gramlich, Edward M. "Subprime Mortgages: America's latest boom and bust." Washington, DC: Urban Institute Press, 2007

Immergluck, Dan and Geoff Smith. "Risky Business: An Econometric Analysis of the Relationship Between Subprime Lending and Neighborhood Foreclosures." Woodstock Institute, March 2004.

____. "The External Costs of Foreclosure: the impact of single-family mortgage foreclosures on property values." Housing Policy Debate, 17, 1, 57–79, 2006

Kendrick, Kim. Written Statement of Kim Kendrick to the Committee on Financial Services, Subcommittee on Oversight and Investigations of the US House of Representatives, July 2007. Retrieved from: http://frwebgate.access.gpo.gov/cgi-bin/getdoc.cgi?dbname=110_house_hearings&docid=f:38394.pdf., pp. 138–147.

Kushner, James A. and Allen J. Fishbein. "Federal Efforts to Combat Discrimination in the Housing and Mortgage Markets." Housing Policy Debate, 3, 2, 537–599, 1992.

Leadership Conference on Civil Rights Education Fund. "Long Road to Justice: the Civil Rights Division at 50," September 2007.

Lauria, Mickey and Vern Baxter. "Residential Mortgage Foreclosure and Racial Transition in New Orleans." Urban Affairs Review, 34, 6, 757–786, 1999.

Mansfield, Cathy Lesser. The Road to Subprime "HEL" was Paved with Good Congressional Intentions: Usury Deregulation and the Subprime Home Equity Market. South Carolina Law Review, 51(3), 473–587, 2000.

Munnell, A., L.E. Browne, J. McEneaney and G.M.B. Tootell. 1992. "Mortgage Lending in Boston: Interpreting HMDA data." Federal Reserve Bank of Boston, Working Paper No. 92–7, October 1992.

National Fair Housing Alliance. "Dr. King's Dream Denied: Forty Years of Federal Enforcement,: 2008. Available at: http://www.nationalfairhousing.org/Portals/33/reports/2008%20Fair%20Housing%20Trends%20Report.pdf.

Ritter, Richard. 1996.The Decatur Federal Case: A Summary Report. In Goering and Wienk, 445–450, 2004.

Schwemm, Robert G. "Introduction to Mortgage Lending Discrimination Law" in *A Fair Lending Symposium: Litigating a Mortgage Lending Case*, John Marshall Law Review, Winter 1995, 28 J. Marshall Law Review 317, Winter 1995.

____. Housing Discrimination: Law and Litigation. St. Paul: West Group, 2000.

Schloemer, Ellen, Wei Li, Keith Ernst and Kathleen Keest. "Losing Ground: Foreclosures in the Subprime Market and Their Cost to Homeowners." Center for Responsible Lending, 2006. Available at: http://www.responsiblelending.org/mortgage-lending/research-analysis/foreclosure-paper-report-2–17.pdf.

Shlay, Anne B. and Ira Goldstein. "Proving Disinvestment: The CRA Research Experience." Unpublished manuscript, 1993.

Squires, Gregory D. (ed). "Redlining to Reinvestment: Community responses to urban disinvestment. Philadelphia:" Temple University Press, 1992.

____. "Capital and Communities in Black and White. Albany:" State University of New York Press, 1994

____. "Why the Poor Pay More: How To Stop Predatory Lending. Westport CT:" Praeger/ Greenwood Publishing Group, 2004.

____. "Predatory Lending: Redlining in Reverse." Shelterforce Online, 139, Jan/Feb, 2005.

Taylor, John, Josh Silver and David Berenbaum. "The Targets of Predatory and Discriminatory Lending: Who are they and where do they live?" In Squires, 25–37, 2004.

The Reinvestment Fund. Mortgage Foreclosure Filings in Maryland, 2008. Available at: http://www.trfund.com/resource/downloads/policypubs/MarylandForeclosure.pdf.

____. Mortgage Foreclosure Filings in New Jersey. Forthcoming, 2008.

____. Mortgage Foreclosure Filings in Newark. Forthcoming, 2008.

____. Mortgage Foreclosure Filings in Baltimore, Maryland, 2006. Available at: http://www.trfund.com/resource/downloads/policypubs/MD_Foreclosure_2006.pdf

____. Mortgage Foreclosure Filings in Delaware, 2006. Available at: http://www.trfund.com/resource/downloads/policypubs/Delaware_Foreclosure.pdf.

____. Mortgage Foreclosure Filings in Pennsylvania, 2005 Available at: http://www.trfund.com/resource/downloads/policypubs/Mortgage-Forclosure-Filings.pdf.

US Department of Housing and Urban Development, "Unequal Burden: Income and Racial Disparities in Subprime Lending in America," 2000.

United States of America v. Decatur Federal Savings and Loan Association. Complaint. Retrieved from: http://www.usdoj.gov/crt/housing/documents/decaturcomp.htm.

United States of America v. Decatur Federal Savings and Loan Association. Consent Decree. Retrieved from: http://www.usdoj.gov/crt/housing/documents/decatursettle .htm.

Wienk, Ronald E. "Discrimination in Urban Credit Markets: What we don't know and why we don't know it." Housing Policy Debate, 3, 2, 217–240, 1992

Zandi, Mark M. "Financial Shock: a 360° look at the subprime mortgage implosion, and how to avoid the next financial crisis." NJ:FT Press, 2009.

NOTES

1. See, for example: Squires, "Capital and Communities in Black and White." 1994.

2. Schwemm, "Introduction to Mortgage Discrimination Law." 1995.

3. Goering and Wienk, "Mortgage Lending, Racial Discrimination and Federal Policy." 1996.

4. For a complete legislative history of HMDA and more information about the CRA, see these pages on the website of the Federal Financial Institutions Examination Council (FFIEC): For the HMDA, http://www.ffiec.gov/hmda/history2.htm; for the CRA, http://www.ffiec.gov/cra/history.htm. Accessed 10/21/2010.

5. For a review of the limitations of early HMDA studies, see Benston, "Mortgage Redlining Research: A Review and Critical Analysis," 1981; Galster, "Research on Discrimination in Housing and Mortgage Markets: Assessment and Future Directions," 1992; or Wienk, "Discrimination in Urban Credit Markets: What we don't know, and why we don't know it," (1992).

6. For a thorough description of the pre- and post-1988 FHAct provisions and an evaluation of HUD's early enforcement efforts, see Kushner and Fishbein "Federal Efforts to Combat Discrimination in the Housing and Mortgage Markets," 1992.

7. The term pattern or practice in this context generally refers to the notion that an act of discrimination within a lending institution is not a single isolated act; rather, the discrimination is a regular and routine part of the way the institution does business. For a more thorough description, see Schwemm, "Housing Discrimination: Law and Litigation," 2000.

8. See: United States of America v. Decatur Federal Savings and Loan Association (http://www.justice.gov/crt/housing/documents/decatursettle.php).

9. See, for example: Apgar, et al. "The Dual Mortgage Market: The Persistence of Discrimination in Mortgage Lending," 2005.

10. See, for example: Goldstein, "Lost Values: A Study of Predatory Lending in Philadelphia," 2007; Taylor, et al. "The Targets of Predatory and Discriminatory Lending: Who are they and where do they live?" 2004; Goldstein, "Understanding Predatory Lending: Moving towards a Common Definition and Workable Solutions," 1999.

11. See, for example: Hargraves v. Capital City Mortgage Corp. C.A. No. 98–1021 (U.S. District Court, D. D.C.) A complete cataloging of the case can be found at: http://www.clearinghouse.net/detail.php?id=10095.

12. See, for example: Taylor, et al., v. McGlawn and McGlawn, et al. (http://www.aopc.org/OpPosting/CWealth/out/2763CD04_1–13–06.pdf) or Commonwealth of Massachusetts v. H&R Block, Inc. (http://www.mass.gov/Cago/docs/press/2008_06_03_option_one_suit_attachment1.pdf).

13. See, for example: Mansfield (2000); Gramlich, "Subprime Mortgages: America's latest boom and bust," 2007; Ernst, et al. "Legal and Economic Inducements to Predatory Lending," 2004.

14. TRF identified $633.7 billion of loans carrying a reportable rate spread in the 2006 HMDA data. Coleman et al. estimated $600 billion based on data from Inside Mortgage Finance; Mark Zandi reports $615 billion. They each report an additional $395 billion to $400 billion in Alt-A lending volume in 2006. Coleman, et al. "Subprime Lending and the Housing Bubble: Tail wags dog," 2008; Zandi, "Financial Shock: a 360o look at the subprime mortgage implosion, and how to avoid the next financial crisis," 2009.

15. See: Avery, et al. "New Information Reported under HMDA and Its Application in Fair Lending Enforcement," 2005.

16. In Philadelphia, for example, as of March 2008, 5.4% of prime loans were delinquent, while 21.9% of subprime loans were delinquent.

17. See: National Fair Housing Alliance, "Dr. King's Dream Denied: Forty Years of Federal Enforcement," 2008.

18. See: Kendrick, Written Statement, 2007.

19. Data provided by HUD's Mid-Atlantic Homeownership Center to TRF show that in the first half of calendar year 2008, FHA endorsed 11,713 purchase money mortgages in Pennsylvania and 7,402 purchase money mortgages in Maryland. In calendar year 2005, FHA endorsed 11,102 purchase money mortgages in Pennsylvania and 5,413 purchase money mortgages in Maryland.

20. See, for example: Goldstein, 1999; Carr and Kolluri, "Predatory Lending: An Overview," 2001; Engel and McKoy, "A Tale of Three Markets: The Law and Economics of Predatory Lending," 2002; Gramlich, 2007; and Goldstein, 2007.

21. While we can trace the foreclosure filing to the address of the collateral property with some precision, there is no way—short of contacting each and every person in default—of knowing the race of the person facing foreclosure. Thus this research has been limited to understanding the differential spatial impacts of foreclosures on communities.

22. Section 810 of the FHAct states that there is a one year statute of limitations on filing a discrimination complaint with the secretary of HUD, and Section 813 of the FHAct states that there is a two year statute of limitations for private rights of action.

Chapter Six

Subprime Lending in the City of Cleveland and Cuyahoga County

Jeffrey D. Dillman

The economic crisis that began in 2007 had devastating effects on nearly every area of the country. States such as Arizona, California, Florida, and Nevada, where "exotic" loans such as option-ARMs and interest-only mortgages were common, faced unprecedented foreclosure rates and declines in property values. While the drop in property values in many Rust Belt cities was not as great, the economic situation in many of these cities became in many ways equally, if not more, desperate. Having suffered through the decline in industrial manufacturing and resulting population loss, many of these cities never experienced the huge increase in home prices that had occurred on the coasts. An examination of the rise in subprime lending in the city of Cleveland and surrounding Cuyahoga County, Ohio, provides a useful example of what many of these older industrial cities have faced over the past twenty years, and of the challenges that the crisis has presented.

Cleveland reached its peak in population in 1950, when it was the seventh largest city in the nation with a population of 914,808. However, beginning in the 1950s, Clevelanders began to leave the city, first to the inner ring suburbs, and eventually to regions further and further away. By 2000, Cleveland's population was 478,403, and by 2005–2007, it was estimated to be down to 405,014, just 44% of its peak in 1950.[1]

In some Cleveland neighborhoods, the decline has been profound. For example, the population of the Fairfax neighborhood on the east side of Cleveland dropped from 39,380 in 1950 to 7,352 in 2000, an 81.3% decline. The population declines in the adjacent neighborhoods (which were between 93% and 97% African American in 2000) were nearly as high, with the Central neighborhood experiencing a population decrease of 82.6% compared to 1950, the Hough neighborhood a 75.1% decrease, and the Kinsman neighborhood a 73.6% decrease.[2]

The vast majority of the decline in Cleveland's population has been due to the decrease in its white population, as can be seen in Figure 6.1.[3]

In 1930, whites accounted for 91.90% of the city's population, with African Americans making up 8.00%. By 1950, the African American population of Cleveland had doubled to 16.20%, while the white population had dropped to 83.70%. In the next 30 years, Cleveland's African American population grew from 148,199 to 251,334, while the white population decreased dramatically, going from 765,694 to 306,995. Although the rate of white flight decreased somewhat after 1980, the overall number of white residents, as well as the percentage of whites in the city, continued to decrease so that by the 2005–07 period, African Americans outnumbered whites, accounting for 52.80% of the population (at 213,847) compared to 39.40% (at 149,576).

Cleveland was not alone in this trend. Census data shows that many Rust Belt cities followed this same trajectory, reaching their peak population in the 1950s or 1960s, followed by declines that by 2000 ranged from 49% to 80% of their peaks.[4] (See Table 6.1.)

While cities such as Chicago and Milwaukee have retained much of their peak population, others, such as Buffalo, Detroit, and Pittsburgh have experienced large population declines similar to Cleveland.

These changes in Cleveland's population coincided with persistent racial segregation for African Americans. Prior to the Civil War, African Americans in Cleveland "did not reside in ghettos but lived throughout the city."[5] By the 1870s, however, the "ghettoization of African Americans [in Cleveland] had begun," and what had been referred to as "the 'city of immigrants' had by

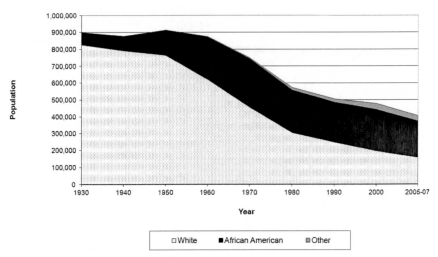

Figure 6.1. Population City of Cleveland.

Table 6.1. Population of Selected Rust Belt Cities

| City | Maximum Population | | 2000 Population | |
	Number	Year	Number	% of Max.
Akron	290,351	1960	217,074	74.76
Albany	134,995	1950	95,658	70.86
Buffalo	580,132	1950	292,648	50.45
Chicago	3,620,962	1950	2,896,016	79.98
Cleveland	914,808	1950	478,403	52.30
Detroit	1,849,568	1950	951,270	51.43
Milwaukee	741,324	1960	596,974	80.53
Pittsburgh	676,806	1950	334,563	49.43

Source: U.S. Census.

1920 become 'the segregated city.'"[6] The "Great Migration of the World War
I era accelerated the residential segregation … and [by] 1930, twelve census
tracts on the city's East Side were between 60% and 90% black."[7] In contrast
to white ethnics, Cleveland's African American population increased in size
while becoming more, rather than less, segregated.[8]

   An examination of the dissimilarity segregation index shows dramatically
the spatial segregation African Americans faced—and continue to face—in
Cleveland. The dissimilarity index measures the percentage of a group's
population that would have to move in order to have that group evenly spread
throughout an area. A score of 100 indicates complete segregation and that all
of a group's population would have to move in order to achieve integration,
while a score of zero would indicate that the area is completely integrated.[9]
While the methodology has varied somewhat over the years,[10] as can be
seen in Table 6.2, African Americans experienced increasing segregation in
Cleveland from 1870 through 1940, when the level reached 92.0, indicating

Table 6.2. African-American Segregation in Cleveland

| | *(Dissimilarity Index)* | |
		Unit of Analysis
1870	49.0	ward
1910	69.0	ward
1940	92.0	block
1950	91.5	block
1960	91.3	block
1970	89.0	block
1980	85.4	tract
1990	82.4	tract
2000	76.8	tract

that 92% of African Americans would have to move in order for them to be integrated evenly throughout the community.

While the number dropped somewhat from 1980 through 2000, the overall rate of segregation still placed the Cleveland metropolitan area as the sixth-most segregated region in the country for African Americans based on the dissimilarity index, and the third-most segregated area in the country considering an average of five segregation indices.[11] During this period, the Cleveland Metropolitan Statistical Area (MSA) actually became more segregated for Hispanics/Latinos, with the dissimilarity index increasing from 57.5 in 1980 to 57.7 in 2000, although the region moved from being the seventh-most segregated area for Hispanics/Latinos to the eleventh-most, reflecting an increase in segregation in other areas.[12] While this does indicate some improvement in terms of racial segregation of African Americans, that progress has been extremely slow, and at current rates, it will take decades, if not centuries, for the region to become integrated.

THE RISE OF SUBPRIME LENDING

The mortgage lending industry has undergone profound changes in the past fifty years. Historically, mortgage lending was conducted by depository institutions—savings and loans, banks, and credit unions—which primarily offered 30–year fixed rate mortgages. Loan decisions were, on paper at least, made based on the borrower's ability to repay (evaluated primarily based on income) and the value of the collateral (i.e., the value of the home being purchased or refinanced). Evaluating these variables often entailed examining a borrower's debt-to-income (DTI) ratio to ensure that the borrower had sufficient income to pay the loan as well as any other debts and expenses and therefore would be unlikely to default on the loan. The value of the collateral was measured using loan-to-value (LTV) ratios to ensure that, if the borrower did default, there was sufficient equity to allow the lender to recoup its investment after foreclosing on the property. The underlying assumption of these considerations was that lenders wanted to ensure that borrowers had sufficient money to repay their loans. In the event that a prospective borrower did not meet the underwriting criteria set by the lender, he or she was denied a loan.

This lending system worked well for many middle- and upper-income borrowers, especially whites, allowing them to become homeowners and accumulate wealth through the process. But residents of African American and Latino neighborhoods often were denied access to mortgage credit through redlining based on the perceived risk of lending money in those neighborhoods.[13] Redlining dates at least to the 1930s through the rating system devised by the

Home Owners Loan Corporation (HOLC) that coded the riskiest urban neigh-borhoods, which would receive few if any loans, with the color red. Citing the research of Kenneth Jackson, Douglas Massey notes, "Black neighborhoods [were] always coded red, and even those with small percentages of black residents were usually rated as hazardous and placed in the lowest category."[14] Although the HOLC did not invent the racialized standards that correlated real estate value to whiteness, it played a key role in institutionalizing them in policies which would later be adopted by federal agencies such as the Federal Housing Administration (FHA) and Veterans Administration (VA). For example, a 1939 FHA underwriting manual warned against "inharmonious racial or nationality groups" and stated that for neighborhoods to retain stability, and therefore property values, "it is necessary that properties shall continue to be occupied by the same social and racial classes."[15]

The social movements of the 1960s and early 1970s gave rise to an attempt to prohibit some of the more abusive of these practices through the passage of the federal Fair Housing Act,[16] the Equal Credit Opportunity Act,[17] the Home Mortgage Disclosure Act (HMDA),[18] and the Community Reinvestment Act (CRA).[19] Despite these statutes, numerous researchers have found continuing racial and ethnic disparities in mortgage lending.[20] Early research into mortgage lending disparities often examined differences in loan denial rates in order to help gauge possible discrimination. To the extent that African Americans or Latinos (or other racial and ethnic groups) were denied loans at a disproportionate rate compared to whites, this provided evidence of possible discrimination in the mortgage lending market in that members of these groups were not being provided with adequate access to credit.[21]

In the 1980s and 1990s, the traditional system of lending through depository institutions evolved in several important ways. Risk-based pricing was introduced, which allowed lenders to offer mortgage products to individuals who might not otherwise have qualified for a loan. Through risk-based pricing, a lender uses a consumer's credit report and other similar data in "setting or adjusting the price and other terms of credit offered or extended to a particular consumer."[22] The theory behind this lending model is that some borrowers might not have adequate income or other credit profile characteristics to qualify for a traditional (prime) 30–year, fixed-rate loan. But rather than simply deny them the loan, the lender offers the borrower a loan at a *higher* rate. Because these loans are made to borrowers whose credit profiles are lower than that used for traditional prime borrowers, they are considered "subprime." The theory behind charging more for such a loan is that the increased cost is designed to help protect the lender from the higher risk of default on the part of the borrower. That is, because the borrower's credit risk is higher than a "prime" borrower's, there is a higher risk that he or she will default on the loan.[23]

While subprime loans were a logical product on one level, they also contained an inherent contradiction. The higher interest rate of a subprime loan makes the loan more expensive overall, generally with higher monthly payments and other onerous terms, *which themselves make default more likely*. Thus the very borrower who might have a harder time successfully purchasing a home and making the required payments on his or her mortgage loan is given a loan with higher payments than a borrower with higher income.[24]

This rise in subprime lending also coincided with, and was furthered by, the rise of mortgage brokers (independent salespeople who worked to obtain loans for borrowers). Although many borrowers assumed mortgage brokers were looking out for their best interests, trying to find them loans with the best rates and other features, compensation structures often paid brokers more in the event that a borrower was in a less suitable higher-cost loan. For example, brokers paid through a "yield spread premium" were paid a fee ("premium") for putting a borrower in a *higher* interest rate loan than he or she qualified for based on credit. In addition, most brokers' fees were based on a percentage of the loan principal. That gave them an incentive to push individuals into borrowing more money than they otherwise might need, including obtaining cash back in the transaction, refinancing other debt (credit card, car loan, etc.) or completely refinancing an existing mortgage loan rather than obtaining a second mortgage to make repairs. Encouraging borrowers to take on increased debt through increasing the amount borrowed and increasing the interest rate put borrowers at greater risk for default, but independent mortgage brokers did not bear any risk for this action because they made their profit and completed their transaction at the time of origination.

The rise of the secondary mortgage market and securitization also changed incentives in the mortgage industry. Whereas in the past, the originating lender often retained the loan on its books and/or continued to service it throughout its life, by the 1990s, an increasing percentage of loans were either sold on the secondary market or securitized into investments to be sold on Wall Street. In both scenarios, the originating lender sold the loan shortly after it was made (sometimes on the same day) and therefore bore little if any risk in the event of a borrower's default. Thus, incentives to ensure that a borrower would repay the loan and that the collateral was sufficient were greatly diminished, if not removed altogether.[25]

Whereas redlining had resulted in a denial of credit to minority neighborhoods, the changes in the mortgage industry described above contributed to the rise of what came to be known as "reverse redlining." In contrast to traditional redlining, reverse redlining was a deliberate targeting of these neighborhoods by mortgage lenders (often non-depositories, although some depository institutions did engage in the practice either directly or through non-depository subprime affiliates). These neighborhoods, often historically deprived of adequate access to credit, were preyed upon by these lenders, who pushed predatory and subprime loans on individuals who had few if any other options for obtaining mortgage credit.[26] The effects of reverse redlining can be seen when one considers the fact that up to one-half of all subprime borrowers could qualify for a prime-rate loan with a lower interest rate.[27]

Subprime Lending in Cleveland: 1995–2005

The effect of the changes in the mortgage industry described above can be seen in the growth of lending by subprime lenders in the Cleveland region from the mid-1990s to the mid-2000s.[28] In 1995 in the city of Cleveland, subprime lenders made only 3.23% of home purchase loans. By 1998, this had increased to 19.07%, and from 1999 through 2003, the percentage remained in the lower twenties, until 2003, when it increased to 29.46%, followed by a jump to 45.26% in 2004. Home purchase lending by subprime lenders showed similar increases in Cuyahoga County, although the overall percentages were lower. (See Figures 6.2 and 6.3.)

Throughout this same period, the percentage of refinance loans made by subprime lenders was higher overall, starting at 45.78% in Cleveland in 1995 and remaining in the forty and fifty percent range through 2000, after which they decreased to the lower thirties before rising back to 45.87% in 2004. Cuyahoga County refinance loan originations by subprime lenders showed a similar trend, although, as with home purchase loan originations, the overall rate was lower than in Cleveland.

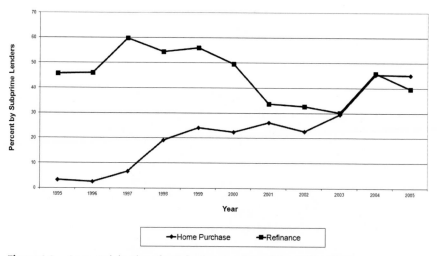

Figure 6.2.   Loan Originations by Subprime Lenders, City of Cleveland.

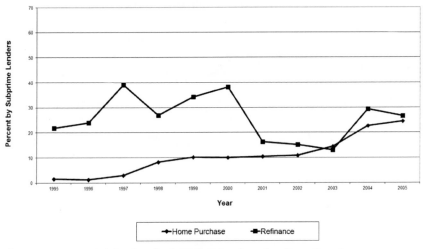

Figure 6.3.   Loan Originations by Subprime Lenders, Cuyahoga County.

The higher rates of subprime refinance lending compared to home purchase lending in the mid-1990s is likely a result of the way the predatory and subprime lenders operated during this period. Much of the initial growth in this sector of the lending industry occurred in the early-to-mid 1990s, when brokers and lenders used public records to identify individuals who had equity in their homes. These borrowers, disproportionately elderly and/or long-time homeowners, were targeted for refinancing that extracted home equity that had been built up over many years. Many of these initial lenders and brokers were relatively small operators who reached their targets through mail, phone, and door-to-door solicitations. As the industry grew and consolidated in the late 1990s, it became more mainstream, with television, radio, and print advertising, thereby spreading to include a much larger percentage of home purchase loans.

As was noted above, subprime lending carries an increased risk of default, as borrowers who obtain such loans must generally devote a larger amount of money to housing costs in the form of higher monthly payments compared to a prime-rate loan.

RECENT MORTGAGE LENDING
TRENDS IN THE CLEVELAND AREA

The concept of "fair lending" encompasses two important elements: access to credit (i.e. whether lending is made available to groups in an equitable manner) and the terms of that credit (i.e. is that lending made on "fair" terms). An examination of mortgage lending in the city of Cleveland and

Cuyahoga County in recent years provides evidence of persistent racial disparities on both of these measures of fair lending. The data used for this analysis consisted of home purchase and refinance loans reported by lenders under the Home Mortgage Disclosure Act (HMDA) for the years 2005, 2006, and 2007 in the city of Cleveland and Cuyahoga County for one-to-four unit properties. Access to credit was examined by considering denial rates by racial and ethnic group to determine whether members of certain groups were denied mortgages disproportionately compared to members of other groups.[29] The terms of credit were evaluated by examining high-cost lending rates, to evaluate whether these groups received a disproportionate percentage of mortgage loans with high interest rates, compared to prime-rate loans.

Denial Rates

The greatest racial disparities in denial rates were found in home purchase loans. In the city of Cleveland for each of the years from 2005 through 2007, not only were African Americans denied home purchase loans more often than whites when comparing the same income groups, but *upper income* African Americans were denied home purchase loans more often than *low income* whites.[30] For example, in 2005, upper income African Americans were denied home purchase loans 34.67% of the time, compared to 27.52% of the time for low income whites and 19.19% of the time for upper income whites. In 2006, the disparity increased, with upper income African Americans being denied home purchase loans 42.66% of the time, compared to 30.25% for low income whites and 21.01% for upper income whites. Although the disparity decreased somewhat in 2007, even in this year upper income African Americans were denied home purchase loans 44.42% of the time, more than twice the rate of upper income whites (at 19.44%) and at one and one-quarter times the rate of low income whites (33.00%). (See Figure 6.4.)

In Cuyahoga County, the racial disparities in home purchase lending were even greater than in the city of Cleveland. (See Figure 6.5.) Upper income African Americans were denied loans at one and one-half times the rate of low income whites (and at over three times the rate of upper income whites) in each year from 2005 through 2007. For example, in 2005, upper income African Americans were denied home purchase loans 30.60% of the time, compared to 20.97% of the time for low income whites and 9.48% of the time for upper income whites. This disparity increased in each of the following years, so that by 2007, upper income African Americans were denied home purchase loans at one and three-quarters times the rate of low income whites (41.00% of the time compared to 23.38%).

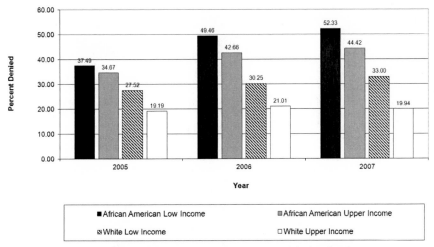

Figure 6.4. Denial Rates for Home Purchase Loans, City of Cleveland.

Refinance lending in the city of Cleveland showed much smaller racial disparities. (See Figure 6.6.) As with home purchase lending, African Americans at each income level were denied more refinance loans than whites at the same level. The denial rates of upper income African Americans were slightly lower than that for low-income whites for the years 2005 and 2006 and approximately the same in 2007; in each of these years, African Americans were denied loans at higher rates than whites within each income group. In Cuyahoga County, racial disparities in refinance

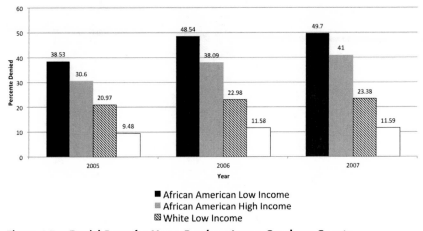

Figure 6.5. Denial Rates for Home Purchase Loans, Cuyahoga County.

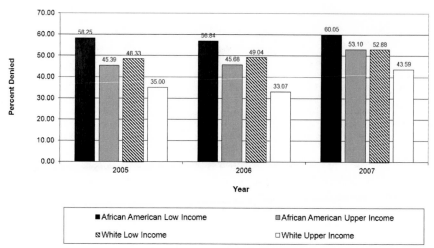

Figure 6.6.   Denial Rates for Refinance Loans, City of Cleveland.

lending was also much smaller than for home purchase lending, with upper income African Americans being denied loans at approximately the same rates as low income whites for each of the years. (See Figure 6.7.)

While the disparities in denial rates were smaller for refinance lending than home purchase lending, the existence of these disparities at all is cause for concern. One would expect that upper income individuals of any race would be denied fewer loans than low income individuals, and the fact that the de-

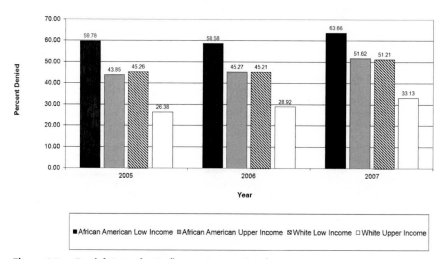

Figure 6.7.   Denial Rates for Refinance Loans, Cuyahoga County.

nial rates for upper income African Americans were even close to that for low income whites is troubling.

Discussions with local advocates provide a possible explanation for some of the difference in disparity rates between home purchase and refinance lending. As can be seen from the figures above, overall denial rates for both African Americans and whites are much higher for refinance loans compared to home purchase loans. Thus, the smaller racial disparities between African Americans and whites in refinance lending are due in some part to the higher denial rates of whites in obtaining these loans.

High-Cost Lending Rates

An examination of high-cost lending rates in both Cleveland and Cuyahoga County also reveal widespread racial disparities between whites and African Americans.[31] For the years 2005–07, African Americans in every income group in Cleveland received more high-cost home purchase and refinance loans than whites of comparable incomes.

Overall in the city of Cleveland, 55.44% of all home purchase loans were high-cost in 2005. For African Americans, the rate was 71.96%, compared to 38.26% for whites and 37.16% for Hispanics/Latinos. In Cuyahoga County in 2005, 33.57% of all home purchase loans were high-cost. Although the overall rate was lower in Cuyahoga County, the racial disparities between races was higher, with African Americans receiving high-cost loans 65.57% of the time, compared to 20.04% for whites and 16.43% for Hispanics/Latinos. The primary reason for the increased disparity in Cuyahoga County compared to the city of Cleveland is that the rates of high-cost lending for whites in the county were substantially lower than the rates in Cleveland (20.04% compared to 38.26%).

Even more disturbing, upper income African Americans received more high-cost home purchase and refinance loans than low income whites. For example, in 2005 upper income African Americans received high-cost home purchase loans at over one and one-half times the rate of low income whites in the city of Cleveland (71.69% of the time compared to 42.37%); in 2006 upper income African Americans received high-cost home purchase loans 73.74% of the time, compared to 31.03% for low income whites; and in 2007 the rates were 52.91% and 27.27%, respectively. (See Figure 6.8.)

While these numbers do show a large decrease in high-cost lending to upper income African Americans in 2007, it is disturbing that this group, with incomes of at least 120% of the area median income, wound up with

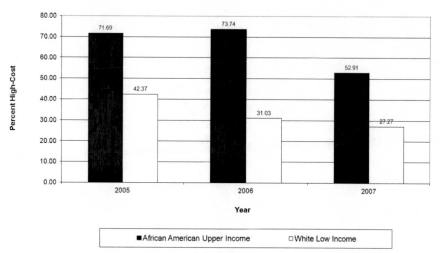

Figure 6.8.   High Cost Home Purchase Lending, City of Cleveland.

high-cost loans at nearly twice the rate of whites whose income was less than 50% of the median income.

Although the rates of high-cost lending in Cuyahoga County were somewhat lower for each racial group compared to their rates in Cleveland, the disparities *between* African Americans and whites in the county as a whole were greater. In Cuyahoga County in 2005, upper income African Americans received high-cost home purchase loans 60.53% of the time, almost two and one-half times the rate for low income whites (24.73%). In 2006, upper income African Americans received high-cost home purchase loans at over three times the rate of low income whites (64.28% compared to 20.45%). By 2007, the rates of high-cost home purchase lending for both groups had decreased significantly, although upper income African Americans were still more than twice as likely to obtain such loans (39.56%) compared to low income whites (17.03%).[32] (See Figure 6.9.)

Refinance lending in both Cleveland and Cuyahoga County revealed similar, although somewhat smaller, disparities between African Americans and whites throughout this time period, with upper income African Americans receiving more high-cost loans than low income whites. (See Figures 6.10 and 6.11.)

As with home purchase lending, the rates of high-cost lending were higher for both African Americans and whites in the city of Cleveland, compared to the county as a whole, although the disparities between upper income African Americans and low income whites were greater in the county.

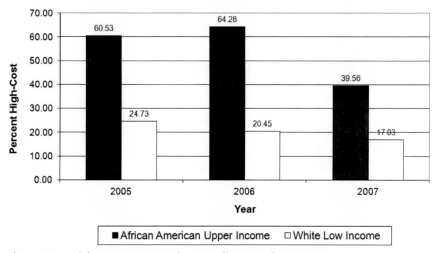

Figure 6.9.　High Cost Home Purchase Lending, Cuyahoga County.

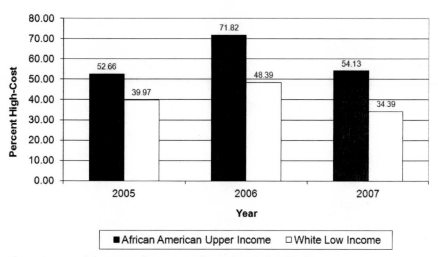

Figure 6.10.　High Cost Refinance Lending, City of Cleveland.

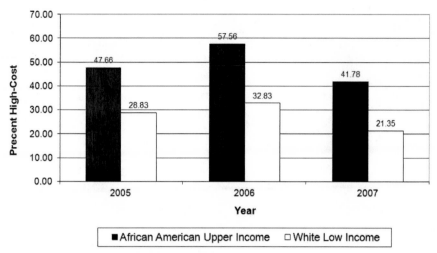

Figure 6.11. High Cost Refinance Lending, Cuyahoga County.

THE EFFECTS OF UNFAIR LENDING ON CLEVELAND

The effects of the extremely high rates of subprime lending, as well as the racial disparities in mortgage lending in Cleveland and Cuyahoga County, can be felt throughout the region. During much of the 2000s, Ohio has had one of the highest foreclosure rates in the nation.

Economic changes, such as the decline in manufacturing, the rise in unemployment, and the rise of poverty in the region—in 2008, 30.3% of Clevelanders had incomes below the poverty level—certainly played a part in the growth in foreclosures.[33] Yet statewide as well as local data show that the number of foreclosures has climbed regardless of the change in the un-employment rate from 1995–2009. In fact, even as unemployment decreased from 5.6% in 1994 to 4.0% in 2000, Ohio's foreclosure rate doubled in the same period, rising from 17,026 to 35,377. By 2006, with unemployment at 5.4% statewide—still below the rate in 1994—foreclosures had doubled again, reaching 79,435.[34] (See Figure 6.12.)

Moreover, these trends are also reflected in local data, which show that Cuyahoga County experienced a similar rise in foreclosure filings starting in 1994, when there were 4,335 foreclosures filed, to 2007, when the num-ber reached 14,946. As with statewide foreclosures, this growth occurred irrespective of the change in the county's unemployment rate, growing particularly quickly from 2003 to 2007 at a time when the unemployment

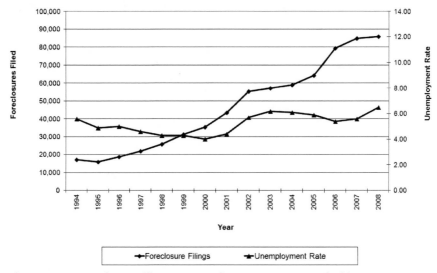

Figure 6.12.   Foreclosure Filings & Unemployment Rate, State of Ohio.

rate went from 6.2% to 5.7% in 2006, and then back to 6.2% in 2007.[35]
(See Figure 6.13.)

A 2008 study by researchers at Case Western Reserve University made
clear the relationship between mortgage lending and foreclosures, and
particularly the racial disparities discussed above. The study examined the

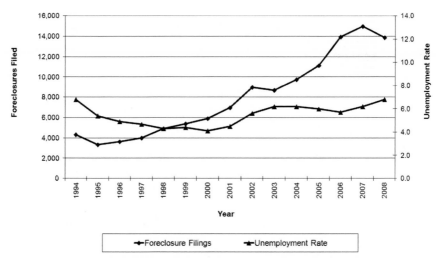

Figure 6.13.   Foreclosure Filings & Unemployment Rate, Cuyahoga County.

relationship between high-cost lending and foreclosure filings in Cuyahoga County in 2005 and 2006, finding that:

> . . .by far the strongest predictor of a loan foreclosing is its status as a high cost subprime loan. Holding other factors constant, home purchase loans that were high cost subprime had an 816 percent higher chance of going into foreclosure than other loans. Indeed, subprime lending accounted for 84 percent of the fore-closures on home purchase and refinance loans [in 2005 and 2006].[36]

The researchers further noted that the racial disparity in loan originations, in which African Americans (even with upper incomes) received more high-cost loans than whites, was reflected in foreclosure rates: "African American borrowers had the highest foreclosure rates (28.25 percent), Non-Hispanic whites had the lowest (7.58 percent), and Hispanic borrowers had moderate foreclosure rates (12.83 percent)."[37]

Research from the Federal Reserve Bank of Cleveland similarly found a strong correlation between race and foreclosure filings in Cuyahoga County: the neighborhoods with the highest foreclosure rates had the highest percent-age of high-cost loans and the highest percentage of African American resi-dents. Moreover, these neighborhoods were concentrated mainly in Cleve-land's east side, which is home to a high percentage of African American residents.[38]

Although the city of Cleveland, and especially the predominantly Afri-can American east side, suffered the effects of subprime lending and the foreclosure crisis more greatly than Cuyahoga County as a whole, by 2009 data suggested that suburban areas (and the whiter west side of Cleveland) would likely see an increasing impact in their communities. According to data provided by the Center on Urban Poverty and Community Develop-ment at Case Western Reserve University, while nearly twice the number of mortgage loans in the east side of Cleveland were "at risk" of foreclosure in the 2009–2011 period compared to the predominantly white west side, the rates on the east side appeared to be slowing.[39] Additionally, by 2009 there were more "at risk" loans in the suburbs of Cuyahoga County (13,756 loans) compared to the city of Cleveland (10,438).[40]

The rise in foreclosures has contributed to a widespread decline in the qual-ity of life in many Cleveland and Cuyahoga County neighborhoods as fore-closures lead to increases in vacant and abandoned property, which contribute to crime and other social costs. According to an estimate from Cuyahoga County Treasurer Jim Rokakis, in 2009 there were approximately 15,000 vacant properties awaiting demolition in the county, with 10,000 to 11,000 of those in the city of Cleveland.[41] Moreover, vacancies have been increasing in length. In 2009 in the city of Cleveland, "36.6% of all vacant residential addresses [had] been empty for three years or more."[42]

The high number of these foreclosures has also contributed to a decrease in property values. Although the overall volume of property sales in Cuyahoga County has changed little from 2000 to 2009, the percentage of transactions involving properties that have undergone a foreclosure has skyrocketed. In 2000, 92% of sales in Cuyahoga County, and 84% of sales in the city of Cleveland, involved properties that were not tainted by foreclosure.[43] By 2008, only 52% of county sales and 29% of Cleveland sales were not tainted by foreclosure. Research by the Woodstock Institute has shown that in Chicago, foreclosures can decrease property values of properties within an eighth of a mile by as much as 0.9–1.136%.[44] Locally, the huge increase in the number of sales involving foreclosed homes is reflected in a corresponding drop in sales prices during the same period. In Cuyahoga County, the median sales price of single family homes dropped from $102,000 in 2000 to $72,000 in 2008, while in the city of Cleveland it dropped from $65,000 in 2000 to $13,000 in 2008. Removing properties tainted by foreclosure, however, shows that countywide the median sales price increased from $107,000 in 2000 to $125,000 in 2008, while values in Cleveland decreased slightly from $67,000 in 2000 to $65,000 in 2008.[45]

CONCLUSION

Addressing the racially disparate subprime lending and the resulting foreclosure crisis will require a broad-based effort. While there were many causes to this crisis—including actions by governments at all levels as well as private individuals and institutions such as mortgage brokers, lenders, loan servicers, and those involved in the Wall Street securitization process—an underlying assumption of much of the mortgage lending industry in the past 30 years (and the economy more broadly) has been that the market does better than government in evaluating risk, offering financial products to consumers, and regulating itself.

This assumption derives from a discourse, initially promoted by conservatives in the 1980s but often adopted by liberals since that time, that not only delegitimizes the state as a potential solution to social problems but also considers government itself as the problem. The belief that government could help bring about a more equitable society has been replaced by a narrative of individualism and laissez faire capitalism, with the market as the solution. Thus, we are left to attempt to provide market incentives to reduce discrimination, to support integration, to build accessible housing, and so on.[46]

In order to succeed in addressing the racial disparities in mortgage lending and the foreclosure crisis in the country, advocates must directly challenge this conservative narrative. In the wake of the global financial crisis, much of the public seems to intuitively grasp that "the market" failed. However, the response even of many in the Obama Administration has been tepid, offering what are often minor adjustments in policy without fundamentally challenging the conservative narrative about government. Ending housing discrimination and segregation is inherently a radical act, and one that is threatening to those who support and benefit from such conditions. Just as the gains of the Civil Rights and other social movements were won with broad-based progressive activism, challenging and ending housing discrimination and segregation will likewise require advocates to become activists.

NOTES

1. U.S. Census Bureau, "Historical Census Statistics on Population Totals by Race, 1790 to 1990, and by Hispanic Origin, 1970 to 1990, For Large Cities And Other Urban Places in the United States," Population Division Working Paper No. 76, February 2005, Table 36; U.S. Census Bureau, Census 2000; U.S. Census Bureau, "Population of the 100 Largest Cities and Other Urban Places in the United States: 1790 to 1990," Population Division Working Paper No. 27, June 1998, Table 1.

2. Randell McShepard & Fran Stewart, "Rebuilding Blocks: Efforts to Revive Cleveland Must Start by Treating What Ails Neighborhoods," (PolicyBridge, October 2009), pp. 5–6.

3. U.S. Census Bureau, "Historical Census Statistics on Population Totals by Race, 1790 to 1990, and by Hispanic Origin, 1970 to 1990, For Large Cities And Other Urban Places in the United States," Population Division Working Paper No. 76, February 2005, Table 36; U.S. Census Bureau, Census 2000 (for 2000 data); U.S. Census Bureau, 2005–07 American Community Survey 3–Year Estimates.

4. U.S. Census Bureau, "Population of the 100 Largest Cities and Other Urban Places in the United States: 1790 to 1990," Population Division Working Paper No. 27, June 1998, Table 23 (for maximum data); U.S. Census Bureau, Census 2000 (for 2000 data).

5. David C. Perry, "Cleveland: Journey to Maturity," in *Cleveland: A Metropolitan Reader*, W. Dennis Keating, Norman Krumholz, & David C. Perry, eds. (Kent, OH: Kent State University Press, 1995), p. 22. During this pre-Civil War period, African Americans made up less than two percent of the population. Id.

6. Id., citing Kenneth L. Kusmer, *A Ghetto Takes Shape: Black Cleveland, 1870–1930* (Urbana: University of Illinois Press, 1976), p. 35.

7. Edward M. Miggins, "Between Spires & Stacks," in *Cleveland: A Metropolitan Reader*, W. Dennis Keating, Norman Krumholz, & David C. Perry, eds., p. 193.

8. Id.

9. U.S. Census Bureau, "Racial and Ethnic Residential Segregation in the United States: 1980–2000," August 2002, p. 8.

10. Sources: 1870 and 1910 data: Douglas S. Massey & Nancy A. Denton, *American Apartheid: Segregation and the Making of the Underclass* (Cambridge, MA: Harvard University Press, 1993), p. 21, Table 2.1; 1940–1970: Massey & Denton, *American Apartheid*, p. 47, Table 2.3; 1980–2000: U.S. Census Bureau, "Racial and Ethnic Residential Segregation in the United States: 1980–2000," August 2002, p. 69, Table 5–4. As Massey & Denton note (p. 31), the unit of analysis can affect the dissimilarity index rates, with the shift from wards to blocks adding at least 10 points to the index. The change from block to tract likely resulted in a decrease in the scores from 1970 to 1980. *See, e.g.*, John Iceland & Erika Steinmetz, "The Effects of Using Census Block Groups Instead of Census Tracts When Examining Residential Housing Patterns," U.S. Census Bureau Working Paper, July 2003. In addition, the earlier analyses examined the city of Cleveland only, while the 1980–2000 analysis covered the entire Metropolitan Statistical Area, which includes five counties.

11. U.S. Census Bureau, "Racial and Ethnic Residential Segregation," p. 69, Table 5–4.

12. Jeffrey D. Dillman, Carrie Pleasants & Samantha Hoover, "The State of Fair Housing in Northeast Ohio: April 2009," p. 20, citing U.S. Census Bureau, "Racial and Ethnic Segregation in the United States: 1980–2000."

13. *See, e.g.*, HUD Preamble I, 53 Fed. Reg. 44998 (November 7, 1988).

14. *See, generally*, Douglas S. Massey, "Origins of Economic Disparities," in *Segregation: The Rising Costs for America*, James H. Carr & Nandinee K. Kutty, eds. (New York: Routledge, 2008), pp. 69–71.

15. Id., pp. 71–72.

16. 42 U.S.C. §3601, *et seq*. Passed in 1968, the Fair Housing Act prohibited discrimination based on race, color, religion, and national origin. Later amendments prohibited discrimination based on sex (Housing and Community Development Act of 1974, Pub. L. No. 93–383, §808), as well as familial status and handicap (Fair Housing Amendments Act of 1988, Pub. L. No. 100–430).

17. 15 U.S.C. §1691, *et seq*. The Equal Credit Opportunity Act (ECOA), passed in 1974, prohibits discrimination in the extension of credit based upon race, color, religion, national origin, sex, marital status, and age.

18. 12 U.S.C. §2801, *et seq*. HMDA, passed in 1975, requires most mortgage lenders located in metropolitan areas, including depository institutions as well as non-depository mortgage and consumer finance companies, to report certain data regarding their mortgage loan applications and originations to the federal government and members of the public. While reporting requirements vary by year, they generally require a lender to report information on all applications received and loans made for home purchase, refinance, and home improvement loans. Lenders without offices in a metropolitan areas and/or who originate or accept fewer than five applications in a metropolitan area are exempt from HMDA reporting requirements. In addition, lenders with small assets size are not required to report data for the following year. *See, e.g.*, FFIEC, "2006 Reporting Criteria for Depository Institutions," and "2006 Reporting Criteria for Nondepository Institutions," available at http://www.ffiec.gov/

hmda/reportde2006.htm and http://www.ffiec.gov/hmda/reportno2006.htm. Although not all lenders are required to provide data under the Act, HMDA data is generally regarded as providing the most thorough information available on mortgage lending. Data reported include the race, ethnicity, gender, and income of an applicant; the disposition of the application; and, since 2004, whether or not an originated loan constituted was "high-cost."

19. Passed in 1977, the Community Reinvestment Act (CRA), 12 U.S.C. §2901, *et seq.*, was intended to address the failure of many banks and thrifts (savings and loans) to adequately invest in low- and moderate-income neighborhoods by requiring periodic examinations of their lending practices in such communities and considering the results of such exams when federal regulators evaluated whether to approve mergers and other actions by those institutions. While the CRA has resulted in substantial investments in such communities, the exams have been criticized as *pro forma*, with virtually every institution receiving a high score, much like Garrison Keillor's Lake Wobegon, where every child is above average.

20. *See, e.g.*, National Community Reinvestment Coalition, "Income is No Shield Against Racial Differences in Lending II: A Comparison of High-Cost Lending in America's Metropolitan Areas," July 2008; Allen J. Fishbein and Patrick Woodall, "Subprime Locations: Patterns in Geographic Disparity in Subprime Lending," Consumer Federation of America, September 5, 2006; Debbie Gruenstein Bocian, Keith S. Ernst & Wei Li, "Unfair Lending: The Effect of Race and Ethnicity on the Price of Subprime Mortgages," Center for Responsible Lending, May 31, 2006; Alicia H. Munnell, Lynn E. Browne, James McEneaney & Geoffrey M.B. Tootell, "Mortgage Lending in Boston: Interpreting the HMDA Data," Federal Reserve Bank of Boston Working Paper No. 92–7 (1992).

21. *See, e.g.*, 42 U.S.C. §3605. *See also* HUD, "Unequal Burden: Income and Racial Disparities in Subprime Lending in America (April 2000), available at http://www .huduser.org/Publications/pdf/unequal_full.pdf; Alicia H. Munnell, et al., "Mortgage Lending in Boston," Federal Reserve Bank of Boston Working Paper No. 92–7 (1992).

22. *See* Federal Reserve Board and Federal Trade Commission, Press Release, "Agencies Issue Proposed Rules on Risk-Based Pricing Notices," May 8, 2008, available at http://www.federalreserve.gov/newsevents/press/bcreg/20080508a.htm.

23. This increased credit risk was sometimes based on "objective" criteria, such as higher debt-to-income (DTI) ratios and loan-to-value (LTV) ratios. In theory, a higher DTI ratio signifies that a borrower has less income available with which to pay the mortgage loan and other living expenses and therefore is more likely to miss a payment and default on the loan. A higher LTV ratio signifies that the borrower has invested less of his or her money in the property. This could result both in the borrower being more likely to "walk away" in the event he or she has financial difficulties as well as the lender being unable to fully recoup its loan costs in the event of foreclosure, as the cost of the outstanding loan balance and the foreclosure costs could be greater than the value of the property.

24. Elizabeth Renuart, "Toward One Competitive and Fair Mortgage Market: Suggested Reforms in *A Tale of Three Markets* Point in the Right Direction," 82 *Texas Law Review* 421, 427 (2003).

25. While some of the securitization agreements did contain features requiring originating lenders to buy back underperforming or defaulting loans, in practice these clauses did not result in originating lenders making loans in a more responsible manner. For a discussion of market failures in subprime and predatory lending, *see* Kathleen C. Engel and Patricia A. McCoy, "A Tale of Three Markets: The Law and Economics of Predatory Lending," 80 *Texas Law Review* 1255, 1280–1297.

26. *See* Ray Brescia, "Subprime Communities: Reverse Redlining, the Fair Housing Act and Emerging Issues in Litigation Regarding the Subprime Mortgage Crisis," 2 *Albany Government Law Review* 164, 179 (2009).

27. *See* Freddie Mac, "Automated Underwriting: Making Mortgage Lending Simpler and Fairer for America's Families" (September 1996), p. 24 ("Preliminary Freddie Mac estimates suggest that between 10 and 35 percent of borrowers who obtained mortgages in the subprime market could have qualified for a conventional loan. A recent poll of the 50 most active subprime lenders supports this conclusion. The survey found that up to 50 percent of subprime mortgages could qualify as investment-grade mortgages, although some of these loans would fail to meet certain secondary market criteria." (footnotes omitted)) and Remarks Prepared for Delivery by Franklin D. Raines, Chairman and CEO, Fannie Mae, Rainbow/PUSH Wall Street Project Conference, New York, NY, January 14, 2000 ("[A]bout half of the borrowers in the high-cost subprime market could qualify for lower-cost conventional financing.").

28. During this period, information on whether a loan was prime or subprime (or high-cost or not high-cost) was not available publicly. However, the U.S. Department of Housing and Urban Development maintained a list of "subprime lenders." These lenders, who were primarily self-identified, made primarily subprime loans. While counting loans by subprime lenders likely undercounts many subprime loans (i.e. it does not include a subprime loan made by a prime lender) and overcounts others (i.e. assumes that all loans made by these institutions were subprime), over time it gives a picture of the overall trend in subprime lending.

29. For reasons of space, this paper focuses on racial disparities between whites and African Americans. HMDA data reveal that Latinos/Hispanics, who made up 4.1% of the population of Cuyahoga County in 2007, were also denied loans at higher rates than whites, although at a much lower rate than African Americans. For details on mortgage lending by Latinos in Northeast Ohio and throughout the state, *see* Housing Research & Advocacy Center, "Persisting Racial and Ethnic Disparities in Ohio Mortgage Lending," February 2009, available at http://www.thehousingcenter.org/Publications/Research-Reports.html.

30. "Upper income" individuals had incomes at least 120% of the median rate for the region, while "low income" individuals earned less than 50% of the median income.

31. High-cost lending refers to lending in which the interest rate is at least 3% (or, for second-lien mortgages, 5%) above the rate on Treasury securities of comparable maturity. This rate was chosen by the Federal Reserve Board for all HMDA-reporting lenders as the threshold for lenders to report certain pricing information about their mortgage loans to the federal government beginning with the 2004 HMDA submissions. The Federal Reserve Board indicated that it chose the 3% and 5% thresholds in

the belief that it would exclude the vast majority of prime-rate loans and include the vast majority of subprime-rate loans. Federal Reserve Board, "Frequently Asked Questions About the New HMDA Data," p. 4, *available at* http://www.federalreserve.gov/news-events/press/bcreg/bcreg20060403a1.pdf. "High-cost" lending is not synonymous with "subprime lending." High-cost lending is a narrower category than "subprime" lending.

32. Interestingly, upper income African Americans received high-cost loans at a higher rate than lower income African Americans. The HMDA data do not provide an explanation for this result, which is inconsistent with what one would expect.

33. *See* McShepard & Stewart, "Rebuilding Blocks," p. 9.

34. In 2007, there were 84,751 foreclosures statewide, and in 2008, the number reached 85,782.

35. In Ohio, foreclosure cases are filed in county Courts of Common Pleas. Prior to November 1, 2005, foreclosure filings in Cuyahoga County Common Pleas Court were not searchable based on the location of the property, but only based on the address of the property owner, making it difficult to determine foreclosure trends in the city of Cleveland.

36. Claudia Coulton, Tsui Chan, Michael Schramm, Kristen Mikelbank, "Pathways to Foreclosure: A Longitudinal Study of Mortgage Loans, Cleveland and Cuyahoga County, 2005–2008" (June 2008), p. 1. The study noted that the 84% figure was an underestimate of the total impact, because some of the loans originated in 2005 and 2006, the years studied, were likely to go into foreclosure in the future.

37. Id., p. 7.

38. Lisa Nelson, "Foreclosure Filings in Cuyahoga County: A Look Behind the Numbers," Federal Reserve Bank of Cleveland, Fall 2008, available at http://www.clevelandfed.org/Our_Region/Community_Development/Publications/Behind_the_Numbers/2008/0908/BTN_20080929.cfm.

39. On the east side, 6,700 loans were considered "at risk," compared to 3,700 on the west side. The report considers loans to be "at risk" if they are an adjustable rate mortgage, a high-cost mortgage, a mortgage from a subprime lender, or are already in active foreclosure. Frank Ford, "Foreclosure and Housing Market Facts and Trends: Cleveland and Cuyahoga County, October 1, 2009 (unpublished report relying on data from NEO CANDO data system, Center on Urban Poverty and Community Development, Case Western Reserve University), p. 1.

40. Id., p. 1.

41. McShepard & Stewart, "Rebuilding Blocks," pp. 12–13.

42. Id., p. 7.

43. Properties were considered "tainted" by foreclosure if there was a sheriff's deed recorded for the property during the time period 1995–2009, indicating that the property had been sold at a sheriff's sale during this time period.

44. Dan Immergluck and Geoff Smith, "There Goes the Neighborhood: The Effect of Single-Family Mortgage Foreclosures on Property Values" (June 2005), available at http://www.woodstockinst.org/publications/download/there-goes-the-neighborhood%3a-the-effect-of-single%11family-mortgage-foreclosures-on-property-values/.

45. Frank Ford, "Foreclosure and Housing Market Facts and Trends: Cleveland and Cuyahoga County, p. 2.

46. *See* Jeffrey D. Dillman, "New Strategies for Old Problems: The Fair Housing Act at 40," 57 *Cleveland State Law Review* 197, 206–07 (2009).

Chapter Seven

Bending Toward Justice

An Empirical Study of Foreclosures in One Neighborhood Three Years after Impact and a Proposed Framework for a Better Community

Mark Ireland

North Minneapolis, Minnesota is not very different from the dozens of other neighborhoods in large metropolitan areas around the country. Like those neighborhoods, North Minneapolis was among the first hit by the foreclosure crisis. The majority of people who live in North Minneapolis are people of color.[1] Over one-third of the neighborhood is comprised of rental property, rather than owner-occupied.[2] And, approximately one-fifth of the families who live in North Minneapolis are living at or below the poverty level.[3]

As other demographic statistics are evaluated and the neighborhood's history is explored, it also becomes clear that the foreclosure crisis is not the only crisis adversely affecting the lives of people who live and work in this community. There is also a health care crisis, an educational crisis, and a living-wage crisis, which each have unique causes and affects. Ultimately, all of these individual forces feed upon each other to create an environment that undermines an ability to live a stable and healthy life.

This chapter uses statistics and empirical research to focus on foreclosures in North Minneapolis. It then uses this information to begin a larger conversation about moving toward more equity and more fairness in our society. Part I is a summary of research related to Minneapolis and foreclosures with a specific focus on North Minneapolis. It is not intended to paint North Minneapolis as a monolithic entity, because that would be false. The limits of statistics are well recognized and documented.[4] Part I is intended, instead, to provide a baseline for discussion, using certain statistics to draw-out specific issues that may otherwise be overlooked. Part II is a brief analysis of the research in the context of questions raised by the origination of predatory loans and their aftermath in North Minneapolis. The questions are essential in understanding the context behind the statistics presented in Part I, as well as other statistics presented by other sources. Finally, Part III concludes with a discussion of the framework for a grassroots recovery and creating lasting, systemic change based upon a speech by Dr. Martin Luther King, Jr. entitled, "Where do we go from here?"

AN EMPIRICAL STUDY OF THE FORECLOSURE CRISIS AND ITS IMPACT ON NORTH MINNEAPOLIS

This empirical study of foreclosures in North Minneapolis is divided into four parts.[5] Part one provides a general overview of the demographics of North Minneapolis. Part two describes specific information related to the foreclosures that occurred in North Minneapolis and compares that information to the broader community. Part three identifies specific lending patterns as well as the lenders whose loans ultimately resulted in foreclosure. Part four focuses on a sample of foreclosed properties and tracks what happened to these properties three years after the foreclosure Sheriff's Sale.

General Demographic Information about North Minneapolis

Two zip codes generally encompass the area of Minneapolis that is considered North Minneapolis." These two zip codes are 55411 and 55412. Within these zip codes there are primarily two neighborhoods—Near North (55411) and Camden (55412)—with a dozen smaller niche communities within Near North and Camden. These neighborhoods sometimes exceed the 55411 and 55412 boundaries, or do not reach these boundaries. The amount that the neighborhoods exceed or other neighborhoods encroach along the 55411 and 55412 boundaries, however, is not significant. Therefore, this study of North Minneapolis limits itself to these two zip codes in order to simplify data gathering and analysis.

There are approximately 55,000 people who live in North Minneapolis. It is a diverse community:

- More than half of the people living in North Minneapolis are people of color. Specifically, in the 55411 zip code, 76% are people of color, and, in the 55412 zip code, 46% are people of color;
- There is also a significant population of renters; more than 48% of housing units are rental properties in 55411; for 55412 it is 22%;
- Approximately 25% of North Minneapolis residents have not graduated high school;
- Approximately 20% speak a language other than English at home; Between 20–to-25% live below the poverty level;
- 28% of the people living in 55411, and nearly 20% in 55412, identify themselves as having a disability.[6]

Foreclosures in North Minneapolis

The number of foreclosures in Hennepin County, including Minneapolis, was relatively stable from the mid-1980s to 2002. The total number of foreclosures was around 1,100 per year, sometimes slightly over and sometimes dropping below 1,000 per year. But, beginning in 2004 and continuing to the present, the number of foreclosures far exceeds the normal historical fluctuations. Figure 7.1 provides a historical retrospective of foreclosures in Hennepin County for the past twenty years. As evidenced by Figure 7.2, the dramatic spike in the number of foreclosures did not correlate with any of the leading economic indicators, such as unemployment rate or long-term interest rates. For North Minneapolis and Hennepin County, the spike in foreclosures occurred several years *before* the economic crisis and recession of 2008.

The primary factor that changed within this time period was the dramatic increase of subprime and Alt-A (option ARMs, no/low documentation, stated income) loans. The percentage of these loans increased from less than 10% of the overall market to approximately 40% of the overall mortgage market. Based upon Home Mortgage Disclosure Act data, the first place that subprime mortgages had a substantial market-share in Hennepin County and Minneapolis market was in North Minneapolis. The number of subprime originations throughout Hennepin County, including Minneapolis, and Ramsey County, including Saint Paul, are relatively scattered. But, there was a high concentration of sub-prime originations, more than 10%, in 55411 and 55412.

Since many subprime mortgages had adjustable interest rates that adjusted to a high level after two or three years, commonly referred to as 2/28s or

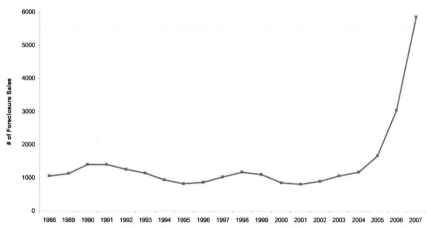

Figure 7.1.   Hennepin County Foreclosure Sheriff Sales. Foreclosure Sales Data is from the Hennepin County Sheriff's Office.

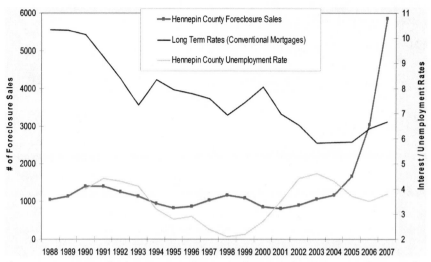

Figure 7.2. **Hennepin County Foreclosure and Economic Data. Foreclosure Sales are from Hennepin County Sheriff's Office; Unemployment Rate from the Minnesota Department of Employment and Economic Development, and Interest Rates from the Federal Reserve Board.**

3/27s, the echo of these 2002 originations are seen in the foreclosure increases in 2004 and 2005 (Figures 7.1 and 7.2).

By 2006, more than half of the foreclosures that occurred in Minneapolis took place in just these two zip codes. Specifically, there were 1,610 foreclosures in Minneapolis. Of those foreclosures, 50.5% occurred in North Minneapolis. This concentration of foreclosures was unmatched anywhere else in the city.

In North Minneapolis, the foreclosure rate as a percentage of households was approximately six times higher than Hennepin County and four times higher than Minneapolis.[7] But, what is more telling is data related to the underlying toxicity of the mortgage loans that were foreclosed upon.

The mean number of months from the date of origination for mortgage loans in North Minneapolis to the date of foreclosure was approximately 21 months. Specifically, 26% of the foreclosed mortgage loans were foreclosed upon less than a year after origination.[8] Another 48% were foreclosed upon less than two years after origination, and only 3% were mortgage loans older than five years.[9] In other words, 97% of the foreclosed mortgage loans in 2006 were originated after 2001, which correlates with the rise of the subprime and Alt-A mortgage industry.[10]

Based on Sheriff's Sale auction data, it is also clear that North Minneapolis homeowners had made very few payments toward the principal balance of their foreclosed mortgage loan. Rather than having equity, the amount due at

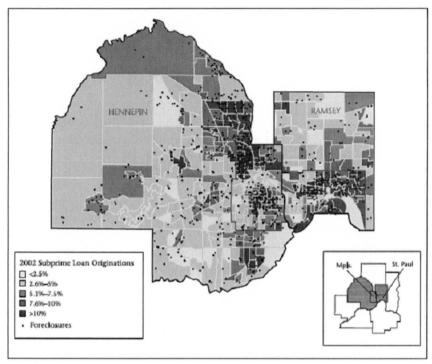

Figure 7.3. 2002 Subprime Originations and Foreclosures. Home Mortgage Disclosure Act Data (HMDA), 2002.

sale was approximately 4–5% *higher* than the original principal balance of mortgage loan.[11]

The high number of investment properties is also evidenced by the high percentage of people who had two or more foreclosed mortgage loans within the 55411 and 55412 zip codes that were foreclosed upon in the same year.[12] In 55411, nearly 16% of the foreclosures related to a person who had been foreclosed upon more than twice in 2006;[13] in 55412, that number was 5.5%.[14]

A study recently released by the University of Minnesota confirms the high number of rental property that was foreclosed upon, and the significant impact of foreclosures on renters in North Minneapolis.[15] Specifically, the study found that non-homesteaded (rental) property comprised 61% of all foreclosures that occurred in North Minneapolis in 2006–07.[16] The other key finding of the study was that households with children were disproportionately affected by the foreclosure crisis.[17]

Of the foreclosed addresses, almost 40% were households that had children in the Minneapolis public schools,[18] yet based upon census statistics, only about 16% of Minneapolis households have a child in public schools.[19] Thus, the incidence of children in school was roughly two and a half times higher for foreclosed households than the general population of the city.[20]

When the ethnicity of the foreclosed households with children in school is determined, the study finds that 60% were African-American.[21] That percentage is almost double the percent of African-American households in Minneapolis.[22] In contrast, there is a significant under-representation of white households.[23] While 50% of Minneapolis' households with children in school are white, only about 10% of foreclosures matched school records for a white household.[24]

Lending Patterns in North Minneapolis.

There are three questions that were examined as it relates to lending patterns in North Minneapolis. First, who was originating the loans in North Minneapolis? Second, of those originating the loans in North Minneapolis, were their lending practices different than elsewhere in the metropolitan area? Third, who originated the loans that ultimately failed and was foreclosed upon in 2006?

To answer the first two questions, data obtained through the Home Mortgage Disclosure Act (HMDA) indicates that the most active lenders in North Minneapolis were "sub-prime" lenders. These subprime lenders primarily worked through mortgage brokers, and, based upon the nature of these lenders, it is assumed that most, if not all, of these loans were ultimately securitized. Overall, 1.8 % of the Minneapolis-Saint Paul Metropolitan Statistical Area's home purchase and 2.0 % of the area's refinancing loans were issued in North Minneapolis.

Of those originations, 49% of these home purchase loans were subprime and 46.8% of refinance loans were subprime. In the rest of the region, the corresponding rates are 13.5% for home purchase loans and 20 % for refinancing loans. In other words, a home purchase loan in North Minneapolis was 3.6 % more likely to be subprime than a loan for a home located elsewhere. Likewise, a refinancing loan for a home located in North Minneapolis was 2.3 times more likely to be subprime than a refinancing loan located elsewhere in the area.

Data from the HMDA further shows that many subprime lenders did a disproportionate amount of their lending in North Minneapolis, while many prime lenders did disproportionately little lending in North Minneapolis.[25]

For example, Wells Fargo Bank (generally considered a prime lender) made 286 of its home loans in North Minneapolis and 34,233 loans in the rest of the area. This means that Wells Fargo made 0.8 percent of its loans in North Minneapolis. If North Minneapolis had received a proportionate amount of Well Fargo's loans, 635 loans would have been originated there, 349 fewer than were actually issued in the area. Similarly, CitiMortgage,

Table 7.1. Data Related to Purchase Origination Lending Patterns of Prime Lenders

Home Purchase	Percentage of All Loans Issued in North Minneapolis (1.8% Overall)	Percentage of Northside Loans that are Subprime	Percentage of Loans Issued in the Rest of the Metro that are Subprime	Northside Denial Rate Total	Northside Denial Rate Racial Minority	Total Northside Loans/Total Loans	Total Northside Records with No Race in HMDA
Wells Fargo Bank NA	0.8%	8.0%	2.2%	16.0%	26.4%	286/35272	46
US Bank NA	0.9%	0.0%	1.2%	10.6%	15.6%	75/8645	4
PHH Mortgage	0.7%	4.1%	0.6%	1.6%	0.0%	49/6751	4
Bell America	0.6%	7.1%	3.7%	5.4%	20.0%	28/5082	2
ABN Amero	0.5%	0.0%	0.3%	18.5%	33.3%	16/3024	4
PHH home loans	0.5%	7.7%	2.1%	0.0%	0.0%	13/2774	9
Bankers Mortgage Co.	0.3%	0.0%	4.3%	0.0%	0.0%	8/2661	1
Universal American Mortgage	0.0%	N/A	0.7%	0.0%	No applications	0/2322	0
CTX Mortgage	0.2%	0.0%	0.8%	14.3%	20.0%	5/2207	0
Marketplace Home Mortgage	0.5%	11.1%	3.2%	0.0%	0.0%	9/1785	0
CITI Mortgage	0.8%	9.1%	4.7%	12.5%	0.0%	11/1375	3
Voyager	0.6%	0.0%	0.4%	13.3%	66.7%	10/1616	0
Xpulte	0.0%	N/A	0.2%	N/A	N/A	0/1112	0

Table 7.2. Data Related to Purchase Origination Lending Patterns of Sub-Prime Lenders[i]

Home Purchase	Percentage of All Loans Issued in North Minneapolis (1.8% Overall)	Percentage of Northside Loans That Are Subprime	Percentage of Loans Issued in the Rest of the Metro That Are Subprime	Total Northside Loans/Total Loans	Total Northside Records with No Race in HMDA
Argent Mortgage	9.7%	84.2%	79.6%	241/2481	29
BNC Mortgage	10.8%	99.0%	99.3%	196/1821	69
New Century	6.5%	83.1%	75.7%	154/2359	0
Long Beach	12.2%	93.7%	85.2%	63/516	8
Accredited Home	10.6%	85.7%	76.7%	42/398	17
Mila	3.8%	76.5%	73.5%	34/890	30
Resmae	7.0%	100%	95.4%	33/470	92
Decision One	3.7%	92.1%	94.9%	59/1581	11
Fieldstone	5.4%	89.3%	69.5%	28/514	10

[i]Other subprime lenders doing ten percent or greater of their total business in North Minneapolis: Finance America, First Guarantee Mortgage Corp., The CIT group, Acoustic Home Lenders, Express Capital Lending, Aegis Funding Corporation, Community Lending Incorporated, Saxon Mortgage, Sunset direct lending, Ocwen Loan Servicing, Chapel Mortgage, Hic-star Corp., First NLC financial services, First NLC Financial Services, Nation One Mortgage Co., Academy Mortgage Corp., First NLC financial Services, Nation One Mortgage Co., Academy Mortgage Corp., First Consolidated Mortgage co., Lime Financial Services, American Business Financial, Meritage Mortgage Co., Boundary Waters Bank, Franklin National Bank, Innovative Mortgage Capital, Southern Star Mortgage, Specialty Mortgage Corporation, Spectrum Funding Corporation, Olympus Mortgage Company, Ace Mortgage Funding,

Table 7.3. Data related to Refinance Loan Originations of Sub-Prime Lenders[i]

Refinance	Percentage of All Loans Issued in North Minneapolis (2.0% Overall)	Percentage of Northside Loans That Are Subprime	Percentage of Loans Issued in the Rest of the Metro That Are Subprime	Total Northside Loans/Total Loans	Total Northside Records with No Race in HMDA
Argent	6.2%	69.8%	61.3%	295/4773	37
Ameriquest	3.8%	63.6%	48.1%	173/4605	538
Town & Country	5.8%	78.8%	50.9%	118/2027	65
New Century	3.7%	79.8%	68.6%	104/2785	42
BNC	6.8%	95.8%	94.9%	95/1400	40
Option One	4.5%	59.5%	66.5%	79/1745	40
Encore	5.2%	86.0%	83.2%	43/830	24
Accredited Home Lenders	4.7%	94.9%	75.0%	39/822	36
Aames	5.6%	56.4%	53.7%	39/695	24
Aegis	4.7%	84.2%	73.5%	38/809	32

[i]Other subprime lenders with ten percent or more of their total refinance market in North Minneapolis: Finance America, First Guarantee Mortgage Corp., The CIT group, Acoustic Home loans, Aegis funding, Community Lending Inc., Sunset Direct Lending, Ocwen Loan Servicing, Chapel Mortgage, Hic-Star Corp., First NLC Financial Services, Nation One Mortgage Co., Weststar Mortgage, Academy Mortgage, First Consolidated Mortgage, Lime Financial Services, Steward Financial, American Business Financial, Mertiage Mortgage Corp., Boundary Waters Bank, Specialty Mortgage Corp., and ACE Mortgage.

Table 7.4. Data Related to Refinance Loan Originations of Prime Lenders

Refinance	Percentage of All Loans Issued in North Minneapolis (2% Overall)	Percentage of Northside Loans That Are Subprime	Percentage of Loans Issued in the Rest of the Metro That Are Subprime	Northside Denial Rate	Northside Denial Rate Racial Minority	Total Northside Loans/Total Loans	Total Northside Records with No Race in HMDA
US Bank, NA	0.7%	0.0%	0.2%	14.8%	20.0%	43/6562	8
ABN AMRO	0.6%	0.0%	0.1%	9.0%	9.5%	31/5100	23
Provident Funding associates	0.6%	0.0%	0.0%	0.0%	0.0%	19/3174	2
PHH mortgage	0.7%	0.0%	0.0%	4.0%	14.3%	17/2311	3
Mortgage Network	0.8%	0.0%	1.2%	6.7%	0.0%	14/1697	3
Voyager Bank	0.7%	0.0%	0.3%	5.9%	8.3%	14/1974	2
Wells Fargo Funding	0.7%	0.0%	1.0%	0.0%	0.0%	14/1884	1
Principal Residential Mortgage	0.4%	0.0%	0.3%	0.0%	0.0%	9/2008	0
GMAC	0.7%	0.0%	2.7%	61.7%	66.0%	9/1334	40
Summit Mortgage	0.5%	0.0%	0.6%	33.3%	33.3%	8/1526	0

Voyager Bank, and PHH mortgage were among other prime lenders that were disproportionately absent from North Minneapolis loan records.

Conversely, the Minneapolis-Saint Paul Metropolitan Statistical Area's large subprime lenders made a disproportionately large number of loans in North Minneapolis. For example, BNC mortgage made 10.8 percent of its loans in North Minneapolis (196 out of 1821), while Long Beach Mortgage Company made 12.2 percent of its loans in North Minneapolis (63 out of 516).

This pattern continues in the refinancing market in North Minneapolis, however, the disparities are somewhat less extreme.

The percentage of these loans that ultimately resulted in foreclosure largely mirrors the market-share of the individual lenders. Table 7.5 provides a list of the top ten originating lenders of mortgage loans that resulted in a foreclosure for North Minneapolis.

There are two issues that are significant in Table 7.5. First, when the underlying loan documents were researched, the vast majority of mortgage loans that resulted in a foreclosure were originated through a mortgage broker. Based on a review of the companies identified as the "lender," at least 80% were originated using a mortgage broker. According to a report issued by the Center for Responsible Lending, a homeowner who used a mortgage broker to obtain a sub-prime mortgage loan pays more than $1,000 more the first year, and, due to a higher interest rate, pays an average of $35,000 more over

Table 7.5. Originating Lenders of 2006 Foreclosed Mortgage Loans[i]

Rank	Originating Lender	# of Foreclosures	% of Overall Northside Foreclosures
1	BNC	128	12.6%
2	Argent	127	12.5%
3	Fremont Investment and Loan	60	5.9%
4	Ameriquest	34	3.3%
5	Decision One	33	3.2%
6	Wells Fargo	32	3.1%
7	New Century	31	3%
8	Great Northern	24	2.4%
9	Long Beach Mortgage	23	2.3%
10	America's Wholesale	22	2.2%
10	First Guaranty	22	2.2%
10	Maribella	22	2.2%

[i]Housing Preservation Project, *North Minneapolis Originations and Foreclosures* (October 23, 2008) http://www.hppinc.org/_uls/resources/55411-55412_Foreclosure_Ana_2.pdf.

the life of the loan when compared to a homeowner who obtains a sub-prime mortgage through a retail lender or "branch bank."[26] The deep market penetration of broker-originated loans in North Minneapolis indicates a failure of traditional lending institutions to serve this community.

Second, the majority of loans originated in North Minneapolis came from non-bank lenders. As seen in Table 7.5, the number of lenders in North Minneapolis was fractured, but the majority were not federal banks subject to the Community Reinvestment Act.

A STUDY OF FORECLOSED PROPERTY
THREE YEARS AFTER FORECLOSURE

Although there have been many studies on lending practices, there are relatively few studies on post-foreclosure sales and activities. For this chapter, one hundred properties were randomly selected from foreclosures that occurred in the city of Minneapolis. When broken down by zip code, the numbers and percentages of foreclosed properties used in the sample were consistent with the numbers and percentages of foreclosed properties located in North Minneapolis. When comparing statistics derived only from North Minneapolis properties in the sample with all sample properties there was not a significant variation in the findings. Therefore, there is no distinction between Minneapolis and North Minneapolis in the findings.

The findings of the study are as follows:

- The median time from the date of the foreclosure Sheriff's sale to the date that the property sold to another party was 484 days. Assuming a six month redemption period, it took a lender approximately 304 days or ten months for a property to be sold.
- The difference between the amount that a lender purchased a property for at the Sheriff's Sale auction, typically the amount owed on the mortgage loan, and the later sale price was usually a loss of $65,039 (average) or $77,424 (median). As a percentage, the lender later sold the properties for a loss of 25% (average) to a loss of 49% (median).
- 83% of the foreclosed properties had 911 calls post-Sheriff's Sale.
- The average number of 911 calls was eight, while the median was five calls per property.
- The vast majority of 911 calls (74%) occurred after the end of the redemption period when the property was under the control and ownership of either the mortgage loan servicing company or the person who bought the property from the mortgage loan servicing company.

FIVE QUESTIONS AND AN ANALYSIS OF
NORTH MINNEAPOLIS FORECLOSURE DATA

So often statistics are presented and then the questions raised by such statistics are left unaddressed. Part II of this chapter identifies seven basic questions that are either raised or implicated by the statistics provided in Part I. Although the questions and responses focus on North Minneapolis, they are questions that likely relate to neighborhoods across the country. The general responses provided are only meant for moving the discussion forward, whether one disagrees or agrees with the conclusions.

Question One: Were Early Foreclosure Relief Efforts Targeted Appropriately, And How Could They Have Been More Effective?

As it relates to North Minneapolis, the statistics indicate three major assumptions related to foreclosures that were ultimately incorrect, and these incorrect assumptions undermined initial foreclosure mitigation efforts. First, there was an assumption that the mortgage loans that were at-risk of being foreclosed upon were properly underwritten. Second, there was an assumption that there was no need to oversee or regulate the terms of loan modifications. Third, the impact of foreclosures on renters was either misunderstood, minimized, or ignored in foreclosure relief efforts. These assumptions resulted in a narrow and limited initial response to providing relief to the first communities affected by foreclosures, which were also often communities of color.

Failure to Properly Underwrite

The belief that mortgage loans were properly underwritten was an assumption fostered by the rhetoric and opinions of regulators and many policy leaders from the late 1990s through 2007: Why would a bank do something that was not in its best interest?[27] Alan Greenspan, then Chairman of the Federal Reserve, believed that through complex algorithms and computer technology, risk could properly be assessed and avoided by lenders.[28]

It was also an assumption rooted in the traditional notions of mortgagee and mortgagor. Regulators and the public had not yet come to understand that this was not a simple, two-party transaction with each party having a significant stake in the successful repayment of the loan. Rather there were multiple parties involved.[29] In a typical, modern mortgage transaction there is the borrower/mortgagor, mortgage broker, lender/mortgagee, a Wall Street investment firm that provided the lender with a wholesale line of credit to originate the loan, a Wall Street investment firm that pooled and converted the mortgage loans into mortgage backed securities (an agreement that typically existed between the lender and firm long before the loan was originated), the credit rating agencies, the trustee of the securitized loan trust, the servicer of the mortgage loans (different from the investor and owner), the purchasers of the securities or bonds, and the competing regulators that oversee the practices of these various actors.[30]

As aptly summarized by law professor Christopher Peterson, the origins of financing a home mortgage purchase had humble beginnings and changed significantly in the twentieth century.[31] It began as a two-party transaction involving neighbors and friends joined together in a building society.[32] These began in the United States in 1831 and were modeled after similar British institutions.[33] Then, after the Great Depression, the government began to assume a role as an assignee for the original lenders.[34] Thus, the government was encouraging more lending by agreeing in advance to purchasing loans originated by others.[35]

In the past fifty years, there were two additional developments. First, there was the development of a government sponsored securitization market.[36] This was done primarily through Fannie Mae and, to a lesser extent, Freddie Mac.[37] Securitization converted the relatively locked nature of a 30–year fixed mortgage, and then made it far more dynamic and flexible. Second, there was the development of the private, non-government sponsored securitization market.[38] This may also be called "private label" securitization.[39] It is within private label securitization that risky and illegal behavior arguably began and thrived.[40]

The statistics described in Section I indicate that the loans were not properly underwritten by the lenders, and that the cause of the foreclosure went far beyond the traditional reasons for foreclosure, such as job loss, divorce, or medical problems. The mean number of months from the date of origination to the date of foreclosure was approximately 21 months for mortgage loans originated in North Minneapolis, meaning that most borrowers were foreclosed upon within two years of origination. As stated above, 26% of the foreclosed mortgage loans were foreclosed upon less than a year after origination, which meant that the foreclosure process began, at most, nine months after origination.[41] Indeed, most people owed more than the original balance of the mortgage loan, due to mortgage servicer fees, at the time of the foreclosure Sheriff's Sale than was owed on the date of origination.

The assumption the mortgage loans were properly underwritten made it easier for regulators and the public to believe that the initial wave of foreclosures was an aberration, and that the market would quickly correct itself. It also made it easier for regulators and the public to believe that the risky lending patterns were not widespread. Thus, early calls for federal intervention were dismissed as unnecessary or an over-reaction.

Lack of Oversight for Mortgage Loan Modifications

Based on the assumption, stated above, that the owners of mortgage loans would not do anything that was not in their own best interest, there was minimal oversight of the types of loan modifications that were occurring. Often loan modification studies or reports indicate that there is a very high failure rate of modified loans, and people then interpret that high failure rate as a basis to conclude that loan modifications are pointless. When the loan modifications themselves are categorized and defined, a much clearer picture of the problem emerges. Specifically, the loan modifications that occurred were inherently flawed and did not substantively change the terms of the mortgage loan to be sustainable. Further, the loan modifications that occurred were very small relative to the total number of foreclosures that were occurring. Thus, the large number of foreclosures has been wrongly conflated with the large number of "modified" loans that re-default.

A major study funded by the Ford Foundation found that the high re-default rate of modified loans was based on the quality of the loan modifications[42] Specifically, the study compared different mortgage modification scenarios, including interest rate reduction, principal balance reduction, monthly payment reduction, or simple restructuring, which includes an increased monthly payment.[43] Not surprisingly, the loan modifications that resulted in a lower monthly payment combined with a principal balance reduction were the most sustainable and most likely not to re-default.[44] Yet, many mortgagers, particularly at the beginning of the foreclosure crisis, modified mortgage loans in a manner that resulted in higher monthly payment.[45] Not surprisingly, most of these modified loans re-defaulted within a year.

Even worse, the vast majority of delinquent modifications were not modified at all.[46] A study released by the Federal Reserve Board in Boston found that less than 8% of seriously delinquent loans received any loan modification.[47] The study examined a large sample of mortgage loans from across the United States that was originated between 2005 and 2007.[48] Ultimately, the study concluded that the widespread opinion that a sustainable loan modification is a win-win is either a myth or mortgage loan servicers, as an industry, are systematically not acting in their own best interest.[49] The two propositions are mutually exclusive.

Misunderstanding, Minimizing, and Ignoring
The Impact of Foreclosures On Renters

In Section I, the statistics indicate that there were a large number of renters adversely affected by the initial wave of foreclosures. The findings of the

University of Minnesota study were that over 60% of the properties that were foreclosed upon were non-homesteaded, exceeding the proportion of rental property in the neighborhood. Yet, the vast majority of initial foreclosure prevention efforts, both local and national, were designed only to help homeowners with little or no mention of renters.

Elected officials took pains to distinguish between homeowners and investors, noting that its foreclosure prevention programs would not assist investors and would only cover owner-occupied property.[50] While from a public policy and public relations perspective this is an important and justified distinction, in practice it fails to recognize the issues encountered by the renters who live in these foreclosed properties.

For example, many renters who live in investment properties that are displaced by foreclosure are forced to incur moving costs that were not budgeted, and that they may not be able to afford. Renters in foreclosed properties often risk utility shut-offs or delayed maintenance and repair. Renters may also lose their security deposits because landlords or investors disappear after the foreclosure. Today, three to four years after the foreclosure crisis began, there is still no comprehensive, nationwide plan to protect renters facing foreclosure. There is also no significant effort to try and compensate renters for lost income, unreturned security deposits, or relocation expenses.

Question Two: Did The Community Reinvestment Act Force Lenders To Make Loans In North Minneapolis To Unqualified, Minority Borrowers?

There are some who blame the foreclosure crisis on the Community Reinvestment Act.[51] Enacted over twenty years ago, the Community Reinvestment Act, aimed at preventing red-lining and reverse red-lining, prohibited federally insured banks and thrifts from limiting loans or prohibiting loans offered in certain neighborhoods.[52] Critics of the Community Reinvestment Act argue that the government itself was to blame for the current economic crisis by forcing innocent lenders to originate loans to high-risk black and Hispanic borrowers.[53] Thus, it was not speculators, fraudulent brokers, or negligent lenders who are to blame for predatory loans originated in North Minneapolis. Instead, they argue, it was the government's fault.

For example, Ann Coulter wrote an article entitled, *"They Gave your Mortgage to a Less Qualified Minority."*[54] Ms. Coulter argues that the foreclosure and economic crisis was caused by "political correctness being forced on the mortgage lending industry in the Clinton era."[55] She then posits that banks were forced to ignore credit scores and lend based on "nontraditional measures of credit-worthiness, such as having a good jump shot or having a missing child named Caylee."[56]

This theory, related to the Community Reinvestment Act, has largely, if not entirely, been de-bunked.[57] The most high-risk lending occurred through non-bank lenders that were not even covered by the Community Reinvestment Act.[58] Some estimates are that three-quarters of the sub-prime loans that were originated by non-bank lenders during the real estate boom were not subject to the Community Reinvestment Act.[59]

The breakdown of mortgage loans originated in North Minneapolis is consistent with such estimates. Therefore, the Community Reinvestment Act cannot be blamed for compelling people who are not even subject to the Act for behaving in a certain manner. This is, of course, assuming that the Act requires lenders to give loans to people who have good jump shots, which it does not.

Question Three: Is There Any Correlation Between Race And The Likelihood That A Minority In North Minneapolis Would Receive A Sub-Prime Or High-Cost Mortgage Loan?

Every study that has examined the correlation between race and the likelihood that a minority in North Minneapolis or the Minneapolis-Saint Paul metropolitan region would receive a high-cost, predatory loan has concluded that there was an extremely high correlation. In a study by the National Community Reinvestment Coalition, the Minneapolis-Saint Paul metropolitan statistical area ("MSA") had the second largest disparity in the entire country between white and non-white applicants in receiving predatory, high cost loans.[60] When focused on congressional district, African American men were more than three times likely to receive a high-cost, sub-prime loan than their white counterparts in the congressional district that encompasses North Minneapolis.[61]

Another recent study, conducted by the University of Minnesota's Institute on Race and Poverty, found similar results.[62] Not only were persons of color five times more likely to be given a high-cost, subprime loan, the University of Minnesota study also found a large disparity in the denial rates between different races.[63] For example, very high-income blacks, Asians, and Hispanics (making more than $157,000 a year) in the MSA were more likely to be denied a mortgage loan than whites making less than $39,250.[64] The denial rate for blacks with incomes above $157,000 was 25%, while it was just 11% for whites making $39,250 or less.[65]

Question Four: Does Federal Funding To Address Vacant And Abandoned Houses Target The Neighborhoods That Have The Greatest Need?

By far, the largest recovery program created by the federal government, relating to the vacant and abandoned houses created by the foreclosure crisis, is the Housing and Economic Recovery Act of 2008.[66] Specifically this Act contained a provision that created a pool of money to help communities recover from the foreclosure crisis. This fund and its administration are generally referred to as the National Stabilization Program ("NSP").[67] Approximately $6 billion of NSP grants were distributed to states across the country, and the states were then required to give "priority emphasis and consideration to those ... areas with the greatest need."[68]

Yet, in Minnesota, the funds were not provided to the geographic areas of the greatest need.[69] North Minneapolis and certain neighborhoods in Saint Paul have unquestionably been the State's most negatively impacted areas by almost any measure, but, based upon the formula developed by the State of Minnesota, at least $9 million of Minnesota's $17 million NSP award was automatically directed to other areas of the state.[70] In fact, the State of Minnesota created its own factor (not suggested or authorized by Congress) to create a formula that is "balancing the distribution of funds between the Twin Cities metro area and Greater Minnesota."[71]

This "balancing" is irrelevant to the goal of targeting funds to areas of greatest need, like North Minneapolis, and ignores the reality of the foreclosure crisis.[72] It also violates the intent and language of the statute.[73] The distribution of funds away from areas of greatest need was mitigated in later awarding of funds, because more money was distributed directly to cities and counties and not left to the discretion of state entities. The issue, however, is important when analyzing all recovery efforts (not just housing).

For example, there are questions related to whether transportation funds are being spent in areas of greatest need. Most people live in large metropolitan areas (two-thirds) and the metropolitan areas are where the biggest impact of the foreclosure crisis has been felt. Yet, urban areas received less than half of transportation stimulus dollars.[74] It raises the issue of how our transportation system and other federal recovery spending would look differently if the spending is focused on the specific inner-city and urban areas that most need the funds.

An article in the *New York Times*, which profiles its study of stimulus spending, concludes with the following:

> We have a long history of shortchanging cities and metropolitan areas and allocating transportation money to places where few people live," said Owen D. Gutfreund, an assistant professor of urban planning at the City University of New York who wrote "20th Century Sprawl: Highways and the Reshaping of the American Landscape. (Oxford University Press, 2004)
>   Professor Gutfreund said that in some states the distribution was driven by statehouse politics, with money spread to the districts of as many lawmakers as possible, or given out as political favors. In others, he said, the money is distributed by formulas that favor rural areas or that gives priority to state-owned roads, often found far outside of urban areas.

Mayors had lobbied Congress to send the money directly to cities, but in the end, 70 percent of the money was sent to the states to be divided, and 30 percent was sent to metropolitan planning organizations, which represent the local governments in many metropolitan areas.[75]

Question Five: Is This Crisis Really Just Part Of A Pattern?

Looking at the foreclosure crisis and the impact on North Minneapolis, it is clear that the foreclosure crisis did not occur in isolation of many other issues of race and economics. It is also clear that the foreclosure crisis is not the first confluence of these various issues. In the past twenty years, North Minneapolis experienced a high number of house flipping in the late 1990s,[76] then from 2002–2006, North Minneapolis experienced a high-level of equity strippers,[77] and from 2006 to present, North Minneapolis has had the highest rates of foreclosure in the region.[78] So the answer to the question is yes, the foreclosure crisis is part of a pattern of exploitation and marginalization of a community. The better question is how to stop it.

Bending Toward Justice

In an address to the Tenth Anniversary Convention of the S.C.L.C. in Atlanta, Georgia on August 16, 1967, Dr. Martin Luther King, Jr. made an address entitled, "Where do we go from here?"[79] The title of this speech was also the title of Dr. King's last book, entitled "Where do we go from here: Chaos or Community?"[80] Historically, 1967 was thirteen years after the US Supreme Court issued its decision in *Brown v. Board of Education.*[81] It was six years after the Freedom Rides, four years after the march on Washington, and three years after the passage of the Civil Rights Act.[82]

It was at a time of historic victories, but much work remained and communities were anxious for change and prosperity. Indeed, the summer before Dr. King's speech a series of riots and disturbances erupted in major cities across the United States.[83] The incidents received significant media attention, some exaggerated, which heightened tension.[84] It is in this national environment in which Dr. King made this important speech.

In his speech, Dr. King set forth a framework for renewal and progress.[85] First, he identified "where we are" and then demanded that persons of color "massively assert our dignity and worth."[86] Second, Dr. King stated that the community must identify the basic challenges that it faces.[87] Third, Dr. King stated that we must develop a program and commit to a path of nonviolence.[88] He said that the "whole structure must be changed," and then concluded with the following:

When our days become dreary with low-hovering clouds of despair, and when our nights become darker than a thousand midnights, let us remember that there is a creative force in this universe, working to pull down the gigantic mountains of evil, a power that is able to make a way out of no way and transform dark yesterdays into bright tomorrows. Let us realize the arc of the moral universe is long but it bends toward justice.[89]

Isn't that the framework that we must adopt in the wake of the foreclosure and economic crisis? A crisis that undermined, in many cases, decades of work and progress toward a more equal society. A crisis that depleted the wealth of communities of color. A crisis that undermined neighborhoods and displaced thousands of families.

This chapter is intended to start the process of defining "where we are at." But, that is only the beginning. We need to define where we are at as a nation, not just where we are at in North Minneapolis. Doesn't the largest financial crisis in modern history deserve its own government commission to hold the mirror up to ourselves? And then, together, we will begin steps two and three—bending the arc of the moral universe toward justice.

NOTES

1. United States Census, American Fact Finder Zip Code Tabulation for 55411 and 55412, http://factfinder.census.gov (last visited August 13, 2009).

2. *Ibid.*

3. *Ibid.*

4. For example, there are no statistics that can quantify the dedication of community board members or the number of loving parents who are standing on the sidelines of the baseball field at Fairview Park and that are cheering on their children. Studies and measurements are also limited to what the research is looking for and intends to measure, but they are only a snapshot and an incomplete snapshot at best.

5. The data used in this study focuses on the 55411 and 55412 zip codes. Although the dimensions of these zip codes do not exactly track the borders of what is considered "North Minneapolis," the differences do not significantly alter the analysis. The geographic differences are largely on the fringes, resulting in a small under-count in some census tracts and a small over-count in others.

6. United States Census, American Fact Finder Zip Code Tabulation for 55411 and 55412, http://factfinder.census.gov (last visited August 13, 2009).

7. Housing Preservation Project, *Analysis of Detailed Sheriff's Sale Data: Includes 2005–2006 Data for zip codes 55411 and 55412* (March 6, 2008) http://www.hppinc.org/_uls/resources/55411–55412_Foreclosure_Ana.pdf.

8. *Ibid.*

9. *Id.*

10. *Id.*

11. *Id.*

12. *Id.*

13. *Id.*

14. *Id.*

15. Ryan Allen, *The Unraveling of the American Dream: Foreclosures in the Immigrant Community of Minneapolis*, Report to Minneapolis Public Schools REA Division at 3 (March 2009) http://www.hhh.umn.edu/people/rallen/pdf/unraveling_american_dream.pdf;Steve Perry, *Who's Getting Hurt? UM Study crunches the numbers on foreclosures in Minneapolis,* MinnPost (Feb. 19, 2009) http://www.minnpost.com/steveperry/2009/02/19/6811/whos_getting_hurt_um_study_crunches_the_numbers_on_minneapolis_foreclosures.

16. *Id.*

17. *Id.*

18. *Id.*

19. *Id.*

20. *Id.*

21. *Id.*

22. *Id.*

23. *Id.*

24. *Id.*

25. Data collection and assistance with analysis was provided by research assistants at the University of Minnesota's Institute for Race and Poverty. *See also* Myron Orfield, *Communities in Crisis: Race and Mortgage Lending in the Twin Cities*, Institute on Race and Poverty (February 2009) http://www.irpumn.org/uls/resources/projects/IRP_mortgage_study_Feb._11th.pdf;

26. The Center for Responsible Lending, *Steered Wrong: Brokers, Borrowers, and Subprime Loans* (April 2008).

27. Alan Greenspan, Chairman, Bd. of Gov of the Fed. Reserve Sys., Remarks to the Federal Reserve System Community Affairs Research Conference (Apr. 8, 2005), at 5 (transcript available at http://fraser.stlouisfed.org/historicaldocs/ag05/download/29243/Greenspan_20050408.pdf).

28. *Id.* ("With these advances in technology, lenders have taken advantage of credit-scoring models and other techniques for efficiently extending credit to a broader spectrum of consumers . . . . Where once more-marginal applicants would simply have been denied credit, lenders are now able to quite efficiently judge the risk posed by individual applicants and to price that risk appropriately.")

29. Kathleen C. Engel & Patricia A. McCoy, *Turning a Blind Eye: Wall Street Finance of Predatory Lending*, 75 Fordham L. Rev. 2039, 2070 (2007).

30. *Id.*

31. Christophe L. Peterson, *Predatory Structured Finance,* 28 Cardozo L. Rev. 2185, 2186–2213 (2007).

32. *Id.* at 2191.

33. *Id.*

34. *Id.* at 2194.

35. *Id.*

36. *Id.* at 2198.

37. *Id.*

38. *Id.* at 2200.

39. *Id.*

40. *Id.*

41. *Id.*

42. Roberto G. Quercia, Lei Ding, and Janneke Ratcliffe, *Loan Modifications and Redefault Risk: An Examination of Short-term Impact,* Center for Community Capital, The University of North Carolina at Chapel Hill (March 2009 http://www. ccc.unc.edu/documents/LM_March3_%202009_final.pdf); *See also* Office of the Comptroller of the Currency, *Comptroller Dugan Highlights Re-Default Rates on Modified Loans,* Press Release (December 8, 2008) last visited September 11, 2009 http://www.occ.treas.gov/ftp/release/2008–142.htm.

43. *Id.*

44. *Id.*

45. *Id.*

46. Manuel Adelino, Kristopher Gerardi, and Paul S. Willen, *Why Don't Lenders Renegotiate Home Mortgages? Redefaults, Self-Cures, and Securitization,* Public Policy Discussion Papers No. 09–04, Federal Reserve Bank of Boston (July 6, 2009) http://www.bos.frb.org/economic/ppdp/2009/ppdp0904.pdf.

47. *Id.*

48. *Id.*

49. *Id.; See also* Peter S. Goodman, *Lucrative Fees May Deter Efforts to Alter Loans,* New York Times (July 29, 2009) ("But industry insiders and legal experts say the limited capacity of mortgage companies is not the primary factor impeding the government's $75 billion program to prevent foreclosures. Instead, it is that many mortgage companies are reluctant to give strapped homeowners a break because the companies collect lucrative fees on delinquent loans. Even when borrowers stop paying, mortgage companies that service the loans collect fees out of the proceeds when homes are ultimately sold in foreclosure. So the longer borrowers remain delinquent, the greater the opportunities for these mortgage companies to extract revenue—fees for insurance, appraisals, title searches and legal services." http://www.nytimes. com/2009/07/30/business/30services.html.

50. *See e.g.* House Committee of Financial Services, *House Passes American Housing Rescue and Foreclosure Prevention Act,* Press Release (May 8, 2008) ("Only primary residences are eligible: NO speculators, investment properties, second or third homes will be refinanced."); United States Dept. of the Treasury, *Relief for Responsible Homeowners One Step Closer Under New Treasury Guidelines: Updated Fact Sheet,* Press Release (March 4, 2009) ("[W]hile attempting to prevent the destructive impact of the housing crisis on families and communities. It will not provide money to speculators, and it will target support to the working homeowners…") http://treas.gov/press/releases/reports/housing_fact_sheet.pdf.

51. Michael Aleo & Pablo Svirsky, *Foreclosure Fallout: The Banking Industry's Attack on Disparate Impact Race Discrimination Claims Under the Fair Housing Act and the Equal Credit Opportunity Act*, 18 B.U. Pub. Int. L.J. 1, 10–11 (2008) (summarizing and citing various commentaries blaming the Community Reinvestment Act for the foreclosure crisis).

52. *Id.* at 11.

53. *Id.*

54. *Id.* (citing Ann Coulter, *They Gave Your Mortgage to a Less Qualified Minority*, Human Events Online, Sept. 24, 2008, *available at* http://www.humanevents. com/article.php?id=28714).

55. *Id.*

56. *Id..*

57. *See id.* at 12–14.

58. *Id.* at 12.

59. *Id.* at 13–14.

60. National Community Reinvestment Coalition, *Income Is No Shield Part III* at 3 (June 2009).

61. National Community Reinvestment Coalition, *Black 2006 Subprime Disparity Index by Congressional District* (2009) http://www.ncrc.org/images/stories/pdf/ research/black%20subprime%20disparity%20by%20congressional%20district.pdf.

62. Myron Orfield, *Communities in Crisis: Race and Mortgage Lending in the Twin Cities*, Institute on Race and Poverty (February 2009) http://www.irpumn. org/uls/resources/projects/IRP_mortgage_study_Feb._11th.pdf; *See also* Jeffrey Crump, *Subprime Lending and Foreclosure in Hennepin and Ramsey Counties* at 15, CURA Reporter (Summer 2007) http://www.cura.umn.edu/reporter/07–Summ/ Crump.pdf .

63. *Id.*

64. *Id.*

65. *Id.*

66. Housing and Economic Recovery Act of 2008, P.L. 110–289, § 2301(c)(2) (2008).

67. *Id.*

68. *Id.*

69. Housing Preservation Project, Harrison Neighborhood Association, and the Northside Residents Redevelopment Council, *Administrative Complaint to HUD* (December 16, 2008).

70. *Id.*

71. *Id.*

72. *Id.*

73. *Id.*

74. Michael Cooper and Griff Palmer, *Cities Lose Out on Road Funds From Federal Stimulus,* New York Times (July 8, 2009) http://www.nytimes.com/2009/07/09/ us/09projects.html?_r=1.

75. *Id.*

76. Federal Reserve Bank of Minneapolis, *Property Flipping in the Twin Cities* (November 2002) ("The property flippers recruited buyers from homeless shelters, laundromats and churches. Most of the homebuyers were low-income, and the flips were geographically concentrated in North Minneapolis neighborhoods.")

77. Jonathan Kaminsky, *Steal this House,* City Pages (May 16, 2007) (describing a North Minneapolis victim of equity stripping).

78. Housing Preservation Project, *Analysis of Detailed Sheriff's Sale Data: Includes 2005–2006 Data for zip codes 55411 and 55412* (March 6, 2008) http://www.hppinc.org/_uls/resources/55411–55412_Foreclosure_Ana.pdf.

79. Martin Luther King, Jr., *Where do we go from here?* Indiana University, Democracy: Historical Texts http://www.indiana.edu/~ivieweb/mlkwhere.html.

80. Dr. Martin Luther King, Jr., *Where do we go from here: Chaos or Community?* Harper & Row (1967).

81. *Brown v. Board of Education of Topeka*, 347 U.S. 483 (1954).

82. The Civil Rights Act of 1964 (Pub. L. 88–352, 78 Stat. 241, July 2, 1964).

83. Kerner Commission, Report of the National Advisory Commission on Civil Disorders (February 29, 1968) http://www.eisenhowerfoundation.org/docs/kerner.pdf.

84. *Id.*

85. *See supra* note 85.

86. *Id.*

87. *Id.*

88. *Id.*

89. *Id.*

Chapter Eight

The Foreclosure Crisis and Fair Credit Access in Immigrant Communities

Deyanira Del Rio

Immigrants face multiple barriers to fair housing opportunity, in both the rental and home purchase markets. Obstacles include discrimination by landlords and real estate professionals based on immigrants' race, country of origin, and real or perceived immigration status. Language barriers impede many immigrants' access to information about housing opportunities and their rights under fair housing and other anti-discrimination laws. Immigrants who are new to the country or have avoided debt may lack formal credit histories, which are frequently reviewed by landlords when considering prospective tenants, and are vital to securing mortgages on fair terms.

Housing affordability is also a pervasive issue affecting immigrants, who are more likely than people born in the U.S. to live in cities and to spend a larger percentage of their incomes on housing. In New York City, where immigrants make up 37% of the population and 46% of the workforce, low income renters typically spend more than half of their incomes on rent.[1] As a result of affordable housing shortages, immigrant families are more likely than others to live in overcrowded housing conditions, as well as in informal or illegally converted housing units.[2] In recent years, affordable housing in New York and other high-cost cities has been further threatened by "predatory equity" schemes, in which private equity companies have purchased large apartment buildings, with the intent of forcing out rent-regulated (often immigrant) tenants, and increasing rents many times over.[3]

Local governments have also taken actions that undermine immigrants' rights under the federal Fair Housing Act and other anti-discrimination statutes.[4] In recent years, dozens of municipal governments throughout the country have passed ordinances prohibiting landlords from renting apartments to undocumented immigrants.[5] While many of these ordinances have been struck down or are being challenged in court, their passage and the anti-immigrant sentiment they help fuel have had negative consequences on local housing conditions—not only for undocumented immigrants, but for legal residents and US citizens, as well. Many families and workers have reportedly moved out of these communities as a result of the hostile climate, contributing to a decline in local economies and housing markets.[6]

Immigrant communities have suffered the effects of the subprime lending boom, as well as the resulting foreclosure crisis. Housing and legal services advocates cite particularly abusive practices by "one-stop shops," in which real estate agents, appraisers, mortgage brokers, and attorneys collude to steer homebuyers into purchasing homes at inflated values and with unaffordable mortgages. These schemes were rampant in immigrant communities, where language and cultural barriers often result in greater reliance on brokers to navigate the complicated home-buying process.

In particularly egregious cases, unscrupulous real estate professionals targeted undocumented immigrants for predatory loans or scams involving mortgage fraud. In New York City, for example, nonprofit housing and immigrant advocates have collaborated to identify and assist undocumented immigrants at risk of foreclosure because of predatory loans. In multiple cases, advocates found that predatory mortgage and real estate brokers had instructed immigrants to provide false information on loan applications, or to recruit friends or family members willing to sign for mortgage loans. These schemes cost many families their life savings, while exposing all parties involved to serious legal risks.

At the same time that undocumented immigrants were frequent targets for abuse, they also had—in some parts of the country—greater access to credit in the years leading up to the foreclosure crisis. Over the past decade, a small but growing number of lenders began making mortgage loans to individuals who did not have Social Security numbers or traditional credit histories. Instead they accepted those individuals' IRS-issued Individual Taxpayer Identification Numbers (ITINs) and developed underwriting criteria that considered alternative payment and credit histories. ITIN loans have consistently outperformed even prime mortgage loans. Nonetheless, the availability of ITIN loans has diminished drastically as a result of the mortgage crisis, among other factors, curtailing opportunities for homeownership among undocumented immigrants.

Immigrants make up a growing share of the U.S. population, including in parts of the South and Midwest where their presence was virtually nonexistent ten or fifteen years ago. Demographers and housing policy analysts have pointed to the critical role that immigrants will play in the nation's recovery from the current housing crisis and in ensuring future housing demand.[7] Strengthening and enforcing fair housing and fair lending protections—including those provided for by the federal Fair Housing Act—is increasingly vital, not only to protect the rights of the country's growing immigrant population, but to stabilize and preserve housing markets and local economies going forward.

HOMEOWNERSHIP IN IMMIGRANT COMMUNITIES

Homeownership, the primary vehicle for wealth and asset development in the United States, is lower for immigrants as a whole than for the US-born population, notwithstanding gains made in the past two decades.[8] In 2008, 53% of immigrant-headed households owned their homes, compared to 70% of households headed by US-born people. The immigrant population is, of course, not monolithic, and homeownership rates vary among immigrants based on ethnicity, countries of origin, length of time in the United States, and areas of settlement in the United States, among other factors. Roughly 45% of foreign-born blacks and Latinos owned homes, for example, compared to 58% of foreign-born Asians and 66% of foreign-born whites. Naturalized citizens are nearly twice as likely to own homes (67%) as non-citizens (35%); and after 20 years, immigrants are almost as likely as their native-born peers to own their homes.[9]

Immigrants face a host of obstacles to homeownership, including the high cost of housing in cities, where 96% of immigrants live (compared to 78% of those born in the United States).[10] Limited English proficiency, lack of familiarity with the financial services system, and discrimination by home sellers and real estate professionals in some markets further impede immigrants' ability to navigate the home-buying process safely. Among some immigrant groups, homeownership may be valued less than higher education or business ownership, and family resources may accordingly be spent toward those pursuits.[11] Many immigrants send money (remittances) to support family members in their home countries, or may intend to move back themselves, making homeownership in the United States economically unviable or undesirable.

Access to fair mortgage loans is limited for some immigrant groups, even where homeownership may be an affordable option. New immigrants, for example, typically have little or no credit history, which makes it difficult to access credit on fair terms.[12] Immigrants are also more likely than people born in the United States to be self-employed, or to have informal or pooled sources of income, making them prime candidates during the housing boom for "stated income" and other nontraditional loans that were often predatory.

On a fundamental level, immigrants are less likely than those born in the United States to have bank accounts—a critical entry point to the formal financial services system. An estimated 32% of foreign-born households in the U.S. do not have a bank account, compared to 18% of those born here.[13] Immigrants face multiple barriers to account ownership, including prohibitive identification requirements imposed by some banks, high fees and minimum balance requirements, and concerns about their ability to access funds if they are detained or deported. Without bank accounts, it can be extremely difficult for individuals to save, demonstrate their income, or build relationships with financial institutions from which they might obtain future loans, including mortgages.

PREDATORY LENDING AND FORECLOSURES IN IMMIGRANT COMMUNITIES

The continuing subprime lending and foreclosure crisis has reversed many of the gains made in homeownership over the past decade, particularly among people of color. Extensive research has documented racial and ethnic dispari-ties in mortgage lending, even when controlling for income and credit scores. In 2006, for example, black and Latino New Yorkers were four times and three times respectively as likely as white borrowers to receive subprime loans to purchase their homes.[14] Among borrowers who received subprime loans in 2006, 61% had credit scores that should have qualified them for prime loans, according to a study completed for the *Wall Street Journal*. African Americans and Latinos were also more likely to receive interest-only and Option Adjustable Rate Mortgages (ARMs) than white borrowers at all levels of income, debt loads and credit scores.[15]

Communities of color have long-received a disproportionate share of subprime loans, as documented through research using publicly available Home Mortgage Disclosure Act (HMDA) data. HMDA data does not include information about loan applicants' countries of origin, making it difficult to estimate the percentage of subprime loans made to native- vs. foreign-born borrowers. However, GIS mapping of mortgage lending patterns in New York City, by census tract, reveals that high-cost mortgage loans are over-whelmingly concentrated in neighborhoods of color, including those where large shares of immigrants live. *(See Figure 8.5.)*

Similarly, limited data and research exists on the impact of foreclosures on immigrant- vs. U.S.-born homeowners. Pew Research Center, for example, has found on the one hand that counties with higher shares of immigrants have higher rates of foreclosure. On the other hand, between 2006 and 2008, the homeownership rate fell less sharply for immigrants than it did for native-born people—by 0.4% among immigrants, compared to 1.5% among the US-born.[16]

In New York City, the highest number of foreclosure filings on one-to-four family homes was in Queens County, where almost half the population (46%) is foreign-born (Table 8.1.).[17] GIS mapping of foreclosure patterns in 2008 shows that among neighborhoods hardest-hit by foreclosures, many have higher shares of immigrants than the city as a whole. (*See Figure 8.6.*)

Chhaya Community Development Corporation, based in Jackson Heights, Queens, has estimated that in some zip codes in Queens, more than 50% of homeowners in default on their mortgages are South Asian.[18] The organization, which provides home purchase as well as foreclosure prevention counseling, has noted that many of the mortgage brokers who steered immigrants into unaffordable loans have converted to for-profit "foreclosure rescue" and "loan modification" outfits—essentially promising to bail out the same homeowners they helped steer into bad loans.

Overcrowding in immigrant communities has worsened, as many homeowners have rented out rooms or basement units in their homes in order to keep up with mortgage payments. Chhaya notes that helping homeowners secure affordable loan modifications is difficult, particularly among immigrants who are self-employed or work for cash and have underreported income; this makes it difficult to verify homeowners' income and their eligibility for loan modifications under the federal Home Affordable Mortgage Program (HAMP) guidelines.[19]

Asociación Tepeyac, a New York City-based organization serving Latino immigrants, began working on foreclosure issues in 2007, responding to a surge in predatory lending and foreclosure cases among low income and undocumented immigrants they served. In virtually every case identified by Tepeyac, unscrupulous realtors and mortgage brokers steered families into buying homes at inflated values, with abusive subprime mortgages. Undocumented immigrant families, which typically made significant down payments and paid thousands of dollars in up-front fees, received among the most egregious loans that foreclosure prevention attorneys in NYC had seen.[20] (*See Figures 8.1. and 8.2.*) News stories about similar scams in other parts of the country abound.[21]

Table 8.1. Foreclosure Actions Filed* New York City

Borough	2005	2006	2007	2008
Bronx	808	1,128	1,585	1,619
Brooklyn	2,557	3,307	4,895	4,746
Manhattan	39	43	62	65
Queens	2,666	3,624	5,789	5,660
Staten Island	803	986	1,500	1,604
NYC Total	6,873	9,088	13,831	13,694

*Based on lis pendens of mortgage default filings filed on 1–4 family homes (Source: Profiles Publications)

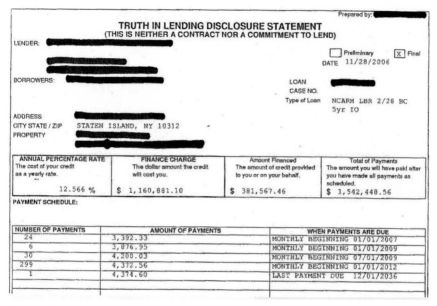

Figure 8.1.

Truth in Lending Disclosure Statement – Mr. and Mrs. R

Mr. and Mrs. R, who are undocumented immigrants from Mexico, received a high-cost mortgage loan to purchase their home in 2006. The Rs were steered by a broker to a subprime lender, which made them a loan for $380,000. In spite of their strong income and credit history, the Rs received a 2/28 Adjustable Rate Mortgage, with interest-only payments for the first five years. The loan, had an initial interest rate of 12.6%, due to increase after two years; over the life of the loan, the interest rate could increase to as high as 18%. The Rs made on-time payments for more than two years, paying more than $100,000 in interest–on top of a $50,000 down payment–without reducing their principal by a single penny.

Figure 8.2.

Brokers typically were aware of borrowers' immigration status and seemingly preyed on families that they suspected would be unlikely to report the abuse, even warning the members of one family that they could be deported if they sought help. Although the brokers could have pursued legitimate ITIN mortgages for these families, they instead instructed homebuyers to falsify loan applications or to find family members or friends with Social Security numbers willing to sign loan documents.

WHAT HAPPENED TO ITIN MORTGAGES?

Beginning in the early 2000s, a growing number of financial institutions began accepting IRS-issued ITINs to open bank accounts and, in some cases, to make mortgages and other loans.[22] The emergence of so-called "ITIN mortgages" provided a path to homeownership for immigrants who lacked Social Security numbers and formal credit histories, but could otherwise qualify for and sustain loans. Criteria for ITIN mortgages were typically more flexible than for other loans in terms of acceptable income and down payment sources that borrowers could provide, as well as alternative credit and bill payment histories that lenders would consider.

By 2005, at least 20 banks and credit unions offered ITIN loans, with Chicago and other midwestern banks at the forefront of this new market.[23] As of 2008, immigrants borrowed between $1–$2 billion in ITIN mortgages, according to estimates by the National Association of Hispanic Real Estate Professionals (NAHREP) and Hispanic National Mortgage Association (HNMA).[24] Before the economic downturn, NAHREP estimated that more than 216,000 undocumented Latino immigrants could purchase homes and sustain upwards of $44 billion in mortgages.[25]

ITIN mortgages consistently outperformed other mortgages, including prime loans. According to HNMA, less than 1% of ITIN loans were in foreclosure as of mid-2008, compared with 1.2% for prime mortgages and nearly 11% for subprime mortgages.[26] In spite of their strong performance, ITIN mortgages were never purchased by government-sponsored enterprises Fannie Mae and Freddie Mac.[27] HNMA and other entities attempted to establish alternative secondary market sources for these loans, but these efforts were relatively small in scale and faced formidable challenges.[28] Lack of a large-scale secondary market was a major barrier to the growth of ITIN mortgages, as lenders had no choice but to maintain these loans in their portfolios.

From its inception, the ITIN mortgage market was complicated by political issues and uncertainties. There are no US laws that prohibit financial institutions from serving undocumented immigrants, or that restrict property ownership to US citizens or green card holders. However, widespread anti-immigrant sentiment—including within some financial institutions—has undermined efforts to bring undocumented immigrants into the financial mainstream. Many banks have cited, among their reasons for not serving undocumented immigrants, fears of anti-immigrant protests at their branches, backlash from existing customers, and negative press coverage.[29] Some banks have offered ITIN mortgages but not publicized them, relying instead on word-of-mouth within immigrant communities to attract borrowers. Others have offered ITIN loans only in certain markets, or even branches, within their service areas.

Regulatory Issues and Immigrants' Financial Access

Section 326 of the USA PATRIOT Act requires financial institutions to collect, at a minimum, the following information from new customers: name, date of birth, street address, and an identification number. For non-U.S. citizens, the identification number may be a Social Security number, Individual Taxpayer Identification Number (ITIN), or the number from a US or foreign government-issued ID that includes the person's photo or similar safeguard, and nationality or residence.

While these requirements are flexible and permit banks to accept, for example, foreign passports and consular identification cards (such as Mexico's matricula consular), they nonetheless have caused confusion among many financial institutions. While some banks have adopted flexible identification requirements in compliance with the law, others have developed policies that go far beyond what the law requires and that arguably have discriminatory impact on immigrants–for example, accepting only Social Security Numbers to open accounts or make loans.

For more information, see: NEDAP, *Promoting Financial Justice for Immigrant New Yorkers* (Aug. 2006); and *A Survey Report on Barriers Faced by Low Income Immigrants in NYC* (Feb. 2009).

Figure 8.3.

Concerns about immigration law enforcement have also chilled efforts to bring immigrants into the formal banking system. In the wake of stepped-up immigration raids in many communities, some banks feared becoming targets of law enforcement agencies, or expressed concerns about what recourse they would have to collect on loans if a borrower was detained or deported. On several occasions, members of Congress have introduced legislation to prohibit financial institutions from making mortgages or issuing credit cards to undocumented immigrants.[30] While these proposals have consistently failed, they have contributed to the sense among some banks that doing business with undocumented immigrants would expose their institutions to excessive political and legal risks.[31]

Advocates have also expressed concerns about ITIN mortgages, including excessively high fees and interest rates associated with ITIN loans made by some non-bank mortgage lenders. While some added cost to borrowers could arguably be justified by the more intensive underwriting required for ITIN loans, as well as lenders' need to maintain these loans in portfolio, a number of brokers and lenders have seemingly exploited the limited options available to homebuyers with ITINs.

Advocates have also raised concerns about the privacy of immigrant borrowers' information, in cases where ITIN mortgage loans have been sold or where financial institutions may have filed Suspicious Activity Reports (SARs) about borrowers.[32] A representative of a large national bank told advocates in 2006 that the bank routinely filed SARs on ITIN mortgage loan borrowers, not because the bank believed they had committed any crimes, but as a way to protect the institution against possible scrutiny or sanctions by examiners. FinCEN reported an increase in mortgage loan fraud SARs filed involving individuals with ITINs, beginning in 2004, which suggests that other banks may have followed similar practices. These filings raise concerns around unwarranted risks to which banks may be exposing immigrant home-buyers.[33] *(See Figure 8.4.)*

Like other mortgages loans, ITIN loans largely dried up with the collapse of the financial markets in 2008. Banco Popular suspended its ITIN mortgage lending outside of Texas in August 2008, citing "turbulent times" in the mortgage industry. Wells Fargo, which had begun a pilot-lending program in Los Angeles and Orange County, California, in 2005, never expanded it to other states. A representative of HNMA Funding Co., which had purchased approximately $200 million of ITIN mortgages before ending its secondary market program in June 2008, told a reporter that, "If the market closed for plain-vanilla loans, it is now more than closed for loans that fall outside the traditional mortgage pattern."[34] MGIC Investment Corp., which began offering mortgage insurance on ITIN loans in 2004, also exited the market in 2008, citing lack of sufficient demand.[35]

Not all lenders, however, have stopped making ITIN mortgages. Several community development credit unions and small banks continue to successfully lend to people with ITINs. Latino Community Credit Union, for example, with branches throughout North Carolina, has made close to 400

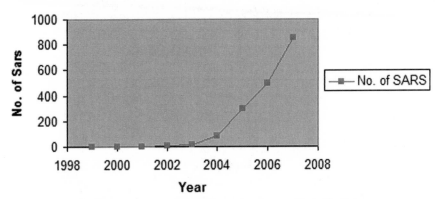

Figure 8.4. Mortgage Loan Fraud SARs Regarding Borrowers with ITINs.

mortgages to families where one or more borrowers provided an ITIN. In spite of the economic decline, the credit union has foreclosed on only four borrowers to date.[36]

RECOMMENDATIONS

Policymakers and enforcement agencies should expand fair housing and fair lending opportunities in immigrant communities by:

- *Amending fair housing and fair lending laws—including the federal Fair Housing Act—to explicitly prohibit discrimination against non-citizens and undocumented immigrants.* The Fair Housing Act, for example, currently prohibits discrimination on the basis of race, color, national origin and familial status, among other factors, but does not explicitly prohibit discrimination against non-citizen or undocumented immigrants. Some local governments have passed laws prohibiting housing discrimination on the basis of citizenship or immigration status, which can serve as models to strengthen federal statutes.[37]
- *Pressing regulated financial institutions to provide equitable banking and credit access in immigrant communities.* Low income and undocumented immigrants, in particular, face formidable barriers to fair financial services access, and are frequently relegated to high-cost and predatory financial services providers. Regulatory agencies that supervise banks should, at a minimum:
  - Jointly issue clear guidance to financial institutions affirming the legality under existing laws to open bank accounts and provide loans, including mortgages, to individuals regardless of their immigration status.
  - Train bank examiners and ensure consistent enforcement of rules. Many banks cite examiner scrutiny and fears of a "regulatory crackdown" as the basis for maintaining policies that effectively discriminate against immigrants.
  - Educate regulated institutions on ways to offer equitable banking and credit access to all communities within safety and soundness of banking laws, and in compliance with the Community Reinvestment Act and other statutes.
- *Evaluating the extent to which banks meet the credit needs of immigrant communities in Community Reinvestment Act examinations.* Consideration is already given to banks' provision of low-cost money transfer (remittance) services; the same could be done to encourage, for example, the opening of bank accounts and provision of credit to immigrants, including

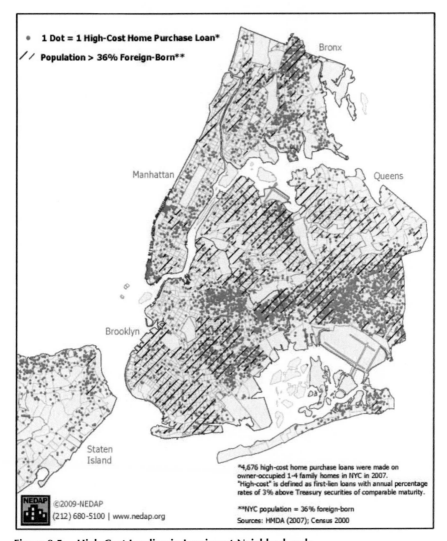

Figure 8.5.   High-Cost Lending in Immigrant Neighborhoods.

with ITINs. This should particularly apply to banks located in areas with high shares of low or moderate income immigrants.

- *Examining banks and lenders for possible discrimination against foreign-born individuals.* Regulators should flag and address instances in which financial institutions inquire about a customer's immigration status, for example, or offer costlier or inferior products to customers based on their immigration or citizenship status.

Figure 8.6.   Foreclosures in Immigrant Neighborhoods.

CONCLUSION

Immigrants represent an ever-growing percentage of residents in rural, urban and suburban communities throughout the United States. Additional
research is needed to identify the scale and nature of lending abuses leveled
at immigrants during the subprime lending boom, as well as the impact of
the foreclosure crisis on immigrant homeowners and communities. A better

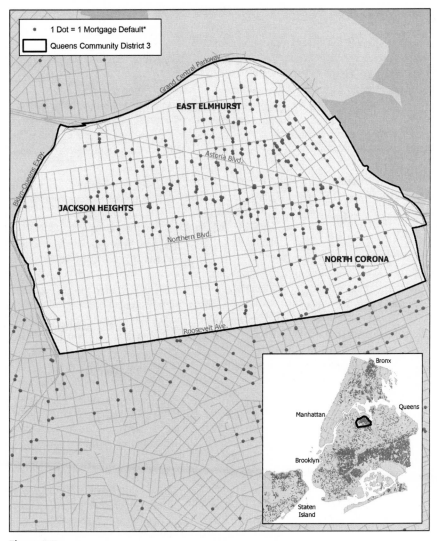

Figure 8.7.

understanding of barriers that different immigrant groups face in the housing and credit markets will be critical to policymakers, advocates and other stakeholders, as they work to reform the financial services system and expand fair lending and consumer protections. Addressing immigrant concerns must be viewed not as a marginal issue, but as increasingly fundamental to the enforcement of anti-discrimination statutes and to ensuring a fair and robust housing market going forward.

NOTES

1. Pratt Center for Community Development and New York Immigrant Housing Collaborative, *Confronting the Housing Squeeze. Challenges Facing Immigrant Tenants, and What New York Can Do* (October 2008).

2. Informal or illegally converted units include apartments created in the basements or attics of existing one- or two-family homes, without required permits. In many cases, immigrant homeowners struggling to make mortgage payments undertake these conversions to generate needed rental income. *See* Chhaya CDC, *Finding a Path to South Asian Community Development. A Report on the Housing Needs of South Asian Americans in New York City* (2001).

3. *See* Association for Neighborhood and Housing Development, *The Next Sub-Prime Loan Crisis: How Predatory Equity Investment is Undermining New York's Affordable Multi-Family Rental Housing* (2008).

4. The Fair Housing Act, Title VIII of the Civil Rights Act of 1968, prohibits discrimination in the sale, rental, and financing of homes on the basis of race, color, national origin, religion, sex, familial status and disability. Citizenship and legal immigration status are not explicitly covered under the Act; however, attempts to discriminate on these bases may violate FHA insofar as they result in unfair treatment of individuals of a particular race, national origin or other protected class.

5. National Commission of Fair Housing and Equal Opportunity, The Future of Fair Housing: Report of the National Commission on Fair Housing and Equal Opportunity (2008) ("Anti-immigrant ordinances are a particularly egregious example of the use of land use regulation to erect barriers to fair housing....Without the authority or expertise to determine a potential tenant's immigration status, a landlord may refrain from renting or leasing to anyone he suspects could be an undocumented immigrant, a behavior likely to lead to racial and ethnic profiling and discrimination against people of color, and most commonly, Latinos.")

6. Jill Esbenshade, Immigration Policy Center, American Immigration Law Foundation, *Division and Dislocation: Regulating Immigration through Local Housing Ordinances* (2007). *See* also "Towns Rethink Laws Against Illegal Immigrants," *available at* http://www.nytimes.com/2007/09/26/nyregion/26riverside.html.

7. *See*, e.g., Joint Center for Housing Studies, Harvard University, *The State of the Nation's Housing* (2009), *available at* http://www.jchs.harvard.edu/son/index.htm.

8. Joint Center for Housing Studies at Harvard University, *New Americans, New Homeowners: The Role and Relevance of Foreign-Born First-Time Homebuyers in the U.S. Housing Market* (Aug. 2002).

9. Pew Hispanic Center, *Through Boom and Bust: Minorities, Immigrants and Homeownership* (May 2009).

10. Pew, *Through Boom and Bust*.

11. Migration Policy Institute, *Immigrants and Homeownership in Urban America: An Examination of Nativity, Socio-Economic Status and Place* (2004).

12. 22% of Latinos, for example, have thin credit files or no credit history at all, compared to 4% of whites. Michael Stegman et al., "Automated Underwriting: Getting to 'Yes' for More Low-Income Applicants" (2001 presentation to the Research Institute for Housing America Conference).

13. 2000 Survey of Income Program Participation.

14. Subprime (or "high-cost") loans are defined in the Home Mortgage Disclosure Act as first-lien loans with annual interest rates of 3% or more, or second-lien loans with annual interest rates of 5% or more, above Treasury securities of comparable maturity.

15. Consumer Federation of America, *Exotic or Toxic? An Examination of the Non-Traditional Mortgage Market for Consumers and Lenders* (May 2006).

16. *See* Pew, *Through Boom and Bust, Minorities, Immigrants and Homeownership*. Pew found, for example, that of two counties with similar economic and demographic characteristics, the one whose immigrant share of the population was 10% higher than the other had a foreclosure rate that was 0.6% higher.

17. Neighborhood Economic Development Advocacy Project estimates, based on *lis pendens* filings obtained from Profiles Publications, Inc.

18. See http://www.chhayacdc.org/images/Chhaya Press Release and Supporting Materials 1 12 2009.pdf.

19. Interview with Seema Agnani, Executive Director, Chhaya CDC.

20. Interviews with Teresa Garcia, Asociación Tepeyac.

21. *See, e.g.,* Kirstin Downey, "Foreclosure Wave Bears Down on Immigrants," *Washington Post* (Mar. 6, 2007), and Brigid Schulte, *"'My House. My Dream. It Was All an Illusion,'"* *Washington Post* (Mar. 22, 2008).

22. ITINs are unique, nine-digit numbers issued by the IRS to individuals who are required to file tax returns or report other information to the IRS and who do not qualify for Social Security numbers. The IRS has issued more than 13 million ITINs since 1996. ITINs may be accepted, in conjunction with other identifying information, by financial institutions to open accounts and make loans.

23. Mari Gallagher, *Alternative IDs, ITIN Mortgages, and Emerging Latino Markets. See* also Miriam Jordan, "Home Loans to Illegal Immigrants Sturdy But Show Some Cracks," *The Wall Street Journal Online* (October 15, 2007). ("Illinois, Georgia, Indiana, Wisconsin and Texas are the top producers of ITIN mortgages, accounting for about 70% of the volume insured by MGIC.")

24. Nancy Mullane, "Politics Undercut Mortgages for Illegal Workers," NPR, *available at* http://www.npr.org/templates/story/story.php?storyId=96557544.

25. Rob Paral and Associates, *The Potential for New Latino Homeownership Among Undocumented Latino Immigrants*, prepared for the National Association of Hispanic Real Estate Professionals.

26. Miriam Jordan, "Mortgage Prospects Dim for Illegal Immigrants," *available at* http://online.wsj.com/article/SB122463690372357037.html.

27. Fannie Mae does not require that borrowers have a SSN, but it requires that they be lawfully present in the United States. *See* http://www.efanniemae.com/sf/formsdocs/forms/1003.jsp. Freddie Mac cited "political issues" that would need to be resolved before the agency looked into ITIN loans. *See* http://www.americancity.org/magazine/article/web-exclusive-undocumented-dream-gallagher.

28. Illinois and Wisconsin instituted programs to purchase ITIN and other nonconforming mortgages, but both stopped their programs after a few years—in the case of Wisconsin, after a state law was passed prohibiting ITIN mortgages. The National Federation of Community Development Credit Unions purchases nonconforming

loans—including ITIN mortgages—from member credit unions, offering a small secondary market for these institutions.

29. New South Federal Savings Bank in Birmingham, AL, for example, received hostile calls and emails, and was even threatened with a lawsuit for racketeering. *See* http://www.businessweek.com/magazine/content/05_29/b3943001_mz001.htm. These concerns have been fueled by prominent examples of media and customer backlash, e.g., against Bank of America after *The Wall Street Journal* reported that the bank was issuing credit cards to people who did not have Social Security Numbers. *See:* http://www.bankofamericaboycott.com.

30. In 2007, for example, Rep. John Doolittle, R-Calif, introduced H.R. 480 to amend the Truth in Lending Act to prohibit issuance of residential mortgages to any individual who lacks a Social Security Number.

31. Various state bills have similarly sought to prohibit banks from accepting Mexico's matrícula consular card as a valid form of identification to open accounts. Other states have attacked immigrants directly, by taxing their remittances sent to family members back home and arguably discouraging immigrants from using formal financial services channels.

32. Financial institutions are required to file Suspicious Activity Reports about customers' known or suspected criminal activity. The number of SARs filed by financial institutions has skyrocketed over the past decade, with depository institutions alone filing 732,563 SARs in 2008, compared to 203,538 in 2001. *See*: FinCEN, *The SAR Activity Review—By the Numbers*, Issue 13 (Jan. 2010).

33. The U.S. Department of Treasury's Financial Crimes Enforcement Network (FinCEN), which receives and tracks SARs, has attributed the increase in SARs to "defensive filing" by financial institutions that were "becoming increasingly convinced that the key to avoiding regulatory and criminal scrutiny under the Bank Secrecy Act is to file more reports, regardless of whether the conduct or transaction identified is suspicious." *See:* Statement of William J. Fox, Director FinCEN, Before the U.S. House of Representatives Committee on Financial Services Subcommittee on Oversight and Investigations (May 26, 2005).

34. Miriam Jordan, "Mortgage Prospects Dim for Illegal Immigrants."

35. Phone interview with Katie Monfre, MGIC (October 2009).

36. Interview with Luis Pastor, CEO of Latino Community Credit Union (January 2010).

37. *See*, e.g., NYC Human Rights Law, *available at* http://www.nyc.gov/html/cchr/html/hrlaw.html.

Chapter Nine

An Ethnographic View of Impact

Asset Stripping for People of Color

Hannah Thomas

I finished the interview with Edna and then used her bathroom, taking the opportunity to poke my head around the rest of the house. It was small. The bathroom was off the TV room and had a door through to the kitchen on the other side. In the dining room, the dining table was laid out with a full dinner set and tablecloth. There was a sofa and armchair in the living room area. It felt middle class, but not excessive; respectable, but certainly not extravagant. There were few knick-knacks or clutter in the house in general. The bathroom held a minimum of "stuff"—just hand soap and a small vase. The towels matched, but were frayed, indicating use and age. She came into the kitchen and opened up the blinds "to let fresh air into the house." She explained how her neighbor would help her out, and she'd help out the neighbor, like taking each other's trash out.

Edna was a grandmother. She'd been married, but was now separated and had bought a small home in a community in the southern part of Boston to look for a quieter, safer place to live. Two guys at a local mortgage company offered to help her buy the home, but they inflated her income on the loan application. She couldn't afford the mortgage payments, so she started using her 401K (retirement plan) to manage the mortgage payments and cover the deficit. She didn't feel like she had a choice.

An older woman, her health had started taking its toll and she was struggling to stay at work, meanwhile rapidly building up medical debts. She was in foreclosure now, about to lose her home, and any assets that she'd accumulated had been poured into the mortgage to save the house. She was a single, elderly African American woman.

We climbed into her car. She was wearing the housekeeping uniform for her job, so I asked her about her work. It was the second job that she'd taken on to afford the mortgage and it was on the other side of the city. She'd been sick this week and unable to work her first job, also in housekeeping. I asked about her family. Originally she was from Birmingham, Alabama. Her father was Jamaican. She had three kids and said it was rough at the moment; life was hard. When she asked, I told her I was studying inequality. She laughed, saying that I would find out about inequality through living it.

Edna was by no means unique. In the thirty-five interviews that I did with individuals in foreclosures around the city of Boston, Massachusetts, I encountered many situations like hers: people working hard to save their homes and using up their assets, like retirement plans and savings accounts, to do so. Most of the people I talked to bought a house to provide safety and stability, to live the "American Dream," and to secure a future for themselves and their children. But these individuals got caught up in the turbulence of a speculative housing market, where subprime mortgages were propelled by profit-driven Wall Street investors and the mortgage lenders and brokers who capitalized on the seemingly never-ending increases in housing prices, and the fees and interest rates they could extract.[1] In the following chapter, I plan to explore some of these stories and draw out some themes about what the current foreclosure crisis might mean in terms of losses, not just of people's homes, but also of their asset cushions, like retirement savings and their children's college savings.

FORECLOSURES

To date, policy reports have mainly focused on large scale studies of foreclosure, looking at the characteristics of the loans, with few studies of the details of people who are in foreclosure (race, age, family structure, class), let alone documenting their stories and experiences. As a result, we have a good idea of the types of loans that are going into foreclosure—subprime high loan-to-value ratios, often adjustable rate mortgages or interest-only mortgages with prepayment penalties and balloon payments (Affairs 2006; Center for Responsible Lending 2008; Ernst et al. 2006; Foote et al. 2008; Foote, Gerardi, and Willen 2008; Gerardi, Shapiro, and Willen 2007; Immergluck and Smith 2005; Newburger 2006; Quercia, Stegman, and Davis 2007). And we have a sense that these loans, and the associated foreclosures, have been disproportionately located in communities of color through spatial analyses of foreclosure filings and foreclosure sales (Reid 2009).

We also have a sense of some of the impacts of earlier waves of foreclosures on individual households in Europe from studies in Britain and Sweden that focused on health and psychological impacts. Nettleton (1998) found that the impact of mortgage arrears increases the frequency of visits to family practitioners in Britain. Nettleton suggested this was related to the basic lack of security and a social context in Britain where individuals were held responsible for foreclosure (repossession) (Nettleton and Burrows 1998).

Another study by Nettleton and Burrows (2001), based on interviews with 30 families, demonstrated increased autonomy (agency) as families fought to save homes at the same time as they experienced negative impacts on their health and emotions. Nettleton and Burrows describe this as the "new landscapes of precariousness."[2]

A study of repossessions in Sweden in the 1980s provides insight into the experiences of homeowners in that country (Bjork 1994). This study is particularly relevant since it followed a similar methodology to the current study, using interviews with homeowners who are experiencing loss of homeownership. The study also addresses a similar question of the experience of a home repossession (foreclosure). A critical observation from the study was that loss of homeownership was equivalent to loss of identity for homeowners. Bjork (1994) described the "general scheme of grief" she observed from her interviews: an initial stage of denial of the problem, followed by shock, then blame, action, bitterness, and finally constructive action. Bjork noted that many were forced to make decisions when they were at inappropriate stages of this "scheme of grief." Importantly, Bjork pointed to the tension between the commodity or investment value of the home, and the use-value of the home to the inhabiting family. These studies point to the social and psychological impacts on families, but they do not describe the financial impacts of repossession.

While the aggregate studies give us some sense of the scale of foreclosure, we are not able to clearly see the financial impact that foreclosures have on a family beyond just the actual loss of the house. The studies completed to date at the individual level offer insight into psychological and emotional processes, but they do not provide us with a clear picture of the financial impacts of foreclosure. We might expect that there are impacts on credit scores, financial savings and debts, on families' assets and wealth, and on the ability of parents to provide wealth to pass on to their children.

This study makes a first attempt to look at the financial impact of foreclosure on a family. It does not attempt to provide a representative sample of families in foreclosure, nor does it claim to look at the full range of possible impacts. Instead, it offers a detailed picture of a sample of families (n=30) who were in different stages of foreclosure in Boston in 2007 and 2008, exploring the financial path to foreclosure as well as the resulting impacts on the family's financial balance-sheet. The families in this study are predominantly families of color, and as we'll see, this follows the pattern of foreclosure petitions and foreclosure sales being disproportionately located in communities of color in Boston.

METHOD AND DATA—SAMPLE AND RECRUITMENT

The interviews used in this chapter were completed in two stages: as part of a partnership with the City of Boston; and subsequent interviews funded by the Department of Housing and Urban Development (HUD). The first set of data comes from semi-structured interviews with individuals who were in foreclosure and who lived in Boston. Interviews were not recorded, but detailed notes were taken. The second set of data comes from analysis of an additional five interviews in Boston with individuals who were in foreclosure between January and August 2008. These interviews were fully recorded and transcribed. The following analysis is based on coding and analysis of both sets of interviews.

Individuals were recruited through the City of Boston's database of foreclosures. Where phone numbers were publicly available, individuals were contacted and asked if they wished to participate in this research, with a full explanation of what was involved in the research. A time was scheduled that was convenient for the individual, or couple, and at a place chosen by the participant. In some cases this was their home that was in foreclosure; in other cases, participants felt more comfortable meeting in a coffee shop, local community facility, or other public space. The interview lasted between one-and-two hours, and covered how the person came to own a home, details of their mortgage, their financial situation including assets, debts, and other monthly payments, credit scores, approach to finances and details of how they came to be in foreclosure.

This set of interviews is geographically representative of the locations of foreclosures in Boston. Since there is no data at the individual level to know the racial distribution of foreclosures, it is unclear whether the interview sample was representative of the economic, demographic and social backgrounds of those in foreclosure. However, the themes emerging from the interviews are very similar, suggesting data saturation (Charmaz 2005). The purpose of this chapter is exploratory, and not broadly generalizable. This research, however, follows other studies that have attempted to look at similar questions, and it has struggled with the same set of challenges in recruiting individuals to take part in the process (Bjork 1994). Some of those challenges include: families being in a particularly stressful moment in their lives and as a result unwilling to speak with the interviewer; families no longer living at the address of the property in foreclosure; disconnected telephone numbers as a result of financial difficulties; and a general unwillingness to share personal financial information with the interviewer.

BOSTON FORECLOSURES

Foreclosures in Boston have, as in many cities (see Cleveland, Ohio for example), been predominantly located in communities of color. In California, black and Hispanic borrowers with good FICO scores were four times more likely to receive a higher-cost mortgage (proxy for subprime) than were white or Asian borrowers (13), with the result that the percentage of black and Hispanic home purchase borrowers in default (the stage prior to foreclosure) were four-to-five times higher than for white borrowers (28) (Reid and Laderman 2009). For Massachusetts, Gerardi and Willen (2008) found that African American borrowers were as much as 2.3 times more likely to go into foreclosure than whites. For Boston, by mapping out where foreclosures are located, we can quite easily see the alignment of foreclosures with all their associated negative impacts, with census tracts predominantly black or Hispanic (see Figure 9.1).

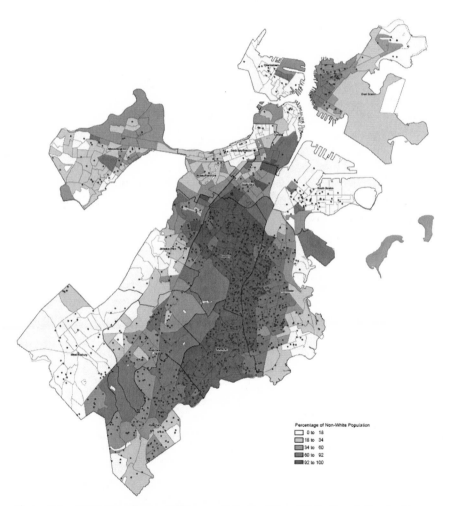

Figure 9.1.   2006 Foreclosure Petitions and Percent Non-White Population by Census Block Group (provided courtesy of the City of Boston).

The interviews that I conducted were predominantly with black immigrants, or African American individuals and their families, or Latinos. I did not interview any Asian American families, and I was only able to recruit two white families in foreclosure. There is likely a bias in my sample, however, as with all studies of foreclosure. I was unable to determine whether my sample was representative demographically of the full population currently in foreclosure since we do not yet have the ability to describe the full population of foreclosures, for example in terms of race, income, family structure.[3] While we can understand patterns of foreclosures at the neighborhood level, and some studies are beginning to describe the race of individual borrowers in foreclosure, this has yet to happen in Boston, nor for national data. Table 9.1 at the end of this chapter provides a breakdown of the demographics of the participants interviewed, with comparisons for foreclosures in Boston where available.

There are generally two types of foreclosures that occur in the United States depending on the state's legal process: judicial and non-judicial. In a judicial state, the foreclosure process includes a court hearing where the borrower has an opportunity to challenge the foreclosure. Massachusetts in a non-judicial state and so no opportunity exists for a homeowner to challenge a foreclosure in a court hearing. So, once a mortgage is delinquent for 90 days, i.e. the servicer or bank has not received payment for 90 days, foreclosure proceedings begin, and a letter is sent to the debtor, asking for full payment. If full payment is not received, the lender/servicer will begin foreclosure proceedings. Usually, somewhere between three and six months later (although this is currently potentially longer because of the volume of foreclosures and as a result of the moratorium), there will be a foreclosure auction where the house is sold to the highest bidder, which is often the bank. The property is then held by the bank as a real-estate owned (REO) property, and attempts are made to sell it, sometimes in bulk, and sometimes as an individual property.

FROM BUYING TO LOSING THE HOME

With the exception of the two white homeowners who had received a foreclosure petition, all the families I interviewed had subprime mortgages. This is perhaps no surprise because subprime mortgages have a far higher rate of foreclosures. It should also be of no surprise then to learn that all of these subprime mortgages were adjustable rate mortgages, which analysis has shown to be at a 50% higher likelihood of entering foreclosure (Quercia, Stegman, and Davis 2007), and that all of them had very high loan-to-value ratios—the mortgage being around 90–100% of the value of the house. From basic loan underwriting, this is a risky proposition. Families of color in Boston whom I interviewed were in inherently risky subprime mortgage products.

In addition, many of these families spoke about the mortgage being unaffordable from the start. They understood that the mortgage payment was too high to be affordable at loan closing, and they recalled telling the mortgage broker about their observation, only to be told that they could refinance six months later. For others, they had discovered, through the process of foreclosure counseling, that they had been subject to fraudulent activity in which their income had been inflated without their knowledge. Again, no surprise, as the Massachusetts attorney general has litigated several lawsuits against subprime mortgage lenders. For example, a judge issued a ruling of unfair and deceptive lending against Fremont Investment and Loan and its parent Fremont General Company under Massachusetts Consumer Protection laws.[4] What the interviews started to reveal was the cycle that families moved into once they had purchased a house with a toxic subprime loan. Figure 9.1 shows the cycle that families now find themselves within.

The household or individual encountered a financial emergency, such as any combination of an unaffordable mortgage, loss of a job, divorce, or other economic hardship.[5] At this point, the household had various options: to sell the house, to continue trying to pay the mortgage or let the mortgage go into default.

How did I arrive at foreclosure?

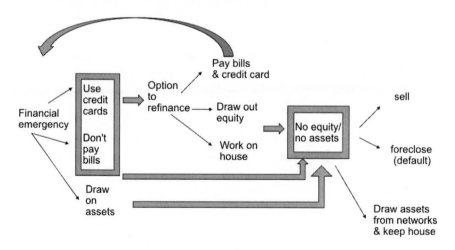

Context of a subprime loan makes financial emergency more like financial crisis

Figure 9.2.   The path to foreclosure.

Usually the household in my interviews decided to continue trying to pay the mortgage. To then cope with the financial emergency, the household or individual would use their credit cards,[6] not pay other household bills described as "robbing Peter to pay Paul",[7] or draw on savings and other assets available to the household.[8] If there was still equity in the house, the household might refinance and use the equity from the house to pay off credit cards or bills that had become delinquent. Alternatively, the household could refinance earlier in the cycle instead of using credit cards or not paying the bills. In some cases, individuals refinanced their houses believing that it would make the mortgage payments more affordable, a solution, as they saw it, to their financial predicament.[9]

Using such methods, the household could recover apparent financial stability. But the reality was that the entire financial situation was not sustainable. Another financial emergency might create urgency and stress again, further exacerbating this cycle. Eventually at some point in the cycle the household had no equity or assets remaining, and the household either attempted to sell the property, or most often defaulted on the mortgage payments, or both. In some cases, at this final point, a household might be able to draw some assets from family or friends and could maintain the property for some additional time, but this was rare in this study.

HOME AS STABILITY AND SECURITY: CONTEXTS FOR FINANCIAL DECISION-MAKING

The decisions that are made along the way towards foreclosure for the household are taken in the context of life position and meanings associated with the home. In other words, the decisions to make the mortgage payment and build up credit card debt, or to make the mortgage payment at the expense of not paying other bills, will be made in the context of what the house means to a household, family or individual.

For example, drinking a coffee after he'd talked to me about why he bought a house, Charles, a Haitian immigrant living in Roslindale, spoke about his motivations as he tried to explain his current decisions about his home in light of being in foreclosure:

> *I mean everything I do, I do it for my daughter. I mean I don't do it for myself. I'm done. I'm a done deal. I'm living life. ...So I think the good Lord will come up for me, and show me, lead me to the right place. And get things back for, provision for her. She will be, cause I want her to be happy, not struggling like I'm struggling. This thing will ride out for her.*

This quote gives a real picture of the way that Charles was making decisions about his home based on his daughter. All the specific meanings associated with the home, and the resulting decisions he was making, were within this broader framework of looking out for his daughter's future. His role of being a father was informing how he struggled to make sure that he was providing her with a financially secure future, ensuring that he continued to own a home. The house specifically became a means to provide future economic security for his daughter.

Richard was a self-employed 61–year-old African American man whose income had declined each year. He had bought the house to stabilize his housing costs, but instead had ended up in a subprime adjustable rate mortgage where the payments were becoming too much to handle.

". . .the rentals were as high as the mortgage... in this point in our life, we needed to have, something that we owned so we could, as I said, try to have a steady cost we could fix within my fixed income."

Richard saw the house as a way to provide a more secure situation for himself and his wife as they approached retirement.

As heads of households found themselves in a mortgage they couldn't afford, unable to see a clear way out, they were trying to make the best of it, and find a way to keep the house, a place full of meaning for themselves and their families, even if it meant spending down their assets built up over years.

ASSET STRIPPING

In conventional lending banks want to make sure that the potential borrower has sufficient financial assets to allow continued repayment of the loan in a period of unemployment or sickness. Responsible lenders will take into account savings and other financial assets in thinking about this ability to repay. But responsible lenders also try to make sure that the loan they give to a borrower is affordable and not inherently set up to continually be more expensive than the borrower can afford, nor to consistently and regularly increase. In contrast, the subprime mortgages that were being made between 2000–07 were often not only ignoring a borrower's ability to repay, but were frequently also set up to constantly increase (e.g. hybrid ARMs and Option ARMs).

The mortgages of those interviewed were large (median $304,925), reflecting high house prices in the Boston metropolitan region. As a result, the mean annual mortgage-payment-to- income ratio was 58.44%, and the median was 54.04%. The minimum was 21.25% and the maximum 167.29% (based on current income, and current monthly mortgage payment). This mortgage-payment-to-income ratio does not account for payment increases anticipated from scheduled adjustable rate mortgages. The Department of Housing and Urban Development considers that for a housing payment to be affordable, it should not be more than 30% of the monthly income. Only two individuals were not paying more than 30% of their monthly income on the mortgage payment alone (not including taxes and insurance). This is certainly far from the ideal of responsible lending described above.

The interviews suggest that the only way many borrowers had to try and make the monthly mortgage payments and keep their house was to draw on cash reserves and other financial assets they might have (savings, retirement plans, college savings plans), or to increase their debt levels (home equity, credit cards, personal loans). This process is one that in a best-case scenario prevents a family from building up protective assets, and in a worse case scenario steadily strips a household of what little assets it might have. This process is not necessarily problematic if the use of assets is to respond to a temporary cash-flow challenge or a temporary income reduction. But in the case of these subprime mortgages, the monthly payment was usually unsustainable from the beginning, with temporary financial emergencies hastening the instability. Instead of assets providing a temporary buffer, they were rapidly being depleted with little chance of replenishment.

Drawing on the strength of a borrower's desire to own and keep their house, a lender can draw large amounts of regular monthly payments that are structured to provide homeownership at a premium (through higher interest rates), as well as extracting a variety of late, and other fees from the savings that a family has been attempting to accrue. As families headed towards delinquency and foreclosure, their credit scores sank lower and lower.[10] The implication is that all aspects of these families' lives are now impacted. A low credit score can make it harder to get insurance, to access new loans, to find an apartment or even to find employment. Coupled with the asset stripping, this extends the financial losses of a family beyond just the loss of the house and assets.

Charles, introduced above, had bought a house that ended up needing more repairs than his housing inspector had found. He'd originally bought the house to build equity to send his daughter to college and provide a home for her. A Haitian immigrant, the American Dream of social mobility sounded loud and clear. To buy the house, he got 100% financing with a subprime mortgage that was clearly too expensive for the income he received from driving taxis. He described how he'd decided to use the modest amounts of money he'd managed to save for his seven-year-old daughter's college tuition to keep paying the mortgage, after he'd exhausted the $8,000 he had in savings. Now he was losing the house, finally giving up the battle he'd been fighting to keep some social mobility and opportunity for his daughter. His credit score had "crashed" into the 400s and he owed extensive credit card debt, having poured more than $22,000 into house repairs, while trying to meet his monthly mortgage payment.

Doris met me in a coffee shop in Jamaica Plain. She'd lived in Boston her whole life and in her current house for more than 20 years, which had been owned by her grandmother before her. She had two young sons, and due to mental health problems she had recently lost her job as a special education teacher. She described a systematic and ongoing process of asset stripping, from predatory contractors in the 1990s that did shoddy work at great expense, to a mortgage well beyond her current ability to afford today. Particularly egregious, she and her husband got caught with a $20,000 pre-payment penalty prior to the passage of a 2005 Massachusetts anti-predatory lending law. That penalty quickly reduced the equity in their home when they refinanced to a lower interest rate. She desperately wanted to keep her grand-mother's house, especially because of her children. But real estate agents had begun showing the property and she was resigning herself to losing it.

These stories represent an unknown, but likely important percentage of homeowners who are currently in foreclosure in Boston's communities of color. They represent families who were slowly working towards middle-class status—college education for themselves with 401K plans, college aspirations for their children, and growing levels of homeownership. The reality is that as this foreclosure crisis worsens, more of these families who had been gaining some social mobility will be losing their financial footing, sliding back into a financially-precarious situation.

In Massachusetts, evidence is mounting that a traumatic story of distress and asset stripping in communities of color is occurring. Prior to 2006, the increases in black homeownership paid off for families when they were able to sell their homes.. But by 2007, if a black homeowner was moving out of homeownership it was mostly through foreclosure (Gerardi and Willen 2008). The gains in homeownership of the 2000s for black and Hispanic families that resulted from the subprime mortgage market start to look like a failed experiment that has left black and Hispanic households in a worse financial condition than if they had never owned a house, not to speak of the psychological distress imposed on these families.

IMPLICATIONS FOR THE NEXT GENERATION

While the interviews offer little direct insight into the picture for the next generation, they do suggest significant impacts. Children who hoped to attend college have fewer options for help from their parents as houses and any equity and assets owned by the families are lost. Charles, the Haitian immigrant, had started a small college savings fund for his young daughter, but he used it to keep up with the mortgage payments for an unaffordable subprime loan. He was precariously close to losing the house and any hope of future home equity when I spoke with him in 2008. We know from work by Thomas Shapiro (Shapiro 2004) of the important role that parents play in helping out at key moments by leveraging their own assets for their children.

On the other end of the spectrum, as parents age, the security provided by owning a home and the possibility of using home equity as the means to cover retirement costs will no longer be available. This study points to the possible impacts of older black and Hispanic families being unable to finance their retirement through their homes. As noted by Richard, an African American man in his sixties who'd cared for his own parents, and put his children through college: *"What's happened with my father was… he was able to sell the house and have a nice nest egg to go into his independent living place. I have no nest egg and this house probably in ten years would've been a nice little nest egg to have." … plans just didn't work out the way I had envisioned them to."* The question is, who is going to pay for Richard's retirement? Will it be his children?

If Gerardi and Willen's study bears out beyond Massachusetts, the increases in black-and-Hispanic homeownership during the last decade may well have been lost in foreclosure and distressed sales. It seems not a question of whether, but more of how the specific details of this intergenerational impact will play out. These questions have yet to be answered.

POLICY IMPLICATIONS

This study can only suggest the full picture of what is happening for families of color in cities across America. We need to look more closely at the patterns of asset use during financially difficult times across different demographics to understand to what degree the patterns we can see here play out for a broader range. Particularly for black and Hispanic families, studies are pointing to the disproportionate impacts of foreclosures. Understanding the processes of asset loss playing out for these families, we must conclude that there will be substantial impacts from this foreclosure crisis on the racial wealth divide.

There are significant ways that policy-makers can act at both the macro and micro level. At the macro level, they need to look at the system of mortgage lending that has created such disproportionate levels of subprime mortgage lending and foreclosures in communities of color. We have seen

Table 9.1. **Characteristics of Interview Participants with Comparable Data for Boston (where available)**

Category	Interviews	City of Boston Foreclosure Petitions (Where Available 2006)
African American or black immigrant	24 (80%)	unknown
White	2 (7%)	unknown
Hispanic	4 (13%)	unknown
Immigrant	12 (40%)	unknown
Mean age	50.2 years	unknown
Median time in house	2.5 years	3.7 years
Married or living with partner	14 (47%)	unknown
Single	16 (53%)	unknown
Female headed	11 (37%)	unknown
Neighborhood		
Dorchester	11 (37%)	430 (27%)
Roxbury	3 (10%)	283 (18%)
Mattapan	5 (17%)	190 (12%)
Hyde Park	4 (13%)	200 (13%)
Central	1 (3%)	16 (1%)
Jamaica Plain	1 (3%)	56 (4%)
East Boston	2 (7%)	64 (4%)
South End	1 (3%)	25 (2%)
Roslindale	2 (7%)	
Current Household Annual Income		
<80% Area Median Income	17 (57%)	unknown
80–100% Area Median Income	5 (17%)	unknown
>100% Area Median Income	7 (23%)	unknown
Education Level		
Graduate School	4 (13%)	unknown
Completed College	3 (10%)	unknown
Some college	8 (27%)	unknown
Beyond high school not college	3 (10%)	unknown
High school graduate	7 (23%)	unknown
High-school Drop-out	2 (7%)	unknown
Renters present	14 (47%)	unknown
Housing Type		
Condo	6 (20%)	29.6%
Single Family	10 (33%)	25.1%
Two Family	10 (33%)	25.2%
Three Family	4 (13%)	20.1%
Median amount of mortgage	$304,925	$311,920[i]
Median purchase price of house	$292,000	$300,000[ii]

[i]Suffolk Registry of Deeds, Department of Neighborhood Development internal Policy Development and Research department analysis of foreclosure petitions between 1/1/2006 and 12/31/2006. Data available for 89% of records.
[ii]Ibid. Data available for 81% of records.

from programs such as the Community Advantage Program at Self-Help Credit Union, as well as with Neighborhood Services of America (NHSA), that safe mortgage products are less risky with risky borrowers, (i.e., lower priced mortgage products can mean successful homeownership with low overall foreclosure rates.) By expanding such programs and incentivizing prime mortgage originators to extend credit to communities of color, and by addressing the hesitancy of people like those I interviewed about going to their bank (for they all had checking and savings accounts), we might find ways to build sustainable homeownership in communities of color.

At the individual level we need to start thinking about ways to build and protect assets. How can mortgage originators take account of the asset vulnerability of potential borrowers? And are there ways that we can collectivize some of the risk so that we build programs and structures that can assist asset-vulnerable populations when they encounter financial emergencies, such as community resource pools available to help borrowers cover the mortgage payment during a period of temporary unemployment.

In protecting assets, we can structure earlier counseling to help borrowers, before they become delinquent, develop a strategy to work with their financial goals, such as retirement security or saving for their children's college education. If we understand the motivational contexts for their financial decisions, the counseling may be more effective. Currently, foreclosure counseling kicks in after the borrower is delinquent, and as a result the strategy must be one of crisis management rather than proactively considering the whole financial picture that envelops a borrower.

BIBLIOGRAPHY

Affairs, Texas Department of Housing and Community. "A Study of Residential Foreclosures in Texas." edited by H. a. C. Affairs, 2006

Bjork, Mia. 1994. "Investigating the experience of repossession: A Swedish example." *Housing Studies* 9:511–530.

Center for Responsible Lending. "Updated Projections of Subprime Foreclosures in the United States and Their Impact on Home Values and Communities." Center for Responsible Lending, Durham, North Carolina, 2008.

Charmaz, Kathy. "Grounded Theory in the 21st Century: Applications for Advancing Social Justice Studies." *The SAGE Handbook of Qualitative Research*, edited by N. Denzin and Y. Lincoln, 2005.

Ernst, Keith, Kathleen Keest, Wei Li, and Ellen Schloemer. "Losing Ground: Foreclosures in the Subprime Market and their Cost to Homeowners," 2006.

Foote, Chris, Kristopher Gerardi, Lorenz Goette, and Paul Willen. "Subprime Facts: What (We Think) We Know about the Subprime Crisis and What We Don't." Federal Reserve Bank of Boston, 2008.

Foote, Christopher L., Kristopher Gerardi, and Paul Willen. "Negative Equity and Foreclosure: Theory and Evidence." *Public Policy Discussion Paper*. Boston: Federal Reserve Bank of Boston, 2008.

Gerardi, Kristopher, Adam Hale Shapiro, and Paul Willen. "Subprime Outcomes: Risky Mortgages, Homeownership Experiences and Foreclosures." Federal Reserve Bank of Boston, 2007.

Gerardi, Kristopher and Paul Willen. 2008. "Subprime Mortgages, Foreclosures, and Urban Neighborhoods." in *Public Policy Discussion Papers*: Federal Reserve Bank of Boston.

Immergluck, Dan and Geoff Smith. "Measuring The Effect Of Subprime Lending On Neighborhood Foreclosures." *Urban Affairs Review* 40:362–389, 2005.

Nettleton, Sarah and Roger Burrows. "Mortgage debt, insecure home ownership and health: an exploratory analysis." *Sociology of Health & Illness* 20:731–753, 1998.

"Families coping with the experience of mortgage repossession in the 'new landscape of precariousness'." *Community, Work & Family* 4:253–272, 2001.

Newburger, Harriet. "Foreclosure Filings and Sheriff's Sales Experienced by Low-Income, First-Time Home Buyers." *Housing Policy Debate* 17:341–387, 2006.

Petersen, Chris. "Predatory Structured Finance." *Cardozo Law Review* 28, 2007.

Quercia, Roberto, Michael Stegman, and Walter Davis. "The Impact of Predatory Loan Terms on Foreclosures: The Special Case of Prepayment Penalties and Balloon Payments." *Housing Policy Debate* 18:311–146, 2007.

Reid, Carolina. "The Untold Costs of Subprime Lending: The Impacts of Foreclosure on Communities of Color in California. " Federal Reserve Bank of San Francisco, 2009.

Reid, Carolina and Elizabeth Laderman. "The Untold Costs of Subprime Lending: Examining the Links among Higher-Priced Lending, Foreclosures and Race in California." Paper presented at the Institute for Assets and Social Policy, Brandeis University, 2009.

Shapiro, Tom. *The Hidden Cost of Being African American*, 2004.

NOTES

1. The subprime mortgage market transitioned from including three stakeholders in the 1970s to over 40 by 2007, Petersen, Chris. 2007. "Predatory Structured Finance." *Cardozo Law Review* 28..

2. Nettleton's notion of a "landscape of precariousness" is embodied in work by Jacob Hacker (2006) in his book *The Great Risk Shift*. Hacker suggests families are living in a world where risk is being taken on increasingly by the individual or family, instead of institutions and governments. This creates a precarious existence that Nettleton suggests increases stress.

3. There is a lack of available data on the distribution of foreclosures by race and other demographic details. There has been some attempts to merge Home Mortgage Disclosure Act data with other sources of data that include loan performance, but we still do not have detailed breakdowns at the city level available.

4. Commonwealth of Massachusetts v. Fremont Investment & Loan & Fremont General Corporation. No. 08–J-118. May 2, 2008. By the Court (COHEN, J.).

5. Many of the people interviewed had experienced a small negative shock, such as a brief period of unemployment, loss of rental income, and temporary property tax increases that led to missing one or two mortgage payments. These events impacted them financially, but for some of these individuals it appeared realistic to get back on a payment plan with their mortgage. However, servicers were reported as being hard to reach, unresponsive, inflexible, and refused to take payment. Arrearage quickly built up where an interviewee had been trying to negotiate, and quickly tens of thousands of dollars were owed. Without large asset pools to draw on, families found they couldn't get back on track with payments. This lack of flexibility appears to be amplifying the effects of negative economic shocks to a family's ability to maintain the mortgage.

6. Twenty-three people (77%) had credit card debt. The mean outstanding balance was $7,066, the median was $5,000, the maximum $29,600 and the minimum $80. Other debts included medical debts, student loans and car loans. Many individuals identified themselves as debt averse, even though they did have some level of debt. This ranged from statements such as making attempts to pay off all their credit card debt to become debt free, to discussing the use of minimal debt to achieve necessary goals, to literally only paying cash for items needed. Several individuals used their mortgage refinance to consolidate their credit card debt into the mortgage, usually at the suggestion of the mortgage broker. This will mean that the credit card debt reflected above is lower for some than it might otherwise have been.

7. Many families were *"robbing Peter to pay Paul,"* choosing which other bills not to pay, in order to make sure they paid the mortgage, since they wanted to avoid losing the house at all costs. This led to declining credit scores, and mounting utility bills, putting them in a more precarious financial position for the long-term. Families reported high levels of stress from worrying about how to pay the mortgage. This stress was adversely impacting family relationships and their own health. Families were trying to remain self-sufficient, not wanting to be a burden to anyone, until their financial situation had become a crisis.

8. Twenty-four people, or four out of five of those interviewed either currently had, or had had in the recent past 401Ks or equivalent retirement accounts. Fourteen (47%) had depleted their 401Ks and equivalents to pay the mortgage and bills, or to complete repairs on the house. Every person interviewed had a savings account, the vast majority (n=27) of them had depleted their savings accounts to pay for their mortgages and other bills.

9. Eleven households (37%) refinanced to lower their monthly mortgage payments.

10. Most of those interviewed presented a picture of confusion, fear and lack of power in dealing with their credit score. They knew their credit score if they had attempted to refinance recently. Many described their fear in looking at it, noting that it was a "depressing" and "stressful" experience. Most also anticipated that their credit score was not very good at the moment. " *it's not very good. What would I look at it for? I know what it's going to say…*" CN1 "*I try not to look at my credit score. I can't take it.*" YE1.

Three of those interviewed looked at their credit scores regularly and spoke with some sense of control about their score. Despite usually not knowing their credit scores, those at risk of delinquency or foreclosure knew and anticipated that their credit score would soon be going down due to likely problems paying bills on time. This indicates that there is a general level of understanding about the credit report system, but a lack of engagement in managing their credit score. A few individuals identified their low credit score as of concern if they lost the house, particularly in gaining a new place to live.

Chapter Ten

Affirmatively Furthering Fair Housing

A Critical Component of the Neighborhood Stabilization Program

Ira Goldstein, Kennen Gross, and
Dan Urevick-Ackelsberg

In August 2009, Westchester County (New York) and the Anti-Discrimination Center (ADC), a New York City, New York based non-profit group that "...works to prevent and remedy all forms of discrimination in housing, employment, education and public accommodations through advocacy, litigation, education, outreach, monitoring, and research"[1] reached a very novel settlement of its lawsuit filed under the False Claims Act (the Claims Act). ADC alleged that Westchester County violated the Claims Act by repeatedly falsely certifying that the county was in compliance with the affirmatively-furthering-fair-housing provisions of the federal Fair Housing Act (FHAct). Specifically, ADC's lawsuit alleged that while applying for, and in receipt of federal housing dollars, Westchester County misled federal officials as to what it was doing to uphold its federally-mandated responsibility to *affirmatively further fair housing* (AFFH).[2]

The FHAct and regulations implementing the Community Development Block Grant program require that recipients of federal funds administer their programs in a manner that affirmatively furthers fair housing. The ADC alleged that despite continuing high levels of segregation in many of its municipalities, Westchester County repeatedly certified that it was in fact acting to AFFH. After three years of litigation, the ADC and Westchester County settled this dispute. The settlement agreement (Agreement) resulted in Westchester County agreeing to build 750 units of affordable housing in areas that are virtually all white, and to then aggressively market those units to African Americans and Hispanics so as to purposefully work to reverse the highly segregated settlement pattern in the county.[3] Regrettably, the "Amended Monitor's Report" to the court notes that six months after settlement, little progress had been made toward the specific terms of the Agreement.[4]

The Fair Housing Act

Sec. 808 (d)   Cooperation of Secretary and executive departments and agencies in administration of housing and urban development programs and activities to further fair housing purposes.

All executive departments and agencies shall administer their programs and activities relating to housing and urban development (including any Federal agency having regulatory or supervisory authority over financial institutions) in a manner *affirmatively to further* the purposes of this subchapter and shall cooperate with the Secretary to further such purposes. [Emphasis added]

Figure 10.1.

Thus, while the legal strategy of the Westchester complaint and Agreement was novel, it fits squarely within Congress' clear intention that the FHAct should be used to overcome racially segregated communities. In this instance, the Agreement required that the recipients of federal funds use those funds to *affirmatively* undo the pattern and impacts of this racially segregated county.

NEIGHBORHOOD STABILIZATION

At the same time as the ADC was reaching its agreement with Westchester County, cities across the country were completing applications for the second round of funding under the Neighborhood Stabilization Program (NSP). NSP is a program first passed and enacted towards the end of the Bush Administration ("NSP- 1")[5] as the housing and subprime-lending crisis reached a fever pitch. NSP was allocated a second round of funding ("NSP-2") in the American Recovery and Reinvestment Act of 2009. In general, NSP was designed to help municipalities stabilize "communities that have suffered from foreclosures and abandonment."[6] While cities could use the money for a number of different activities, including acquisition, demolition, rehabilitation, and land banking, the regulations and allocation-targeting formula prepared by HUD ensures that investments will be de-

Housing and Economic Recovery Act of 2008

Sec. 2301. EMERGENCY ASSISTANCE FOR THE REDEVELOPMENT OF ABANDONED AND FORECLOSED HOMES.

(c) Use of Funds-
    (2) PRIORITY – Any State or unit of general local government that receives amounts pursuant to this section shall, in distributing such amounts give priority emphasis and consideration to those metropolitan areas, metropolitan cities, urban areas, rural areas, low-and moderate-income areas, and other areas with thegreatest need, including those –
        (A) with the greatest percentage of home foreclosures;
        (B) with the highest percentage of homes financed by a subprime mortgage related loan; and
        (C) identified by the State or unit of general local government as likely to face a significant rise in the rate of home foreclosures.

Figure 10.2.

ployed in areas hardest hit by foreclosures and vacant properties. Because NSP funds are federal, like those involved in the Westchester County case, all NSP recipients are required to certify that they are spending NSP funds in a manner that is consistent with AFFH.

As the program's name implies, Congress' intent for NSP was to focus on specific *areas* damaged by the vacant property and foreclosure crisis, rather than on *individuals* personally facing foreclosure. Thus, while cities can build affordable housing with NSP funds, as the rules were originally written, they could not provide direct financial assistance to homeowners struggling with their mortgage payments, or engage in foreclosure-prevention efforts. While this may make sense for a program that was designed to be a place-based response to the foreclosure crisis' impact on cities and communities, there is an important consequence of the NSP's formula that housing advocates have warned HUD about since the program was promulgated.[7] Specifically, the FHAct requires that federal funds be spent in a manner that affirmatively furthers fair housing, but the singularity of the place-based implementation of NSP makes it difficult to reduce existing levels of segregation and may, in fact, further entrench racial segregation.

In an attempt to operationalize Congress' use of the phrase "areas with the greatest need," HUD created a scoring mechanism for both allocating funds to recipients and then highlighting areas within the recipient's area that should be prioritized for NSP funds.[8] Data problems aside, this was an extraordinary undertaking for HUD. However, researchers and fair housing advocates have repeatedly demonstrated that minority neighborhoods disproportionately experienced the adverse effects of subprime lending and the foreclosure crisis.[9] Oftentimes, those same communities became targets of abusive lenders as the absence of more mainstream lending sources created a void that predatory lenders could exploit.[10,11] It is not surprising then that a HUD risk score that looks at both the vacancy and foreclosure risks of a neighborhood, including a variable reflective of subprime lending activity as one of the key components, will certainly identify more minority neighborhoods as high risk than those that are predominantly white.

With respect to NSP implementation, HUD prescribed that NSP-2 funds be targeted to neighborhoods that scored at least an 18 (out of 20) on HUD's

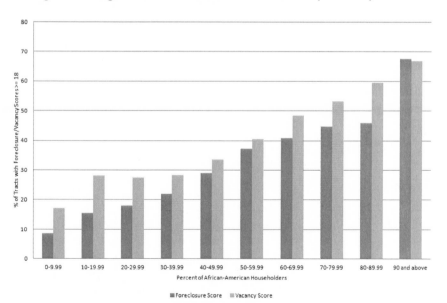

Figure 10.3. HUD Foreclosure and Vacancy Risk Scores.

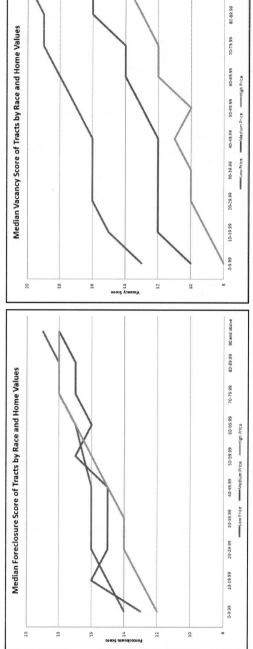

Figure 10.4.   Persistent Correlation Between African American Percentage and HUD Risk Scores (despite similar home prices).

foreclosure or vacancy index; in the alternative, HUD guidance offered that if areas with scores under 18 were addressed with NSP funding, the average risk score of all areas touched by NSP needed to be 18 or higher.[12] These elevated scores and their relationship to neighborhood racial composition is reasonably straightforward. That is, minority areas generally have higher scores and white areas generally lower scores.[13]

As the above chart and tables demonstrate, there is a straightforward relationship between the percentage of households in a neighborhood that is African American and the likelihood that the same neighborhood meets or exceeds the HUD prescribed NSP eligibility threshold. While neighborhoods that are virtually all white are fairly unlikely to be eligible for NSP-2 funds, areas that are mostly African American are much more likely to be eligible for funds. The relationship between racial composition and HUD risk scores holds even when tracts are grouped by whether they have high, medium or low priced homes.

In sum, the HUD risk scores increase the likelihood that communities will deploy their NSP funds in minority communities. Thus, most demolition, acquisition and rehabilitation and land banking will address properties in minority areas. On its face, this is a logical result given the nature of the problem. But add to this the requirement that affordable housing created with NSP funds must be preserved as affordable for the longest period possible, and the implication is that NSP may hinder minority communities from reaping the benefit of price appreciation when America's housing markets finally stabilize. In essence, the logical implication of creating NSP singularly as a place-based initiative that concentrates NSP activities predominantly in minority communities is that NSP, at best, removes some blight in minority areas without any impact on the racial segregation of communities. At worst, it may further concentrate permanently low- priced housing in minority areas, thereby exacerbating economic segregation. That is contrary to one of the key programmatic objectives of HUD's Community Development Block Grant program.

HOW CAN NSP BE ADMINISTERED TO MEET ALL OF CONGRESS' INTENTIONS, INCLUDING AFFH?

In order to meet the legal obligation to AFFH, NSP recipients must: (1) consciously and purposefully administer their programs, taking account of the racial composition of where funds are being obligated; (2) view NSP as one of several federal programs available to recipients, all of which have obligations to AFFH; (3) as regulations allow, administer NSP and other related federal programs as if there are both place-based and people-based components; and (4) utilize objective market data to design an implementation strategy because it is these data that can help HUD and its grantees succeed at the collection of its objectives.

CONCLUSION

Meaningful commitment to AFFH requires that grantees prioritize the stabilization of racially diverse communities–something that absolutely can be accomplished with commitment and creativity. To be most effective at AFFH, adding in a people-based component to NSP is critical. The people-based component could work in a few ways and may actually require grantees and HUD to look at NSP as one of several federal tools–in addition to CDBG–that allows them to help people and communities suffering from foreclosure and vacancy. For example, grantees could use CDBG to help lower income individuals in integrated communities to weather the recession. Pre-purchase and default and delinquency counseling, bridge loans, and other such interventions are all legitimate uses of CDBG funds. A complementary strategy is the more traditional affirmative marketing of properties and counseling of prospective homeowners in a manner that promotes desegregative moves. As in Westchester, affirmatively market properties to racially and ethnically diverse customer groups. By being purposeful and strategic both in the acquisition/ rehabilitation phase and in disposition phase, recipients could stabilize communities and meet their technical and substantive AFFH objectives. Each pot of federal funds may, taken alone, have provisions that make it difficult to AFFH. But taken together these federal funding programs can work to realize the goals of AFFH.

What are the challenges? First, NSP funding under rounds 1 and 2–and more recently under round 3–is inadequate for most locales to address even a small portion of their vacancy and foreclosure problems.[14] Second, nearly two-thirds of NSP-1 funds are used for acquisition and rehabilitation; another 10% are being used for new construction.[15] In that pursuit, recent research also shows that municipalities confronted a number of difficulties deploying those funds including: (1) locating real estate owned (REO) properties for acquisition; (2) competition from the private sector for these REO properties; (3) an absolute shortage of REO inventory in some markets; (4) the complexity of the federal (and local) requirements.[16]

NSP remains perhaps a once-in-a-lifetime opportunity to address the blighting influence of vacancy and foreclosure in communities, and it would be regrettable and contrary to the intentions of Congress to allow this to pass without meaningful compliance with AFFH.

NOTES

1. "About Us." The Anti-Discrimination Center, accessed 10/20/2010: http://anti-biaslaw.com/about-us.

2. Craig Gurian, Esq. "False Claims Act Complaint and Demand for Jury Trial." United States District Court, Southern District of New York. April 12th, 2006. http://www.antibiaslaw.com/sites/default/files/files/WestchesterFCAcomplaint_0.pdf. Accessed 10/20/2010.

3. United States District Court, Southern District of New York. "Stipulation and Order of Settlement and Dismissal." No. 06 Civ. 2860 (DLC). Document 320. Filed 08/10/2009. http://www.antibiaslaw.com/sites/default/files/files/SettlementFullText.pdf. Accessed 10/20/2010.

4. United States District Court, Southern District of New York "Amended Monitor's Report Regarding Implementation of the Stipulation and Order of Settlement and Dismissal for the Period of August 10, 2009 through February 10, 2010." No. 06 Civ 2860 (DLC). http://www.antibiaslaw.com/sites/default/files/files/0328–1.pdf. Accessed 10/20/2010.

5. NSP 1 was created as part of the Housing and Economic Recovery Act (HERA) passed in 2008. For more information on NSP-1 and the Housing and Economic Recovery Act, see HUD's website at http://www.hud.gov/offices/cpd/community development/programs/neighborhoodspg/nsp1.cfm.

6. U.S. Department of Housing and Urban Development. "Neighborhood Stabilization Program Grants: Introduction." For a general program description of NSP, see: http://hud.gov/offices/cpd/communitydevelopment/programs/neighborhoodspg/. Accessed 10/20/2010.

7. See, for example, letter to HUD Deputy Assistant Secretary Nelson Bregon, re: "Fair housing issues in the implementation of the Neighborhood Stabilization Program," March 24, 2009. Available at http://www.prrac.org/pdf/HUD_re_NSP ARRA_3–24–09.pdf, Accessed 10/20/2010. See also letter to HUD Secretary Shaun Donovan, February 6, 2009, available at http://www.prrac.org/pdf/HUD_stimulus_ 2–6–09.pdf. Accessed 10/20/2010.

8. HUD's estimation of local risk was based on an analysis of: (1) OFHEO data on decline in home values; (2) high cost loan data from HMDA; (3) unemployment rate; and (4) long term vacancy. Note that racial composition is not one of the variables used to estimate risk. For a complete description of HUD's method, see: http://www.huduser.org/datasets/nsp_target.html.

9. As examples of this research, see:
Debbie Gruenstein Bocian, Wei Li, and Keith S. Ernst. "Foreclosures by Race and Ethnicity: The Demographics of a Crisis."The Center for Responsible Lending,

June 18, 2010. Available at: http://www.responsiblelending.org/mortgage-lending/ research-analysis/foreclosures-by-race-and-ethnicity.pdf, accessed 10/20/2010.

or Debbie Gruenstein Bocian, Keith S. Ernst, and Wei Li. "Unfair Lending: The Effect of Race and Ethnicity on the Price of Subprime Mortgages." The Center for Responsible Lending, May 31, 2006. Available at: http://www.responsiblelending.org/mortgage-lending/research-analysis/rr011–Unfair_Lending-0506.pdf, accessed 10/20/2010.

or Debbie Gruenstein Bocian, and Richard Zhai. "Borrowers in Higher Minority Areas More Likely to Receive Prepayment Penalties on Subprime Loans." The Center for Responsible Lending, January, 2005. Available at: http://www.responsiblelending.org/mortgage-lending/research-analysis/rr004–PPP_Minority_Neighborhoods-0105.pdf, accessed 10/20/2010.

or U.S. Department of Housing and Urban Development. 2000. Unequal Burden: income and racial disparities in subprime lending in America.

or U.S. Department of Housing and Urban Development. 2000. Curbing Predatory Home Mortgage Lending. Bradford, Calvin. 2002.

"Bringing Subprime Mortgages to Market and the Effects on Lower Income Borrowers." Joint Center for Housing Studies of Harvard University, Building Assets, Building Credit Working Paper BABC 04–7.

10. See, for example, the Final Order issued by the Commonwealth Court of Pennsylvania in the case of Reginald McGlawn v. Pennsylvania Human Relations Commission (No. 2763 C.D. 2004 and No 6 C.D. 2005) accessed on 11/4/2010 from: http://www.aopc.org/OpPosting/CWealth/out/2763CD04_1–13–06.pdf.

11. See: Ira Goldstein. "Lost Values: A study of predatory lending in Philadelphia." Philadelphia, PA: The Reinvestment Fund, 2007. Available at: http://www. trfund.com/resource/downloads/policypubs/Lost_Values.pdf. Accessed 10/20/2010.

12. See: Housing and Urban Development, "Neighborhood Stabilization Program 2: Frequently Asked Questions," p. 3. Available at: http://www.hud.gov/offices/cpd/communitydevelopment/programs/neighborhoodspg/pdf/nsp2faq.pdf. Accessed 10/20/2010.

13. To see HUD Foreclosure and vacancy data for any neighborhood in the United States, visit PolicyMap, TRF's mapping and information tool, at www.PolicyMap.com.

14. Ira Goldstein. "Maximizing the Impact of Federal NSP Investments through the Strategic Use of Local Market Data." REO & Vacant Properties. Boston: The Federal Reserve Banks of Boston and Cleveland and the Federal Reserve Board, 2010. P. 66, Table 1. Available at http://www.bos.frb.org/commdev/REO-and-vacant-properties/ 65–Goldstein.pdf, accessed 10/20/2010.

15. See "HUD NSP-1 Reporting, August 2010 Snapshot Report," p. 2. Available at http://hudnsphelp.info/media/snapshots/08-31-2010/1PW-SUMMARY-08312010. pdf, accessed 10/20/2010.

16. Harriet Newburger, "Acquiring Privately Held REO Properties with Public Funds: The Case of the Neighborhood Stabilization Program." See also Craig Nickerson, "Acquiring Property for Neighborhood Stabilization: Lessons Learned from the Front Lines." Both contained in REO & Vacant Properties. Boston: Federal Reserve Banks of Boston and Cleveland and the Federal Reserve Board, 2010.

Chapter Eleven

Fannie, Freddie, and the Future of Fair Housing

Jillian Olinger

Research and analysis of Fannie Mae and Freddie Mac (the Enterprises) reveals two key takeaways. First, Fannie and Freddie were neither outright responsible for the current subprime and foreclosure crisis, nor will their restructuring alone eradicate the problem without broader financial reform. Second, sustainable homeownership, especially for marginalized borrowers, is not just about turning on the spigot of credit. Sustainable homeownership is about many factors, including human capital and mobility. We need to address the bigger picture of sustainable homeownership, research the different paths that lead to sustained homeownership for marginalized groups, and then determine how Fannie and Freddie can best be restructured to be more responsive to targeted groups' needs. The literature to date is largely silent on how policy in general, and Fannie and Freddie in particular, could be restructured or managed differently to improve sustainable homeownership in neighborhoods of opportunity.

This chapter represents a first step in that direction. It begins with a brief discussion on the key players influencing Fannie and Freddie, past and present; next, it provides an abbreviated history of how the Enterprises' roles and missions have changed through the years. It goes on to discuss the Enterprises' obligations to affirmatively further fair housing, and the outcomes of the Enterprises' activities with regards to low- and moderate-income borrowers, respectively. The chapter concludes with a call to action for developing an affirmative fair housing agenda for Fannie and Freddie.

INTRODUCTION

The spectacular failure of Fannie Mae and Freddie Mac in 2008 and their subsequent conservatorship has drawn increasing attention to what went right, and what went wrong, with Fannie and Freddie, as policymakers, advocates, and analysts alike grapple with what the future holds for the Enterprises, and for the US housing financial system as a whole. As we continue in this debate, it is critical to bear in mind that Fannie and Freddie were not the sole source of the current subprime and foreclosure crisis, nor is their restructuring the only solution. Indeed, "the systemic failures stemmed from the proliferation of poorly underwritten mortgages channeled through the so-called shadow banking system of unregulated private label securities."[1] The US mortgage system is best characterized as a dual, "separate and unequal" credit delivery system, where "all too often, lower-income and minority communities are served by a distinctly different set of organizations offering a distinctively different mix of products."[2] These distinctively different products are more representative of discriminatory terms of credit, epitomized by predatory loans, as opposed to an outright denial of credit, which had historically been the case. Nationally, the subprime and foreclosure crises that resulted in the Great Recession provide compelling evidence that we cannot sustain racially disparate policies and practices in our provision of credit and housing. The segregated housing and credit markets have deep roots, beginning in the 1930s when racialized home financing federal policies, such as redlining that denied credit to entire neighborhoods, were institutionalized by the Federal Housing Agency (FHA). During the 1990s, the predatory and subprime markets exploded, and many qualified borrowers of color were channeled into subprime loans. Communities of color, historically the recipients of targeted disinvestment, found themselves flooded with high-cost credit, often of a predatory nature. The system simply imploded after 70–plus years of mounting pressure. In the continuing aftershocks of the financial collapse,

> ...the lesson policymakers should be taking away from the crisis is that level playing fields are necessary, particularly when it comes to affordable [and fair] access to credit. When safe, affordable, and well-underwritten loans must compete against unregulated, exotic mortgage products priced without regard to underlying asset value or risk and marketed by brokers with misaligned incentives, the results are disastrous, both for homeowners and the larger economy. We must ensure that parallel systems cannot again emerge....[3]

Nonetheless, Fannie and Freddie's status as mortgage giants in the US financial system necessitates an honest and urgent assessment of their impact and significance in the US mortgage markets. Critics have argued that the Enterprises weren't well-regulated, and were highly leveraged and thus posed significant risk to the mortgage market. Supporters have argued that Fannie and Freddie successfully generated an efficient secondary market and improved credit access for low- and moderate- income borrowers. Whatever your position, clearly Fannie and Freddie are *the* key players in the mortgage market—by the second quarter of 2008, the combined GSE market share of new mortgage business stood at 84%, compared to 46% by the second quarter of 2007.[4] As of the second quarter of 2009, Fannie, Freddie, and the FHA purchased or guaranteed nine out of ten new mortgages.[5]

But the discussion of the future of Fannie and Freddie cannot exclusively focus on issues of safety and soundness. There are essentially two broad policy objectives that must be pursued: decreasing the systemic risk posed by the Enterprises (for example, by limiting their mortgage portfolios), and connecting marginalized borrowers and communities to sustainable home-ownership opportunities. These are not necessarily incompatible goals, yet the discussions by the media and officials for the most part have pitted them against each other. For example, in the most recent hearing on the Enter-prises, committee members still wrongly argued that the affordable housing goals were the primary drivers that led to the collapse of the Enterprises, even though there is substantial evidence to the contrary.[6] Although increasing the safety and soundness of Fannie and Freddie will take concentrated effort and time, it is in the realm of the doable. Solutions have been debated for years, and are fairly straightforward, such as increasing capital requirements and imposing portfolio size limits. However, these regulations—*if not properly designed*—could have a negative impact on their affordable housing mis-sion. The Enterprises have long held a responsibility to increase lending and improve housing opportunity for marginalized borrowers and communities. The 1992 GSE Act instituted affordable housing goals as a means to achieve their affordable housing mission. Whether the Enterprises were successful in meeting these expanded affordable housing obligations is a matter of debate. Although the Enterprises have generally met numeric lending goals set forth, this has not necessarily translated into overall improved housing market outcomes and homeownership opportunities for marginalized borrowers and communities.

The indisputable racial footprint of the subprime and foreclosure crisis, and the larger economic recession, further begs the question of whether the Enterprises have a duty to affirmatively further fair housing, and if so, whether their past actions have achieved this.[7] Importantly, this is not the same question as to whether the Enterprises have achieved their stated affordable housing goals. Affirmatively furthering fair housing is a ques-tion not only of access to sustainable credit, but of *where* the housing is located—whether marginalized homebuyers have the opportunity to pur-chase housing in stable or appreciating neighborhoods and thereby access the opportunity to build wealth as well as gain access to other opportunity structures critical for achieving one's full potential: good schools, quality grocery stores, access to health care, and so forth. Before delving into a more targeted discussion of the missions of the Enterprises, a few more fundamental issues are reviewed, including who is deciding what happens to Fannie and Freddie, and the identity of key players; also, what were the Enterprises' roles and requirements before, what are they now, and what can they do going forward?

WHO'S RUNNING THE SHOW

There are a variety of key players—people with power and interest over the Enterprises—and this composition has changed over the course of the Enterprises' history. The following is a brief list of past and current players, and their interests related to the Enterprises.

Previous Players

The Federal Housing Enterprise Financial Safety and Soundness Act of 1992 (the GSE Act) created the Office of Federal Housing Enterprise Oversight (OFHEO), an independent agency within the Department of Housing and Urban Development (HUD) charged with the duty to oversee and enforce the capital requirements and safety and soundness of Fannie and Freddie. There were important limitations to this agency, however, including inadequate resources for monitoring and the inability to take enforcement actions if it was found that the safety and soundness of the government sponsored enterprises (GSEs) was deteriorating, unlike the authority available to federal bank regulators.[8] The GSE Act also granted the HUD secretary expanded authority to regulate and enforce the affordable housing goals (and extended them to Freddie), which had been authorized in 1968 for Fannie but lacked any enforcement mechanism. It further granted the Secretary authority to approve any new mortgage program unless it was found to violate the GSEs' charters or the public interest.[9]

Given their structure as private, for-profit enterprises with government-chartered missions, the board and shareholders had clear power over Enterprise decisions. In the early 2000s, numerous media reports revealed excessive risk-taking practices, internal memos discussing the increasing pressure to recapture market share and therefore profits (especially through the intentional targeting of the subprime market), and numerous accounting scandals that inflated returns.[10] The accumulation of these risky practices and irresponsible management decisions led to a buildup of credit risk that ultimately led to their conservatorship.[11]

Current Players

The Federal Housing Finance Agency (FHFA) was created as part of the Housing and Economic Recovery Act (HERA) of 2008[12] on July 30, 2008. The creation of the new, independent federal agency represented a consolidation of regulatory and supervisory authorities previously under the purview of OFHEO, HUD, and the Federal Home Finance Board, regulator of the twelve Federal Home Loan Banks (FHLBs). Broadly, the FHFA was created to improve the safety and soundness supervision of Fannie, Freddie, and the FHLBs, as well as improve the mission supervision of these agencies. In response to the financial meltdown in October 2008 and rapidly deteriorating economic conditions, and after an intense review of the Enterprises that revealed substantial market, credit, and operational risks, FHFA was authorized to serve as conservator of Fannie and Freddie and help stabilize the housing market.[13]

The Administration is also a key player, and has used the Enterprises to inject some stability and confidence back into the US housing market, specifically through loan modification and foreclosure mitigation programs (discussed below). However, at this writing, the Administration was not expected to reveal their longer term plans for the Enterprises until the announcement of the 2011 Budget, in February, 2011. Questions over the future form of the Enterprises remain unanswered, but there are three general proposals (wholly government-owned, re-constitution as GSEs, and privatization) that seem to have gained the most traction, and for which the GAO released an analysis in September 2009. While these three broad forms have been at the center of recent discussions for restructuring Fannie and Freddie, it is becoming more and more apparent that the extremes are not likely to gain much support, and that reconstituted GSEs, with better regulation, is the most likely candidate.[14] Please refer to Addendum A for a brief review of the proposed forms.

The Federal Reserve, through expanded authority granted under HERA, has been a critical player in the Enterprises' activities. In September 2008, the Federal Reserve committed to supporting the mortgage market and the Enterprises by purchasing their debt obligations and mortgage-backed securities (MBS) in order to reduce the costs and increase the availability of credit for home purchases. As of March 2009, the Federal Reserve committed to purchasing Enterprise debt up to $200 billion each, and purchasing MBS up to $1.25 trillion.[15] However, the Federal Reserve will begin winding down its support of the Enterprises, beginning in the first part of 2010.

The Treasury Department also has a vested interest in the Enterprises. HERA expanded Treasury's scope of authority to provide stability to the Enterprises and increase investor confidence in Enterprise debt and MBS.[16] It is currently the main stockholder of the Enterprises at 79.9%, and has to date provided $111 billion in funding. Recent activity, however, has changed the nature of that aid. On Christmas Eve 2009, the Administration and Treasury pledged unlimited support to the Enterprises by lifting the portfolio caps the previous administration had put in place (in the hopes of avoiding a sharp increase in interest rates once the Fed winds down its assistance), and lifting the cap ($400 billion) on the level of assistance the Treasury could offer the Enterprises.[17] In doing so, the Administration has provided the Enterprises with increased flexibility and capacity to carry out its activities, specifically the mortgage modification programs, without worrying about incurring losses, as well as providing the opportunity for a more aggressive approach to the continuing housing market crisis.

Future Players

Who the key future players are will depend on the form the Enterprises take. For the immediate term, even the next several years, we can expect a continued influence of Treasury as the Enterprises continue to pay their commitments to Treasury (through their Senior Preferred Stock Purchase agreements), and of the Administration, as interest in and need for programs targeted at helping distressed homeowners avoid foreclosure continues. The ultimate details will be worked out in Congress.

In the meantime, the Administration has convened a task force, made up of officials from FHFA, Treasury, HUD, the National Economic Council, and the Council of Economic Advisors, to begin discussing the options for moving forward.

ENTERPRISES' ROLES: PAST, CURRENT, AND FUTURE

The Enterprises have undergone significant structural and mission-related changes throughout their history. Created as a government agency in 1938, Fannie Mae was initially charged with the duty to purchase and sell FHA-guaranteed and VA-guaranteed loans in the 1930s and 1940s. It operated in this capacity until the 1950s, when it was charged with the mission to increase liquidity through creating a secondary mortgage market for FHA and VA loans, and to reduce regional disparities in interest rates. In 1968, Fannie was reorganized as a government-sponsored enterprise, and the authority and responsibility to serve LMI borrowers was granted. Freddie Mac was created in 1970 to develop a secondary market for conventional mortgage loans; it did not have a housing mission. In 1989, Freddie was reorganized as a government-sponsored entity. The 1992 GSE Act was passed in response to increasing concerns over the safety and soundness of both GSEs, especially in light of the recent Savings and Loan crisis. The Act clarified the housing finance and expanded the housing mission responsibilities for both of the GSEs.

In 2008, the Enterprises were placed in conservatorship. While in conservatorship, their missions have focused on mortgage affordability and availability, foreclosure mitigation, and general housing market stabilization.[18] Addendum B provides a more detailed timeline of events.

The Enterprises' future roles and activities is of course the subject of much debate. The outcomes of these debates are especially important for affordable housing advocates for the four following reasons:[19]

Their ability and willingness to provide long- term, fixed-rate financing which provides a sustainable means to homeownership;

Their importance in multi-family housing. Their involvement with, and in some cases guarantees on, multi-family loans have enabled the completion of a substantial number of developments, including a substantial number of LIHTC projects, purchasing approximately 40% of credits in past years.[20] Their importance in times of economic crisis is even more pronounced for the multifamily housing sector: between October 2007 and September 2008, the Enterprises together provided 82% of net new multifamily financing;[21]

Their willingness to buy and/or securitize loans from any bank that meets their underwriting standards helps to "level the playing field" some for smaller community banks; and lastly,

Their potential to provide additional resources for affordable housing activities, for example, through the Housing Trust Fund requirements.[22]

A DUTY TO AFFIRMATIVELY FURTHER FAIR HOUSING

Fannie and Freddie are under a general obligation to not discriminate against purchasers of mortgages,[23] and to assist HUD in discovering information on lenders with which they do business to ensure that the lenders are not violating the Fair Housing Act (FHA).[24] Fannie and Freddie must also comport their underwriting and appraisal guidelines to the FHA.[25] In addition to any obligations made by virtue of government sponsorship or HUD funding to affirmatively furthering fair housing, the Enterprises are under a duty to abide by the FHA.[26] Under the 1992 GSE Act, the Enterprises also have a duty to assist HUD in investigating and bringing enforcement actions against fair housing and fair lending violators.[27] HUD and the Department of Justice also share enforcement responsibility in all Title VIII claims.[28] However, despite these obligations, fair housing and fair lending enforcement is negligible at best.[29]

WHY AFFIRMATIVELY FURTHERING
FAIR HOUSING MATTERS

Fannie and Freddie are part of a system of credit and housing that has historically been marked by racial discrimination in housing policy. The federal government has a well-documented history of racializing federal policy. For example, the Home Owners Loan Corporation (HOLC), established in 1933 in an effort to provide mortgage relief to homeowners and lenders in the wake of the foreclosure crisis during the Great Depression, developed racial underwriting and appraisal practices. Specifically, HOLC created a neighborhood-ranking system that judged credit-worthiness based on the following four categories:

> . . . the highest category going to new, racially homogenous, all-white neighborhoods. Outlying Jewish and white working-class neighborhoods were given a second grade, while neighborhoods near a contiguous African American neighborhood were assigned a third category of housing value. The lowest appraisal value was given to allAfrican American neighborhoods, regardless of the age of the dwellings or the income of the residents.[30]

The Federal Housing Authority, created in 1934 as part of the New Deal legislation, incorporated the policies of HOLC, including the racially discriminatory appraisal methods, neighborhood ranking system, and amortized payment schedule.[31] Both HOLC and FHA required private institutions to adopt "land use tools and subdivision regulations to protect property values," and staff warned developers and realtors that "if a neighborhood is to retain stability it is necessary that properties shall continue to be occupied by the same social and racial classes" and lenders to "not insure mortgage on homes unless they were covered by a racially restrictive covenant, located in racially homogenous neighborhoods, and removed from blighting influences such as poor schools and older housing."[32] In short, "the FHA institutionalized a racially separate and unequal system of home financing that favored suburban building for whites while precluding insurance for homes in racially mixed and nonwhite neighborhoods in the inner city."[33] Fannie Mae, as the offspring of the FHA, inherited this legacy.

This story has gotten lost in the recent debates over not only reforming Fannie and Freddie, but reforming the broader financial system. For example, in discussing the housing market, advocates and analysts hold up the 30–year, fixed-rate mortgage as the triumph of the US housing finance system, a product introduced by HOLC, standardized under the FHA, and continued through the Enterprises. While the innovation of this "modern long-term, fixed-rate mortgage that we all take for granted...."[34] undoubtedly expanded the possibility of homeownership to millions of Americans since its inception (homeownership rose from 44% in the late 1930s to 64% by the mid-'60s alone),[35] these loans were exclusively offered to white suburban homeowners, to the neglect of households of color and inner city homes. Indeed, the historic exclusion of households of color and continued disinvestment in urban communities of color created credit-starved communities ripe for exploitation through predatory products. Exclusion of credit today is less about outright denial of credit, and more about the terms of credit—borrowers of color were 30% more likely to receive a high-cost loan than white borrowers, even after controlling for differences in risk and other factors, such as borrower income and property location.[36] Hispanic and African Americans borrowers were channeled into the subprime market, even though they could have qualified for a prime loan (i.e. long-term amortizing, fixed-rate mortgage).

Subsequent laws have been passed attempting to correct for these policies, such as the Fair Housing Act (1968), the Equal Credit Opportunity Act (1974), and the Community Reinvestment Act (1977). However, other laws have been passed that work against them. For example, layered on top of an already-uneven landscape of opportunity came waves of financial deregulation. Beginning in the 1980s and culminating in the Gramm-Leach-Bliley Act in 1999, Congressional legislation effectively dismantled the system of protections—for both banks and borrowers—established in the 1930s. These acts included the Deregulation and Monetary Control Act of 1980 (DIDMCA), which eliminated state interest rate ceilings on home mortgages where the lender has a first lien; the Alternative Mortgage Transaction Parity Act of 1982 (AMTPA), which dismantled state regulations over alternative mortgage transactions; and the Tax Reform Act of 1986, which disallowed consumer tax deductions on credit cards, but allowed tax deductions on mortgage interest. While the intent of the deregulation legislation was to attract global capital to a competitive market and protect depositories from interest rate risk,[37] it also opened the floodgates to unscrupulous practices and incentivized consumers to gamble with their home equity. As Jesus Hernandez summarized,

> . . . [these] federal financial policies set the condition for the new subprime market to boom. They eliminated the interest rate caps, so you could charge whatever interest rate you wanted. They allowed for adjustable rate mortgages and balloon payments. They overrode local government restrictions on high-cost lending products. They eliminated the tax write-offs on consumer credit, making high cost mortgages less expensive than your credit card…so everybody put the debt onto their house.[38]

Affirmatively furthering fair housing, therefore, is more than just providing homeownership to those historically excluded. It means homeowners have the ability to buy a house in a neighborhood that will offer an opportunity to build wealth while providing access to resources such as health care and good schools. . This is different from setting and meeting numeric affordable housing goals. Research shows that meeting these affordable housing goals has not necessarily improved marginalized homeowners' access to improved housing market outcomes, such as the ability to buy in a stable neighborhood. Achieving homeownership in a declining neighborhood does not improve one's ability to achieve wealth and the American Dream. In order to realize this objective we must also pursue affirmative fair credit, where appropriate loans are offered to homeowners based on their situation—achieving home-ownership through highly risky credit products does not provide a means to sustainable homeownership. It is clear that in order to fix the housing market, and affirmatively further fair housing, we also need to fix the credit system, and affirmatively further fair credit.

RESEARCH REVIEW: MOVING THE
MISSIONS FORWARD

It will take time and effort to increase the safety and soundness of Fannie and Freddie, but it can be done. Solutions have been debated for years, and are fairly straightforward, such as increasing capital requirements and imposing portfolio size limits. However, these regulations—*if not properly designed*—can have a negative impact on affordable and fair housing goals. Several proposals to achieve reduced risk have been offered: regulating more tightly what kind of mortgages could be held; imposing fees for issuance of debt; directly limiting the size of the portfolio; and increasing the capital require-ments.[39] However, these all reduce profit, and therefore might ultimately limit housing goals.

The Enterprises are expected to improve housing market conditions be-cause they have to meet established numeric lending goals. Generally, the three categories the goals target include low-income borrowers, underserved areas, and special affordable borrowers.[40] The goals specify a percentage of loans purchased that must qualify for the single family goals and a specified number of units for multi-family goals. The focus of these goals is to improve homeownership rates for low- and moderate-income (LMI) borrowers, and improve housing conditions for LMI borrowers and neighborhoods.

The research to date, however, has shown limited improvements in housing market conditions for LMI borrowers, and underserved areas as a result of increased GSE activity. Various studies have assessed housing market condi-tions along a number of indicators, including homeownership rates, vacancy rates, median house values, and single family home prices, to name a few. For example, one study found that in assessing borrowing activity and homeownership rates in tracts designated as "underserved," there was no positive GSE effect on conforming mortgage lending activity and homeownership.[41] This conclusion was reached despite the fact that the GSEs had apparently met their housing goals. One possible explanation is that the increase in GSE activity is crowding out other secondary mortgage market actors. In this study, the researchers suggest that the increased activity in the conforming sector may come at the expense of lending activity in the non-conforming sector, or may crowd out other private, un-subsidized secondary market intermediaries. The study did find, however, positive effects of Community Reinvestment Act (CRA) activity in the non-conforming sector, and a positive but small effect on homeownership rates, suggesting that the CRA does in fact increase the supply of credit in marginalized communities. Another study focused on the ability of the GSE affordable housing goals to improve housing market conditions and homeownership rates.[42] The study assessed three indicators of housing market conditions—homeownership rates, vacancy rates, and median house value—and found that GSE-targeted tracts in the study area did not show statistically significant improvements in housing market conditions, suggesting that the affordable housing goals of the GSEs did little to improve local homeownership rates or improve local housing conditions. The implicit expectation that improving access to credit for marginalized borrowers or areas would increase homeownership and in the process create healthier neighborhoods has not been supported by research.[43]

Policy decisions dictating Enterprise activity, for example the numeric levels at which the goals are set, have impacts on affordable housing goals of other market participants. Policymakers must consider the full range of impacts of Enterprise goals on these other participants' activities to mitigate the chance for 'substitution effects'—we want policies to complement each other, not to crowd each other out. For example, CRA (private market-oriented) and FHA (government-led) policies target similar borrowers as those in the Enterprise affordable housing goals. Research has indicated that one explanation for less-than-optimal homeownership outcomes from increased GSE activity is that this increased activity essentially substituted for FHA loans—the Enterprises were able to "cream" the best credit-quality borrowers who otherwise would have qualified for FHA loans; as a result, and faced with a higher risk pool, the FHA tightened its underwriting standards and reduced its loan volume.[44] Other research has indicated that the Enterprises lag other institutions in improving credit access to low- to moderate-income borrowers (LMI), with possible explanations that this may be a result from increased enforcement of the CRA during the 1990s.[45]

Yet the picture becomes more complex. There may be positive effects of "GSE crowd out." One study found that a ten percent increase in GSE market share corresponded to a 2.7% decrease in subprime market share, representing a potential cost savings of about $100 million.[46] Greater GSE activity was associated with a reduction of subprime activity in a neighborhood, and was also found to be more pronounced in neighborhoods with high concentrations of minority households. When contextualized with the findings that anywhere from 30–50% of subprime borrowers could have qualified for prime loans, growth in GSE activity may prove on balance, beneficial.[47] The study also found that increases in FHA market share corresponded to decreases in subprime market share, but with a smaller magnitude than that found with GSE market share. The negative relationship found between both GSE and FHA market share with subprime market share lends support for government involvement, in some form, in promoting *sustainable* homeownership opportunities for historically marginalized borrowers. This observation differs from the absence of significant effects on homeownership or housing market conditions when assessing GSE impact alone.

The relationship between subprime lending activity and GSE activity bears some emphasis. Not only have the Enterprises been targeted as one of the instigators of subprime lending in an effort to achieve their affordable housing goals—a charge which does not bear out in fact[48]—but their presence in the secondary mortgage market may actually serve to protect marginalized borrowers from the abuses of predatory lending. While the non-covered subprime market has collapsed, targeted affordable lending programs do work and offer alternatives for going forward. Research comparing community reinvestment loans facilitated under the CRA with prime-type characteristics performed better than subprime loans originated with a broker (thus originated outside the scope of regulations, and often with excessively risky features, such as adjustable rates and prepayment penalties).[49] In fact, broker-originated loans with risky terms were four to five times more likely to default than community reinvestment loans.[50]

A key finding from research on Freddie and Fannie outcomes is that access to prime credit is not the only barrier—maybe even not the most important barrier—facing marginalized borrowers, or more accurately, different groups of marginalized borrowers. For example, the issue of mobility may be a substantial barrier for transient populations such as immigrants, given the high entry and exit costs of homeownership relative to renting.[51] Research indicates that interest rates—which have been a selling point of the GSEs—may have little influence on long run homeownership trends.[52] One study found no direct impact from interest rate changes on long run homeownership; changes in interest rates may change the timing of homeownership (accelerate it for some) but not the long term affordability of homeownership, and may increase housing starts in the short term.[53] A study assessing FHA lending found similar results—FHA lending was not found to *enable* homeownership for those who would never be able to buy but for the FHA, but rather, was found to accelerate it (or allow borrowers to consume more housing than they would be able to from conventional lenders).[54] The study also found that renters who qualified as "FHA only" borrowers waited years after qualifying for the FHA loan before purchasing homes. This lag between qualifying and purchasing may indicate that there are other barriers or considerations in homeownership beyond credit access. Results indicated that income and demographic factors may play a more important role in homeownership rates, and that these factors can be different for different racialized groups. For example, Painter et.al. (2000) found that differences in income, immigrant status, and education can fully explain the gap between Latino and white homeownership rates, but only part of the gap between black and white homeownership rates. For the former group, interventions targeted at affordability and human capital may be more beneficial than credit policies.[55] This differentiates between access to credit and the cost of credit, finding that the cost of credit may not be directly as important a barrier to homeownership as other barriers, such as perpetual low income or less wealth, which may speak more to the continuing racial disparities in education, labor, and health. More generally, changes in interest rates—the cost of borrowing—will benefit those for whom the cost of credit is the main barrier,[56] but not impact borrowers struggling with the *cumulative* effects of marginalization. Therefore, lowering interest rates may improve access somewhat, but there are other remaining income and demographic factors that are critical for making homeownership a sustainable opportunity for these borrowers.

Another study found that despite the increases in homeownership in the 1990s, substantial homeownership gaps persisted—in 2001, the black-white homeownership gap was about 26 percentage points, and the Hispanic-white homeownership gap was about 30 percentage points.[57] During the study period from 1983 to 2001, credit barriers were found to account for only 5 percentage points of the white-minority gaps in homeownership, even though the 1990s was a period during which a variety of new mortgage products (i.e. subprime lending, notably the explosion of PLS, use of ARMs, and low-doc loans) were introduced to (supposedly) improve access to mortgage credit.[58] Conversely, differences in household attributes were found to explain about two-thirds of the white-minority homeownership gaps.[59] Again, this suggests that we may not fully understand the pathways to homeownership that matter the most for targeted groups. Careful consideration of these findings is critical for determining how Fannie and Freddie in particular, and the housing finance system in general, can best be restructured to improve sustainable homeownership in neighborhoods of opportunity.

The Enterprises could take a lead role in encouraging sustainable non-prime or prime-type lending, similar to what private, federally insured depositories undertake through the CRA. Tighter regulations of the type or quality of sub-prime loans allowed to qualify towards affordable housing goals should also be reinstated and vigorously enforced.[60] For example, Immergluck (2004) discusses how though there were HUD restrictions eventually placed on the types of loans the Enterprises could include towards their LMI lending goals, and the Enterprises enacted voluntary restrictions on purchases of loans with certain features, these were not comprehensive enough to seriously limit the abuses visited on borrowers. The greater influence of the Enterprises in the secondary markets and these restrictions *could have* reduced the excessive pricing on subprime loans if these restrictions had been more comprehensive (across all abusive loan features) and more strict (lower 'thresholds' for what qualified as 'high cost'), because the Enterprises would not (hypothetically) purchase loans with certain features. Therefore independent mortgage companies had an incentive to make more responsible subprime loans if they wanted to improve their liquidity.

CONCLUSION: DEVELOPING A FAIR HOUSING AGENDA FOR FANNIE AND FREDDIE

There is a clear disconnect between policy objectives and policy outcomes. As we have seen, there has been little to no net improvement in housing market conditions or homeownership rates for the intended beneficiaries, despite the fact that the Enterprises have been "successfully" meeting their affordable housing goals. It is also not clear the extent to which the crowd-out effect posed by Enterprise activity harms or helps marginalized communities; on the one hand, they may crowd out subprime activity. On the other hand, they may crowd out FHA activity. And by most accounts, the Enterprises do not perform as well as other institutions in meeting the credit needs of these communities. These findings have several implications for developing an action plan for the Enterprises to affirmatively further fair housing.

First, we have about two decades or more of critique over not only their structure as GSEs, but of their performance regarding their affordable housing mission. However, there has been no consideration of their activities as they relate to fair housing, and no affirmative action plan developed in response to these criticisms. Research surrounding the housing market outcomes of GSE activity has for the most part stopped short of providing concrete solutions for improving affordable housing outcomes—to say nothing of affirmatively furthering fair housing—instead remarking upon the inadequacies of the current policies and structures.

Second, and related, the incentives under which the Enterprises operate—and the subsequent form they take—are critical, and offer a real leverage point for change. Although the Enterprises have more or less consistently met their affordable housing goals, there has been no demonstrable improvement in housing market outcomes for targeted groups. Not only have the Enterprises not been the best provider for meeting these goals—lagging other secondary market actors—but their activities have generally not been shown to have positive impacts for their target populations (i.e. no positive effect on LMI homeownership; no positive effect on housing and neighborhood conditions). This is alarming because the GSEs *are* being deemed successful in meeting the goals dictated to them. Again, it is important to note the geography of GSE activity, which tends to be more affluent neighborhoods that *just* qualify as an underserved area; in other words, activity may not be extending far enough into those neighborhoods with the most need for stabilization because it is more costly to do so.[61] GSE shares tend to be lower in central cities, lower in tracts with the highest minority concentrations, and lower in tracts with high vacancy rates.[62]Analysis by An et.al. (2007) showed that loan-purchase activity declines with tract median income, and purchase activity decreases as minority shares increases. For example, census tracts with area median incomes (AMIs) at 120% had a purchase activity of 35%; for tracts at 80% AMI or below, purchase activity dropped to about 18%. Likewise, purchase activity was about 30% for census tracts with minority shares at 30% or below, but dropped to 20% for tracts where the minority share was above 30%.[63] Together, these observations suggest that the way the goals are structured needs to be revisited.

Third, the Justice Department must be more involved—the federal government is not doing enough to curb discrimination in lending. Because of the plenary authority to act on behalf of victims of housing and lending discrimination, the rampant abuses of lending agents (and the complicity of the Enterprises in this regard, having purchased "junk" private label securities of Wall Street investors),[64] and the Enterprises' affirmative role in fair housing, it is crucial that the Justice Department act to curb and remedy the lending and housing situation in the United States. The Department must not only continue to investigate pattern and practice discrimination, but also to use its discretionary power to join private discrimination suits under Title VIII. Housing and lending discrimination in violation of the Fair Housing Act leads to plummeting neighborhood housing values, loss of home equity, an uneven credit market for marginalized borrowers, and the continuation of discrimination and blocked opportunity for marginalized borrowers. The Justice Department has the ability to address this and must continue to take remedial action for fair housing and fair lending violations.

Finally, there is no coordinated, explicit focus on Fannie and Freddie reform as it pertains to affirmatively furthering fair housing. The Justice Department represents just one entry point for change—albeit an important one—but we would be well-served to highlight different intervention points in an effort to create a more robust advocacy platform. Such a position recognizes that objectives for affirmatively furthering fair housing operate within a larger system of housing finance and affordable housing policies, both within and beyond the scope of Enterprise "jurisdiction." Within this system, there are several actors charged with the goal to provide fair housing. Policies directed at one actor will therefore necessarily interact with the activities and outcomes of policies directed at a different actor. Exploring these interactions, feedback loops, and rebound effects is critical for the design and implementation of a comprehensive, effective, and affirmative fair housing policy. Currently, the major actors within this system are not talking to each other. A general observation is that while advocates agree that the restructuring of Fannie and Freddie is of critical importance, they feel there is too much else going on at the moment that takes precedence. For example, some are focusing their attention on CRA reform. These are not necessarily different issues, and neglecting one to focus on the other limits our opportunity to make significant inroads in addressing fair housing. This segmented approach sets the stage for incremental changes that essentially maintain the current overall structure of affordable housing, which in turn will continue to dictate less than optimal results. These are not independent reforms: changes in one area will have impacts in the other areas. Policymakers, experts, and advocates in each of these areas—CRA, FHA, and the Enterprises at a minimum—must be engaged together in a broader conversation about affirmatively furthering fair housing. To truly promote an affirmative fair housing agenda, especially as it relates to Fannie and Freddie, we must ensure that we keep a mindful balance between advocating for remedial actions pursued by the Justice Department, as well as developing affirmative and creative strategies that encourage the Enterprises to be leaders in fair housing and fair credit.

ADDENDUM A, A REVIEW OF PROPOSED FORMS FOR THE ENTERPRISES

Following is a brief review of the proposed forms, their potential functions, and elements of regulatory structure and oversight.[65]

Proposal 1: Government Corporation. Functions would include focusing on purchasing qualifying mortgages and issuing MBS, but eliminating mortgage portfolios, and transferring responsibility for homeownership to targeted groups to the Federal Housing Agency (FHA). Key elements of regulatory structure and oversight include: risk-sharing agreements with private lenders or mortgage insurers; appropriate disclosures in the federal budget of risks and liabilities (previously off-budget status as GSE); and robust congressional oversight of operations.

Proposal 2: Re-establish as GSE, for-profit with government oversight. Proposal calls for restoring the Enterprises to their pre-conservatorship status but with additional controls to minimize risk, such as eliminating or reducing the Enterprises' mortgage portfolios, or subjecting the Enterprises to public-utility type regulation (i.e. business activity restrictions and profitability limits) and establishing executive compensation limits. Another proposal calls for converting the Enterprises from publicly-traded, shareholder owned corporations to cooperative associations owned by mortgage lenders. Key elements of regulatory structure and oversight include reducing or eliminating portfolios to increase safety/soundness; establishing capital standards that reflect risks; additional regulations (i.e. executive compensation, or public utility-type regulations); financial disclosures in budget; and strong congressional oversight.

Proposal 3: Privatize. Proposal calls for abolishing the Enterprises in their present form and dispersing their mortgage lending activities and risk management throughout the private sector. Some propose the establishment of a federal mortgage insurer to help protect mortgage lenders against catastrophic mortgage losses. Key regulatory structure and oversight elements include: establishing an appropriate oversight structure for a new federal mortgage insurer, which might include appropriate regulations and capital standards, the disclosure of risks/liabilities in the federal budget, and congressional oversight.

ADDENDUM B, TIMELINE OF FANNIE AND FREDDIE ROLES AND ACTIVITIES

Following is a brief review of important structural and mission-related changes through their history.[66] In setting up this timeline, however, it is critical to note the parallel history of housing discrimination in the United States, especially as it relates to the racialization of federal housing policy, as the Enterprises emerged within this context.

1933: Home Owners Loan Act is passed, creating Home Owners Loan Corporation, in response to the foreclosure crisis precipitated by the Great

Depression. HOLC was commissioned to buy mortgages of distressed bor-rowers, and refinance them into more affordable terms.[67] However, there was a clear racial impact. HOLC developed a neighborhood ranking system for credit-worthiness of the housing it financed that favored white, homogenous, new neighborhoods over older, mixed, or African American neighborhoods (regardless of income or age of dwellings).

1934: The Federal Housing Agency (FHA) was created to provide govern-ment insurance to mortgage lenders. The precedent of overtly racist under-writing and appraisal practices, introduced under HOLA, were carried on by the FHA.[68] The FHA is credited with setting industry standards in underwrit-ing and origination. Because the FHA employed discriminatory policies, the adoption of FHA practices facilitated the institutionalization of racial discrimination in housing finance in the private market.[69]

1938: FHA created a national mortgage association, which would become Fannie Mae. During the late '30s and the '40s, this association's duty was to buy and sell FHA-guaranteed loans. In 1948 it received authority to also buy and sell VA-guaranteed loans.

1954: Fannie Mae was chartered to provide liquidity in the secondary market, and provide support in times of economic stress. The Housing Act of 1954 also reorganized Fannie as a mixed-ownership corporation, with both the federal government and mortgage lenders as shareholders.

1950s and 1960s: Limits on interest rates that thrifts could offer, and state regulations that limited banks' ability to branch into different states, contributed to liquidity constraints on banks/thrifts and regional disparities in mortgage interest rates. Fannie's ability to purchase nationwide alleviated these constraints.

1968: Fannie was divided into two agencies. Ginnie Mae was created to guarantee (i.e. full faith and credit of US government) the FHA and VA loans from within HUD. Fannie was reorganized as a private, shareholder-owned entity, but with the federal charter overseen by HUD (i.e. a GSE), which included a general authority to require a "reasonable portion of mortgage purchases to serve LMI borrowers."

1970: Freddie Mac was created to develop a secondary market for conven-tional mortgage loans; it was owned by the Federal Home Bank Board.

1971–72: Freddie created the first mortgage-backed security. Fannie bought its first non-FHA/VA conventional loan.

Early 1980s: Fannie experiences mortgage portfolio troubles from climb-ing interest rates (S&L failures); Fannie issues first MBS.

1989: Freddie becomes publicly traded (GSE).

1992: The 1992 GSE Act established OFHEO as independent oversight agency within HUD to ensure safety and soundness of the GSEs. Expanded the affordable housing mission by setting annual numeric housing goals, established by HUD. Three targets for the goals: purchase of mortgages serving LMI families; special affordable housing for families (i.e. families in low-income areas, and very low-income families); and housing located in central city, rural, and other "underserved" areas.

1990s: Rapid growth of the Enterprises.

2000s: Housing bubble bursts; GSEs engage subprime markets; practice bad accounting; conservatorship.

Early 2000s: start buying Alt-A and subprime securities.

2003–04: accounting scandals uncovered by OFHEO at both GSEs.

2008: HERA passed, created FHFA.

September 2008: FHFA as conservator of Fannie and Freddie; abolished OFHEO; HUD's mission authority over affordable housing goals transferred to FHFA.

2008–09: Administration/FHFA use Fannie and Freddie to focus on mortgage affordability, mortgage availability, and foreclosure mitigation, in efforts to stabilize the housing market, through:

Foreclosure moratorium from November 2008–January 2009.

Making Home Affordable Program[70]: helped develop with Administration, Treasury, and HUD. Designed to help prevent foreclosures for homeowners that qualify. Freddie is charged with servicer compliance; Fannie works with servicers to implement the program. The key elements of the program:

Home Affordable Modification Program: loan modification guidelines and incentives for servicers, borrowers and lender/investors to engage in successful loan modifications.

Home Affordable Refinance Program: homeowners with conforming loans owned or guaranteed by Fannie Mae or Freddie Mac to refinance their loans into more affordable mortgages.

NOTES

1. Andrew Jakabovics, Center for American Progress. "The Future of the Mortgage Market and the Housing Enterprises Testimony Before the US Senate Committee on Banking, Housing and Urban Affairs." October 9. 2009. Page 1.

2. William Apgar et al. at the Joint Center for Housing Studies, Harvard University. "Credit, Capital and Communities: The Implications of the Changing Mortgage Banking Industry for Community-Based Organizations." March 9, 2004 Report. Accessed at http://www.jchs.harvard.edu/publications/communitydevelopment/ccc04–1.pdf.

3. Supra n. 1 at 5.

4. Remarks by Treasury Secretary Henry M. Paulson Jr. on the Role of the GSEs in Supporting the Housing Recovery before the Economic Club of Washington, January

7, 2009. Accessed September 23, 2009 at http://www.treas.gov/press/releases/hp1345. htm.

5. Timiraos, Nick. "Industry Seeks Fannie, Freddie Overhaul." *The Wall Street Journal* September 2, 2009. Accessed November 2, 2009 at http://online.wsj.com/article/ SB125186013970178403.html.

6. Financial Services Committee Subcomittee on Capital Markets, Hearing on "The Future of Housing Finance: A Progress Update on the GSEs." September 15, 2010.

7. See Korman, Henry. "Furthering Fair Housing, the Housing Finance System, and the Government Sponsored Enterprises." Updated September 4. 2010. in *Fair Credit and Fair Housing in the Wake of the Subprime Lending and Foreclosure Crisis: Findings from the Kirwan Institute Initiative,* Chapter 13.

8. United States Government Accountability Office. "Fannie Mae and Freddie Mac: Analysis of Options for Revising the Housing Enterprises' Long-term Structures." September 2009. Page 17.

9. *Id.*

10. Duhigg, Charles. "Pressured to Take More Risk, Fannie Reached Tipping Point." *The New York Times*, October 5, 2008.

11. Supra n. 8 at 7, stating "...the [E]nterprises incurred substantial credit losses on their retained portfolios and their guarantees on MBS. These losses resulted from pervasive declines in housing prices, as well as specific enterprise actions such as their guarantees on MBS collaterized by questionable mortgages, and their investment in Private Label MBS backed by subprime loans."

12. The Housing and Economic Recovery Act 2008 is a comprehensive piece of legislation designed to address the housing market instability that became apparent throughout 2007, and markedly so during the early part of 2008. The Act includes provisions for housing finance reform (including reforms of federal housing regulatory agencies), foreclosure prevention provisions, and tax-related provisions.

13. James B. Lockhart III (Director, Federal Housing Finance Agency) "Statement on the Appointment of FHFA as Conservator for Fannie Mae and Freddie Mac before the Senate Committee on Banking, Housing, and Urban Affairs." September 23, 2008. Page 3. Available at http://www.fhfa.gov/webfiles/17/92308FHFAHearing Statementcorrected092608.pdf.

14. Supra n. 5. Timiraos.

15. Supra n. 8 at 10. The Fed has provided similar support to Federal Home Loan Banks.

16. To this end, three facilities were developed: (1.) Senior Preferred Stock Purchase Agreements, which provided an effective guarantee for investors of GSE obligations (any negative equity at either GSE will be offset by Treasury investment); support was initially capped at $200 billion for each GSE. Under this agreement, shares carry a 10% coupon, and a quarterly dividend payment as compensation for the commitment; limits were also placed on their portfolio size pursuant to this agreement, not to exceed $850 billion on December 31, 2009, and since lifted. (2.) GSE MBS Purchase Program, scheduled to expire 12–31–2009. (3.) GSE Credit Facility which allows the Enterprises to borrow funds if they are unable to issue debt in the

financial markets, scheduled to end December 31, 2009 (as of September 2009, the Enterprises hadn't used this authority.)

17. Timiraos, Nick. "Questions Surround Fannie, Freddie." *The Wall Street Journal.* December 30, 2009. Accessed January 6, 2010 at http://online.wsj.com/article/SB10001424052748704234304574626630520798314.html?mod=dist_smartbrief.

18. James B. Lockhart III (Director, Federal Housing Finance Agency) "Statement on the Present Condition and Future Status of Fannie Mae and Freddie Mac." Before the House Financial Services Committee, Subcommittee on Capital Markets, Insurance, and Government Sponsored Enterprises. June 3, 2009. Page 4.

19. Zigas, Barry. "What does the Future Hold for Fannie and Freddie?" *Shelterforce*, Fall 2009. Available at www.shelterforce.org/article/print/1769.

20. The Federal Reserve Board of Governors and the Federal Reserve Bank of St. Louis. "Innovative Ideas for Revitalizing the LIHTC Market." November 2009. Page 4. Available at http://www.federalreserve.gov/communitydev/other20091110a1.pdf.

21. Supra n. 1 at 3.

22. Supra n. 8 at 41. HERA established a Housing Trust Fund, to be funded through assessments on Enterprises' unpaid principal balance on new business, equal to 4.2 basis points (or .042%). 65% of this assessment would go to HUD and the Trust Fund; 35% would go to Treasury's CDFI trust fund. However, given the current financial conditions of the Enterprises, and the economy in general, assessments have been stalled.

23. 12 U.S.C. § 4545 (2009) (Stating that HUD shall "prohibit each enterprise from discriminating in any manner in the purchase of any mortgage because of race, color, religion, sex, handicap, familial status, age, or national origin, including any consideration of the age or location of the dwelling or the age of the neighborhood or census tract where the dwelling is located in a manner that has a discriminatory effect").

24. *Id.* The Enterprises are also required by regulation to assist the Secretary in investigations of potential violations of the Equal Credit Opportunity Act (ECOA). Should violations of either FHA or ECOA be found, the Enterprises are instructed to take remedial actions against the violating lenders, "including suspension, probation, reprimand, or settlement."

25. *Id.* (Stating that HUD must "periodically review and comment on the underwriting and appraisal guidelines of each enterprise to ensure that such guidelines are consistent with the Fair Housing Act . . .").

26. Title VIII of the Civil Rights Act of 1968 requires that the U.S. Department of Housing and Urban Development (HUD) and all executive departments and agencies "affirmatively further the Fair Housing Act." 42 U.S.C. § 3608(d) (2008).

27. 24 C.F.R. §81.44 (2010 ed.).

28. 42 U.S.C. §§ 3612–3614 (2008).

29. Supra n. 7.

30. Gotham, Kevin Fox. "Racialization and the State: The Housing Act of 1934 and the Creation of the Federal Housing Agency." *Sociological Perspective*, Vol. 34, No. 2: 291–371. Summer 2000. Page 306.

31. *Id.*

32. *Id.* at 307.

33. *Id.*

34. Supra n. 1 at 4.

35. Kuttner, Robert. "The Bubble Economy." *The American Prospect.* September 24, 2007. Accessed April 24, 2009 at http://www.prospect.org/cs/articles?article=the_ bubble_economy.

36. Bocian, Debbie Gruenstein, Keith S Ernst, and Wei Li. "Unfair Lending: The Effect of Race and Ethnicity on the Price of Subprime Mortgages." Center for Responsible Lending. May 31, 2006. Page 3. Available at http://www.responsiblelending.org/mortgage-lending/research-analysis/rr011exec-Unfair_Lending-0506.pdf.

37. Richard K. Green and Susan M. Wachter, "The Housing Finance Revolution," Prepared for the 31st Economic Policy Symposium: Housing, Housing Finance & Monetary Policy, Federal Reserve Bank of Kansas City. See p. 21 ff. http://www.kansascityfed.org/publicat/sympos/2007/PDF/2007.08.21.WachterandGreen.pdf.

38. Jesus Hernandez, presentation on panel "Reverse Redlining, Foreclosure and the Wealth Gap" at The Kirwan Institute's National Convening Subprime Lending, Foreclosure and Race, October 2–3, 2008. Transcript available at http://4909e99d3 5cada63e7f757471b7243be73e53e14.gripelements.com/pdfs/events/Panel_1_Transcript.pdf.

39. Jaffee, Dwight M. and John M. Quigley. "Housing Subsidies and Homeowners: What Role for Government Sponsored Enterprises?" January 2007. Presented at the Brookings-Wharton Conference on Urban Affairs, Washington DC, October 19–20, 2006.

40. FHFA, *2010–2011 Enterprise Affordable Housing Goals; Final Rule*, The 2008 HERA reformed the housing goals established in the 1992 GSE Act, creating separate low-income single family purchase and refinance goals for borrowers at 80% AMI or below; a low-income area home purchase goal for families in census tracts up to 80% AMI; a multi-family housing goal for families at or below 80%, regardless of location; and a special affordable multi-family subgoal for very low-income families at or below 50% AMI.

41. Gabriel, Stuart and Stuart Rosenthal. "The GSEs, CRA, and Homeownership in Targeted Underserved Neighborhoods." Paper presented at the Conference on the "Built Environment: Access, Finance, and Policy," Lincoln Institute of Land Policy, Cambridge MA, December 7–8, 2007. The authors also observe that the limited effects of increased GSE activity on homeownership may be due to a 'crowding out' of the alternate, non-conforming loan market segment (i.e. increases in conforming loan sector are offset by decreases in the non-conforming sector).

42. Bostic, Raphael W. and Stuart A. Gabriel. "Do the GSEs matter to low-income housing markets? An assessment of the effects of the GSE loan purchase goals on California housing outcomes." *Journal of Urban Economics* 59: 458–475. 2006.

43. Freeman, Lance, George Calaster and Ron Malega. "The Impact of Secondary Mortgage Market and GSE Purchases on Home Prices: A Cleveland Case Study." *Urban Affairs Review* 42(2): 193–223. November 2006. Finding no significant relationship between secondary market purchasing rates of home-purchase mortgages and home prices for under-served census tracts in Cleveland, Ohio.

44. An, Xudong and Raphael Bostic. "GSE Activity, FHA Feedback, and Implications for the Efficacy of the Affordable Housing Goals." *Journal of Real Estate Finance and Economics* 36: 207–231. 2008.

45. Supra n. 43, at 208, citing Evanoff and Segal (1996). See also Gabriel and Rosenthal (2008), who found that although the CRA and GSE affordable housing goals were both met, only the CRA activities had a positive impact on homeownership rates and mortgage lending activity.

46. An, Xudong and Raphael Bostic, "Have the Affordable Housing Goals been a Shield against Subprime? Regulatory Incentives and the Extension of Mortgage Credit." Working paper with the School of Policy, Planning, and Development Lusk Center for Real Estate, University of Southern California, April 2006.

47. *Id.* at 17, citing Carr and Scheutz (2001).

48. Duhigg, Charles, "Pressured to Take More Risk, Fannie Reached Tipping Point." *The New York Times,* October 5, 2009. Accessed September 29, 2009 at http://www.nytimes.com/2008/10/05/business/05fannie.html.

The subprime market took off between 2001 and 2004, growing from $160 billion to $540 billion. Fannie did not make significant forays into the market until 2004/05; between 2005 and 2008, it purchased or guaranteed at least $270 billion in risky loans, almost three times over all previous years combined. In large part, this was in an effort to regain market share—and thus profits—lost to subprime lenders.

49. Ding, Lei and Wei Lei. "Risky Borrowers or Risky Mortgages? Disaggregating Effects Using Propensity Scoring Methods." Working Paper with Center for Community Capital, University of North Carolina, December 2008.

50. *Id.* at 1.

51. Painter, Gary and Christian L. Redfearn. "The Role of Interest Rates in Influencing Long Run Homeownership Rates." *Journal of Real Estate Economics* 25(2/3): 243–267. 2002.

52. *Id.*

53. *Id.*

54. Goodman, John L and Joseph B. Nichols, "Does FHA Increase Home Ownership or Just Accelerate It?" *Journal of Housing Economics* 6: 184–202. 1997.

55. Supra n. 51 Painter and Redfearn, at 260.

56. *Id.* at 249.

57. Gabriel, Stuart A and Stuart S. Rosenthal. "Homeownership in the 1980s and 1990s: aggregate trends and racial gaps." *Journal of Urban Economics* 57: 101–127. 2005. Page 121.

58. *Id.*

59. *Id.*

60. An article in *The Washington Post* also refers to remarks by Allen Fishbein, adviser to former Assistant HUD Secretary William C. Apgar, that HUD failed to use its regulatory power to disallow the GSEs from counting subprime securities toward their affordable housing goals, "contrary to good lending practices." Leonnig, Carol. "How HUD Mortgage Policy Fed the Crisis." *The Washington Post* June 10, 2008. Accessed September 28,2009 at http://www.washingtonpost.com/wp-dyn/content/article/2008/06/09/AR2008060902626.html.

61. Bhutta, Neil. "GSE Activity and Mortgage Supply in Lower-Income and Minority Neighborhoods: The Effect of the Affordable Housing Goals." Federal Reserve Board *Finance and Economic Discussion Series*, Division of Research & Statistics and Monetary Affairs. Working Paper, 2009–03. Stating that "insofar as these stable neighborhoods are a relatively low priority for advocates, these results demonstrate how a broadly targeted GSE Act might interact with the GSE profit-motive to yield effects that are out of line with the intent of the law." Page 18.

62. Supra n. 43 An and Bostic, at 218.

63. An, Xudong, Raphael Bostic, Yongheng Deng, and Stuart Gabriel. "GSE Loan Purchases, the FHA, and Housing Outcomes in Targeted, Low-Income Neighborhoods." Brookings-Wharton Papers on Urban Affairs: 2007.

64. See Christopher L. Peterson, "Fannie Mae, Freddie Mac, and the Home Mortgage Foreclosure Crisis." Loyola University New Orleans Journal of Public Interest Law, Vol. 10, pp. 149–170, 2009. Private label securitization (PLS) on Wall Street took off during the 1990s; at that time, Fannie and Freddie steered clear of these securities that were backed by subprime and Alt-A loans. However, amidst declining market share, the GSEs both increased their presence in the subprime markets: in 1998, Freddie had purchased about $25 billion in PLS, and in 1997, Fannie had purchased only $18.5 billion. However, by the end of 2007, Freddie owned $267 billion in PLS, and Fannie owned $127.8 billion. Between 2003 and 2005 alone, the Enterprises' combined PLS holdings increased from 9.9% of their total combined mortgage portfolio, to 22% (162–163). It was the losses on these private label securities, backed by subprime and predatory loans, that ultimately necessitated the conservatorship of the Enterprises—some losing as much as 90% of their value from their date of purchase. Theresa R. DiVenti, "Fannie Mae and Freddie Mac: Past, Present, Future." *Cityscape: A Journal of Policy Development and Research*, Vol. 11, No. 3, pp. 231–242, 2009. Available at http://www.huduser.org/portal/periodicals/cityscpe/vol11num3/ch11.pdf.

65. Adapted from GAO report, supra n. 8 at 29–37.

66. Adapted from GAO report, *Id.* at 11–12.

67. Peterson, Christopher L. "Predatory Structured Finance." *Cardazo Law Review* Vol. 28, No. 5: 2185. 2007. Page 2195.

68. *Id.*

69. Fox Gotham, Kevin. "Racialization and the State: The Housing Act of 1934 and the Creation of the Federal Housing Administration." *Sociological Perspectives,* Vol. 43, No. 2, pp. 291–317.

70. However, only 4% of loan modifications have made it past the trial modification phase of the program to a permanent loan modification. Renae Merle, "Foreclosure relief program is stuck in first: JUST 4 PERCENT IN FINAL STAGE: Thousands now risk losing mortgage help," *The Washington Post*, December 11, 2009. http://www.washingtonpost.com/wp-dyn/content/article/2009/12/10/AR2009121003834.html.

Chapter Twelve

Fannie Mae and Freddie Mac

How Can We Improve Their Support of the Mortgage Market?

Thomas H. Stanton

In September 2008, Fannie Mae and Freddie Mac failed and went into government hands. Since their failure a year ago, Fannie Mae and Freddie Mac have absorbed more than $100 billion of taxpayer funds to make up for losses at the two companies. The Treasury has committed to cover future losses as well.

The Obama Administration is reviewing a range of options for the future of the two insolvent companies. This chapter proposes using Fannie Mae and Freddie Mac as wholly owned government corporations, i.e., government agencies, to support the mortgage market for the next five years. That support might include (1) funding new mortgages with lower borrowing costs, including prudent affordable housing loans, (2) providing help for troubled mortgage borrowers, (3) improving consumer protection for borrowers, and (4) supporting other government housing programs, especially the Federal Housing Administration (FHA). At the end of five years, when the housing market has stabilized, policymakers can decide on the ultimate future of the two organizations.

The first section of this chapter discusses how Fannie Mae and Freddie Mac failed and explores the sometimes-unmanageable tension between private profits and their public missions. The second section discusses the continuing tension between private profits and public purpose now that the companies are in government hands, but with shareholders still in possession of a minority of stock of each company. This section also introduces the government corporation as an organizational form. The third section presents advantages of the government corporation in providing multiple forms of support for the mortgage market in ways that reflect the substantial taxpayer investment in Fannie Mae and Freddie Mac. The chapter concludes with the judgment that potential benefits over the next five years could be substantial. After that, when the financial system and housing market have stabilized, policymakers will have a better idea what form the two government corporations should take to provide the support that may be needed for the longer term.

THE FAILURE OF FANNIE MAE AND FREDDIE MAC

Fannie Mae and Freddie Mac committed serious misjudgments that helped to bring about their insolvency. The most serious misjudgments involved the companies' resistance to accepting more effective supervision and capital standards.

High Leverage

For years, starting with their successful efforts to weaken the legislation that established their safety-and-soundness regulator,[1] the two companies managed to fend off capital standards that would have reduced their excessive leverage and provided a cushion to absorb potential losses. They held about half of the capital that competing banks and thrift institutions would have needed to hold to support a similar book of business.

The companies fought for high leverage because this benefited their shareholders and managers, at least until the companies failed. Freddie Mac reported returns on equity of over 20% for most years since it became an investor-owned company in 1989, reaching highs of 47.2% in 2002 and 39.0% in 2000. Fannie Mae reported earnings of almost as much, reaching a high of 39.8% in 2001.[2] The two companies fought higher capital requirements because more capital would have diluted those returns to shareholders.

While high leverage was profitable for the owners and managers of the two companies, it also made them much more vulnerable to financial collapse in the event that the mortgage market became troubled.

Poor Business Decisions

The two companies compounded their self-inflicted structural vulnerabilities with a series of misjudgments that involved taking on excessive risk just at the point that housing prices were peaking. According to press reports, the chief executives of both Fannie Mae and Freddie Mac disregarded warnings from their risk officers and sought to catch up with the market by greatly increasing their purchases of risky loans.[3]

Freddie Mac reported that, "Total non-traditional mortgage products, including those designated as Alt-A and interest-only loans, made up approximately 30% and 24% of our single-family mortgage purchase volume in the years ended December 31, 2007 and 2006, respectively."[4] Fannie Mae reported that purchases of interest-only and negative amortizing ARMs amounted to 7% of its business volume in 2007 and 12% in each of 2006 and 2005. Moreover, Alt-A mortgage loans "represented approximately 16% of our single-family business volume in 2007, compared with approximately 22% and 16% in 2006 and 2005, respectively."[5] Both companies also invested in highly rated, private-label mortgage-related securities that were backed by Alt-A or subprime mortgage loans, amounting to total holdings by the two companies of more than $200 billion in 2007.[6]

In short, Fannie Mae's and Freddie Mac's managers made unwise business decisions that they knew, or at least their risk officers knew, could inflict serious harm on the two companies. Because they persisted in operating with high leverage and thin capitalization, neither company could withstand the resulting losses.

Fannie Mae and Freddie Mac were the largest companies in a group of organizations known as government-sponsored enterprises (GSEs). [7] In making their mistakes, Fannie Mae and Freddie Mac revealed the inherent vulnerabilities of the GSE as an organizational form. First, the GSE lives or dies according to its charter and other laws that determine the conditions under which it operates. That means that GSEs select their chief officers in good part for their political connections and savvy rather than their ability to manage two of the largest financial institutions in the world.

Second, the GSE combines private ownership with government backing in a way that creates a virtually unstoppable political force. Because of their government backing and low capital requirements in their charters, Fannie Mae and Freddie Mac gained immense market power. They doubled in size every five years or so until at the time of their failure the two companies funded more than $5 trillion of mortgages, about 40% of the mortgage market.

Their market power gave them political power. Whenever someone would urge regulatory reform, such as higher capital standards to reduce the GSEs' dangerous leverage, huge numbers of constituents could be expected to flood Capitol Hill.[8] That political power in turn entrenched the GSEs' market power.

The GSE is characterized by an unusual combination of private ownership and public purpose. Under the law, the officers and directors of a privately owned corporation have a fiduciary responsibility to serve shareholders and the corporation. Other purposes are secondary. This principle applies to shareholder-owned GSEs as well. The Treasury Department reported many years ago on "the tension between profit and public purpose" inherent in the GSEs and noted that, "As a private company, the GSE will act to fulfill its fiduciary responsibilities by promoting and protecting the interests of its shareholders."[9]

It can become difficult if not impossible to manage the tension between the needs of private shareholders and those of stakeholders with differing views of the companies' public purposes. Former Fannie Mae CEO Daniel Mudd testified in December 2008 that the conflicting pressures are so unmanageable that the GSE should be ended as an organizational form:

> I would advocate moving the GSEs out of No Man's Land. Events have shown how difficult it is to balance financial, capital, market, housing, shareholder, bondholder, homeowner, private, and public interests in a crisis of these proportions. We should examine whether the economy and the markets are better served by fully private or fully public GSEs.[10]

Mr. Mudd speaks with the voice of someone who has struggled to deal with the complexities of a government-sponsored enterprise. His recommendation to end the GSE as an organizational form is consistent with lessons from the public administration literature as well.[11]

TURNING FANNIE MAE AND FREDDIE MAC INTO WHOLLY OWNED GOVERNMENT CORPORATIONS

The question then becomes whether the mortgage markets continue to need governmental support. If not, privatization of the GSEs would be the answer. However, for the next five years government support is likely to be a high priority. In the second quarter of 2009, Fannie Mae and Freddie Mac, now in government hands, funded almost three quarters of newly originated home mortgages. Most of the remainder was funded with support from the Federal Housing Administration (FHA). In this context, privatization of the GSEs is out of the question. The continuing weak state of the economy means that the mortgage market is likely to require extensive government support for perhaps five years. After that, depending on the state of the mortgage market, one hopes that much less support would be needed.

FANNIE MAE AND FREDDIE MAC IN CONSERVATORSHIP

The government placed Fannie Mae and Freddie Mac into conservatorship rather than receivership. Unlike receivership, the voluntary acceptance of conservatorship by Fannie Mae or Freddie Mac was not subject to legal challenge, which could have further disturbed the financial markets.

Technically, conservatorship means that the government is working to restore the companies to financial health. As the head of the Federal Housing Finance Agency (FHFA), the federal agency that oversees the two companies, recently testified, "...FHFA's duties as conservator mean just that, conserving the Enterprises' assets."[12]

Consistent with this view, but inconsistent with the fact that the two companies are insolvent with a substantial negative net worth, the government has preserved private shareholders in the two companies and allowed their stock to trade freely. Until shareholders are removed, the officers and directors of the two companies will face conflict as to their fiduciary responsibilities. Do they price mortgage purchases low to support the market or do they price higher to replenish the companies' shareholder value? As the companies themselves pointed out in filings with the Securities and Exchange Commission, they face conflicts among multiple objectives that "create conflicts in strategic and day-to-day decision making that will likely lead to less than optimal outcomes for one or more, or possibly all, of these objectives."[13]

Conservatorship and the preservation of shareholders are largely inconsistent with the pressing need to use the two companies to support the mortgage market. With shareholders still in the equation, government cannot use the two companies as a source of strength for the rest of the mortgage market, except as this can be justified as a means of conserving Fannie Mae's and Freddie Mac's assets.

It is time to remove the shareholders from the insolvent companies and turn Fannie Mae and Freddie Mac into wholly owned government corporations. At that point policymakers can use the two companies to support the mortgage market in many ways that are not being done today.

THE WHOLLY OWNED GOVERNMENT CORPORATION

What form should government support now take? Mr. Mudd has it right: if government cannot make the GSEs fully private, then they should become fully public. That means turning Fannie Mae and Freddie Mac into wholly owned government corporations.

The wholly owned government corporation is a special type of government agency that is supposed to keep its accounts and manage its affairs on a businesslike basis.[14] To the extent that a government corporation is financially self-sustaining, it does not need annual appropriations and instead funds itself from revenues that it generates from its activities. The US Postal Service sells mail delivery services, the Tennessee Valley Authority sells power, and Ginnie Mae charges a fee for guaranteeing mortgage-backed securities.

Wholly owned government corporations have provided support to housing and community development for many decades. Fannie Mae, established in 1938 as a secondary market institution to help revitalize the housing sector, began as a wholly owned government corporation. Only in 1968 did the government separate the Federal National Mortgage Association (Fannie Mae) into two parts, (1) Ginnie Mae, which remains a wholly owned government corporation, and (2) Fannie Mae, which became a government-sponsored enterprise, owned and controlled by private shareholders. More recent examples of government corporations include the Resolution Trust Corporation, which helped to resolve the savings and loan debacle, and the Community Development Financial Institutions Fund. The Clinton Administration proposed transforming the FHA into a wholly owned government corporation as a way to increase its capacity, but the proposal did not become law.[15]

HOW GOVERNMENT CORPORATIONS COULD SUPPORT THE MORTGAGE MARKET

Once they become wholly owned government corporations, we can use Fannie Mae and Freddie Mac as agents of reform for the mortgage market. The benefits could be substantial:

- They could fund mortgages in a manner targeted to meet pressing public purposes, including providing affordable housing in a financially prudent manner.
- They could deliver government support for borrowers facing foreclosure and especially for the increasing number who default on their mortgages because they lose their jobs.
- They could provide essential consumer protections for borrowers, such as Alex Pollock's one-page mortgage disclosure form, borrower counseling, and increased pre-foreclosure loss mitigation services.[16]
- They could adapt their Automated Underwriting Systems and other systems and capabilities for use by other federal agencies and programs, starting with the FHA.

In short, the government could turn the insolvency of Fannie Mae and Freddie Mac into an opportunity to begin to upgrade the quality of federal support for delivery of credit by federal agencies. Consider each of these advantages in turn.

Because they are in conservatorship, with private shareholders as well as government ownership, Fannie Mae and Freddie Mac do not operate with the lowest possible borrowing costs. The markets charge somewhat more to the two failed companies because they operate with government backing that is somewhat less than a full-fledged government guarantee, known as a "full-faith-and-credit" guarantee of the federal government. Turning Fannie Mae and Freddie Mac into wholly owned government corporations would allow them to borrow with a full government guarantee. Because they merely need to make a surplus, and not additional profits for shareholders, the government corporations could lower mortgage rates more than is possible for a GSE.

As government corporations, Fannie Mae and Freddie Mac could do even more to support affordable housing. With shareholders out of the picture, the two companies could set aside a small fraction of their incomes each year for a form of the Affordable Housing Trust Fund. That kind of fund, which had been intended for the two companies as government-sponsored enterprises, would be a practical program for two wholly owned government corporations to implement. Money from the trust fund could be used to reduce borrowing costs for qualified affordable housing applicants, to provide counseling and other costly but necessary services, support innovative programs such as those of NeighborWorks, and other purposes that policymakers might authorize.

As government corporations, Fannie Mae and Freddie Mac also could experiment with eligibility criteria for nontraditional borrowers. It has long been understood that credit scores, now ubiquitous in determining the eligibility of middle class loan applicants, may not apply as well to low income or other nontraditional types of borrowers.[17] Because they do not need to subordinate their public purposes to the interests of shareholders, the two government corporations could experiment with flexibility in credit and mortgage scores. Pilot programs could test various parameters to see whether substitutes might be available that make nontraditional borrowers creditworthy even though they do not meet the standard criteria. Especially given lessons from today's troubled mortgage market, these pilot programs could be important means of adjusting credit scores to inform the difficult judgment of how much credit to offer what types of borrowers to support homeownership without extending credit that a borrower would be unlikely to repay.

The corporations also could experiment with allocations of subsidy amounts from available Affordable Housing Trust Fund monies to try to determine how much and what kinds of financial, counseling or other support are most effective with what types of nontraditional borrowers. By publishing results from these experiments the corporations could help to influence constructive actions of private lenders, and inform policymakers of the most cost-effective policies that might be considered to carry out affordable housing and community reinvestment and other such purposes.

By limiting the experiments to pilot programs, the government corporations could limit their financial risk (and also the potential financial harm to
participating nontraditional borrowers). If a pilot program proved successful,
then the government corporations could expand their overall lending criteria
in a prudent manner to take account of the results.

PROVIDING HELP FOR TROUBLED
MORTGAGE BORROWERS

The number of foreclosures continues to rise. Millions of people are defaulting on their mortgages and being forced from their homes. Defaults are coming in three waves: (1) the borrowers who took out mortgages (many of the
subprime, Alt-A, option-adjusted ARMs, etc.) that they never should have
had; (2) borrowers who took out mortgages with teaser rates that are reset-
ting to levels that the borrower cannot afford to repay; and (3) an increasing
number of people who had been current on their mortgages until losing their
jobs in the recession.

The Administration has tried to prompt Fannie Mae, Freddie Mac, and
lenders with government assistance to offer loss mitigation programs. FHA
is also available to help borrowers to refinance. However, none of these programs serve the wave of people who default on their mortgages when they
lose their jobs.[18] Moreover, there is indication that some lender reluctance to
modify loans has a practical basis: many unmodified delinquent loans cure
themselves and many modified loans default.[19] In between are millions of
mortgage loans that are likely to default and lead to foreclosure.

One result will be an increasing number of families who are traumatized
by being put out on the street. Another result will be the collapse of property values and community vitality in neighborhoods affected by multiple
foreclosures. The possibility of blight is serious. Evidence from one major
lender shows that foreclosed properties lose almost two-thirds of their value
in liquidation sales.[20]

What should be done? The Administration and private lenders fear that
supporting people who are foreclosed upon could create incentives for millions of other people, and especially those whose mortgages exceed the value
of their homes, to default. Practical answers are available; the country has
faced this problem before.[21]

Perhaps policymakers should take the view that many people suffered from
a huge real estate bubble that cannot be sustained. While we may not be able
to keep everyone in their home, we at least should mitigate the hardship and

let them down easy. That appears to be a good part of the logic behind the massive government support for banks and auto companies.

What kind of government support could Fannie Mae and Freddie Mac provide as wholly owned government corporations? One answer might be a program of government rental assistance that would allow a family to remain in its home for up to three years after foreclosure. If the lender was able to sell the property in that time, the voucher would become portable to allow the family to rent elsewhere. Because it could be more difficult to sell an occupied home, the government might provide funds for an increased commission for selling a foreclosed home when the family still occupies it.

The value of using a government corporation to reduce dislocation of households and communities is that the corporation could monitor success of the program and, according to the amount of discretion that the enabling legislation allows, adapt the program to meet local conditions in various markets, within specified parameters. In contrast to a GSE, a government corporation merely needs to cover its costs, not make a profit. Because a government corporation is a part of government, it can administer subsidized programs as well, so long as appropriations are available. The wholly owned government corporation is an organizational form well suited to providing such support to the housing market.

IMPROVING CONSUMER
PROTECTION FOR BORROWERS

At this writing, the Congress continues to deliberate whether to create a Consumer Financial Protection Agency and the extent that such an agency will receive the legal authority and organizational capacity to do its job. The record of other consumer protection agencies is not completely encouraging in this regard. If the agency actually comes into being, it is likely that the same stakeholders that now seek to kill the agency would continue to exert pressure over coming years.[22]

The value of a government corporation is that it is active in the market. In contrast to a consumer protection agency that must regulate and enforce its decisions, a government corporation can set conditions as a requirement of doing business. In 1971, when Fannie Mae still had much of the culture of a government corporation and when Freddie Mac was just starting business, the two companies joined to standardize mortgage forms. The result was a great increase in the efficiency of the mortgage market as mortgage terms, with appropriate variations, were standardized across the country.[23]

In the same way, the government corporations could set requirements that would enhance market efficiency in current circumstances. One clear need is for improved consumer disclosure. Alex Pollock of the American Enterprise Institute has proposed a one-page mortgage disclosure form. It would require a lender, for example, to disclose the highest monthly payments that are possible under the mortgage, thereby putting the borrower on notice about "teaser rates" and other variable rates that have turned mortgages into impossible burdens for so many households.

The government corporations also could place requirements for streamlined loss mitigation procedures into their seller-servicer guides, require counseling for affordable housing buyers, and otherwise ensure consumer protections that enhance the efficiency of the markets. It bears emphasis that the current market, in which millions of people are losing their homes and major mortgage lenders have blown themselves up, requires increased consumer protection, not only because this is fair, but also to promote market efficiency.

SUPPORTING OTHER GOVERNMENT HOUSING PROGRAMS AND ESPECIALLY THE FEDERAL HOUSING ADMINISTRATION (FHA)

Then-HUD Secretary Steve Preston pointed out in November 2008 that the volume of FHA mortgage insurance trebled over the prior year. He was candid in his assessment that FHA is not strong enough, either in statutory authority or administratively, to carry the load of a substantial increase in volume without causing significant potential losses to taxpayers. Secretary Preston objected to Congress' refusal to allow FHA to implement modest risk-based pricing for the agency's mortgage insurance program. He also pointed to problems with FHA's patchwork of IT systems, noting that FHA's core loan processing system is still written in COBOL.[24]

The HUD Inspector General and other housing experts also worry that fraud may overtake the FHA program as subprime lenders and others move their loan production to FHA. Kenneth M. Donahue, HUD's Inspector General, has warned that "It looks like an incoming tsunami." FHA lacks the capacity to monitor and respond quickly to fraud. Moreover, the agency's protracted procedures do not allow for prompt removal of fraudulent or abusive lenders from the program.[25]

Fannie Mae and Freddie Mac possess the needed systems and facilities to support FHA and ensure capable implementation of the FHA's single-family and multifamily mortgage insurance programs. As government corporations they could either provide technical assistance to FHA to upgrade its loan processing platforms and systems and models or, because of the continuing growth of FHA's workload, might themselves process FHA loans, at least until FHA's own capacity can be enhanced. Taxpayers have paid dearly for Fannie Mae and Freddie Mac and their systems, and may as well benefit from that investment by strengthening the FHA so that it does not collapse under the weight of its new responsibilities.[26]

CONCLUSION: AFTER FIVE YEARS

It is clear that government will need to provide extensive support of the mortgage market until it recovers from the current boom-and-bust, perhaps in five years. Until that time, because of the disruption that reorganization could cause, it is probably wise to maintain Fannie Mae and Freddie Mac as distinct corporations. In five years policymakers will have a better idea both of the needs of the mortgage market at that time and also of the consequences of the economic losses the nation has suffered from the debacle.

Then, depending on the needs that policymakers perceive at that time and the resources available to address those needs, it may be time to turn Fannie Mae and Freddie Mac into a single government corporation with a clear mandate to serve the most pressing housing needs. Those needs might include service to first-time homebuyers in the single-family market and support of the multifamily market, for example. The relationship of the new government corporation to FHA and Ginnie Mae would need to be determined by, among other factors, the financial and operational state of FHA at that point.

Whatever happens in five years, the bottom line today is clear: (1) the mortgage market needs much greater government support right now, and (2) that support could come from Fannie Mae and Freddie Mac as government corporations in a manner and to the extent that no other organization could provide.

NOTES

1. Among the many reports documenting the successful efforts of Fannie Mae and Freddie Mac at weakening the regulator and their capital standards, see, e.g., Carol Matlack, Getting Their Way, *National Journal*, October 27,1990, pp. 2584–2588; Jill Zuckman, "Bills To Increase GSE Oversight Move Ahead in House, Senate," CQ Weekly, August 3, 1991; Stephen Labaton, "Power of the Mortgage Twins: Fannie and Freddie Guard Autonomy," *New York Times*, November 12,1991, p. D1; Kenneth

H. Bacon, "Privileged Position: Fannie Mae Expected to Escape Attempt at Tighter Regulation," *Wall Street Journal*, June 19,1992, p. A1.

2. These and other statistics on the two companies may be found in the historical data tables of each annual report of their regulator, the Federal Housing Finance Agency. The 2008 report is available at: http://www.fhfa.gov/webfiles/2335/FHFA_ReportToCongress2008508rev.pdf.

3. David S. Hilzenrath, "Fannie's Perilous Pursuit of Subprime Loans: As It Tried to Increase Its Business, Company Gave Risks Short Shrift, Documents Show," *Washington Post*, August 19, 2008, p. D01; Charles Duhigg, "At Freddie Mac, Chief Discarded Warning Signs," *New York Times*, August 5, 2008; Charles Duhigg, "The Reckoning: Pressured To Take More Risk, Fannie Reached Tipping Point, *New York Times*, October 5, 2008.

4. Freddie Mac, *Annual Report*, 2007, p. 13.

5. *Ibid*, pp. 128–9.

6. Fannie Mae, *Annual Report*, 2007, p. 93; Freddie Mac, *Annual Report*, 2007, p. 94.

7. A government-sponsored enterprise is a government chartered, privately owned and privately controlled institution that, while lacking an express government guarantee, benefits from the perception that the government stands behind its financial obligations. See, Ronald C. Moe and Thomas H. Stanton, "Government Sponsored Enterprises as Federal Instrumentalities: Reconciling Private Management with Public Accountability," *Public Administration Review*. July/August 1989. This definition is consistent with the definition Congress enacted in amendments to the Congressional Budget Act of 1974, codified at 2 U.S.C. Section 622 (8).

8. Observers have long noted this pattern. "Builders, real estate brokers and bankers across the country rely so heavily on Fannie Mae for mortgage funds that they live in fear of offending the firm and routinely defend it in Washington." David A. Vise, "The Money Machine: How Fannie Mae Wields Power," *Washington Post*, January 16, 1995, p. A14.

9. US Department of the Treasury, *Government Sponsorship of the Federal National Mortgage Association and the Federal Home Loan Mortgage Corporation*, July 11, 1996, p. 81.

10. Daniel H. Mudd, Written Statement, Before the Committee on Oversight and Government Reform U.S. House of Representatives, December 9, 2008, available at http://oversight.house.gov/images/stories/Hearings/110th_Congress/Fannie_Freddie/Testimony_Daniel_H_Mudd.pdf , accessed February 7, 2009. Similarly, in August 2008 the *Washington Post* reported the views of Freddie Mac's CEO at the time, Richard Syron:

"Freddie Mac chief executive Richard F. Syron…said yesterday that conflicting demands on the government-chartered mortgage giant have made his job 'almost impossible.'

"On the eve of Freddie Mac's quarterly earnings report, Syron said that the McLean company has been whipsawed by the dual tasks of creating profit for private investors and serving the public by boosting the housing market. 'What this organization is all about is balancing among the different missions,' Syron said in an interview. 'It makes the job almost impossible.'"

11. See, e.g., Harold Seidman, *Politics, Position, and Power: The Dynamics of Federal Organization,* Fifth Edition (New York: Oxford University Press, 1998), p. 213:

"Intermingling of public and private purposes in a profit making corporation almost inevitably means subordination of public responsibilities to corporate goals. We run the danger of creating a system in which we privatize profits and socialize losses."

See also, Thomas H. Stanton, "Government-Sponsored Enterprises: Reality Catches up to Public Administration Theory," *Public Administration Review*, July/August, 2009.

12. Statement of Edward J. DeMarco, Acting Director Federal Housing Finance Agency before the U.S. Senate Committee on Banking, Housing and Urban Affairs "The Future of the Mortgage Market and the Housing Enterprises" October 8, 2009, p. 6.

13. Fannie Mae Form 10Q filing for the quarterly period ended September 30, 2008, p. 7; Freddie Mac Form 10Q filing for the quarterly period ended September 30, 2008, p.5.

14. See, e.g., Thomas H. Stanton and Ronald C. Moe, "Government Corporations and Government Sponsored Enterprises," Chapter 3 in *Tools of Government: A Guide to the New Governance*, Lester M. Salamon, Editor, Oxford University Press, 2002; Office of Management and Budget, *Memorandum on Government Corporations*, M-96–05, December 8, 1995; and U.S. Government Accountability Office, *Government Corporations: Profiles of Existing Government Corporations*, GGD-96–14, December 1995.

15. U.S. Department of Housing and Urban Development, *HUD Reinvention: From Blueprint to Action*, March 1995, pp. 49–72.

16. Alex Pollock's one page mortgage form can be found at http://www.aei.org/scholars/scholarID.88/scholar.asp. His analysis is attached below.

17. See, e.g., Thomas H. Stanton, *Credit Scoring and Loan Scoring: Tools for Improved Management of Federal Credit Programs*, PwC Endowment for the Business of Government, July 1999, available at http://www.businessofgovernment.org/sites/default/files/Credit.pdf

18. For a cogent explanation why middle class families have become increasingly vulnerable to defaulting on their mortgages, see, Elizabeth Warren and Amelia Warren Tayagi, *The Two-Income Trap: Why Middle-Class Parents are Going Broke*, Basic Books, 2003.

19. Manuel Adelino, Kristopher Gerardi, and Paul S. Willen, "Why Don't Lenders Renegotiate More Home Mortgages? Redefaults, Self-Cures, and Securitization," Public Policy Discussion Paper, Federal Reserve Bank of Boston, July 6, 2009.

20. Gretchen Morgenson, "So Many Foreclosures, So Little Logic," *New York Times*, Sunday Business, July 5, 2009, p. 1

21. Thus, the Emergency Housing Act of 1975 offered support to homeowners to try to prevent foreclosure but specified rules to prevent homeowners from arbitrarily defaulting on their loans; a current program with similar rules which is intended to prevent foreclosures is the Pennsylvania state Homeowners' Emergency Mortgage Assistance Program (HEMAP). A list of those protective measures, found at https://www.hemap.org/hemap/secure/help.aspx?HelpID=HEMAPQualifications, could be adapted for the rent support program suggested here.

22. The Consumer Product Safety Commission (CPSC), to give but one example, suffered continuing erosion of its staffing authority from 900 people in 1977, shortly after it began operations, to less than half that number thirty years later. Recent concern over imports of dangerous consumer products led to new legislation in 2008 that, among other measures, streamlined the agency's cumbersome rulemaking procedures and required an increase in the agency's staffing. See, Bruce Mulock, "Consumer Product Safety Commission: Current Issues," Congressional Research Service, June 17, 2008; and Margaret Mikyung Lee, "Consumer Product Safety Commission Improvement Act 2008, P.L. 110–314," Congressional Research Service, September 22, 2008.

23. See, Committee on Banking, Housing, and Urban Affairs, United States Senate, "Federal National Mortgage Association Public Meeting on Conventional Mortgage Forms, Sponsored by the Federal National Mortgage Association and Federal Home Loan Mortgage Corporation," April 5 and 6, 1971, 92nd Congress, 1st Session, Document No. 92–21.

24. HUD Secretary Steve Preston, Prepared Remarks at the National Press Club, November 19, 2008, available at http://www.hud.gov/news/speeches/2008–11–19. cfm, accessed October 16, 2009.

25. Barry Meier, "As FHA's Role Grows, So Does the Risk of Fraud," *New York Times*, December 10, 2008.

26. The two government corporations might also provide support for other federal housing programs including the direct loan program for homeowners (part of the disaster loan program) of the Small Business Administration. The needs of FHA are especially pressing and deserve to be a priority.

Chapter Thirteen

Furthering Fair Housing, the Housing Finance System, and the Government Sponsored Enterprises

Henry Korman[1]

INTRODUCTION:
ENTERPRISES IN TRANSITION

The Federal National Mortgage Association, known as Fannie Mae, and the Federal Home Loan Mortgage Corporation, or Freddie Mac, are secondary market entities chartered by Congress to provide liquidity and stability in the residential mortgage markets.[2] These government sponsored enterprises (GSE) purchase homeowner and multifamily mortgage loans from lenders, who use the proceeds to make new loans. The GSEs either hold the loans in portfolio, or securitize the acquired mortgages into mortgage backed securities (MBS), selling shares of the right to the principal and interest payments to investors, and guaranteeing payment of the loans in the event of default by borrowers on the underlying mortgages. They are both stock corporations. The GSEs also set national underwriting and appraisal standards for the conventional or "conforming" loans they purchase and securitize, based on characteristics such as borrower creditworthiness, loan-to-value ratios, the age of the dwelling, conditions in the market area of the loan location, and other factors.[3] The underwriting standards are intended to facilitate consistency in prime mortgage loan products, promote efficiency in the market, and reduce costs for lenders and borrowers.[4]

Enterprise business activities are not limited to the purchase of conforming loans and MBS issues, and risky business practices proved to be their undoing. Like other financial institutions, in the run up to the financial downturn, they traded in so-called private label mortgage-backed securities (PLS) backed by subprime mortgages. By mid-2007, PLS were made worthless by foreclosures. As financial conditions deteriorated, the value of the mortgages in enterprise securities portfolios declined precipitously with an escalation in conforming mortgage foreclosures. GSE capitalization levels began to drop below safety and soundness levels as enterprise debt outstripped the value of holdings.

The downward financial spiral of the GSEs was compounded by efforts to fulfill the charter mandate of promoting stability in the mortgage market through the purchase of increasing amounts of mortgages. GSE financial conditions deteriorated to such an extent that Congress overhauled oversight legislation in the summer of 2008. Facing $5.3 trillion of losses in combined amounts of guaranteed MBS and outstanding debt, regulators determined that enterprise financial failures threatened a further collapse of financial markets. In September 2008, both enterprises were placed under the conservatorship of a new federal oversight agency, the Federal Housing Finance Agency (FHFA).[5] Propped up with trillion dollar investments from the Treasury Department, the GSEs play an important role in the Obama Administration's efforts to slow home foreclosures and support lending for affordable rental housing.

The GSEs are successors to Depression-era federal agencies that institutionalized and standardized redlining; the practice of refusing to extend home mortgage credit on the basis of the race and ethnicity of individual borrowers and the inhabitants of a neighborhood. Enterprise oversight legislation requires the US Department of Housing and Urban Development (HUD) to assure that GSE activities do not discriminate based on race, color, religion, sex, disability, family status, age, or national origin. The enterprises operate under a mandate to assist HUD and other federal agencies in the investigation and enforcement of fair lending obligations under the Fair Housing Act (Title VIII) and the Equal Credit Opportunity Act (ECOA). HUD is obligated to ensure that GSE underwriting guidelines are consistent with Title VIII. The Fair Housing Act and corresponding HUD regulations forbid discrimination in the securitization of mortgages and the purchase and sale of home loans. Equally crucial for fair housing purposes is the mandate imposed by Title VIII on all "executive departments and agencies" to "administer their programs and activities relating to housing and urban development (including any Federal agency having regulatory or supervisory authority over financial institutions) in a manner affirmatively to further the purposes of" the Fair Housing Act.[6]

At this writing (September 2010), significant questions remain about the future of Fannie Mae and Freddie Mac, including whether they should continue to do business as private corporations with dominant positions in the secondary mortgage market, whether they should be abolished and their secondary market functions left entirely to the private market, or whether their charters should be reformulated to limit their activities to specific purposes.[7] Within these discussions are additional questions about the effectiveness and continued viability of housing goals imposed by current law that are intended to facilitate home mortgage credit for low- and moderate-income purchasers, loans for multifamily rental housing serving low-income households, and investment in single family and multifamily loans made in low-income areas and neighborhoods of color. Among the many issues open for debate is the proper balance between achieving housing goals and reclaiming and sustaining financial soundness.

More significantly, the discussions about the future of the enterprises are now taking place within the context of emerging federal proposals to reform the system of housing finance of which the GSEs are a part, and the necessity of recalibrating the role of government within that system. Despite the historic GSE link to redlining, despite the fact that oversight laws incorporate civil rights considerations, and despite the continuing persistence of discrimination in conventional mortgage lending, fair housing and fair lending issues are lacking from the debate about the future of the enterprises and the financial structures that facilitate the private secondary mortgage markets.

The purpose of this chapter is to use the activities of Fannie Mae and Freddie Mac to examine, within the concept of the duty to further fair housing, the workings of the secondary mortgage market to highlight the civil rights considerations that require attention as policymakers take on both the future of the enterprises, the shape of the housing finance system, and the role of government within the housing finance system.

AFFIRMATIVELY FURTHERING FAIR HOUSING

The obligation to further fair housing codified in Title VIII derives from the Congressional recognition of the long and well documented history of the use of federal housing activities to create and perpetuate widespread patterns of residential racial segregation, in both homeownership and rental housing programs. As interpreted by the courts, the responsibility has several elements. Federal agencies must not engage in acts of housing discrimination, or acts that establish or perpetuate segregation, and must ensure that entities under agency supervision involved in housing activities do not engage in discrimination. Agencies must also gather information about and understand whether the actions of entities under their supervision advance housing opportunity or instead perpetuate segregation. They must take affirmative steps in funding and supervisory activities to break down patterns of residential segregation and create truly open housing markets.[8] An agency may not disregard these duties. However, once an agency acts to carry out the responsibility, it is entitled to considerable deference.[9]

The first GSE, the Federal Home Loan Bank Board (FHLBB), was a linchpin of the efforts at establishing segregation, and there is a symmetry between the racialized origins of GSEs during the Great Depression and the current foreclosure crisis visited primarily on people and neighborhoods of color. The FHLBB was created in 1932 to provide low cost advances to member banks for home mortgage lending. A companion agency, the Homeowners Loan Corporation (HOLC) was established "to exchange government bonds for delinquent mortgages with lenders and provide homeowners with new low-interest, 15–year fully amortized mortgages and the chance to save their home."[10] Around the same time, the Federal Housing Administration (FHA) was created to insure similar long term, amortizing loans with standardized features.

It was the FHA, and HOLC at the direction of the FHLBB, that devised appraisal approaches that devalued properties in areas predominated by African Americans. It was the FHA, and HOLC at the direction of the FHLBB, that created the maps that redlined the black neighborhoods where no loans could be made, and it was the FHA that institutionalized the practice of lending to create or preserve racial homogeneity within urban and suburban communities. These acts are held responsible for establishing the patterns of residential segregation that still characterize most metropolitan areas.[11]

The GSEs are inheritors of this legacy. Fannie Mae was created in 1938 to buy FHA's mortgages.[12] Freddie Mac was created in 1970 to serve the same function for members of the Federal Home Loan Bank system, and when first established, it was wholly owned by FHLBB members.[13]

As a legal matter, it is unsettled whether the statutory duty to further fair housing applies to the GSEs. Judicial remedies for the violation of the duty to further fair housing are most often imposed where there is direct evidence that a federal agency, or a local agency under the supervision of a federal agency, engages in activities that either deliberately fosters segregation, or has a discriminatory effect.[14] There is no indication that the GSEs ever utilized the segregationist underwriting standards pioneered by FHA and HOLC. Moreover, Title VIII cases against federal agencies are decided under the federal Administrative Procedure Act (APA). It is less than clear that the GSEs are considered "agencies" for APA purposes, and can be held responsible for violating the Title VIII obligation to further fair housing like other grantees of federal funds.[15]

Even with this lack of clarity, it is beyond question that HUD and FHFA are federal agencies subject to the APA, and they must exercise their supervisory authority over the enterprises consistent with the obligation to further fair housing.[16] Together with the GSEs, they are inheritors of a system for funding home mortgages that is responsible for establishing patterns of residential segregation that persist to the present day. Their supervisory activities, while defined by enterprise oversight laws, must be consistent with the responsibility to further fair housing. Their record of doing so is equivocal at best.

FAIR LENDING ENFORCEMENT AND THE GSES

The Fair Housing Amendments Act of 1988 amended the Fair Housing Act to forbid discrimination based on race, color, religion, sex, disability, familial status, and national origin in the "purchasing of loans" secured by residential real estate; that is, in secondary mortgage market transactions.[17] HUD fair housing rules define prohibited conduct to include: the purchase or securitization of loans in some areas but not others based on the protected characteristics of the people living in the area; pooling or securitizing loans for purchase and sale based on protected characteristics; and the use of different terms and conditions in purchase, sale, or securitization of mortgages because of loan features related to protected characteristics.[18]

There appear to be few, if any, judicial or administrative decisions involving complaints of discrimination in secondary mortgage market transactions. It is clear, however, that Congress intended to enlist the enterprises in identifying and bringing enforcement actions. The Federal Housing Finance Regulatory Reform Act of 1992 (the 1992 Reform Act) was enacted as part of a larger effort to establish financial safety and soundness standards and to improve government oversight of the enterprises.[19] Section 1325 of the 1992 Reform Act imposed fair housing responsibilities on both HUD and the enterprises:

- The enterprises are prohibited from discrimination in the purchase of any mortgage because of race, color, religion, sex, disability, familial status, age, or national origin, "including any consideration of the age or location of the dwelling or the age of the neighborhood or census tract where the dwelling is located."
- The GSEs must submit lender data to HUD and other federal agencies to assist in investigations of failures to comply with Title VIII and ECOA.
- HUD is required to obtain information from other federal, state, and local agencies regarding violations of the Fair Housing Act and ECOA, and to direct the enterprises to take enforcement action against lenders that are found to be in violation of fair lending laws.[20]

Under HUD regulations, the GSEs are obliged to submit lender data only at HUD's request.[21] Provisions for the exchange of information between

HUD and the enterprises as part of a fair lending enforcement strategy appear to have yielded no results. That outcome is part of a pattern of widespread weaknesses among HUD, banking regulators, and the Department of Justice in efforts to carry out fair lending enforcement.

Banking regulators do review financial institution fair lending compliance as part of banking examinations.[22] However, from 2005 through 2008, the five federal bank regulators with supervision authority over more than 16,000 financial institutions made only 118 ECOA and Title VIII referrals to the Justice Department after completing consumer compliance and so-called "outlier" examinations. Nearly half of the referrals involved discrimination based on marital status, a characteristic protected by ECOA but not Title VIII. Outlier examinations, in which Home Mortgage Disclosure Act (HMDA) data is used to identify loan pricing disparities for African-American and Hispanic borrowers, yielded only 10 referrals to the Justice Department for investigation of pattern and practice violations of Title VIII.

Of the seven fair lending cases settled by the Justice Department between 2005 and 2009, only two were based on referrals from banking regulators. Structural issues within the enforcement framework such as inconsistent approaches to examination, and limitations in the content of HMDA data, are obstacles to better enforcement.[23] These overall weaknesses indicate that there must be improvements in the enforcement activities of HUD, the banking regulators, and the Department of Justice before the enterprises can play any meaningful role in fair lending enforcement.

FAIR LENDING AND GSE UNDERWRITING

HMDA data continues to report racial disparities in access to home mortgage credit by people of color, especially blacks.[24] Denial of conventional credit is linked to the correspondingly higher rates of subprime lending to people of color, and research points to significant correlations between high rates of subprime lending to people of color and levels of segregation.[25]

A decade ago, the GSEs underperformed the market in their purchase of loans to African American and Latino borrowers, with especially high disparities compared to the market in purchases of loans made to African Americans, including high-income African Americans.[26] By 2008, Fannie Mae succeeded in eliminating the gap, matching the overall market's loans to blacks, and exceeding it slightly for Latino borrowers. Freddie Mac lagged in the market for African American borrowers by 1% and also exceeded the market in the purchase of loans made to Latinos.[27] Annual Housing Activities Reports (AHAR) filed by the enterprises with FHFA for 2009 show dramatic reversals. The share of Fannie Mae purchases of loans to black borrowers dropped from 5% in 2008 to 3% in 2009; the percentage of purchases of loan to Latinos dropped from 6.6% to 4.9%. Freddie Mac's purchases showed similar trends with reductions in the acquisition of black-originated loans from 4% to 2.5% of all loans, and similar reductions in purchases of loans to Latinos from 6.4% to 4.1%.[28]

It may be that these changes reflect larger dynamics in the home mortgage market, which saw loan applications from black borrowers drop by 48% and applications from Latinos by 55%.[29] Whatever the cause of the GSEs' current performance, it is indicative of a larger disregard for the availability of credit for borrowers of color, considering the chronically persistent level of racially disparate home mortgage loan denials in the private market.

The 1992 Reform Act addressed the poor performance of the GSEs in purchasing loans made to borrowers of color in part by imposing a duty on HUD to review and comment on GSE underwriting and appraisal guidelines "to ensure that such guidelines are consistent with the Fair Housing Act."[30] HUD rules turn this obligation on its head by requiring the enterprises to submit a fair housing analysis of "underwriting standards, business practices, repurchase requirements, pricing, fees, and procedures that affect the purchase of mortgages for low- and moderate-income families, or that may yield disparate results" as part of an AHAR.[31]

Enterprise AHAR indicate some effort to address the potential for discrimination in GSE underwriting. Fannie Mae, for example, "maintains an ongoing comprehensive fair lending risk assessment program that is designed to ensure that its underwriting standards, business practices, repurchase requirements, pricing policies, fee structures, and procedures comply with the fair lending laws and promote fair and responsible lending."[32] The enterprises make automated underwriting systems available to lenders with manual override capabilities that are intended to combine consistency, fairness, and flexibility in loan processing. Beyond considerations of discrimination in underwriting, lack of funds for down payments and lower credit rating scores are also barriers to access to home loans that tend to affect people of color at higher rates.[33] Historically, the GSEs underwrote alternative loan products with reduced loan-to-value requirements and higher risk profiles that are targeted at such borrowers. They also purchased loans made in connection with public programs that often facilitate homeownership by people of color.

It may be that these alternative loan products are a factor in the slight progress made by the enterprises in matching the market's share of loans to borrowers of color in 2008. As addressed in greater detail in later sections, it is equally plausible that the advances in GSE purchase of loans to households of color are tied to purchases of private label securities collateralized with subprime mortgages. In any event, the underwriting of alternative loan products is now stricter with the onset of GSE financial deterioration, and is likely to curtail access to conventional credit for borrowers of color for the foreseeable future. Beginning in 2007, both GSEs reduced acceptable loan-to-value ratios, increased credit score requirements, reduced "back end" borrower debt-to-income ratios, and took other steps that curtailed the efficacy of alternative underwriting tools. They also eliminated the more relaxed underwriting criteria for alternative loan products. These actions were taken in a larger market environment in which both the FHA and private lenders also imposed more conservative loan standards.[34]

Even before the current financial crisis took hold, GSE underwriting and appraisal standards were often controversial. Fannie Mae and Freddie Mac both have been defendants in litigation alleging that their single family automated underwriting software programs unfairly denied the credit applications of borrowers of color and violated Title VIII and ECOA.[35] As the foreclosure crisis gained momentum in 2007, the GSEs added features to their software that identified so-called "declining markets" by zip code. Loan applications submitted to the automated underwriting systems by lenders from borrowers in declining market zip codes delivered a message instructing lenders to seek extra information about the market area and the quality of supporting appraisals. Borrowers in declining markets were subject to more stringent loan-to-value underwriting requirements. Amid criticism of redlining reminiscent of the past segregationist practices of the FHA, the FHLBB, and the HOLC, the enterprises abandoned the practice in favor of stricter, national, uniform loan-to-value requirements.[36]

Enterprise multifamily underwriting has also been the subject of scrutiny. One study found evidence that GSE underwriting causes the enterprises to "lag in three sectors of the multifamily market that may have fair lending implications:

• Purchases of loans in high-minority tracts;
• Purchases of loans on small multifamily properties, which are disproportionately owned by property owners of color; and
• Purchases of loans for multifamily properties in underserved areas."[37]

The collapse of the financial markets has resulted in further reductions in GSE multifamily participations. However, multifamily market conditions related to vacancy rates, falling rents, and declining property values are so weak that private lenders have abandoned the market, meaning that in 2009 the enterprises, according to FHFA, "not only led the multifamily market, they effectively were the market."[38] Although some private capital returned to the market in 2010, the GSEs continued to comprise "a larger than usual portion of the multifamily market."[39]

THE DUTY TO FURTHER FAIR HOUSING
AND PAST GSE PERFORMANCE OF THE
AFFORDABLE HOUSING GOALS

Since at least 1989, GSE charters have directed the enterprises to include within secondary mortgage market purchases, "activities relating to mortgages on housing for low- and moderate-income families."[40] The 1992 Reform Act imposed three housing goals on the enterprises: a goal for the purchase of mortgages on housing for low- and moderate-income homeowners and renters; a goal involving mortgage purchases in central city, rural, and other "underserved markets;" and a goal requiring purchases of homeowner and rental mortgages for very-low-income families and also the "special" unaddressed affordable housing needs of low-income families in low-income areas. Housing goal requirements under the 1992 Reform Act are changing in 2010 because of amendments to GSE oversight legislation in the summer of 2008. However, past performance of the enterprises under the old housing goal framework is one means of understanding the fair housing impact of the duty to expand credit to low-income people, low-income areas, and underserved markets.

Federal housing initiatives in general are plagued by a tension between the duty to comply with the mandate to further fair housing by building affordable housing in low-poverty, racially integrated areas (often in the suburbs), and the structural features of programs that direct investment of resources to deteriorated, high poverty, racially identified areas.[41] The housing goals in the 1992 Reform Act reflect similar tensions. The low- and moderate-income goal and the special affordable housing goal are directed at improving access to credit for *people*, suggesting the possibility that those goals can be directed towards furthering fair housing by expanding choice of location in homeownership to racially integrated areas.[42] Such a result has been observed, for example, from lending that qualifies for credit under the Community Reinvestment Act.[43] On the other hand, an "underserved area" is a *place*, a census tract with a median income at or below 120% of area median income (AMI) and a population of people of color of 30% or more, or a census tract where median income does not exceed 90% of AMI. With racial concentrations as part of the benchmark, this housing goal has the potential for reinforcing existing patterns of segregation.

Much of the research examining the GSE affordable housing missions questions the efficacy of the housing goals, without looking more deeply at whether or not they further fair housing. The General Accountability Office (GAO) observed that "the effects of the housing goals on affordability and opportunities for target groups have been limited."[44] A different study uncovered negative interactions between GSE housing goal purchases and outcomes in FHA single family mortgage insurance programs, with GSE purchases "crowding out" FHA closings by focusing on the highest quality, low-income mortgages in highest income neighborhoods that qualified under housing goal standards.[45] Other research suggests that the relatively high income levels used under the 1992 Reform Act to define low- and moderate-income purchases are "exploited" by the GSEs, "yielding effects that might diverge from the law's intent."[46] Similar results were observed for multifamily activity, where GSE purchases are concentrated "in the middle of multifamily market segment with regard to affordability" because the "great majority of rental units are affordable to families at 100 percent of median income."[47]

The focus of the research on the question of housing goal effectiveness misses a key consideration. The congressional interest in affordable housing goals is to expand access to credit for people and places that face historic barriers to homeownership and investment. This intent is evident from the text of the 1992 Reform Act, which instructed HUD to set the goals in part by taking into account "the ability of the enterprises to lead the industry in making mortgage credit available."[48] Notwithstanding this directive, HUD administered the housing goals not to encourage the enterprises to serve as leaders in expanding fair access to credit, but rather to remedy the GSEs' history of lagging the market in providing credit to low-income families, underserved areas, and affordable housing serving low-income households, including affordable rental housing. From 1996 through 2008, housing goals were established at levels that were often less than, and were never greater than, the high end of HUD's forecast of market performance. In 2009, following the enactment of the Federal Housing Finance Regulatory Reform Act of 2008 (the 2008 Reform Act), FHFA assumed responsibility for administering the housing goals. At that point, FHFA adjusted "the housing goal targets to align them with FHFA's estimates of market activity in the current mortgage market environment." Under this regime, it is not surprising that the GSEs met or exceeded most housing goals from 2002 to 2007.[49]

Evidence that the housing goals provide any kind of benefit to borrowers of color is equivocal. Most research in this regard is focused on lending in racially identified areas, not access to credit by individual people of color, nor access by people of color to integrated areas of opportunity. A 2006 study suggested a possible fair housing benefit to the affordable housing goals by observing that as the GSEs increased market share, subprime lending decreased, especially in areas with high levels of racial concentration.[50] However, one year later, the GAO reached an opposite conclusion, finding that as subprime loans grew in market share of homebuyers of color, GSE share shrank. By 2005, subprime lending occupied a greater share of the market for borrowers of color than either Fannie Mae or Freddie Mac.[51]

The most significant civil rights issue associated with GSE housing goal performance remains to be fully explored. In the implementation of the housing goals provisions of the 1992 Reform Act, HUD authorized the enterprises to acquire non-conventional mortgages as a means of achieving the special affordable housing goals.[52] According to Congressional findings, under this authority the GSEs acquired $175 billion in subprime mortgage securities in 2004, and $1 trillion in subprime and Alt-A loans from 2005 through 2007.[53] Through the intervention of FHFA in 2007, the enterprises were compelled to adopt policies that excluded the purchase of loans that were considered to be predatory under guidelines issued by federal banking regulators, ending the acquisition of subprime loans.[54] Data from FHFA indicates that for the five-year period between 2003 and 2008, when enterprise purchases of subprime PLS are excluded from previously reported goals compliance reports, the GSE achievement of the housing goals falls off markedly, and for several years during that period, it falls below federal benchmark requirements.[55]

The data do not reveal the extent to which GSE purchases of subprime PLS involved loans to borrowers of color. Whatever its volume, it cannot possibly be an activity that furthers fair housing to achieve the housing goals through activities that now plague neighborhoods of color.

HOUSING GOALS UNDER THE 2008 REFORM ACT

Housing goals under the 1992 Reform Act were mostly concerned with the incomes of borrowers or renters, and the income and racial characteristics of the locations of units financed with GSE purchases mortgages, with little emphasis on whether the units consisted of for-sale or rental housing. The low- and moderate-income and underserved area goals focused on homeownership or rental housing only through subgoals, which by statute could not be the basis of an enforcement action by HUD in its capacity as overseer of housing goal compliance.[56]

The 2008 Reform Act, enacted in July 2008 as part of economic stimulus legislation, made several changes to this framework. The goals were reorganized to establish four single family homeownership goals and one multifamily rental special affordable housing goal. The new approach more carefully targets lower income households and areas. The old framework under the 1992 Reform Act's low- and moderate-income goal was aimed at moderate-income households at 100% of AMI, and low-income families at 80% of AMI. That goal was administered as single goal, effectively targeting it to households with incomes at or below 100% AMI. In contrast, the 2008 Reform Act establishes separate single family goals for low-income purchasers at 80% of AMI, and another for very low-income buyers at 50% of AMI. The new structure redefines low-income areas from 90% of AMI under the previous underserved area goal, to 80% of AMI. It retains the measure of a racially concentrated area as a census tract with minority population of 30% or more, but reduces the income limit for such locations from 120% AMI to 100% AMI. The multifamily goal under the 2008 Reform Act is aimed at households at or below 80% of AMI, and the legislation creates a multifamily subgoal for very low-income families with incomes at or below 50% AMI.[57]

Several aspects of the new goals methodologies remain unchanged. Like the predecessor law, the 2008 Reform Act requires FHFA to set the housing goals in part so that the enterprises lead the market.[58] FHFA's goals for 2010 and 2011 retain HUD's previous approach, setting goals that match, but do not exceed the market.[59] HUD rules in effect from 2001 to 2003 established incentives for enterprise purchase of loans secured by multifamily properties with less than 50 units. Small multifamily properties are "disproportionately located in high minority areas and… ownership of multifamily properties by African Americans is concentrated among such properties."[60] When HUD abandoned the incentives in 2004, GSE purchases of small multifamily properties dropped by more than 300%.[61] The 2008 Reform Act requires the enterprises to report on small multifamily purchases, and permits but does not require FHFA to set small multifamily goals.[62] The housing goal rule for 2010 and 2011 declines to impose a small multifamily goal.[63]

NEW CONCEPTS OF UNDERSERVED MARKETS

Under the 1992 Reform Act, the housing goal concept of the underserved market was intended to facilitate the provision of credit to low-income places, and areas of racial concentration. The 2008 Reform Act retains a similar targeting objective as part of the single family goals by defining a low-income area in part by reference to the extent of its racial concentration.[64] In a new definition of "underserved market," the 2008 Reform Act imposes an obligation on the GSEs to develop flexible loan products to facilitate a secondary mortgage market in financing for manufactured housing, rural markets, and for the preservation of HUD subsidized multifamily housing, properties assisted with Low-Income Housing Tax Credits (LIHTC), and comparable state and local programs serving moderate, low, and very low-income families.[65]

This new concept recognizes enterprise activities that do not always qualify for housing goal credit, but still have a significant impact on affordable housing. For example, prior to conservatorship, the enterprises made large purchases of LIHTC, and of tax-exempt single family mortgage revenue and exempt facility multifamily bonds. Fannie Mae's 2007 AHAR reported the purchase of $1.18 billion in LIHTC that year, plus an additional $1.32 billion in LIHTC associated with $934 million in multifamily, tax exempt bond mortgages.

Freddie Mac reported $458.3 million in LIHTC purchases, increasing its overall tax credit investments to more than $7 billion, involving 376,740 apartments in more than 5,000 projects. Freddie Mac's tax exempt bond activities were also extensive. They included $2.2 billion in multifamily tax exempt bond purchases, and $1 billion in mortgage revenue bond purchases that financed housing for victims of Hurricanes Katrina and Rita as part of an overall purchase of $1.8 billion in single family bonds.[66] The GSEs also provide credit enhancements in connection with tax-exempt bond financing such as payment guarantees. While single family mortgage revenue bond purchases and multifamily bond credit enhancements count for housing goal purposes under FHFA's new housing goal rules, tax credit investments and purchases of multifamily, tax-exempt bonds received no credit.[67]

It is difficult to overstate the extent to which the enterprises dominated the bond and tax credit markets, especially the market for purchase of LIHTC. Many commentators attribute the recent precipitous drop in tax credit pricing to the fact that the GSEs stopped making LIHTC investments as they began their own decline into conservatorship.[68] Enterprise participations in these activities offer an illustration of the tensions between financial safety and soundness and the public purpose of facilitating the production of affordable housing. In the fall of 2009, both GSEs stated in public securities filings that the value of their tax credit holdings was declining, further weakening already severely impaired balance sheets. The enterprises sought to sell their tax credit interests to two private investment companies at discount rates, a transaction that many feared would add more steep declines to dropping LIHTC prices. FHFA, as the enterprise safety- and soundness-supervisor, approved the sales. The Treasury Department ultimately blocked the deal because of the disproportionate tax benefits that would accrue to the buyers of the credits, and also, some say, to arrest the expected impact on LIHTC pricing.[69]

The focus of the new concept of "underserved markets" on preservation of existing affordable housing implicates crucial fair housing concerns. HUD multifamily programs and the LIHTC program are often criticized for engaging in siting practices that locate family housing in racially segregated, high poverty locations.[70] The 2008 Reform Act did nothing to change HUD's responsibility to ensure that GSE underwriting guidelines "are consistent with the Fair Housing Act."[71] Despite this civil rights imperative, FHFA's approach to regulating the duty to serve underserved markets says nothing about whether enterprise underwriting standards for multifamily preservation will perpetuate existing patterns of segregation in assisted housing, or will instead promote activities that expand housing choice.[72]

THE USE OF THE ENTERPRISES TO STABILIZE HOUSING MARKETS

The FHFA conservatorships of Fannie Mae and Freddie Mac are not the end of the government's direct involvement in the affairs of the enterprises. Section 1117 of the 2008 Reform Act gave the Treasury Department the authority to purchase GSE issued mortgage backed securities. GSE purchased private label securities, enterprise debt, and preferred stock in the GSEs in order to remove the weakest assets from their balance sheets, and to provide infusions of cash for ongoing operations.[73] By the end of 2009, the Treasury Department purchased $50.7 billion in enterprise stock, plus $220.8 billion in MBS. The Federal Reserve also plays a role in propping up the enterprises with commitments for the purchase of $1.25 trillion in GSE securities, and another $175 billion in GSE debt.[74]

The Treasury Department has used its senior preferred stock position to enlist the GSEs in systemic efforts to stabilize homeownership against threats of foreclosure, and also to provide badly needed assistance to the development of multifamily affordable rental housing. In many ways, these efforts are an extension of previous enterprise activities. Under the "Homeowner Affordability and Stability Plan," Treasury purchased bundles of state housing finance agency (HFA) mortgage revenue bonds to assist in single family financing, and exempt facility multifamily bonds from the GSEs to facilitate loans to tax exempt, bond financed rental projects. The Treasury Department also participated with the GSEs in credit instruments that allow HFAs to repay high cost and maturing bonds in order to ease current financial strains.[75] The GSEs are also central to programs that allow loan modifications and loan refinancing for homeowners facing foreclosure, providing over 2,300 lenders and servicers with automatic program access.[76]

The Treasury Department's stock ownership of Fannie Mae and Freddie Mac means that the federal government now has a direct financial interest in affordable homeowner and rental housing. There is no indication that civil rights considerations about the owners and tenants of that housing, or the location of the housing, play any role in these initiatives.

TITLE VIII, THE SECONDARY MORTGAGE MARKET, AND SECURITIZATION: "IT COULD BE STRUCTURED BY COWS, AND WE WOULD RATE IT."

HUD Title VIII rules forbid the use of race, color, and other protected characteristics in the purchase, sale, and securitization of "loans, or other debt or securities which relate to, or which are secured by dwellings."[77] A great deal of recent attention is focused on the role of securitization of mortgages, including subprime mortgages, in causing the current financial crisis. Like fair lending, it appears that discrimination in the secondary mortgage market receives scant attention and enforcement resources.

It is the enterprises that originated the concept of bundling and selling shares in pools of mortgages.[78] They perform all the functions for GSE-issued securities that are spread among multiple parties in the issuance of private label securities. The GSEs typically own the mortgages that are the collateral for MBS. Conforming loan underwriting requirements serve as a form of rating that offers securities buyers some level of confidence in the quality of the underlying collateral. The enterprises also guarantee the return on the MBS.

In contrast, PLS issues are often created on a "shelf" basis, where the underlying mortgages are traded in and out of the pool, and are not generally owned by the issuer.[79] A significant volume of private label securities are collateralized by subprime loans that, when underwritten, did not document buyer income, were based on questionable appraisals, had high loan-to-value ratios, ballooning interest rates, and early maturity dates that resulted in default. The quality of PLS are rated by rating agencies that are paid by the issuers to rate the securities, and whose procedures and standards for issuing the ratings are opaque, and on occasion, non-existent.[80] PLS are not guaranteed by the issuers. Instead, third party insurers supply credit default swaps that promise to make interest and dividend payments to investors in the event of borrower default.[81] For all intents and purposes, the system for issuance of PLS is an unregulated house of cards that purports to separate almost all participants from the risk of default. As one rating agency employee put it at the height of the subprime PLS frenzy, a PLS issue "could be structured by cows and we would rate it."[82] It is no surprise that when subprime mortgages fell into foreclosure, the entire system collapsed.

A fundamental feature of mortgage backed securities is the way the characteristics of individual loans affect how they are bundled by investors, rated by rating agencies, and priced by securities purchasers for both the cost of the security and the expected return. Some of those characteristics implicate fair housing considerations, including the location of the property, the number and characteristics of any tenants, local and regional vacancy rates and rents, the property's physical condition, the property's management, the terms of the leases of the property's tenants, the strength of the local economy, and possible hazards.[83]

Regulation of asset-backed securities issues and rating agencies is the primary responsibility of the Securities and Exchange Commission (SEC). The SEC's "degree of due diligence" with respect to asset-backed securities "falls short of the more extensive HUD review of the 'affordable lending' initiatives of the GSEs or FHFA's review of whether newly developed mortgage products pose safety and soundness risks."[84]

Existing SEC rules for asset-backed securities and for rating organizations do require a certain level of public disclosure on matters like the regional location of the asset comprising the securities, and on the effects of legal or regulatory requirements such as consumer protection and predatory lending laws. The rules provide for no meaningful SEC oversight of whether the characteristics used to bundle and rate mortgages in a securities pool suggest the possibility of discrimination, such as a targeting of subprime lending at communities or people of color.[85] Proposed SEC rules would require a much more detailed level of disclosure, including information about individual loans making up a mortgage-backed security. However, the proposed rules would require disclosure of information about the location of a loan only at the metropolitan area level, making it virtually impossible to identify patterns in securitization at a level of geography that might reveal patterns of discrimination, such as a census tract or zip code. The SEC's proposal about the geographic level of reporting is based in part on considerations of privacy.[86] In that regard, it is worth observing that under the HMDA, lenders are required to gather and disclose information about the racial and ethnic characteristics of borrowers, and the census tract location of individual loans in a manner that protects individual privacy. Under the authority of the 2008 Reform Act, FHFA requires the same type of disclosures for loans purchased by the GSEs.[87]

The extent of SEC involvement in securities transactions that affect housing means that it is an "agency having regulatory or supervisory authority over financial institutions" engaged in activities related to housing, thus requiring the SEC to act "in a manner affirmatively to further the purposes of" Title VIII. In light of the disproportionate impact of subprime lending and foreclosures on homeowners of color and racially identified neighborhoods, it is apparent that the SEC must become part of any reinvigorated fair-lending strategy, both through improved civil rights-related reported requirements, and through enforcement of fair housing principles regarding securitization and the secondary mortgage market. Such an outcome is especially necessary for the regulation of private label syndicators outside of FHFA oversight, and would be doubly required in the event that the GSEs are privatized entirely or terminated, with their functions left to the private market.

THE FAIR HOUSING FUTURE OF
THE SECONDARY MORTGAGE MARKET

Criticism of the combined private ownership and public purpose characteristics of the GSEs is not new, and is fueled by a history of questionable accounting practices, insufficient capital reserves to support enterprise debt obligations, and purchases of risky MBS and PLS, including securities consisting of bundled subprime mortgages. The debate about the future of the GSEs now centers on the continued creditability and viability of their role in providing liquidity and underwriting consistency in the residential mortgage lending market, and also on whether the enterprises should carry out affordable housing goals, and if so, then in what shape and form. In many respects, the debate is as much about the future of the secondary mortgage market as it is about the enterprises.

In broad terms, policymakers are at this writing considering four possible options: (1) converting the enterprises to one or more government corporations or agencies, with activities limited to affordable housing initiatives and liquidity and stability functions, such as issuance of mortgage backed securities consisting only of conforming loans; (2) restoring the enterprises to financial stability through the conservatorship, and allowing them to continue to do business as GSEs, but under more rigorous public utility-like regulation; (3) privatizing the enterprises by allowing them to do business along with other PLS issuers without the tax benefits and government guarantees available under their current charters; and (4) terminating the enterprises altogether, turning secondary market functions over to the private market.[88]

The risky business practices that led to the enterprise conservatorships are not distinguishable from many of the abuses that characterized the downfall of the market for private label securities. GSEs did use the advantages associated with their public role to enhance profit taking, including access to a Treasury Department line of credit that preceded the conservatorship, exemption from state and local taxes, and a now repealed exemption from SEC registration requirements. Those advantages, however, were applied to the same kind of activities that characterized the PLS industry, including trades in subprime PLS.[89] On matters that relate to furthering fair housing—eliminating racial disparities in access to credit and attending to the civil rights impact of underwriting; standardizing loan products that not only promote liquidity but also diminish the viability of subprime loans to borrowers of color; engaging in credit activities that expand housing choices for people of color outside locations of poverty and racial concentration, and inside areas of opportunity; combating discrimination in the making of home mortgage loans; understanding and acting on the fair housing effects of the purchase and securitization of mortgages; promoting a flow of capital for affordable housing development, especially in places that enhance housing choice for low-income people of color- in all these areas—the

GSEs do no better job than the private market. Thus, the key considerations for the fair housing future of the enterprises are no different than the matters that ought to inform the future of the secondary mortgage market:

1. Underwriting and Access to Single Family Credit. The consensus view is that if the enterprises have accomplished anything, they have brought a measure of consistency and predictability to the home mortgage market through standardized underwriting criteria, and as a consequence they have improved access to credit. Enterprise underwriting standards are shaped by financial safety and soundness considerations that dictate the acceptable risk features of purchased loans. Considerations of that sort were missing in the private label securities market, leading to the current economic crisis. A secondary mortgage market that is entirely privatized could easily abandon standardized underwriting, leading to less predictability, greater risk, and curtailed access to credit.

Beyond that issue is the question of whether GSE underwriting criteria contribute to loan denials for people of color. HMDA data shows continuing disparities in home mortgage loan denials for people of color. The enterprises do no better than to match that market. The advent of stricter underwriting standards, both in the loans purchased by the enterprises and in the private market, has sharply reduced the number of loan applications from households of color. While it is easy to reach the conclusion that an end to standardized underwriting will encourage more subprime lending targeted at borrowers of color, too little is understood about how conventional underwriting activities like automated underwriting result in redlining or disparate outcomes based on protected characteristics. Further research on this topic is warranted.

The 1992 Reform Act made it HUD's responsibility to review GSE underwriting and appraisal guidelines, but implementing regulations turn this duty on its head, and require the enterprises to provide HUD with an annual self-assessment.[90] Press reports in 2004 indicated that a HUD-sponsored study of the fair lending impact of GSE underwriting was near completion. HUD refused to release the report because of questions about the methodology. There are ready templates for gauging the GSE performance in this area, including the fair lending examination procedures utilized by the Federal Financial Institutions Examining Council (FFIEC) for banks under its supervision.[91] A fair housing future for both the enterprises and the secondary mortgage market must include features that lead to a better understanding of underwriting and its affect on access to credit, and adjustments in underwriting criteria to achieve equal access to credit.

2. Improving Fair Lending Enforcement. The unfulfilled prospect that the close relationship between lending institutions and the GSEs could be used to enhance fair lending practices is almost entirely overshadowed by the apparent failure of HUD, banking regulators, and the Department of Justice to engage in any meaningful, coordinated, visible, enforcement effort. There is no fair housing future for a secondary mortgage market that reflects any of the options under consideration without a system that directly connects examinations of underwriting practices, lending outcomes, and actual, comprehensive enforcement.

Activities in this area should include multifamily lending. FFIEC's interagency fair lending examination procedures currently examine bank records for discrimination against both home purchasers and the commercial borrowers who are likely to construct multifamily rental housing. However, to the extent that enforcement actions are undertaken, they appear to focus solely on single family loan products. A refusal to lend to a multifamily borrower based on the protected characteristics of the likely occupants of an apartment complex is as much a violation of the Fair Housing Act as a loan denial to a single-family homeowner.[92] Given the common experience of opposition to multifamily housing in high opportunity areas, a revitalized fair lending enforcement effort might address systemic patterns of discrimination in the single family market, and also engage in targeted activities in the multifamily sector.

3. Title VIII and Securitization. Homeowners facing foreclosure sometimes directly experience the securities markets. Foreclosure deeds often state that the originating mortgage lender is the registration company that tracks ownership and servicing obligations for assets that are traded in and out of private label mortgage pools, and they often show the foreclosing entity as the company that services the mortgage for the loan pool.[93] Under the current system for regulating asset-backed securities, there is no mechanism for examining whether the characteristics of the loan pool implicate fair housing considerations that affect homeowners. Oversight of issuers and rating agencies lacks meaningful fair housing content, and unlike the nominal provisions of GSE oversight legislation, there is no apparent means of linking the fair housing enforcement system to securities regulation.

Financial services reform legislation recently enacted in Congress would improve oversight of the security issuers and rating agencies that are the subject of current regulation, would require oversight of other key components of the system for issuing asset-backed securities, such as issuers of credit default swaps, and creates a new Bureau of Consumer Financial Protection. The legislation offers no new oversight authority and no new resources for enforcing Title VIII's non-discrimination requirements.[94] It rejects approaches offered in early proposals to improve interagency coordination of investigative and enforcement activities across a number of areas related to home mortgage finance, including fair lending.[95]

Ensuring fair housing in a reformulated secondary mortgage market, with or without the GSEs, requires meaningful reporting structures that allow oversight agencies to assess the civil rights affect of the characteristics that are the basis for bundling mortgages and other forms of credit. There will be no real impact of any such provision until HUD, the Department of Justice, FHFA, the SEC, and Bureau of Consumer Financial Protection contribute resources to a meaningful and comprehensive enforcement strategy.

4. The Mandate to Create Open Housing Markets and GSE Affordable Housing Goals. Enterprise housing goals focus on access to credit and housing by people, and also on investment in low- and moderate-income, and racially concentrated places. The goals have the potential to strike a balance between creating meaningful choice for people of color to live in high opportunity locations, and activities that remedy the effects of past discrimination through investments in previously disinvested areas.

Some research suggests that the GSEs accomplish their housing goals by creaming; that is, by purchasing qualifying loans in higher income places. Other sources indicate that past housing goal compliance was achieved largely through purchases of private label, subprime mortgage backed securities. Less well known is whether GSE affordable housing activities have the same integrative effect observed in connection with CRA single family lending, or whether enterprise underwriting criteria deprive homebuyers of color of both credit and housing opportunities. The same questions apply to affordable housing activities in the multifamily context. The redefined concept of "underserved" markets, with its emphasis on the preservation of the kinds of assisted housing that are too often a tool for establishing patterns of segregation, is empty of the kind of civil rights imperatives that derive from the duty to further fair housing—understanding the civil rights impact of funding activities, and taking steps so that over time, segregation is dismantled.

In considering the structures for a reorganized financial system for housing finance, policy makers must consider the role of the system in facilitating homeownership and affordable rental housing for low-, very low-, and extremely low-income people.[96] The duty to further fair housing imposes the additional responsibility to shape policies and initiatives so that over time, affordable housing activity opens up markets for people of color, dismantles residential segregation, and allows for true housing choice. These responsibilities will adhere whether they are carried out by FHFA, or some other regulatory successor in any of the strategies under discussion for reformulating the secondary mortgage market, either in an entirely privatized form without the GSEs, or in some approach that includes restructured enterprises.

5. Fair Housing and the Use of the Enterprises to Stabilize Housing Markets. The use of the GSEs by the Treasury Department to stabilize the single family and affordable multifamily housing markets implicates other civil rights issues. At the threshold, all the issues about site selection and housing opportunity in affordable housing are present in discussions about the affordable housing goals and the effect of GSE participations in LIHTC and tax-exempt bond rental projects.

More immediate issues include disposition of foreclosed properties financed with mortgages held by the enterprises. The Neighborhood Stabilization Program (NSP) is a HUD program designed to stabilize areas affected by foreclosures and abandonment.[97] Anecdotal reports indicate that the GSEs often fail to cooperate in neighborhood-based stabilization strategies devised by NSP grantees. Additional reports center on enterprise refusal to provide certifications to NSP buyers about GSE compliance with NSP environmental criteria, and new federal requirements that limit the ability of foreclosing financial institutions to evict tenant occupants of foreclosed housing. These failures can have the effect of accelerating the deterioration of already disinvested locations, places that are predominantly racially-identified neighborhoods.

Foreclosures are not limited to high poverty, racially-identified locations. A great deal of foreclosed property is in higher income areas with access to good schools and jobs. To the extent the enterprises are the foreclosing institutions for properties in these places, the disposition of the properties through NSP and similar programs creates opportunities to expand housing choice for families of color. Although HUD NSP guidance encourages non-profit grantees to acquire housing in opportunity locations, there are few incentives in the program to carry out that objective.[98]

6. Multifamily Foreclosures on the Horizon. While a great deal of attention is focused on single family homeowners, foreclosures also affect renters.[99] Racial disparities in homeownership mean that disproportionate numbers of people of color are renters who are the most likely to be affected by multifamily foreclosures. Evidence of distress in the multifamily market is growing, with significant increases in delinquencies related to decreasing rents and the inability to secure financing to pay for short term commercial debt.[100] The enterprises hold almost 40% of outstanding multifamily debt, and problems with loan defaults are expected to increase from 2010 through 2013, as over $600 billion in commercial loans mature.[101] Distress in multifamily markets may also affect enterprise-housing goals. Both GSEs invest in commercial mortgage-backed securities (CMBS), which face the same exposure to collapse in value already visited on residential mortgage-backed securities. Freddie Mac's past special affordable housing goal performance was accomplished primarily through CMBS purchases.[102] As consequence, the same stress factors in the single family market that resulted in GSE conservatorship are likely to continue through problems in the multifamily market. These conditions further cloud the future of the enterprises.

Multifamily foreclosures may have a special impact on owners and investors of color. The small multifamily properties that are so predominated by African American ownership are also at the highest risk of default because of higher credit costs. In the past, some of the enterprises' alternative loan products were aimed at meeting the needs of the small multifamily market. These products were largely abandoned and it is unlikely that they will be made available as multifamily credit risks are magnified in the next several years.

CONCLUSION

The policy discussions now beginning about the future of Fannie Mae and Freddie Mac implicate wider questions about the furtherance of fair housing within the context of the system for financing residential mortgages. Oversight legislation presumes that the GSEs will serve as foot soldiers in a wider fair lending enforcement effort, yet there is a lagging commitment to fair lending enforcement among the federal agencies responsible for carrying it out. Mandates for housing goals call on the enterprises to lead the market in facilitating access to credit for the most vulnerable borrowers, yet the GSEs do no better than to match continuing racial disparities in the private market. In an environment where subprime lending was targeted at homeowners and communities of color, and was fueled by the securities industry, there remains little evidence of an acknowledgment of the fair housing, fair credit dimensions of asset-backed securitization among policy makers in Congress, or the federal regulators with overlapping oversight responsibilities. Responding to these conditions requires attention not only in the reformulation of the GSEs, in whatever form, but also in the wider financial markets. It is this challenge that remains to be taken up.

BIBLIOGRAPHY

Abt Associates, *Are States Using the Low Income Housing Tax Credit to Enable Families with Children to Live in Low Poverty and Racially Integrated Neighborhoods?* July 28, 2006.

Abt Associates, Inc., *Study of the Multifamily Underwriting and the GSEs' Role in the Multifamily Market: Expanded Version,* August 2001.

An, Xudong and Bostic, Ralphael, *GSE Activity, FHA Feedback, and Implications for the Efficacy of the Affordable Housing Goals,* Journal of Real Estate Finance and Economics, 2008.

An, Xudong and Bostic, Ralphael, *Have the Affordable Housing Goals been a Shield against Subprime? Regulatory Incentives and the Extension of Mortgage Credit,* April 28, 2006.

Avery, Robert B., Bhutta, Neil, Brevoort, Kenneth P., Canner, Glenn B., and Gibbs, Christa N., *The 2008 HMDA Data: The Mortgage Market during a Turbulent Year,* Federal Reserve Bulletin, September 2009.

Bhutta, Neil, *GSE Activity and Mortgage Supply in Lower-Income and Minority Neighborhoods: The Effect of the Affordable Housing Goals,* Finance and Economics Discussion Series, Divisions of Research & Statistics and Monetary Affairs, Federal Reserve Board, 2009.

Bunce, Harold, HF-011, *An Analysis of GSE Purchases of Mortgages for African-American Borrowers and Their Neighborhoods,* Housing Finance Working Paper Series, U.S. Department of Housing and Urban Development, December 2000.

Burnett, Kimberly, Cortes, Alvaro, and Herbert Christopher E., *Review of Selected Underwriting Guidelines to Identify Potential Barriers to Hispanic Homeownership,* Abt Associates, March 2006.

Congressional Oversight Panel, *February Oversight Report: Commercial Real Estate Losses and the Threat to Financial Stability,* February 10, 2010.

David Reiss, *Subprime Standardization: Home Rating Agencies Allow Predatory Lending to Flourish in the Secondary Mortgage Market*, 33 Fla. St. U. L. Rev. 985, 2006.

Federal Financial Institutions Examination Council, *Interagency Fair Lending Examination Procedures,* August 2009.

Federal Home Loan Mortgage Corporation, *Annual Housing Activities Report for 2007,* March 14, 2008.

Federal Home Loan Mortgage Corporation, *Annual Housing Activities Report for 2008,* March 10, 2009.

Federal Home Loan Mortgage Corporation, *Annual Housing Activities Report for 2009,* March 16, 2010.

Federal Home Loan Mortgage Corporation, Bulletin, May 29, 2008.

Federal Home Loan Mortgage Corporation, Bulletin, November 15, 2007.

Federal Housing Finance Agency, *2010–2011 Enterprise Affordable Housing Goals; Enterprise Book-Entry Procedures; Proposed Rule*, 75 Fed. Reg. 9034, February 26, 2010.

Federal Housing Finance Agency, *2010–2011 Enterprise Housing Goals; Enterprise Book-entry Procedures: Final Rule,* 75 Fed. Reg. 55891 (September 14, 2010)

Federal Housing Finance Agency, *Duty to Serve Underserved Markets for Enterprises: Advance Notice of Proposed Rulemaking and Request for Comment*, 74 Fed. Reg. 38572, August 4, 2009.

Federal Housing Finance Agency, *Final Rule for 2009 Enterprise Transition Affordable Housing Goals*, Federal Reg. Vol. 74, No. 152, pp.39873, August 10, 2009.

Federal Housing Finance Agency, *Mortgage Market Note 10–1 (Update of Mortgage Market Notes 09–1 and 09–1A),* January 20, 2010.

Federal Housing Finance Agency, Mortgage Market Note 10–2, *The Housing Goals of Federal National Mortgage Association and Federal Home Loan Mortgage Corporation,* February 1, 2010.

Federal Housing Finance Agency, *Notice of Order: Revisions to Enterprise Public Use Database,* 75 Fed. Reg. 41180, July 15, 2010.

Federal National Mortgage Association, *2007 Annual Housing Activities Report,* March 17, 2008.

Federal National Mortgage Association, *2008 Annual Housing Activities Report,* March 16, 2009.

Federal National Mortgage Association, *2009 Annual Housing Activities Report,* March 15, 2010.

Federal National Mortgage Association, Announcement 07–11, July 13, 2007.

Federal National Mortgage Association, Announcement 08–10, May 16, 2008.

Federal National Mortgage Association, Form 8K (filed with the Securities and Exchange Commission, November 9, 2009.

Friedman, Samantha and Squires, Gregory D., *Does the Community Reinvestment Act Help Minorities Access Traditionally Inaccessible Neighborhoods?* Social Problems, Vol. 52, Issue 2, pp. 209–231, Society for the Study of Social Problems, Inc., 2005.

Furman Center for Real Estate and Urban Policy, *The High Cost of Segregation: Exploring the Relationship Between Racial Segregation and Subprime Lending,* New York University, November 2009.

Geithner, Timothy, *Written Testimony to the House Committee on Financial Services,* TG-603, March 23, 2010.

General Accountability Office, *Fair Lending: Data Limitations and the Fragmented Financial Regulatory Structure Challenge Federal Oversight and Enforcement Efforts,* GAO-09–704, July 2009.

General Accountability Office, *Federal Housing Administration: Decline in the Agency's Market Share was Associated with Product and Process Developments of Other Mortgage Market Participants,* GAO-07–645, June 2007.

General Accountability Office, Federal National Mortgage Association and Federal Home Loan Mortgage Corporation: "Analysis of Options for Revising the Housing Enterprises' Long-term Structures," GAO-09–782, September 2009.

Gray, Robert and Tursky, Steve, "Location and Racial/Ethnic Occupancy Patterns for HUD-Subsidized Family Housing in Ten Metropolitan Areas," *Housing Desegregation and Federal Policy.* Edited by John Goering, Univ. of North Carolina Press, 1986.

Hillier, Amy E., *Residential Security Maps and Neighborhood Appraisals: The Homeowners' Loan Corporation and the Case of Philadelphia,* Social Science History, Vol. 29, No. 2, 2005.

Jaffee, Dwight M., *The Role of the GSEs and Housing Policy in the Financial Crisis,* Financial Crisis Inquiry Commission, February 25, 2010.

Joint Center for Housing Studies, *Mortgage Market Channels and Fair Lending: An Analysis of HMDA Data,* April 25, 2007.

Joint Center for Housing Studies, *The Disruption of the Low-Income Housing Tax Credit Program: Causes, Consequences, Responses, and Proposed Correctives,* December 2009.

Julian, Elizabeth K., *An Unfinished Agenda,* Shelterforce, Winter 2007.

Lockhart, James B. III, Director Federal Housing Finance Agency, Corrected Statement Before the House Committee on Financial Services on the Conservatorship of Federal National Mortgage Association and Federal Home Loan Mortgage Corporation, September 25, 2008.

Massey, Douglas S. and Denton, Nancy A., *American Apartheid: Segregation and the Making of the American Underclass,* Harvard University Press, 1993.

McCoy, Patricia A., Pavlov, Andre D., and Wachter, Susan M., *Systemic Risk Through Securitization: The Result of Deregulation and Regulatory Failure,* 41 Conn. L. Rev. 1327, May 2009.

Memorandum of Understanding Among the Department of the Treasury, the Federal Housing Finance Agency, the Federal National Mortgage Association, and the Federal Home Loan Mortgage Corporation, October 19, 2009.

Office of Comptroller of the Currency, Board of Governors of the Federal Reserve System, Federal Deposit Insurance Corporation, Department of the Treasury, and National Credit Union Administration, *Interagency Guidance on Nontraditional Mortgage Product Risks,* 71 Fed. Reg. 58609, October 4, 2006.

Peterson, Christopher, *Subprime Lending, Foreclosure and Race: An Introduction to the Role of Securitization in Residential Mortgage Finance,* Kirwan Institute for the Study of Race and Ethnicity, September 25, 2008.

Reiss, David, *Subprime Standardization: How Rating Agencies Allow Predatory Lending to Flourish in the Secondary Mortgage Market,* 33 Fla. St. U. L. Rev. 985, Summer 2006.

Securities and Exchange Commission, *Amendments to Rules for Nationally Recognized Statistical Rating Organizations; Proposed Rules for Nationally Recognized Statistical Rating Organizations; Final Rule and Proposed Rule,* 74 Fed. Reg. 63832, December 12, 2009.

Securities and Exchange Commission, *Asset-Backed Securities; Final Rule,* 70 Fed. Reg. 1506, January 7, 2005.

Securities and Exchange Commission, *Asset-Backed Securities; Proposed Rule,* 75 Fed. Reg. 23327, 23357, May 3, 2010.

Securities and Exchange Commission, *Summary Report of Issues Identified in the Commission's Staff's Examinations of Select Credit Rating Agencies,* July 2008.

U.S. Department of Housing and Urban Development, *The Location and Racial Composition of Public Housing in the United States,* December 1994. U.S. Department of Housing and Urban Development, *The Federal National Mortgage Association (Fannie Mae) and the Federal Home Loan Mortgage Corporation (Freddie Mac) Regulations; Final Rule,* 60 Fed. Reg. 61846, December 1, 1995

U.S. Department of Housing and Urban Development, *24 C.F.R. Part 81, Subpart B, Housing Goals,* 2009 ed.

U.S. Department of Housing and Urban Development, *Notice of Fund Availability (NOFA) for the Neighborhood Stabilization Program 2 under the American Recovery and Reinvestment Act, 2009,* Appendix I, par. S.1, May 4, 2009.

U.S. Department of Housing and Urban Development, *Overview of GSEs' Housing Goal Performance, 2000–2007,* November 2008.

U.S. Department of Housing and Urban Development, *U.S. Housing Market Conditions,* November 2009.

U.S. Department of the Treasury, *Data as of March 4, 2010 on Treasury and Federal Reserve Purchase Programs for GSE and Mortgage-Related Securities.*

U.S. Department of Treasury, *Making Home Affordable Program: Servicer Performance Report Through January 2010,* February 17, 2010.

Urban Institute, *A Decade of HOPE VI: Research Findings and Policy Challenges,* May 2004.

Wardrip, Keith E. and Pelletiere, Danilo, *Properties, Units, and Tenure in the Foreclosure Crisis: An Initial Analysis of Properties at the End of the Foreclosure Process,* National Low Income Housing Coalition, Research Note #08–01, May 6, 2008, revised May 8, 2008.

NOTES

1. The author is a partner at the law firm of Klein Hornig LLP, Boston, Massachusetts.

2. The Fannie Mae charter is codified in the banking title of the U.S. Code along with the charter for another government sponsored enterprise, the Government National Mortgage Association, or Ginnie Mae. *See,* 12 U.S.C. §1716, *et seq.* The Freddie Mac charter is at 12 U.S.C. §1451, *et seq.*

3. Peterson, Christopher, *Subprime Lending, Foreclosure and Race: An Introduction to the Role of Securitization in Residential Mortgage Finance* (Kirwan Institute for the Study of Race and Ethnicity, September 25, 2008).

4. General Accountability Office, *Fannie Mae and Freddie Mac: Analysis of Options for Revising the Housing Enterprises' Long-term Structures* (GAO-09–782, September 2009).

5. Lockhart, James B. III, Director Federal Housing Finance Agency, *Corrected Statement Before the House Committee on Financial Services on the Conservatorship of Fannie Mae and Freddie Mac* (September 25, 2008).

6. 42 U.S.C §3608(d).

7. These concerns were most recently expressed in the sweeping Congressional overhaul of the financial services system. *See,* Pub. L. 111–203, §1491; 124 Stat. 2205 (July 21, 2010) (Dodd-Frank Wall Street Reform and Consumer Protection Act).

8. *See, e.g., NAACP v. HUD,* 817 F.2d 149 (1 Cir. 1987); *Otero v. New York City Housing Authority,* 484 F.2d 1122 (2 Cir. 1973); and *Shannon v. United States Department of Housing and Urban Development,* 436 F.2d 809 (3 Cir. 1970).

9. *Jones v. Office of the Comptroller of Currency,* 983 F. Supp. 197, 203 (D.DC 1997); *Jorman v. Veterans Administration,* 579 F. Supp. 1407, 1408 (N.D. Ill. 1984); *Debolt v. Espy,* 832 F. Supp. 209 (S.D. Ohio 1993).

10. Hillier, Amy E., *Residential Security Maps and Neighborhood Appraisals: The Homeowners' Loan Corporation and the Case of Philadelphia,* Social Science History, Vol. 29, No. 2 (2005).

11. Massey, Douglas S. and Denton, Nancy A., *American Apartheid: Segregation and the Making of the American Underclass* (Harvard University Press, 1993).

12. Peterson, Christopher, *Fannie Mae, Freddie Mac, and the Home Mortgage Foreclosure Crisis,* 10 Loyola J. of Public Interest Law 149 (2009).

13. *See,* Pub. L. 91–351, §304 (July 24, 1970); 84 Stat. 454, enacting 12 U.S.C. §1453 ("The capital stock of the [Freddie Mac] shall consist of nonvoting common stock which shall be issued only to Federal home loan banks."). Until 1989, the Federal Home Loan Bank Board also chartered and supervised thrifts. The Financial Institutions Reform and Recovery Act of 1989 abolished the Board, shifting chartering and supervision of thrifts to the Federal Home Finance Board, and oversight of a system of regionalized Federal Home Loan Banks to the Federal Housing Finance Board (FHFB). The Housing and Economic Reform Act of 2008 abolished the FHFB and assigned oversight of regional Federal Home Loan Banks to FHFA. *See,* Pub. L. 110–289, Div. A, §1311; 122 Stat. 2797 (July 30, 2008).

14. *Thompson v. United States Dep't of HUD,* 348 F. Supp. 2d 398 (D. Maryland 2005), summary judgment denied, *Thompson v. United States Dep't of HUD,* 2006 U.S. Dist. LEXIS 9416 (D. Maryland January 10, 2006).

15. The GSEs are APA "agencies" for purposes of the Freedom of Information Act. 5 U.S.C. §552(f)(1). Several cases hold that the Federal Home Loan Banks are "agencies" within the meaning of the APA. *See, e.g., Fidelity Financial Corp. v. Federal Home Loan Bank,* 589 F. Supp. 885 (N.D. Cal. 1983). There are also a number of cases imposing a duty to further fair housing on HUD grantees, and the outcome in these cases suggests that the duty to further fair housing extends to non-federal entities supervised by federal agencies.. *See, e.g., Langlois v. Abington Housing Authority,* 234 F. Supp. 2d 33 (D. Mass. 2002). While it is fair to conclude that these authorities impose a similar obligation on the enterprises either because the GSEs are APA agencies, or because they are supervised by federal agencies, a full exploration of the question is beyond the scope of this essay.

16. *See, Thompson v. United States Dep't of HUD* at note 13 (HUD); *cf., Jones v. Comptroller of the Currency* at note 7 (duty of agency with supervisory authority over financial system to further fair housing).

17. Pub. L. 100–430, §6(c), 102 Stat. 1622 (Sept. 13, 1988), amending 42 U.S.C. §3605.

18. *See,* 24 C.F.R. §100.125 (2010 ed.).

19. Pub. L. 102–550, title XIII (October 28, 1992), 106 Stat. 3941.

20. 12 U.S.C. §4545.

21. 24 C.F.R. §81.44 (2010 ed.).

22. Federal Financial Institutions Examination Council, *Interagency Fair Lending Examination Procedures* (August 2009).

23. General Accountability Office, *Fair Lending: Data Limitations and the Fragmented Financial Regulatory Structure Challenge Federal Oversight and Enforcement Efforts* (GAO-09–704, July 2009).

24. Avery, Robert B., Bhutta, Neil, Brevoort, Kenneth P., Canner, Glenn B., and Gibbs, Christa N., *The 2008 HMDA Data: The Mortgage Market during a Turbulent Year* (Federal Reserve Bulletin, September 2009).

25. Furman Center for Real Estate and Urban Policy, *The High Cost of Segregation: Exploring the Relationship Between Racial Segregation and Subprime Lending* (New York University, November 2009).

26. Bunce, Harold, HF-011, *An Analysis of GSE Purchases of Mortgages for African-American Borrowers and Their Neighborhoods* (Housing Finance Working Paper Series, U.S. Department of Housing and Urban Development, December 2000).

27. Fannie Mae's 2008 purchases of loans made to blacks comprised 5% of overall purchases and its purchases of Latino loans were 6.6% of its purchases, compared to respective market shares by these borrowers of color of 5% and 6.1%. Freddie Mac's respective percentage purchases were 4% and 6.4%. *See,* Fannie Mae's *2008 Annual Housing Activities Report* (March 16, 2009) and Freddie Mac's *Annual Housing Activities Report for 2008* (March 10, 2009). Information about the 2008 market is from HMDA data compiled by the Federal Financial Institutions Examination Council's (FFIEC) and is available at: http://www.ffiec.gov/Hmda/default.htm.

28. Fannie Mae, *2009 Annual Housing Activities Report* (March 15, 2010); Freddie Mac, *Annual Housing Activities Report for 2009* (March 16, 2010).

29. Federal Housing Finance Agency, *2010–2011 Enterprise Housing Goals; Enterprise Book-entry Procedures: Final Rule* 75 Fed. Reg. 55891 (September 14, 2010).

30. 12 U.S.C. §4545.

31. *See,* 24 C.F.R. §81.43 and §81.63 (2010 ed.).

32. Fannie Mae, *Annual Housing Activities Report for 2009.*

33. Bunce, *An Analysis of GSE Purchases of Mortgages for African-American Borrowers;* Burnett, Kimberly, Cortes, Alvaro, and Herbert Christopher E., *Review of Selected Underwriting Guidelines to Identify Potential Barriers to Hispanic Homeownership* (Abt Associates, March 2006).

34. FHFA, *2010–2011 Enterprise Affordable Housing Goals; Final Rule*, 75 Fed. Reg. 55900.

35. Both cases were dismissed without addressing the issue of whether automated underwriting violates fair lending laws. *See, Beaulialice v. Federal Home Loan Mortgage Corporation,* 2007 U.S. Dist. LEXIS 15846, 20 Fla. L. Weekly Fed. D. 656 (M.D. Fla., March 6, 2007) and *Rahmann v. Federal National Mortgage Association,* Case No. 1:02CV01822 (D.C. D.C., November 2, 2004), on file with author.

36. For more detail about the declining market procedures, *see,* Fannie Mae, *Announcement 07–11*(July 13, 2007) and Freddie Mac, *Bulletin* (November 15, 2007). The procedures were abandoned in favor of the national standards in Fannie Mae, *Announcement 08–10* (May 16, 2008) and Freddie Mac, *Bulletin* (May 29, 2008).

37. Abt Associates, Inc., *Study of the Multifamily Underwriting and the GSEs' Role in the Multifamily Market: Expanded Version* (August 2001).

38. FHFA, *2010–2011 Proposed Enterprise Affordable Housing Goals; Enterprise Book-Entry Procedures; Proposed Rule,* 75 Fed. Reg.9033, 9056 (February 26, 2010).

39. FHFA, *2010–2011 Enterprise Affordable Housing Goals; Final Rule,* 75 Fed. Reg. 55921.

40. The low- and moderate-income directive in the Fannie Mae charter is codified in the National Housing Act at 12 U.S.C. §1716(3). The companion provision in the Freddie Mac charter is in a note to 12 U.S.C. §1451.

41. Julian, Elizabeth K., *Fair Housing and Community Development: Time to Come Together,* 41 Ind. L. Rev. 555 (2008).

42. Under the 1992 Reform Act, moderate-income households are families with incomes not in excess of 100% of AMI. Low-income families are those with incomes

adjusted for household size that are at or below 80% of AMI, and very low-income families are households with incomes not in excess of 60% of AMI.

43. Friedman, Samantha and Squires, Gregory D., *Does the Community Reinvestment Act Help Minorities Access Traditionally Inaccessible Neighborhoods?* Social Problems, Vol. 52, Issue 2, pp. 209–231 (Society for the Study of Social Problems, Inc. 2005).

44. GAO, *Analysis of Options for Revising the Housing Enterprises' Long-term Structures,* page 23.

45. An, Xudong and Bostic, Ralphael, *Have the Affordable Housing Goals been a Shield against Subprime? Regulatory Incentives and the Extension of Mortgage Credit* (April 28, 2006).

46. Bhutta, Neil, *GSE Activity and Mortgage Supply in Lower-Income and Minority Neighborhoods: The Effect of the Affordable Housing Goals* (Finance and Economics Discussion Series, Divisions of Research & Statistics and Monetary Affairs, Federal Reserve Board, 2009).

47. Abt, *Study of the Multifamily Underwriting and the GSEs' Role in the Multifamily Market,* page 9.

48. *See,* 12 U.S.C. §4562(b)(5) (low- and moderate-income families); §4563(a)(2)(D) (special affordable housing goal); and §4564(b)(5) (underserved areas).

49. Federal Housing Finance Agency, Mortgage Market Note 10–2, *The Housing Goals of Fannie Mae and Freddie Mac* (February 1, 2010).

50. An and Bostic, *Have the Affordable Housing Goals been a Shield against Subprime?*

51. General Accountability Office, *Federal Housing Administration: Decline in the Agency's Market Share was Associated with Product and Process Developments of Other Mortgage Market Participants* (GAO-07–645, June 2007).

52. *See,* 60 Fed. Reg. 61846, 61891 (December 1, 1995) (promulgating 24 C.F.R. 81.16(b)(3)(ii)).

53. *See,* Pub. L. 111–203, §1491 (July 21, 2010); 124 Stat. 2205 (Dodd-Frank Wall Street Reform and Consumer Protection Act). The Government Accountability Office and the Financial Crisis Inquiry Commission reached similar conclusions. *See,* GAO, *Analysis of Options for Revising the Housing Enterprises' Long-term Structures,* page 27. *See also,* Jaffee, Dwight M., *The Role of the GSEs and Housing Policy in the Financial Crisis* (Financial Crisis Inquiry Commission, February 25, 2010) at page 5 (total enterprise ownership of subprime, Alt-A, and other high risk loans totaled $1.571 billion as of September 30, 2009).

54. FHFA, *2010–2011 Enterprise Affordable Housing Goals; Final Rule,* 75 Fed. Reg. 55901, note 37, citing Office of Comptroller of the Currency, Board of Governors of the Federal Reserve System, Federal Deposit Insurance Corporation, Department of the Treasury, and National Credit Union Administration, *Interagency Guidance on Nontraditional Mortgage Product Risks,* 71 Fed. Reg. 58609 (October 4, 2006).

55. FHFA, *2010–2011 Enterprise Affordable Housing Goals; Final Rule,* 75 Fed. Reg. 55910. The housing goals rule for 2010 and 2011 explicitly excludes subprime PLS from the count of single family goals qualifying mortgages. *See,* FHFA, *2010–2011 Enterprise Affordable Housing Goals; Final Rule,* promulgating 12 C.F.R. §1282.16(d).

56. *See,* 24 C.F.R. §81.12 (2010 ed.) (low- and moderate-income goal with home purchase mortgage subgoal) and §81.13 (2010 ed.) (underserved-area goal with single family subgoal). HUD was prohibited from enforcing compliance with subgoals by 12 U.S.C. §4562(a) and §4564(a).

57. Pub. L. 110–289, §1128; 122 Stat. 2696.

58. Id, 122 Stat. 2699 (single family goals) and 122 Stat. 2700 (multifamily).

59. FHFA, *2010–2011 Enterprise Affordable Housing Goals; Final Rule,* 75 Fed. Reg. 55916. The Final Rule is actually more lenient with GSE housing goal compliance than HUD. Like HUD's old rule, the new rule measures enterprise performance against a benchmark prediction of the market, but allows for adjustment based on actual outcomes in the market. *See* the new 12 C.F.R. §1282.12.

60. Abt, *Study of the Multifamily Underwriting and the GSEs' Role in the Multifamily Market,* page 116.

61. FHFA, *2010–2011 Proposed Enterprise Affordable Housing Goals,* 75 Fed. Reg. 9055.

62. Pub. L. 110–289, §1128; 122 Stat. 2700.

63. FHFA, *2010–2011 Enterprise Affordable Housing Goals; Final Rule,* page 70 to 71.

64. Pub. L. 110–289, §1128(d); 122 Stat. 2702 (definition of "low-income area").

65. Pub. L. 110–289, §1129; 122 Stat. 2704.

66. Fannie Mae, *2007 Annual Housing Activities Report* (March 17, 2008); Freddie Mac, *Annual Housing Activities Report for 2007* (March 14, 2008).

67. *See,* FHFA, *2010–2011 Enterprise Affordable Housing Goals; Final Rule,* promulgating 12 C.F.R. §1282.16(b)(1) (excluding LIHTC); §1282.16(b)(2) (excluding multifamily bonds); and §1282.16(c)(8) (counting single family mortgage revenue bond purchases to the extent that the bond proceeds are traceable to otherwise goal qualifying mortgages). The 2008 Reform Act requires FHFA to count multifamily bond purchases for purposes of the multifamily housing goal, unless FHFA determines "that such purchases do not provide a new market or add liquidity to an existing market." Pub. L. 110–289, §1128; 122 Stat. 2701.

68. Joint Center for Housing Studies, *The Disruption of the Low-Income Housing Tax Credit Program: Causes, Consequences, Responses, and Proposed Correctives* (December 2009).

69. Fannie Mae, Form 8K (filed with the Securities and Exchange Commission, November 9, 2009).

70. Abt Associates, *Are States Using the Low-income Housing Tax Credit to Enable Families with Children to Live in Low Poverty and Racially Integrated Neighborhoods?* (July 28, 2006); Gray, Robert and Tursky, Steve, "Location and Racial/ Ethnic Occupancy Patterns for HUD-Subsidized Family Housing in Ten Metropolitan Areas" from *Housing Desegregation and Federal Policy* (John Goering, ed., Univ. of North Carolina Press, 1986).

71. 12 U.S.C. §4545.

72. FHFA, *Duty to Serve Underserved Markets for Enterprises: Advance Notice of Proposed Rulemaking and Request for Comment,* 74 Fed. Reg. 38572 (August 4, 2009).

73. 122 Stat. 2683.

74. FHFA, *Mortgage Market Note 10–1 (Update of Mortgage Market Notes 09–1 and 09–1A)* (January 20, 2010); U.S. Department of the Treasury, *Data as of March 4, 2010 on Treasury and Federal Reserve Purchase Programs for GSE and Mortgage-Related Securities.*

75. Memorandum of Understanding Among the Department of the Treasury, the Federal Housing Finance Agency, the Federal National Mortgage Association, and the Federal Home Loan Mortgage Corporation (October 19, 2009).

76. Department of Treasury, *Making Home Affordable Program: Servicer Performance Report Through January 2010* (February 17, 2010).

77. 24 C.F.R. § 100.125(b) (2010 ed.).

78. Peterson, *The Role of Securitization in Residential Mortgage Finance;* Reiss, David, *Subprime Standardization: How Rating Agencies Allow Predatory Lending to Flourish in the Secondary Mortgage Market,* 33 Fla. St. U. L. Rev. 985 (Summer 2006). *See also,* Securities and Exchange Commission, *Asset-Backed Securities; Final Rule,* 70 Fed. Reg. 1506, 1510, note 45 (January 7, 2005) ("For a number of years, mortgage-backed securities were almost exclusively a product of government sponsored entities.").

79. SEC, *Asset-Backed Securities; Final Rule,* 70 Fed. Reg. 1512.

80. Securities and Exchange Commission, *Summary Report of Issues Identified in the Commission's Staff's Examinations of Select Credit Rating Agencies* (July 2008).

81. McCoy, Patricia A., Pavlov, Andrey D., Wachter, Susan M., *Systemic Risk Through Securitization: The Result of Deregulation and Regulatory Failure,* 41 Conn. L. Rev. 1327 (May 2009); Reiss, David, *Subprime Standardization: How Rating Agencies Allow Predatory Lending to Flourish in the Secondary Mortgage Market,* 33 Fla. St. U. L. Rev. 985 (Summer 2006).

82. SEC, *Staff's Examinations of Select Credit Rating Agencies,* page 12.

83. *See,* SEC, *Asset-Backed Securities; Final Rule,* 70 Fed. Reg. 1544 to 1545 (discussing disclosure requirements for asset-backed securities, including those consisting of residential mortgages, and those consisting of commercial mortgages). The SEC rule is concerned also with securities consisting of consumer debt, such as car loans and credit card debt. The term "asset-backed security," or ABS, is used to describe the universe of securitized debt instruments that are regulated by the SEC, including mortgage backed securities, commercial mortgage backed securities, and consumer debt.

84. Joint Center for Housing Studies, *Mortgage Market Channels and Fair Lending: An Analysis of HMDA Data* (April 25, 2007).

85. *See, e.g.,* SEC, *Asset-Backed Securities; Final Rule,* 70 Fed. Reg. 1506; Securities and Exchange Commission, *Amendments to Rules for Nationally Recognized Statistical Rating Organizations; Proposed Rules for Nationally Recognized Statistical Rating Organizations; Final Rule and Proposed Rule,* 74 Fed. Reg. 63832 (December 12, 2009).

86. Securities and Exchange Commission, *Asset-Backed Securities; Proposed Rule,* 75 Fed. Reg. 23327, 23357 (May 3, 2010).

87. *See,* 12 U.S.C. §2803(j)(2)(D) (HMDA data collection at the census tract level); *see also,* section Pub. L. 110–289, §1127, amending 12 U.S.C. §1326 (FHFA data collection). For additional discussion about how to protect the privacy of individual borrowers in loan level data gathered for HMDA and by the GSEs, *see,* FHFA, *Notice of Order: Revisions to Enterprise Public Use Database,* 75 Fed. Reg. 41180, 41181, note 1 (July 15, 2010).

88. GAO, *Analysis of Options for Revising the Housing Enterprises' Long-term Structures,* page 28.

89. Geithner, Timothy, *Written Testimony to the House Committee on Financial Services* (TG-603, March 23, 2010), posted at http://www.treas.gov/press/releases/tg603.htm. GSE exemptions from state and local taxes are codified at 12 U.S.C. §1452(e) (Freddie Mac) and 12 U.S.C. §1723a(c) (Fannie Mae). Exemption from securities registration was repealed in the 2008 Reform Act. *See,* Pub. L. 110–289, §1112; 122 Stat. 2677.

90. 24 C.F.R. §81.43(a) (2010 ed.).

91. Federal Financial Institutions Examination Council, *Interagency Fair Lending Examination Procedures* (August 2009).

92. *U.S. v. Massachusetts Industrial Finance Agency,* 921 F. Supp. 21 (D. Mass. 1996).

93. Peterson, *The Role of Securitization in Residential Mortgage Finance,* page 15.

94. *See,* Pub. L. 111-203, *Dodd- Frank Wall Street Reform and Consumer Protection Act of 2009,* §1027(s) (powers of new consumer protection agency do not affect "any authority arising under the Fair Housing Act").

95. Restoring American Financial Stability Act of 2010 (Senate Banking Committee, Chairman's Mark); http://banking.senate.gov/public/_files/ChairmansMark31510AYO10306_xmlFinancialReformLegislationBill.pdf, last accessed March 27, 2010.

96. Geithner, *Written Testimony to the House Committee on Financial Services.*

97. NSP is authorized by other sections of the same legislation that created FHFA and reformulated the housing goals. *See,* Pub. L. 110–289, §2301, *et seq;* 122 Stat. 2850.

98. U.S. Department of Housing and Urban Development, *Notice of Fund Availability (NOFA) for the Neighborhood Stabilization Program 2 under the American Recovery and Reinvestment Act, 2009,* Appendix I, par. S.1 (May 4, 2009).

99. Wardrip, Keith E. and Pelletiere, Danilo, *Properties, Units, and Tenure in the Foreclosure Crisis: An Initial Analysis of Properties at the End of the Foreclosure Process* (National Low-income Housing Coalition, Research Note #08–01 (May 6, 2008, revised May 8, 2008)

100. U.S. Department of Housing and Urban Development, *U.S. Housing Market Conditions* (November 2009).

101. Congressional Oversight Panel, *February Oversight Report: Commercial Real Estate Losses and the Threat to Financial Stability* (February 10, 2010).

102. FHFA, *2010–2011 Enterprise Affordable Housing Goals; Final Rule,* 75 Fed. Reg. 55917.

Chapter Fourteen

Give Credit Where Credit Is Due

Overhauling the CRA

Mark A. Willis

The Community Reinvestment Act (CRA) is in need of a major overhaul. Since the CRA was enacted in 1977, and since the last major rewrite of the regulations more than 15 years ago, much about the financial services industry has changed and much has been learned about the strengths and weaknesses of both the Act and its regulations. Over this time, the share of financial assets held by banks has fallen as banks faced new competition from non-bank institutions, such as money market funds and independent mortgage companies. A few very large banks have emerged with nationwide branch networks, and the number of banks has declined by half, to about 8,000 nationwide. Newly emerged Internet banks have been able to serve national customer bases without opening local branches. The practice of community development has evolved to encompass not just low-income housing, but also mixed-income housing, jobs, education, health, public safety and more. Further, the shift by bank examiners to more of a focus on production volumes has resulted in unintended consequences that have undermined CRA's effectiveness.

Not only does the CRA need to be brought up to date, it needs to be able to continue to stay current into the future. The regulatory system needs to be redesigned to allow for more regular and timely updates, allowing more rapid responses to what is working and what is not. By being more amenable to continuous improvement, the CRA should be more open to innovation and experimentation given the greater opportunity for making midterm corrections.

This chapter starts with a brief overview of the CRA and its successes. It then outlines some ways to facilitate more regular updating of the CRA regulations, followed by a review of a number of ways to increase the effectiveness of CRA in helping to stabilize and revitalize low- and moderate-income (LMI) communities.

AN OVERVIEW OF CRA

The CRA legislation was enacted to encourage banks to help meet the credit needs of all communities where they take deposits, with the intention of helping to stabilize and revitalize LMI communities, consistent with the safe and sound operation of the institution. The CRA created an affirmative obligation for banks to seek to expand access to credit to underserved consumers and neighborhoods, and unlike many compliance statutes and regulatory schemes, was specifically not structured as a prohibition of certain behavior. The focus on deposit-taking grew naturally out of the banking industry structure that existed then, consisting mainly of local banks taking local deposits and lending ("reinvesting") them back into their local community.

Broad authority to implement the law was delegated to the four regulatory agencies that oversaw the banks (the Office of the Controller of the Currency, the Federal Reserve, the Office of Thrift Supervision, and the Federal Deposit Insurance Corporation). Even today the statute provides few details or restrictions, except that each bank must be given one of four ratings: Outstanding, Satisfactory, Needs to Improve, or Substantial Noncompliance. The ratings must be made public as part of a written document called the Performance Evaluation. Bank examiners evaluate the performance of individual banks and arrive at ratings for those states and multi-state metropolitan areas where the bank takes deposits, and then sums them all up to arrive at an overall rating for the bank.

Working together, the agencies have developed regulations to provide the basis for evaluating a bank's compliance with the Act. The last major re-write of the regulations took place in 1995 when regulators, responding to public concerns that the examinations focused too much on efforts to lend, rather than actual results, shifted from measuring processes to measuring production levels. Since then, the exams for all "large, retail banks," with assets greater than $1 billion (which account for over 80% of deposits in the nation) have consisted of a Lending Test, an Investment Test, and a Service Test, all of which focus on the LMI marketplace. These three tests receive, respectively, a weight of 50%, 25%, and 25% toward the determination of a bank's overall CRA rating.

The evaluation of a bank's performance under the Lending Test primarily considers home mortgage and small business lending. Community development loans, a separate category that includes the financing of affordable housing projects and local retail strips in LMI neighborhoods, receive only secondary recognition and can only be used indirectly to enhance a bank's rating. Also included in this category are loans to community development financial institutions (CDFIs) which are loan funds that specialize in serving the LMI community.

The Investment Test is mainly driven by purchases of CRA-eligible bonds, mortgage-backed securities, and limited partnership interests in projects funded through the Low Income Housing Tax Credit (LIHTC) or the New Markets Tax Credit (NMTC) programs. Yet, it also includes grants to non-profits engaging in community development activities—the dollar total of which is generally relatively small and so receives little weight.

The Service Test places most weight on the geographic distribution of branches and branch services and gives only limited consideration to so-called community development services, which include such activities as providing mortgage counseling to first-time homebuyers. In addition to rating the bank on each of the three tests, any bank that fails to do better on the Lending Test than a "Needs to Improve" is automatically disqualified from receiving an overall rating of "Satisfactory" or better.

Smaller banks and wholesale and special-purpose banks face different sets of testing protocols. Small banks (less than $250 million in assets) are basically judged on the simple ratio of their lending in the local community compared to their deposit base. No consideration is given to how many of the loans serve the LMI community. Banks that are the next size larger (but less than $1 billion in assets) are called "intermediate small banks" and are judged on their lending ratio as well as on a community development test that combines community development lending, investments (including philanthropy), and services. Such a community development test is also at the core of the exams for wholesale and special-purpose banks, but no such test exists for large, retail banks. While every bank has the option of developing its own "strategic plan" as the basis for its exams, few have been willing to undertake the regulatory and public process of getting one approved.

To encourage banks to help meet the credit needs of LMI communities, CRA contains a system of carrots and sticks. CRA's most potent incentive has proven to be the power to delay or reject applications by a bank to merge or acquire another bank based on a finding of inadequate CRA performance. (Regulators have also been given the ability to reject applications to open and close branches based on a bank's CRA record, but it is unclear to what extent this power has been invoked or even quietly threatened in recent years.) The wave of bank mergers that began in force in the 1990s proved to motivate banks to achieve a strong CRA rating, which was thought to allow the regulators to move more quickly to an approval. In no case did the banks want to risk having their applications rejected as happened in 1989 when the Continental Illinois Bank applied to acquire another bank.

The ratings themselves are also thought to have value as a matter of public relations. Most banks care about their public image; they do not want to have a less-than-Satisfactory rating. Moreover, the ratings are also seen to matter when the public has a chance to air their views at public "meetings" which the regulators can convene as part of the process of reviewing an application. These "meetings' provide the regulators with the opportunity to gather oral testimony on a bank's performance in meeting the convenience and needs of its communities—an option they have exercised a number of times, especially for the mergers involving the largest banks. When these situations arise, bankers have been comforted by being able to hold up their "Outstanding" ratings as a way to balance any criticisms voiced by members of the community, advocates, public officials, and others. The result has been that the vast majority of banks have a CRA rating of "Satisfactory" or better, and nearly a fifth have an "Outstanding" rating with the proportion much higher for the very largest banks which relied extensively on acquisitions and mergers to attain their size.

POSITIVE IMPACT

Banks have undertaken many CRA-eligible activities that have helped to stabilize and revitalize LMI communities. Yet, developing statistical proof that CRA has made a difference has been a challenge since it is hard to isolate due to a lack of counterfactual information—what would have happened without CRA? Regardless of the measurement difficulties, it seems clear that CRA has encouraged banks to learn more about how to serve the LMI marketplace in a safe and sound way, to recruit and train specialized staff, and to support the growth of specialized consortia.

Improved Communication

CRA has encouraged banks to build better lines of communication with the community and with community groups. As a result, CRA has helped banks better understand the needs of their communities and correct misperceptions as to market risks and opportunities. Products and services tailored to the needs of the community have emerged and banks have found ways to serve the communities in safe and sound ways. One notable example was the development in the early- to mid-1990s of new underwriting standards for home mortgages, thereby facilitating a dramatic growth in mortgage lending to lower income populations and neighborhoods. New mortgage lending data made available as a result of expanded reporting under the Home Mortgage Disclosure Act (HMDA) revealed untapped market opportunities. Through dialogue and careful testing, banks were able to identify and remove unnecessary barriers to serving this marketplace, resulting in loans that performed (and still perform) well considering the state of the economy overall.

In contrast, the subsequent proliferation of toxic-loan products in the early 2000's had little, if anything, to do with CRA or community involvement (in fact many community groups raised alarms about the growth of predatory lending products and marketing), despite the more recent sensational claims in the media and elsewhere to the contrary. In fact, according to a study by the Federal Reserve, of all the subprime loans made in 2005 and 2006 (the peak years of the housing bubble), only 6% were extended by CRA-covered lenders to LMI borrowers or neighborhoods in the communities for which they had a CRA responsibility, (i.e., where they took deposits) (Krozner, 2008). This fact clearly draws into question any notion that CRA was somehow a driver of the crisis.

Dedicated Staff

Another positive result was the establishment, within many of the larger banks, of dedicated units that became proficient at structuring complex affordable housing or community economic development deals involving multiple sources of subsidies and players. As experience with these types of deals proliferated, loan and credit approval officers learned how to think "outside the box," recognizing that government subsidized rents and sale prices actually lowered the risk by lowering the exposure to the usual ups and downs of the economy. The emergence of these specialized units was seen by many bankers and advocates as a means to facilitate the growth of community development lending and investing, and to build trust between the banks and their communities, strengthening important lines of communication.

Working Together

Finally, CRA helped nurture new bank/community/government partnerships as well as new government programs. Collaborations between banks and community-based organizations helped spawn the development of many CDFIs with specialized skills for serving lower income communities. The banks have provided CDFIs startup funding, technical assistance, loans with interest rates at or below market, and operating support. They collaborated in the development of the Low Income Housing Tax Credit (LIHTC) and New Market Tax Credit (NMTC) programs and are major investors. Banks have also worked with community groups to set up consortia to provide mortgage counseling or other forms of financial education (e.g., credit counseling).

THE CHALLENGE OF MEASURING CRA PERFORMANCE

Measurement of a bank's CRA performance suffers from a core problem—the lack of an easy and direct way to measure the incremental impact of a bank's CRA activities on LMI communities. Since 1995 the regulators have increasingly relied on output measures of production. Not surprisingly, what gets measured gets done. Since the production measures are proxies at best, they have led to unintended consequences. Some have given too much credit for activities that are not directly linked to revitalizing and strengthening communities while giving too little credit to other activities that have a significant incremental impact. Some have even had negative consequences.

The problem of imperfect measures of impact is compounded by the difficulty of determining if a bank has done enough or at least tried hard enough. The examiners have found themselves basing their decisions on the volume of a bank's particular CRA activity or on whether a bank is serving the same share of the LMI market as it is of the middle- and upper-income markets (so called parity measures). The reliance on these types of tests raise a number of questions: Should a bank be expected to serve a certain share of the market or do a certain volume of business regardless of the shares held by competitors or the size of the market? What if the amount expected turns out to be much larger than the market can support, or would preclude other banks from meeting the requirements that CRA places on them? What if a bank cannot serve a market profitably, regardless of the volume? If that is the case and society still thinks the market should be served, should the government provide a subsidy or should the bank be expected to absorb the cost? This situation arises with public goods where society as a whole benefits from the provision of a product or service, but the provider of the service might not be able to charge enough to make a profit. A case in point might be financial education (See Lindsey, 2008). If it turns out that the expectation is too large or too unprofitable, should a bank be allowed to substitute the provision of alternative products or services to meet its obligation to help meet the credit needs of a community?

At first glance, it may seem to make sense to rely on measures of the number or dollar amount of loans a bank has made, or evaluate the bank's share of the LMI marketplace compared to its share of the middle- and upper-income marketplace. But the results can be misleading as they do not take into account the impact of the loans or whether the loans would have otherwise been made. For example, a $50,000 loan to a small business, or a $500,000 loan to a small affordable housing project, may be more critical to the well-being of a community than hundreds or thousands of home mortgage loans that would be made as a matter of course by any number of different mortgage companies. Similarly, philanthropic grants given to support local organizations involved in community development receive little credit because they involve small dollar amounts and so pale in comparison to other investments with which they are paired in the Investment Test. Yet, grants can have a critical and large impact as can relatively small amounts of below-market financing that allow, for example, CDFIs to be able to cover their operating costs and help borrowers by offering low-cost financing.

One way the regulators have tried to control for the size of the market is to look to parity tests where a bank's share of the marketplace is compared to its share of the middle- and upper-income segments of that same market. It may, at first, sound sensible to expect that a bank making a reasonable effort to serve the LMI segment for mortgages would have the same share of that market as it does of the middle- and upper-income segments—if it has 10% of the latter, it should have 10% of the former. Unfortunately, the world is much more complicated. In this example, a bank looking to ensure it achieves a 10% share will aim higher than 10%, especially if it seeks an "Outstanding." If enough banks do the same, then they will collectively be seeking a total of more than 100%—a mathematical impossibility. This problem was made worse by the emergence in the late 1990's of independent mortgage companies that focused on the LMI marketplace. By taking a disproportionately large share of the LMI market, these firms made achieving parity even more mathematically impossible. Basing parity tests on non-market, demographic data (e.g., the number of LMI homeowners) can further remove them from any relationship to a reasonable measure of market opportunity. Similar issues are raised by the parity tests used for small business lending and the location of bank branches.

UNINTENDED CONSEQUENCES
IMPAIR CRA'S EFFECTIVENESS

In order to meet volume and parity measures, banks have sometimes undertaken activities that are a waste of resources, if not counterproductive altogether. Banks have been driven to buy market share by subsidizing borrowers, for example, through significant and costly reductions in fees and rates, and to open unprofitable branches in LMI neighborhoods, sometimes even damaging the economics of local banks that were already there. Banks have even resorted to buying mortgages from each other to boost their mortgage numbers, providing employment for mortgage traders but doing nothing to increase the number of mortgages available in the community. By encouraging investments that do not make economic sense, CRA has had the counterproductive effect of undermining the business case for lending and investing in LMI neighborhoods.

The focus on production has also led banks to rely more on their mainstream businesses and less on specialized units to generate the large volumes consistent with the examination criteria. While mainstream units, with their emphasis on scale and mass production, have been able to turn out impressive production volumes that meet the criteria for CRA eligibility, they rely on systems that often lack the flexibility to offer one-off products or modify product features to respond to variations in local needs. The managers and staff of these units rarely have the time or expertise to interact and collaborate with the community on a regular basis. Moreover, these units also manage to a bottom line which makes them reluctant to devote resources that could be deployed more profitably elsewhere, and causes them to be constantly looking for the lowest-cost, short-term way of meeting their CRA targets.

The shift away from specialized units has, in at least some cases, moved overall responsibility for CRA to non-business areas of the bank such as regulatory compliance and philanthropy. These support functions are often not well positioned to encourage innovation and engage in active collaboration with communities. They lack the specialized staff to offer one-off, high impact (but often low-dollar value) products or services or vary their products and services across localities depending upon local needs.

UNDERVALUING OF COMMUNITY DEVELOPMENT

Another problem is that some products or services that are critical for stabilizing and revitalizing LMI communities are simply undervalued. The best example is the current exam procedures for large, retail banks, which, in essence, relegates community development loans, services, and philanthropic grants to second-class status. As noted earlier, the Lending Test looks to community development loans as only a way to enhance a bank's rating; grants (and so-called "patient capital") receive little weight in the Investment Test, and such important community development services as credit and mortgage counseling receive only minor recognition under the Service Test.

Inconsistent Treatment Persists

The lack of more frequent update of the regulations or the Q&As (the Interagency Questions and Answers that provide more detailed guidance on specific questions faced by both the banks and the examiners) has served to perpetuate inconsistent treatment by regulators. For example, only recently, after many years of complaints by bankers and advocates, did the regulators finally update the Q&As to address differences in how they treated the financing of housing projects where less than 50% of the tenants are LMI. Previously, some mixed-income projects received no credit regardless of their contribution to community development, while some received proportional credit. Even now, differences in the treatment of letters of credit for affordable housing projects persist. Some regulators treat them much the same as they do loans while others do not, even though the bank is just as much at risk for default on the project as it would be if it made a loan.

Diminishing Incentives and Opportunities for Public Input

CRA's power has been seriously affected by the current financial crisis. Preserving the safety and soundness of the banking system has been a driving force behind recent bank mergers and acquisitions, and CRA has clearly taken a back seat. Moreover, the wave of mega-mergers may be over, so the very large banks may no longer place as high a value on an "Outstanding," especially in the face of falling revenues and rising loan losses. Fewer banks seeking or receiving an "Outstanding" could have a domino effect by lessening the peer pressure to undertake the extra effort required. Moreover, fewer major mergers also could mean fewer public meetings. As noted earlier, these meetings have proven to be excellent vehicles for integrating public opinion into the decision making process as well as for attracting media attention to a bank's record in serving low- and moderate-income communities.

SOME IDEAS FOR UNBLOCKING THE ROAD

To maintain its long-term effectiveness, CRA needs to be able to adapt more rapidly to changes in markets, the structure of the financial services industry, and community development best practices. More frequent updates could also remove some of the pressure to update everything at once by allowing smaller but steadier steps and giving more time, where appropriate, for a consensus to build among the stakeholders who include not just members of the community, but advocates, bankers, the regulators, and others. Moreover, frequent updates would also allow the regulators to address more quickly inconsistent evaluation policies within and across agencies. The following outlines some steps to make it easier to update the regulations on a more regular basis.

Encourage a Dialogue to Find Common Ground

One thing the major stakeholders can agree on is that lack of consensus makes it hard to change the rules. There need to be forums where differences can be thrashed out and areas of overlap found. While public hearings provide an important opportunity for the different stakeholders in CRA to air their differing points of view, they do not offer an opportunity for a dialogue among the stakeholders to build trust and explore possible areas of agreement on how to improve the effectiveness of CRA. History, differing perspectives, and the inherently adversarial nature of the protest aspect of CRA make it difficult for such conversations to occur spontaneously. The regulators should convene small groups, each with a cross-section of the stakeholder interests, to engage in an open dialogue.

Take Small, but More Regular Steps

A more regular process of updating the regulations would also allow for change to come in smaller doses, hopefully also allowing more time for additional areas of consensus to evolve among the stakeholders. The longer the time between changes, the more pressure builds up for more extensive changes and the increased likelihood that the players will take sides and hold to more rigid positions.

Move Beyond Zero Sum

The current CRA exam framework makes change difficult because of its "zero sum" nature. The current weighting system serves to play one group against another since giving more weight to one activity will generally reduce the importance of another activity in determining a bank's overall rating. For example, giving more weight to community development lending within the Lending Test would necessarily require that less weight be given to mortgages or small business lending. Thus it is hardly surprising that those who want to preserve the level of attention now paid to home mortgages and small business loans are reluctant to contemplate changes that may lead to a reduction in the importance of these loan activities.

A prototype for escaping this zero-sum trap already exists in the regulations. Banks must achieve at least a minimal "passing" grade on the Lending Test in order to get an overall rating of "Satisfactory" or better. Other products and services or groups of products and services (e.g., a community development test, see below) could receive similar status, making the passing of each of them of equal importance, at least with regard to being able to achieve a passing grade overall.

Designate a Lead Agency

The difficulty of trying to reconcile the many perspectives of all the stakeholders is only compounded by having to reach agreement among all of the bank regulators. There needs to be a way to designate one of the bank regulators as the lead, set a timetable for action, and provide sufficient staffing and analytic resources to carry out the role on an expedited basis. That regulator should also have the ability to be the ultimate arbiter of any disagreements among the parties.

POSSIBLE REFORMS TO THE RULES OF THE ROAD

With the roadblocks reduced, a number of options exist for making the CRA a more effective tool for helping LMI communities. Many can be implemented through regulatory changes. In particular, the exams could be restructured to be clearer, faster, and more specific about what is required or desired from the banks of different types and sizes and in different neighborhoods. Some of the existing tests need to be modified, and in some cases totally replaced. Some reforms, though, do require statutory changes.

Find a Better Mix between Quantity and Quality, Production and Process

Finding the right balance between quantitative and qualitative measures is essential since, as noted earlier, smaller loans can have as much, or more, impact on communities than larger ones. The parity tests need to be eliminated or at least tempered with other measures of the impact on LMI communities. The definition of community development might also be expanded to include the whole array of activities that are essential to creating vibrant communities, including access to jobs, health, safety, education and more.

Process measures of the type that were scorned as part of the 1995 reform could help provide a more nuanced test of community impacts that cannot be identified with existing measures. For example, testing the extent of a bank's efforts to assess the needs of its LMI communities would encourage banks to maintain an on-going dialogue with local leaders. A similar impact could result from a test to gauge if the community truly has access to bank officials with sufficient authority to be responsive to their ideas and concerns. In determining if a bank is doing enough extra to justify an "Outstanding," the test could require evidence of innovative products and services, or of the dedication of sufficient expertise and resources to be able to structure innovative deals. This test would also encourage continued support for separate, specialized lending units. Of course, these types of tests call for examiners to be both well-trained and empowered to make the necessary judgments in the field.

Incorporate a Safety Valve to Guard against Unintended Consequences

As long as the CRA has to rely on imperfect measures for the desired outcome, the exam process should provide for a safety valve to minimize the chances that the regulations will force banks to undertake activities which are of limited or no incremental value to the community and undermine the argument that it can make good business sense to serve these markets. Before being made to over-saturate or over-subsidize the market for a particular product of service covered by the CRA exam, a bank should be allowed to make the case that the community is already being well served (it may not even be optimal for every bank to provide the same product or service), or that the economics simply cannot work (e.g., banks have been known to offer subsidies of $8,000 or more to try to increase their market share of lower income home mortgages). A formal "appeals" process should be established so that banks can have the ability to refute any initial judgment of inadequate performance based on numbers alone. Banks that make the case successfully would then have to find other ways to meet their CRA responsibility, such as by providing a unique, high-impact product or service.

Create a Community Development Test for Large, Retail Banks

The exam protocol for large, retail banks lacks a community development test that combines community development lending, investments, grants, and services. Yet, these activities are critical for stabilizing and revitalizing communities. Such a test would allow each of these activities to receive meaningful recognition. Furthermore, by treating all of these activities under one umbrella, a bank would be free to respond appropriately to the mix of local needs and opportunities, whether they be loans, investments, grants, services or a melding of all four. Consideration might also be given to expanding CRA eligibility for grants to the full range of activities that are integral to a thriving community.

One way to provide a transition to a community development test would be to give banks the option of adding community development loans and services to the existing Investment Test. Banks could also be allowed to increase the weight given to this expanded test (perhaps up to 50 percent) with a concomitant reduction in the weight given to the now narrower Lending Test. The importance of mortgage and small business lending can still be maintained by setting minimum standards as discussed below.

Revise Exam Protocols to More Closely Reflect Institutional Strengths and Characteristics

Additional exam protocols need to be established to take advantage of the geographic reach of Internet banks and others that serve regional or national banks. Currently, loans or investments in a nationwide or regional loan or investment fund earn full CRA credit only if the money is channeled into geographies where the bank itself takes deposits. This approach restricts the ability of these funds to put the money where it can do the most good, and specifically deprives those communities that suffer from a limited presence of deposit-taking institutions of capital.

Banks serving a nationwide market should be offered full credit for CRA-eligible loans, investments, and services made in any geography across the country, as long as they have adequately served the communities in which they take deposits. (An alternative way to accomplish the same goal could be to broaden the geographic boundaries determining CRA eligibility under a community development test to encompass whole regions.) A similar approach might be applied to regional banks that would be able to serve all localities within their region. Such a rule would help to ensure that every LMI community has access to capital at competitive prices and allow for further geographic diversity in the portfolios of Internet banks that now feel pressure to concentrate their CRA activity in their headquarter cities. Moreover, this approach would free the loan funds to find the best deals and allow them to serve all of the LMI communities within their service area.

A new exam protocol for the largest banks is also needed to shorten exams that can currently consume 18 months or longer. These protracted exams tie up the resources of all parties for months, and banks find themselves halfway through their business plans for the next exam before they fully know which rules they should be operating under. The result is an elongated feedback loop that slows the process of continuous improvement for all parties concerned. Exams need to be completed faster, or at a minimum any changes in how activities are being evaluated need to be communicated on a real-time basis. And banks need to be given sufficient advance notice of changes so they can incorporate them in their business plans.

Special rules could also be developed for banks that have affiliates (i.e., other subsidiaries of the holding company) that are relatively large and perform activities that would be included in a CRA exam if they were a direct subsidiary of the bank itself. Currently, the examiners do not look at non-bank affiliates unless the bank itself volunteers to include them in its exam. One approach would be to take into account the size and nature of the affiliates in determining the appropriate level of CRA activity expected from the institution.

Another alternative, particularly for Internet banks that serve national markets but take deposits only in limited geographies, would be to require them to create custom-made "Strategic Plans." Once the plans are approved, a bank would be able to be confident of how much of its efforts can go to communities beyond its hometown. Before adopting this approach, however, it would be useful to better understand the historic reluctance of banks to take up the option of creating strategic plans.

Provide Special Credit for Serving Communities
Otherwise Left Underserved

Advocates are concerned that the current system leaves some communities underserved by CRA. The provision of full credit for investments made directly or through funds covering broader national or regional areas should help remove some of these inequities. However, the existence of banks that serve local markets without having local deposit-taking facilities may in some cases leave local banks smaller and only subject to the small bank lending ratio test that does not even focus directly on serving the low- and moderate-income community. Even if a large national bank has a local deposit-taking presence, it may not pay much attention to a locality that is so small that it has little bearing on the institution's overall rating. In these circumstances, the regulators should follow the precedent set for giving credit for serving designated disaster areas, and offer extra credit to any bank that lends, invests, or provides community development services in these communities, regardless of where the bank takes deposits.

Formalize a Process to Adjust Exams for
Local Market Conditions

Communities in Cleveland, Ohio and Chicago, Illinois have different needs and the CRA should be able to be highly responsive to those differences. One way to do this would be for the regulators to be more proactive in compiling assessments of local needs. In each locality a bank would then have the option of choosing the activities it wants to undertake from the menu so identified. In contrast, under the current system, a bank can try to justify local variations in the products or services it provides by making its case as part of its "Performance Context"—a document it has to prepare as part of the examination process. However, this path is unlikely to be taken because of the danger that the examiners will not give enough credit for those special activities to justify having undertaken them in the first place.

An alternative might again be a "Strategic Plan" which would allow a bank to set out in advance the criteria by which it seeks to be judged on a geography-by-geography basis. Once the plans are approved, banks would be able to set their local business plans accordingly.

Make "Satisfactory" an Explicit Floor and Specify
Required Products or Services

To add teeth to CRA and to clarify its requirements, an overall rating of "Satisfactory" should be made an explicit prerequisite for a bank to apply for any of the regulatory approvals covered by the CRA statute. In addition, the products or services required for a "Satisfactory" should be laid out through a series of minimum standards. Failure to achieve these minimums would result in an overall rating below "Satisfactory." This approach eliminates the zero-sum problem, at least with regard to qualifying for a "Satisfactory," and addresses some of the concerns of advocates that the regulators have not been tough enough "graders" or have not flunked enough banks. It also could provide greater clarity for banks as to what is required.

In particular, minimum levels of performance should be set for individual products or services or for groups of them (just as the existing Lending Test looks at the collective performance of a bank with respect to both home mortgages and small business loans). Groupings make sense particularly when better performance on one component can compensate for a lesser performance on another.

In addition to requiring a minimum performance level for home mortgage and small business loans, there could be a "minimum" test for retail services which could combine an evaluation of the geographic distribution of branches, an examination of the bank's policy with regard to closing branches, and an assessment of the effectiveness of any alternative delivery systems for the same products and services found in branches. Another grouping might include compliance with such consumer laws as those that cover discrimination, consumer safety, and unfair and deceptive marketing practices. Still another might include the components of a community development test as described above.

Calibrating the "height" of these minimums requires an evaluation of the costs of meeting them versus the incentives needed to induce banks to comply. Just as the incentives built into CRA are limited, any requirements that banks supply particular products or services may also have to be limited. If the minimum standards are set too high individually or collectively, then the regulations will run the risk that some banks may choose to live with a failing grade. While those banks that anticipate needing any of the delineated powers in the statute, (e.g., for permission to merge or acquire), will be highly motivated to try to comply, others may not be.

Collect the Necessary Data, Publish Enough to Empower the Public

The issue of data collection can be contentious. Advocates and researchers always seem to be looking for more extensive data under CRA, while banks are concerned about cost (which may be particularly burdensome for small banks), customer privacy, disclosure of proprietary information that could be valuable to their competitors, and fueling a proliferation of law suits. Primary consideration needs to be given to what data the regulators need in order to examine the CRA performance of banks. That data should be collected on a regular basis.

A second major consideration is to provide the public with the information it needs to be active and well-informed participants in the CRA process. The more fact-based the public discussion, the more constructive it can be. Moreover, the public can help identify issues for the examiners to pursue more closely. However, not all the data collected from the banks need be made public. One approach might be to determine what amount of information is necessary to allow advocates and others to make the case that a problem may exist. By making public at least that critical amount of data, the public would be able to present a prima facie case that would shift the burden of proof back to the banks to explain why the facts appear as they do or at least spur the examiners to do more in-depth analyses. The regulators could even give CRA credit to banks that make the data easier to use and understand.

Hold Public Hearings Annually to Review the Latest CRA Data

Input from the public has played a crucial role in highlighting community needs in general and in specific communities, as well as providing insights on how well a bank is meeting those needs. This input is in danger of being lost as fewer mergers and acquisitions will reduce the opportunities for public involvement. The regulators should consider holding joint meetings every year to review the latest CRA data. The agenda of these meetings could also be expanded to include a regular dialogue among stakeholders on ways to make CRA work better for all the parties involved.

Tighten Complementary Laws

Anti-discriminatory laws can be critical to helping lower-income communities thrive. The apparent targeting of minorities with toxic subprime products has hurt many of these communities. Rather than explicitly include race or ethnicity in CRA, a better approach may be to strengthen and effectively enforce existing fair-lending laws. It might also help to add an affirmative obligation to those laws rather than to enmesh the CRA itself in the process of investigating discrimination, which often requires reviewing individual loan files, a process that seems best done as it is now by the regulators as part of their fair-lending examinations.

Beyond Credit

The original sharp focus of CRA on "credit" may be outdated and it may be time to include other kinds of bank products and services. To explicitly require the provision of transaction and savings accounts that serve lower-income communities, for example, may require new legislation, although the current statute seems to provide some latitude to cover non-credit products and services that help expand a person's or business's capacity to access credit.

Rethink the Incentives for an Outstanding Rating

New incentives may be necessary to spur banks to continue to seek "Outstanding" ratings. CRA's power to influence bank behavior has been seriously diminished by the current financial crisis. The limited prospects for mergers and acquisitions, at least for the very largest banks, do not bode well, thus removing a key reason for many banks to seek an "Outstanding." To compensate, additional incentives may be necessary just to maintain the status quo. One way to bolster CRA would be to offer to provide an explicit monetary benefit for achieving an "Outstanding."

In addition the government should consider subsidies for products or services that generate externalities that benefit the community as a whole. It has already been shown that monetary incentives can induce banks (and others) to provide more products and services in lower-income communities. Notable successes have been the CDFI Fund and the LIHTC and NMTC programs.

Beyond Banks

Over time, the share of financial assets held by banks has fallen and banks have faced increased competition from non-bank financial companies (Avery et al, 2008). These changes have led advocates to propose expanding the affirmative obligation of CRA to other financial institutions. Mortgage, securities and insurance firms are often cited. While the logic of bringing more resources to bear on helping to revitalize and stabilize LMI communities seems sensible, the experience with CRA points to the types of issues that need to be addressed individually for each industry. Such issues include: What products and services are going to be covered and how will performance be measured? Will the firms be examined or just subject to additional regulations? Will there be opportunity for the public to weigh in? What incentives will be provided to encourage the firms to make the desired extra effort? Would monetary incentives help, particularly if profitability is an issue? The clearer the answers are to these and other questions, the more effective the legislation regulations can be in helping revitalize and stabilize communities.

SOME CAUTIONARY THOUGHTS

While reform can do much good, it can also have unintended consequences. Of particular concern are four possible directions that reform could take. First is the possibility of trying to do too much in one exam. The CRA cannot be seen as the panacea to address such issues as discrimination when other existing legislation and regulations are not working as well as advocates would like. In this regard, the new Consumer Financial Protection Bureau should be able to handle a number of compliance issues that advocates have wanted to build more formally into the CRA, thus allowing the CRA exams to focus on evaluating a bank's affirmative actions to help LMI communities.

As experience has shown, the proper evaluation of the impact of banks' activities on LMI communities requires time and training. The addition of such issues as race and ethnicity to CRA exams would increase the scope of the exams and so risk diminishing the amount of attention that can be paid to any one part of the exam. The result could be a return to a more mechanical exam that will fail to reward those banks that are truly making a difference in their communities. In addition, the more tasks given to the examiners, the longer the exams will take. The longer the exams take, the more attenuated the feedback loop.

Another instance in which change could have unintended consequences would be if pressure from advocates leads to an arbitrary reduction in the number of "Outstanding" ratings. Hopefully, some of the proposals laid out earlier will help to address concerns that standards are too loose and have led to grade inflation. If, however, fewer banks receive an "Outstanding," then even fewer may seek it. Part of the motivation for at least the largest banks was to match their peers. The danger is that once their peers no longer have an "Outstanding," other banks will start to question if the credential is worth the effort.

A third area regards proposals to expand a bank's CRA responsibility to include all localities where it makes loans (e.g., home mortgages), even ones where it does not collect deposits and may not even have any employees. Advocates are concerned that some communities are underserved by CRA. As mentioned earlier, this problem could be addressed directly by identifying such communities and giving banks credit for serving them, regardless of where they take deposits. The danger in expanding the full set of CRA responsibilities to these communities is that existing resources will simply be spread even more thinly, a result that is especially likely with regard to philanthropic grants and below-market loans, the totals for which are generally set on a corporate-wide basis without consideration of the need or the number of jurisdictions potentially involved.

Moreover, the threshold for triggering coverage could have a result opposite to that intended. It could give the bank an incentive to leave that market entirely, thus reducing the availability of loans in the very communities that the change is intended to help. In a bill now before Congress, a bank that serves as little as 0.5% of a market would incur a local CRA responsibility. Such a low threshold might lead banks to refrain totally from serving a community, thus depriving it of the additional competition and so decreasing access to credit. Lastly, any increase in the geographies covered will, again, only serve to lengthen the exams or diminish the amount of time examiners can spend on communities now covered, thus again potentially forcing examiners to reallocate their time, further attenuating the feedback loop.

A fourth area of concern is a desire by some to look to Congressional action to bring about the needed changes to CRA. While some changes can only be made through legislation, the bulk of the changes can be made by the regulators themselves. Relying exclusively on Congress poses two problems. First, as slow as the regulatory process can be, the legislative process is intentionally designed to be hard to move. This situation is further compounded today by the likely opposition from the many legislators that currently believe that CRA was a driver of the subprime crisis, despite clear evidence to the contrary. Second, the danger with legislative action is that it could produce an even more rigid system by reducing the broad discretion now given to the banking regulators. To the degree that detailed prescriptions become embedded in the statute, regulators would be severely limited in their ability to fix even minor problems as they arise.

CONCLUSION

Much has changed since CRA was enacted and since the last major rewrite of the regulations. The CRA regulations can and should be updated to rectify shortcomings and to adapt to changes in the banking industry and community development best practices. The CRA also needs to be more easily updated on a regular basis to keep it more current in the future. Some aspects of reform also require legislation, but it is critical that statutory changes do not limit regulatory flexibility by being overly prescriptive. The CRA needs to be able to evolve over time to maximize its effectiveness in helping to stabilize and revitalize LMI communities.

BIBLIOGRAPHY

Apgar, William C., and Ren S. Essene. "The 30th Anniversary of the CRA: Restructuring the CRA to Address the Mortgage Finance Revolution." In *Revisiting the CRA: Perspectives on the Future of the Community Reinvestment Act,* 12–29. Boston: Federal Reserve Banks of Boston and San Francisco, 2009. http://www.frbsf.org/publications/community/cra/index.html

Avery, Robert B., Marsha J. Courchane, and Peter M. Zorn. "The CRA Within a Changing Financial Landscape." In *Revisiting the CRA*, 30–46.

Barr, Michael S. "Credit Where it Counts: The Community Reinvestment Act and its Critics." *New York University Law Review*, 2005, 80(2): 513–652.

Bhutta, Neil. *Giving Credit where Credit is Due? The Community Reinvestment Act and Mortgage Lending in Lower-Income Neighborhoods.* Washington, DC: Division of Research and Statistics, Federal Reserve Board, 2008.

Federal Reserve Bank of Dallas. *A Banker's Quick Reference Guide to CRA, as amended effective September 1, 2005.* http://www.dallasfed.org/ca/pubs/quickref.pdf (accessed June 12, 2010).

Gainer, Bridget. "What Lessons Does the CRA Offer the Insurance Industry?" In *Revisiting the CRA*, 138–42.

Immergluck, Dan. *Credit to the Community: Community Reinvestment and Fair Lending Policy in the United States.* Armonk, N.Y: M.E. Sharpe, 2004.

Krozner, Randall. "The CRA and the Recent Mortgage Crisis." In *Revisiting the CRA*, 8–11.

Laderman, Elizabeth, and Carolina Reid. "CRA Lending During the Subprime Meltdown." In *Revisiting the CRA*, 115–133.

Lindsey, Lawrence B. "The CRA as a Means to Provide Public Goods." In *Revisiting the CRA*, 160–166.

Litan, Robert E. et al. *The Community Reinvestment Act after Financial Modernization: A Final Report.* Washington, DC: Department of the Treasury, 2001. http://www.ustreas.gov/press/releases/reports/finalrpt.pdf (accessed July 27, 2010).

Marsico, Richard D. *Democratizing Capital: the History, Law, and Reform of the Community Reinvestment Act.* Durham, NC: Carolina Academic Press, 2005.

National Community Reinvestment Coalition. Testimony by John Taylor, President & CEO, Presented at the Joint Public Hearing on the Community Reinvestment Act held by the Bank Regulators, July 19, 2010 http://www.federalreserve.gov/SECRS/2010/July/20100727/R-1386/R-1386_071210_52042_571072649512_1.pdf

Seidman Ellen. "A More Modern CRA for Consumers." In *Revisiting the CRA*, 105–114.

U.S. Comptroller of the Currency. *Community Reinvestment Act Examination Procedures: Comptroller's Handbook* (1999). http://www.occ.treas.gov/handbook/craep.pdf (accessed June 12, 2010).

White, Lawrence. "The Community Reinvestment Act: Good Goals, Flawed Concept." In *Revisiting the CRA*, 185–188.

Willis, Mark. "It's the Rating, Stupid: A Banker's Perspective on the CRA." In *Revisiting the CRA*, 59–70.

Generous support from the Ford Foundation and the Furman Center for Real Estate and Urban Policy has made this article and Mark Willis's ongoing work on CRA possible. The opinions expressed in this chapter are Willis's own.

Chapter Fifteen

Breaking the Bank / (Re)Making the Bank

America's Financial Crisis and the Implications for Sustainable Advocacy for Fair Credit and Fair Banking

Manuel Pastor, Rhonda Ortiz, and Vanessa Carter

The nation's response to the "Great Recession"[1] has been surprisingly short-sighted. The news stations are starting to report that recovery has begun, albeit slowly, and that the country is getting back on track.[2] But getting the country "back on track" is likely the wrong goal. After all, getting back on track only means getting some people stabilized again—back in homes, back in jobs—and does not address the structure of racial- and class-segregation in America that helped get us into this mess in the first place. Indeed, getting "back on track" is just a Band-Aid, potentially setting us up for another crisis.[3]

For those paying attention, the foreclosure crisis has done more than re-mind us that there is still a race problem in America—it has unmasked the power of the financial elite and their ability to exploit us all. The patterns of foreclosures and predatory lending, after all, have most affected people of color and lower-income individuals. The Kirwan Institute, drawing on a report by United for a Fair Economy, indicates that "people of color are more than three times as likely as whites to have subprime mortgages."[4] Our own research on this issue, done as part of an analysis of regional equity in the San Francisco Bay Area, indicates that people living in the highest foreclosure ridden areas were 72 percent people of color.[5]

But it is more than foreclosure and the disappearance of wealth that this disproportionate impact on people of color signals. Our financial system has a distinctly racial character, one that requires a response rooted in racial and social justice. After all, this is coming on the heels of a history of trying to keep these same individuals from buying homes in certain neighborhoods through redlining—and when community push led to bank shove, the open-ing to credit meant that many were pushed into loans that were detrimental to their livelihoods and their asset accumulation. Nationally, African Americans are 2.7 times more likely to have a high-cost loan than whites, and Latinos

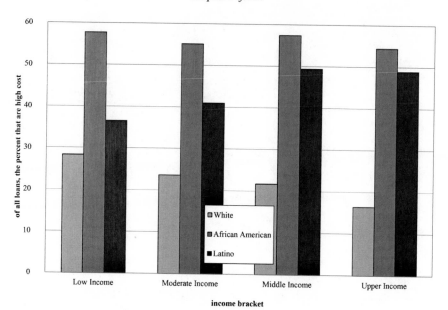

Figure 15.1. High Cost Home Purchase Loans, across 172 cities.

are 2.3 times more likely.[6] What is even more interesting: when that data is disaggregated into income bands, the discrepancy in loan issuance by race is greatest in the wealthiest bracket (see the figure above). Clearly, this is more than an income effect—there are discriminatory factors in play.

It is not just mortgages that have added scars on a landscape of racial inequality. The whole financial system has been rigged against lower-income communities in general and communities of color in particular. The Brookings Institution documented in 2006 that low-income households pay a higher cost for basic financial services.[7] For example, "borrowers pay $4.2 billion every year in excessive payday lending fees," according to estimates from the Center for Responsible Lending; if reversed, it would create a huge boost to income and community development.[8] In areas of concentrated poverty and concentrated minorities, the issue is particularly acute: for example, in largely black and Latino southeast Los Angeles, California, 40% of the residents have never had a bank account, while nearly 31% cash their checks at area supermarkets. In addition, there is only one bank in the area compared to 16 payday lenders, pawnshops or check-casher outlets.[9]

What has led to this situation that leaves the United States resembling something more from the pages of Robin Hood than from the land of opportunity? For starters, the Federal Reserve remains strongly under the oversight of the financial industries—meaning that the regulators are often "captured" by those they are supposed to regulate.[10] Secondly, since the 1980s, there has been a strong trend towards a deregulation of the financial industry. Ira Goldstein and Dan Urevick-Ackelsberg in their paper for the Kirwan Institute[11] identify three laws that led to the rise of subprime lending and the ballooning of predatory lending: the Depository Institutions Deregulation and Monetary Control Act of 1980 (DIDMACA), the Alternative Mortgage Transaction Parity Act of 1982 (AMT-PA), and the 1986 Tax Reform Act.[12] Finally, the Community Reinvestment Act (CRA), originally promulgated to promote banking responsibility and upend financial apartheid, was significantly weakened in its ability to ensure high-quality loans in 1999 when the Gramm-Leach-Bliley Act passed, giving fair passage to investment and securities firms in the mortgage world.[13]

From these changes in law, Wall Street investors have been able to make more money through risky investments. Lenders basically got the go ahead to offer (or, more often, push) subprime loans.[14] The especially painful fact is that many of these customers could actually afford traditional services—"up to 35% of subprime borrowers could qualify for prime mortgage loans"—but brokers profit the most from signing loans with the "highest combination of fees and mortgage interest rates."[15] And this certainly *was* profitable, until the bottom dropped out.

So it is a mess—as evidenced by the financial meltdown—and many have turned to the notion that we will need new regulation, new policy, and new protections. All fine ideas but there is something more fundamental at work: If we are going to turn the financial service industry back into something that benefits the consumer, instead of the financial elites, we have to shift the underlying balance of power.

Money seems to be the easiest way to power, and that is exactly what those victimized by the crisis do not have. But, there are millions of people who have been foreclosed upon, and inner-city residents throughout the nation who have been regular victims of predatory lending. If people get organized, and follow in the great tradition of other American struggles for equity, they can tilt the scales. Social movements provide a vehicle for bringing together allied interests, identifying the most blatant abuse of power, and slowly transferring that power and dignity back into the hands of the people.

Our point is simple. While we do need a new policy package, such advocacy also needs to be embedded in a broader social movement for financial justice. The focus should not simply be on foreclosure relief, but on a new financial frame that has at its heart the restoration of opportunity for all, including those whose voices are typically unheard, but present most accurately the facts on the ground.

If social movements are important, then we are really in a different ball game. Simply preventing communities from the worst effects of asset loss will not change policies. Meanwhile, letting others—such as policy think tanks—advocate on the behalf of financial reform will leave many disadvantaged communities without the capacity to respond to broader injustices, of which financial inequality is just one example. Moreover, working on a single financial issue like subprime mortgages will avoid the root problem. A sustainable social movement for fair credit and banking is what we need.

So how do we dig into this work? What situations or frameworks lead to sustainable advocacy? We do not pretend in this chapter to sketch out what the concrete policy alternatives may be; other chapters that are a part of this project will do that far more successfully. What we do hope to do is examine exactly how sustainable advocacy might be achieved by considering the ways in which social movements can mobilize to change power.

To do this, we draw just a bit from theory, but more often we rely on the practical wisdom our community partners have imparted to us over the years. In what follows, we try to draw lessons from movements that have been successful in the contemporary United States. We offer a frame that puts movements in their place, seeking to look at what we have labeled the troika of social change: projects, policy and power. This leads us to focus on the importance of embedding advocacy into a broader, multi-issue and multi-sector social movement, something that we think differs from the traditional single-issue advocacy that dominates much of the thinking in the financial space. We draw on analytical work we have conducted about what makes for an effective social movement, and explore what this would look like for a movement around fair credit and banking, highlighting along the way both the successes and the challenges we see. In the end, we hope this analysis contributes one piece of the map to a path for long-term advocacy and a changed financial system.

WHAT IS SUSTAINABLE ADVOCACY?

The definitions of advocacy are many. They can include the work of lawyers, community organizers and researchers. Advocacy can be done by individuals, organizations, or the government. The target of advocacy is generally a particular set of government policies; and advocates seek to change the minds and actions of decision-makers.

How does change occur? In our view, it is through a combination of projects, policies and power: projects demonstrate that change is possible, policies make the change standard operating procedure, and power—both understanding it and wielding it—is what changes policy.

The single largest shift in financial relations that benefited low-income communities is the Community Reinvestment Act of 1977; it has brought more than $1 trillion in private investment into urban neighborhoods, often through minority homeownership.[16] The National Training and Information Center (NTIC) and National People's Action (players in the current struggles) spearheaded the mobilization of grassroots organizations to put in place the CRA; legislation that required banks with branches in low-income areas to also lend in those areas.[17] Alex Schwartz puts it eloquently: "The CRA and the HMDA [Home Mortgage Disclosure Act] are both the result and the vehicle of community-based efforts to combat redlining and other discriminatory bank lending practices."[18]

The CRA is structured such that when banks apply for a new charter, a merger, or an acquisition, community groups and other interested parties can use HMDA data to challenge application approvals. Given the trend towards financial consolidation of the 1980s and 1990s, community groups became adept at pressuring banks to expand their activities in low-income and underserved communities. And because of the way CRA oversight is structured, the work of community organizations brings integrity to the application of the law. This is very important as banks are able to choose between four regulatory bodies (FDIC, Federal Reserve, Office of the Comptroller of Currency, and Office of Thrift Supervision) to regulate their work which has the potential to create a race to the bottom in terms of the quality of oversight since the banks also provide these entities with revenue.[19]

In some sense, this reflected exactly the troika we describe. Groups mobilized to attain the law and shift policy accordingly; when banks made loans as a result of the CRA, they began to realize that they were profitable and these "projects" helped demonstrate viability.

But the projects, policy, and power triplet is not confined to the financial sector. In the research for a new book, *This Could be the Start of Something Big: How Social Movements for Regional Equity are Reshaping Metropolitan America*, Manuel Pastor, Chris Benner, and Martha Matsuoka began with a study focused on profiling the best practices of community developers and grassroots advocates who were turning to the regional economy to unlock resources.[20] But they soon found out that it was not just projects and policy. When they talked to the leadership of the Los Angeles Alliance for a New Economy about community benefits agreements (a policy to create local benefits from regional developments), they heard not a treatise about zoning, but rather an analysis of how the community-benefits "frame" paved the way for a new understanding of the economy. When they talked to the directors of Bethel New Life in Chicago about their new transit-oriented development project, they certainly heard about "penciling out" a development, but they also heard about how city dwellers had teamed with suburbanites to save a rail line. When they talked to the organizers of the New Jersey Regional Coalition about their efforts to change a policy that permitted suburbs to avoid their fair share of affordable housing, there was some attention to the character of new housing, but more of a focus on how this effort can help city and suburb see their common fate.

Sure these advocates had ideas about how to redo mass transit, create affordable housing, and secure opportunity. But they were really laser-focused on politics, movement-building, and social change. They had understood two things: first that community-based efforts at what they termed "regional equity" were more likely to succeed with a firm analysis of power and an explicit strategy for organizing. Second, that the work they were doing at a regional level—face-to-face, race-to-race, and place-to-place—could add up to a vision for a new American common ground. They were seeking to change not just the physical and policy landscape of their metro regions, but the political landscape of the country.

We think that this regional equity example is important for thinking about a movement for financial justice in several ways. First, it highlights the differences between organizations focused on projects, policy, and power in a useful way. Pastor, Benner, and Matsuoka,[21] for example, point to community developers as an example of project-related work focused on urban revitalization, think tanks as policy reformers focused on seeking shifts in rules, regulations, and policy makers' attitudes, and social movement regionalism as focused on building a new basis for progressive politics.[22] While they argue that all these groups contribute to the ecosystem of change, they are not agnostic about the relative importance of each. They argue that community developers may be timid politically, partly because they need to work within systems; they suggest that think tanks are disconnected from an organizing base and depend on thin coalitions and policy elites to move policy; they argue that the real linchpin to change is social movements and community organizing.

Pastor, Benner and Matsuoka lift up two other things of importance. First, regions are important—they argue that this is where organizing is made real. Second, social movements have to be multi-issue and multi-constituency.

The analogies to the financial reform field would seem to be relatively clear. Traditional community developers and community development corporations (CDCs), some of whom were helped into being by CRA lending, may be limited in their capacity to make change.[23] This is partly because local politicians and funders help them; agitating too much might break critical relationships that make their work possible—they do not want to bite the hand that feeds them. Groups like NeighborWorks, funded by Congress, are providing important services to help homeowners avoid foreclosures, but it would be unrealistic to expect them to lead the charge against financial injustice.[24] It is also the case that community developers have a mission focused on working within their neighborhoods; as a result, many do not pay as much attention to policy change at the regional, state or national level.

Policy reformers may also face limits: "They seek to identify problems, build networks with politicians and other decision-makers interested in the problems, provide these decision-makers with appropriate research, strategies, and "frames" for understanding and solving the problem, and through this complex combination, influence policy change in a preferred direction."[25] The Center for Responsible Lending (CRL) operates in this niche: doing good research on predatory lending (mortgage and payday lending, overdraft and other consumer loans, and credit cards), informing policymakers, regulators, and others, and offering concrete policy options.[26]

Another example is the work of Matt Fellowes, formerly of the Brookings Institution, who did some of the early research that has resulted in "Bank On" programs throughout the nation. These programs are generally framed as creating a pathway for traditional banks in low-income neighborhoods, and thus winning wealth for the consumer and profits for the banks. This is all good, but the win-win frame can be constraining. As the Bank on San Francisco leaders realized a few years into their implementation, sometimes you also need to just go for the jugular, in this case by using zoning and other tools to freeze out payday lenders.

In our view, such policy entrepreneurs/reformers are an essential part of the ecosystem of change. However, they are not always engaged in direct politics, and like CDCs, may have a fear of burning bridges to get innovative policies passed. Also, because race and poverty remain such touchy subjects, the real needs of people of color and lower-income folks are not always included or addressed explicitly—in the interest of keeping a "broad" frame. Moreover, this approach is generally not attached to community or grassroots leadership development, and thus the positive impact of policy changes on the world may dwindle over time.

Social movements can push for change in the ways that CDCs and policy reformers cannot on their own. CDCs see themselves as working for the betterment of particular neighborhoods, policy reformers target specific issues with specific solutions, but social movements complete the broader fabric of change by building power and long-term infrastructure. They are sustained groupings that develop a frame or narrative based on shared values, that maintain a link with a real and broad base in the community, and that build for a long-term transformation in systems of power—and occasionally produce protests, marches, and demonstrations along the way.

Of course, jumping from the local to the national is a challenge and many social movements—including those of the right—have generally taken a path that first involves trying regional organizing and regional solutions. Movements for fair credit and banking are no different; there is a regional aspect in addition to the organizing aspect, and an analysis of power pointing to the need for a new frame.

The foreclosure crisis and the response to it, in particular, have functioned regionally. Swanstrom, Chapple, and Immergluck profiled regional responses, noting Chicago's Home Ownership Preservation Initiative (HOPI) and Riverside, California's Red Team as the best metropolitan examples.[27] The Red Team (a county-led collaboration funded with Neighborhood Stabilization Funds) works with homeowners in Riverside and San Bernardino Counties to address foreclosures and the region's over-dependency on new single-family home construction to support the economy. The team focuses policy on keeping people in their houses, homeowner education and counseling, and a regional public-private partnership that pools enough resources to buy homes and make a difference in the market.

This is also true of those more focused on organizing and power-building. Among other roles, Empowering and Strengthening Ohio's People (ESOP) of Cleveland, Ohio returns regional benefits to local neighborhoods. Their work began in 1999 with the needs of a few grassroots members who were being foreclosed upon. In 2005, with a regional collaboration they launched a pilot program that has kept homeowners in place by streamlining regional laws, unlocking regional resources, and providing foreclosure prevention services. ESOP also engaged in confrontational organizing tactics that resulted in negotiations with lenders. As a result, homeowners had a much higher mortgage workout rate than those in comparable regions (namely, St. Louis, Missouri).[28]

The California Reinvestment Coalition (CRC), created to leverage the CRA statewide, negotiates between regional, state, and national scales. On June 11, 2009, the National Day of Action, CRC with National People's Action (NPA) and PICO coordinated actions meant to pressure politicians, lenders, mortgage servicers, judges and other key actors (like the Fed) to accept responsibility for easing the pain caused by mortgage foreclosures.[29] CRC affiliates from the Bay Area met with the Fed in Los Angeles and held a press conference in front of a foreclosed apartment building about to evict its residents. They also collaborated to hold four regional community meetings leading up to a press conference at the Federal Building in San Diego, California.[30] CRC provides a platform for those most directly impacted by industry practices and government policies in order to amplify their voices. CRC is an intermediary between those who are typically not heard and those in power—often at the state or federal level.[31]

The "Showdown in Chicago," Illinois, was perhaps the most visible expression of how fair credit and banking issues may be building into a social movement. On October 27, 2009, five thousand people hailing from 20 states marched for financial reform. Their demonstration also coincided with the American Bankers Association convention in Chicago.[32] However, there are many underlying facets of vital importance to this and any other social movement. The Showdown was backed by the training and research done by NPA and the National Training and Information Center,[33] not to mention the work of many smaller organizations in the coalition, that have been careful in their choice of targets, framing, and organizing efforts.[34]

In general, social movements have the capacity to incorporate multiple issues and constituencies. Social movements are distinguishable because they may focus on specific issues at different times, but they are not solely defined by them. In a social movement framework, constituents may take immediate issue with the rate of foreclosures, high interest rates, and discriminatory lending, but the real motivation organizers are trying to tap is anger at the unequal balance of power between the financial elite and everyone else. By way of example, the civil rights movements targeted unequal public accommodations, not because there was anything particularly critical about being able to use a certain bathroom, but to challenge the blatant excess of racism and white power embedded in society. Social movements are more than particularistic interests or episodic coalitions; they are long-term, values-based, and potentially system-transforming.

The key question is whether the movement for foreclosure relief is really building into a broader movement for financial justice and streaming into the river of movements working for economic justice. We think that there is a lot of potential to tap into, but also a long way to go.

WHAT IS A SUSTAINABLE SOCIAL MOVEMENT?

As noted above, projects help us see the possible, policy makes the possible standard practice, and power is what ultimately drives policy reform. Each of the above styles fit within this process. But social movements are usually overlooked in the ecology of change, partly because they are controversial, they are harder to fund, and they are less easily measured and less easily understood.

In 2009, we made some suggestions for funders trying to figure out how to support social movements in a document called "Making Change: How Social Movements Work and How to Support Them."[35] Based on a literature review, interviews, and our experience working with community organizations, we offered ten critical elements that we argued made for a strong and lasting social movement. We have put these ten elements into three buckets for what we hope is conceptual ease.

Bucket One: The Fundamentals

The following three elements define social movements; together, they distinguish a movement from episodic interventions or the efforts of issue-based coalitions. Interestingly, many of these elements have shown up most strongly on the right and, while we do not find too much common ground with them, we have much to learn from them on how to build a solid infrastructure that can change power and policies.

1. Clear Vision and Frame: Social movements rely on frames—conversational constructs that help to set the terms of the debate—allowing individuals of multiple ideologies to stay in the game. Talking about "fair" credit and banking instead of only about the mortgage crisis enables homeowners, renters, and those gouged by payday lenders to come to a common table. Frames also create a sense of urgency, that is, a notion that we need to correct these problems now, because who in America tolerates something "unfair?" These frames help to create vibrancy for moving forward.

   While no one organization has framed this movement, we lift up the work that Americans For Fairness in Lending did to help pass historic reforms, although they became defunct in the process of finalizing this chapter. The organization paid strong attention to messaging to galvanize the movement. In particular, they exposed the broken nature of the current system in a way that makes reform the only sane choice; they helped put the movement on the offense, instead of the defense using both traditional and new media.[36] The "you shouldn't have signed a bad loan" personal-responsibility frame is deeply entrenched, and they helped to shift the dialogue away from individual blame. Crafting a frame that highlights the structural hang-ups, and the benefits and opportunities reform could bring to even middle-class Americans, is pivotal.

2. Solid Membership Base: Social movements make sure to directly involve those with "skin in the game" and make sure that the frames and values are derived from them and not from focus groups conducted by distant intermediaries. Social movements are distinguished by their commitment to organizing as well as their base of members and adherents.

   ACORN members involved in the "Stay Home" campaign have demonstrated their commitment across metropolitan American by literally standing with those about to be evicted because of foreclosures. But they have also been framing up anti-foreclosure policy and winning it in cities like Orlando, Florida; Oakland, California; Los Angeles, California; and Baltimore, Maryland.

3. Commitment to the Long-Haul: Social movements have a long-term perspective—they believe that the problems that their members face are due to misalignments in power and they understand that it takes time to right that ship. Integral to this is taking the time to train leaders and craft relationships.

The Chicago-based advocacy groups—NPA, NTIC, The Illinois Community Investment Coalition, and the Woodstock Institute—have spent more than 30 years pushing against the financial elite. Among other tools, their main one has been the CRA. While they were instrumental in its passing in 1977, NTIC in particular has also guided local implementation; they have been involved in more CRA agreements than any other organization.[37] With the restructuring of the financial industry in the 1990s, the CRA became less powerful,[38] but these groups have remained and now struggle to modernize the Act so that it might, again, have a wide reach.

Bucket Two: Making it Real

Social movements also match their broad vision with practical policy wins so that members can answer the ultimate pragmatic question: What have you done for me lately? Practical wins provide the momentum to secure broader and loftier aims. Winning the Wall Street Reform and Consumer Protection Act, even in its limited form, is momentum toward putting nationwide limits on predatory loans. But, at the same time, social movements are not defined by specific issues or policy victories and they must be nested in a pliable frame.

4. A Viable Economic Model: Because social movements are essentially about the redistribution of resources, they must have an underlying economic model that is viewed as being sensible and viable. Such models cannot simply be assertions—they must be made with research backing and with appropriate modesty and qualifications, such that policy wins will work. While we want to regulate and better the financial industry, we need to be smart in our demands or we will have a system even worse off and ourselves to blame.

There are definitely examples of making change real: In Los Angeles, for example, One-LA, a local IAF affiliate, is organizing immigrant families facing foreclosure to come together and work as a team to approach and negotiate loan terms with banks.[39] But what does seem to be missing from the current broad movement is a clear vision of how to reform broader financial systems with an *alternative* to the current financial market. The movement has outlined needed regulations—caps on interest rates, geographical boundaries on required lending, an agency to protect consumers—but less has been done in lifting up new innovations and making an argument about the role that finance *should* play in facilitating mobility, entrepreneurship, and wealth acquisition. This is not just a problem of community organizers; progressive economists have tended to focus on trade policies or making labor markets work, and not as much on how to grease the economy back to growth with a re-regulated but innovative financial system. It is important to support thinkers and researchers who are infused with community wisdom to shape and fill out this new frame.

5. Vision of Government and Governance: Social movements have a vision of what the government ought to do, not simply in terms of issues, but in terms of its basic relationship to social forces. Progressives have had a tough time crafting a positive vision of government, partly because of widespread (and often justified) mistrust of government bureaucracy in many communities. Framing will matter, especially to deflect accusations of "big government" that have recently gained steam.

As we read it, the movement for financial fairness is framing up government as the protector of, not just the vulnerable, but also the common American resident. The government has been cast in the role to regulate out-of-control industries that violate fairly basic needs for financial services. Similarly, the government gives the common man or woman a chance—government is supposed to keep open the door of opportunity. Getting those thoughts across in a nuanced way is particularly difficult, partly because the image of an inefficient government dominates, and partly because we *do* need to make government more accountable.

6. A Scaffold of Solid Research: Social movements always have an intellectual side in which problems are identified and strategies are explored. Recent social movement groups in the United States have become even more conscious about the power of using research as a scaffold to support and weave together the personal stories generated by base constituencies, both through in-house research capacities and by forging effective alliances with academics and intermediaries.

The Woodstock Institute played a central role in supporting anti-foreclosure groups in Chicago, and is intimately connected with the work of the Illinois Community Investment Coalition.[40] James H. Carr from the National Community Reinvestment Coalition provided written testimony to the House Committee on Oversight and Government Reform using data from the Kirwan Institute's Economic Stimulus Report. The California Reinvestment Coalition has helped organizations think through the best questions to pose to government officials.[41] Of late, it has been particularly important to be able to demonstrate with data that the CRA is not to fault for massive foreclosures, that people of color are given more high-cost loans than whites, and that the financial sector was acting highly irresponsibly.[42]

7. A Pragmatic Policy Package: We need a policy package that looks like it might actually work at alleviating poverty and distress—by securing fair credit and banking practices. The pieces of the package seem to include consumer protection, limits on fees and interest, modernization of

the CRA and HMDA, more oversight for the Fed, and cracking down on predatory lenders. Parts of some of these proposed policies became law in 2010.

The CRA was a winner because it was able to bring investment, and the modernization of such policies will need to accomplish that again. But the policy package to date is mostly proposing regulation and oversight. While that is needed, we also need policies that support more investment and that make real a new vision for fair credit and lending. What would that be, beyond regulation? It might include programs like the Home Owners Loan Corporation (HOLC) that kept tens of thousands of people in their homes in the New Deal Era, or policies that bring banks back to the inner-city, or make homeownership practical for the majority. Such policies would do more than get the industry off the wrong course or re-set its current failures, but actually forge a new and better course.

The challenge is bringing it all together: the movement has a handful of policy prescriptions, but not a plan for health. The existing policies seem more a response to a crisis, and while there is certainly a need for that, we really need to address building a better, healthier system overall. Even the Bureau of Consumer Financial Protection is still regulatory. To round out the policy package, we will have to finish sketching out our viable economic model and then match it with policies to make that model real.

Bucket Three: Bringing it to Scale

In recent years, increasing attention has been paid to the scale or geography of social movements. Movements have won a wave of local living wage laws, community benefits agreements, etc., prior to any such movement on the national front—change has been coming from the region "up" rather than the nation "down." This has to do with a few things: the rise of regions as economic and political units, and businesses finding value in clustering with others associated with their industry, a wrinkle in the off-shoring story. In short, some businesses must remain local; developers, retailers, or, say, banks, need to work with their regional community to make the relationship work. Social movements are making use of this dynamic. Any serious social movement analysis would also acknowledge that the success of the conservative movement was tied to their willingness to work in the trenches of small towns, school boards, and state houses on their way to national power.

8. Recognition of the Need for Scale: While there may be a tendency to think that small organizations must be authentic ones, with the scale of the social problems we face and the extent of power on the other side, we need a scale of organizational capacity to match. We do not mean to dismiss   small

groups, many of which are doing excellent work and are critical in the social ecology of change. Rather, we simply want to remind that organizations with scope, sophistication, and reach are needed to challenge power and policy.

The movement for fair credit and banking has done well on this front: Americans for Financial Reform, the National Community Reinvestment Coalition, National People's Action, ACORN (as it was formerly known), Americans for Fairness in Lending, and the Center for Responsible Lending are (or were) relatively large and sophisticated, and are addressing these issues at the broad systems level. They anchor and provide a common ground and agenda for local affiliates and individual power-building organizations.

9. A Strategy for Scaling Up: There is a geography of power currently being worked out: conservative organizing was built up from local bases, and most social justice organizations are working hard to move from the local to the regional to the state to the national. Such scaling is the stuff of success and is a new arena for research and investment.

People Improving Communities through Organizing (PICO) and National People's Action (NPA) have demonstrated this element. PICO and NPA negotiated with the Federal Reserve to talk with nine local affiliates to show how real people in local communities have been personally devastated by foreclosures. By embedding the local within the national, individual events are connected to a larger story—the unfair financial system, in this case—and the large networks of advocates demonstrates the mounting power to change the norm.[43]

10. A Willingness to Network With Other Movements: No one wins alone. It is critical that social movements focused on particular issues and particular constituencies are able to find their way to potential allies in other movements. Social movement organizations that are too exclusive or too focused on building their own group may fail to strengthen the movement and connect to other groups; the goal is to find those who seem to view their own activities as streams flowing into a raging river of social change.

The first thought here might be that we are talking about the ability to bring divergent actors within the financial equity movement together. That is important. For example, despite a strong collaboration of the public sector and non-profit organizations through Contra Costa Housing Equity Preservation Alliance (HEPA)[44] in the San Francisco Bay Area, when the Fed convened regional partners to address foreclosures, little came of it. Participants reported that each group—the banks, the reinvestment groups, the community-based organizations—were so good at their own work that they did not see much value in collaborating. Interestingly, this region that has historically been on the cutting edge of equity movements responded much more poorly than, say, Riverside, an area not known for its progressive leanings or community capacity. In short, playing well with others can make a big difference.[45]

But what we really want to stress here is that the connection—or lack of it—with other key actors outside of the financial equity arena is crucial in the broader movement for social and economic justice. This means ties with unions, with community organizers and with others.

We note these ten elements, not to say that social movements are easy to construct. They are not, and we ourselves have written that "social movements are marked by tensions and tightropes, with organizations trying to strike a balance between scale and base, organizing and advocacy, vision and research."[46] However, these guideposts can provide some tangible direction to where a social movement around fair credit and banking needs to head. And while no social movement will be perfect, balancing these ten elements will help.

The movement for financial equity has more strong characteristics than not, and might take just a bit more honing to develop into a powerful force. Listening to California advocates, while a frame around financial justice and opportunity is being constructed, much more needs to be done to make it dominant in popular discourse.[47] Developing a viable economic model and the accompanying pragmatic policies is an urgent need, and there are plenty of researchers and think tanks associated with the movement to make that happen. Equally critical, however, is intersecting this movement for financial justice with other movements for economic justice to both make for a more powerful whole, *and* to more firmly place finance within the logic of an alternative economic strategy for jobs, development, and sustainability.

Again, we point these out as places that we think might need some extra attention. But we acknowledge that progressive advocates are already juggling several resource-intensive issues—such as, immigration, climate justice, and ACA implementation—and that resources remain spread thin as we continue coping with this "Great Recession." Working on any of these issues is critical, and collectively may result in a real rebalancing of power. The momentum created by the foreclosure, and broader economic crisis, may be what we need to dig into the knottier areas of the movement for financial equity.

CONCLUSION

As we come to a close, it is important to remember that financial equity plays a particular role in the long-march for economic justice. For the economy to benefit all people, there must be growth, mobility, and standards. Over the past two decades, we have made progress on two of these three fronts. Communities have won strong guarantees of standards via community economic development in the form of Community Benefits Agreements, Project Labor Agreements, and Living Wage laws. Workforce development has increased mobility through new approaches to education like multiple pathways, through constructing career pipelines for the green economy,[48] and through rethinking workforce reintegration for ex-felons. What has been missing from the overall economic justice agenda has been a vision of growth—and it is imperative that one be in place in light of the current crisis.

To improve financial justice is no different—we need to combine all three aspects noted above. Movement builders for financial equity need to develop clear standards that benefit all people, and a starting point should be to define the outcomes we are willing and not willing to tolerate from our economy. This will help insure, for example, that interest rates do not climb to excessive heights or that the financial elite do not siphon the wealth of low-income communities.

The movement should also define the path for mobility—that is, how people can acquire assets and wealth over time. In some ways, this has been the focus: the CRA set standards for the banks, and various organizations facilitated growth in home ownership and access to banks. The problem is that the house of cards is now tumbling down and we are on the defensive on foreclosures rather than on the offensive about extending credit to create a new community-based economy.

To get at that, we need to develop a vision for growth, and in particular, the way in which credit can facilitate development, entrepreneurship and economic expansion. It is a whole new approach and it will require a whole new set of skills. And it will, as we have stressed, require an entirely different balance of power.

The current movements for fair credit and banking are a vital part of the reconfiguration of power necessary to achieve economic justice. We think we are on a roll—the old system has failed, the ideology is up for grabs, and new ideas and organizing are welcome—but there is much more work to be done (and on very thin budgets). In this critical time, we all need to work together in order to step up our game and continue to build the social movement organizations and vision that can help us work towards a new financial and economic system.

BIBLIOGRAPHY

ACORN Fair Housing. "Foreclosure Exposure: A Study of Racial and Income Disparities in Home Mortgage Lending in 172 American Cities." ACORN Housing Corporation, 2007.

Baker, Dean. "Democratizing the Federal Reserve." Washington DC: Americans for Financial Reform, July, 2009.

Carr, James H. "On the Subject of The Silent Depression: How are Minorities Faring in the Economic Downturn?" Written testimony submitted to the United States House of Representatives Committee on Oversight and Government Reform: National Community Reinvestment Coalition, September 23, 2009.

Dreier, Peter. "The Future of Community Reinvestment: Challenges and Opportunities in a Changing Environment." *Journal of the American Planning Association* 69 (Autumn 2003): 341–353.

Fellowes, Matt. "From Poverty, Opportunity: Putting the Market to Work for Lower Income Families." The Brookings Institution Metropolitan Policy Program, 2006.

Fellowes, Matt and Mia Mabanta. "Banking on Wealth: America's New Retail Banking Infrastructure and Its Wealth-Building Potential." Washington, D.C.: The Brookings Institution Metropolitan Policy Program, 2008.

Goldstein, Ira and Dan Urevick-Ackelsberg. "Subprime Lending, Mortgage Foreclosures and Race: How Far Have We Come and How Far Have We to Go?" Paper commissioned for the Kirwan Institute for the Study of Race and Ethnicity at the Ohio State University for its National Convening on Subprime Lending, Foreclosure and Race, Columbus, Ohio, October 2–3, 2008.

Harvard University Joint Center for Housing Studies. "The 25th Anniversary of The Community Reinvestment Act: Access to Capital in an Evolving Financial Services System." Cambridge, MA: Prepared for the Ford Foundation, 2002.

Lee, Joanna and Jennifer Ito. "A Greener Future for Los Angeles: Principles to Ensure an Equitable Green Economy." Los Angeles, CA: Strategic Concepts in Organizing and Policy Education (SCOPE), February, 2009, available at http://www.scopela.org/downloads/2009_SCOPE_A_Greener_Future.pdf.

Pastor, Manuel, Rhonda Ortiz, Jennifer Tran, Justin Scoggins, and Vanessa Carter. "State of the Region: The New Demography, The New Economy, and the New Environment." Los Angeles, CA: The USC Program for Environmental and Regional Equity (PERE), December 15, 2008.

Pastor, Manuel, Chris Benner, and Martha Matsuoka. *This Could be the Start of Something Big: How Social Movements for Regional Equity are Reshaping Metropolitan America.* Ithaca, NY: Cornell University Press, 2009.

Pastor, Manuel and Rhonda Ortiz. "Making Change: How Social Movements Work and How to Support Them." Los Angeles, CA: The USC Program for Environmental and Regional Equity (PERE), 2009.

Rogers, Christy. "Subprime Loans, Foreclosure, and the Credit Crisis: What Happened and Why?—A Primer." Columbus, OH: The Kirwan Institute for the Study of Race and Ethnicity at the Ohio State University, December, 2008.

Schwartz, Alex. "Bank Lending to Minority and Low-Income Households and Neigh-
    borhoods: Do Community Reinvestment Agreements Make a Difference?" *Journal
    of Urban Affairs 20*(1998): 269–301.
Social Compact, Inc. "Los Angeles Neighborhood Market Drilldown: Catalyzing
    Business Investment in Inner-City Neighborhood." Washington DC: The Social
    Compact, Inc., October, 2008.
Swanstrom, Todd, Karen Chapple, and Dan Immergluck. "Regional Resilience in the
    Face of Foreclosures: Evidence from Six Metropolitan Areas." Berkeley, CA: The
    Berkeley Institute of Urban and Regional Development and the MacArthur Foun-
    dation Research Network on Building Resilient Regions, May 27, 2009.

NOTES

1. James H. Carr, "On the Subject of The Silent Depression: How are Minorities Faring in the Economic Downturn?" (Written testimony submitted to the
United States House of Representatives Committee on Oversight and Government
Reform, Washington DC: National Community Reinvestment Coalition, September 23, 2009), 2.

2. Carr, "On the Subject of the Silent Depression," 5.

3. Carr, "On the Subject of the Silent Depression," 37–38.

4. Christy Rogers, "Subprime Loans, Foreclosure, and the Credit Crisis: What
Happened and Why?—A Primer," (Columbus, Ohio: Kirwan Institute for the Study
of Race and Ethnicity at The Ohio State University, December, 2008), 4.

5. Manuel Pastor, Rhonda Ortiz, Jennifer Tran, Justin Scoggins, and Vanessa
Carter, "State of the Region: Growth, Equity and Inclusion in the Bay Area," (Los
Angeles, California: The USC Program for Environmental and Regional Equity,
December, 2008).

6. ACORN Fair Housing, "Foreclosure Exposure: A Study of Racial and Income
Disparities in Home Mortgage Lending in 172 American Cities," (ACORN Housing
Corporation, 2007), 2.

7. Matt Fellowes, "From Poverty, Opportunity: Putting the Market to Work for
Lower Income Families," (The Brookings Institution Metropolitan Policy Program,
2006).

8. Social Compact, Inc, "Los Angeles Neighborhood Market Drilldown: Catalyzing Business Investment in Inner-City Neighborhoods," (Washington DC: The Social
Compact, Inc., October 2008), 17.

9. Social Compact, "Los Angeles Neighborhood Market Drilldown," 8.

10. Dean Baker, "Democratizing the Federal Reserve," (Washington DC: Americans for Financial Reform, July, 2009).

11. Ira Goldstein and Dan Urevick-Ackelsberg, "Subprime Lending, Mortgage
Foreclosures and Race: How Far Have We Come and How Far Have We to Go?" (Paper commissioned for the Kirwan Institute for the Study of Race and Ethnicity at the
Ohio State University for its National Convening on Subprime Lending, Foreclosure
and Race, Columbus, Ohio, October 2–3, 2008).

12. Rogers, "Subprime Loans, Foreclosure, and the Credit Crisis," 8 drawing on Goldstein and Urevick–Ackelsberg, "Subprime Lending, Mortgage Foreclosures and Race: How Far Have We Come and How Far Have We to Go?"

13. Rodgers, "Subprime Loans, Foreclosure, and the Credit Crisis."

14. Matt Fellowes and Mia Mabanta, "Banking on Wealth: Banking Infrastructure and Its Wealth-Building Potential," (Washington DC: The Brookings Institution Metropolitan Policy Program, 2008), 25–26.

15. Rodgers, "Subprime Loans, Foreclosure, and the Credit Crisis," 6.

16. Peter Dreier, "The Future of Community Reinvestment: Challenges and Opportunities in a Changing Environment," *Journal of the American Planning Association* 69 (Autumn 2003): 342. Harvard University Joint Center for Housing Studies, "The 25th Anniversary of The Community Reinvestment Act: Access to Capital in an Evolving Financial Services System," (Cambridge, MA: Prepared for the Ford Foundation, 2002).

17. "Successes," National Training and Information Center, accessed November 10, 2009, http://www.ntic-us.org/index.php?option=com_content&task=view&id=8 8&Itemid=39 .

18. Alex Schwartz, "Bank Lending to Minority and Low-Income Households and Neighborhoods: Do Community Reinvestment Agreements Make a Difference?" *Journal of Urban Affairs* 20 (1998): 270.

19. Interview with Alan Fisher, Executive Director of the California Reinvestment Coalition. Conducted by Vanessa Carter (PERE) on December 1, 2009.

20. Manuel Pastor, Chris Benner, and Martha Matsuoka, *This Could be the Start of Something Big: How Social Movements for Regional Equity are Reshaping Metropolitan America*, (Ithaca, NY: Cornell University Press, 2009).

21. Pastor, Benner, and Matsuoka, *This Could be the Start of Something Big.*

22. Paraphrased from Pastor, Benner, Matsuoka, *This Could be the Start of Something Big*, 19.

23. As Peter Dreier puts it, "The number of nonprofit community development corporations (CDCs) expanded dramatically" because of the CRA. ... For the most part, protest groups shook the money tree, and CDCs collected the rewards." Peter Dreier, "The Future of Community Reinvestment," 345.

24. "Foreclosure Resources," NeighborWorks America, accessed October 21, 2010, http://nw.org/network/foreclosure/default.asp.

25. Pastor, Benner, and Matsuoka, *This Could be the Start of Something Big*, 41.

26. "Mission & History," Center for Responsible Lending, accessed February 6, 2010, http://www.responsiblelending.org/about-us/mission-history/.

27. Todd Swanstrom, Karen Chapple, and Dan Immergluck, "Regional Resilience in the Face of Foreclosures: Evidence from Six Metropolitan Areas," (Berkeley, CA: The Berkeley Institute of Urban and Regional Development and the MacArthur Foundation Research Network on Building Resilient Regions, May 27, 2009).

28. Todd Swanstrom, Karen Chapple, and Dan Immergluck, "Regional Resilience in the Face of Foreclosures: Evidence from Six Metropolitan Areas."

29. "National Day of Action Is Set for June 11 to Pressure Leaders to Accept Responsibility For Easing the Pain of the Economic Crisis," Reinvestment Works...The

Blog, National Community Reinvestment Coalition, March 13, 2009, http://www.ncrc.org/wordpress/?p=91.

30. "Fresno's Ethnic Press Learn About Predatory Lenders," California Reinvestment Coalition, accessed November 12, 2009, http://www.calreinvest.org/newsroom/fresnos-ethnic-press-learn-about-predatory-lenders.

31. Interview with Alan Fisher, Executive Director of the California Reinvestment Coalition. Conducted by Vanessa Carter (PERE) on December 1, 2009.

32. "5000 Converge on American Bankers Association Convention," Service Employees International Union, (Press Release, October 27, 2009, available at http://www.reuters.com/article/idUS202177+27–Oct-2009+PRN20091027).

33. "Showdown in America," Accessed February 6, 2010, http://showdowninamerica.org/.

34. There were also "echo events" put on throughout the nation: "AFR Joins National Mobilization for Financial Reform; Events Across the Country," Americans for Financial Reform, (Press Release, October 26, 2009, available at http://ourfinancialsecurity.org/2009/10/afr-joins-national-mobilization-for-financial-reform-events-across-country/).

35. Manuel Pastor and Rhonda Ortiz, "Making Change: How Social Movement Work and How to Support Them," (Los Angeles, CA: USC Program for Environmental and Regional Equity, 2009).

36. When the first draft of this paper was written, this information could be found at Americans for Fairness in Lending website, *Mission & History*, http://www.affil.org/about/backgrounder.php. Their re-direct page can now be found here: http://americansforfairnessinlending.wordpress.com/

37. When the first draft of this paper was written, this information could be found at The National Training and Information Center webpage, accessed February 6, 2010, http://www.ntic-us.org/index.php?option=com_content&task=view&id=88&Itemid=39. At the time of publication, this website was no longer active.

38. For a description of how the changing financial services industry resulted in the CRA having less influence, see Peter Dreier, "The Future of Community Reinvestment: Challenges and Opportunities in a Changing Environment," 349.

39. Jessica Garrison, "Valley residents make fighting foreclosures a community affair," *Los Angeles Times*, (December 8, 2008).

40. Todd Swanstrom, Karen Chapple, and Dan Immergluck, "Regional Resilience in the Face of Foreclosures: Evidence from Six Metropolitan Areas," 39.

41. Interview with Alan Fisher, Executive Director of the California Reinvestment Coalition. Conducted by Vanessa Carter (PERE) on December 1, 2009.

42. Rodgers, "Subprime Loans, Foreclosure, and the Credit Crisis."

43. When the first draft of this paper was written, this information could be found at "Community Meetings with the Federal Reserve," National Training and Information Center, accessed February 6, 2010, http://www.ntic-us.org/index.php?option=com_content&task=view&id=217&Itemid=1. At the time of publication, this website was no longer active.

44. HEPA provides a single point for families seeking advice related to foreclosures or legal counseling.

45. Todd Swanstrom, Karen Chapple, and Dan Immergluck, "Regional Resilience in the Face of Foreclosures: Evidence from Six Metropolitan Areas," 29–30.

46. Manuel Pastor and Rhonda Ortiz, "Making Change: How Social Movement Work and How to Support Them."

47. Comments at "The Future of Housing and Fair Credit Convening," Oakland, CA: PolicyLink and the Kirwan Institute, 18 December 2009.

48. For an example of this, see Joanna Lee and Jennifer Ito, "A Greener Future for Los Angeles: Principles to Ensure an Equitable Green Economy," (Los Angeles, CA: Strategic Concepts in Organizing and Policy Education (SCOPE), February, 2009, available at http://www.scopela.org/downloads/2009_SCOPE_A_Greener_Future.pdf).

Chapter Sixteen

The Housing and Credit Crisis Revisited

Looking Back and Moving Forward

john a. powell and Jason Reece

In September of 2008, we were in the final weeks of planning for our forth-coming national conference on credit, subprime lending, foreclosure and race at the Kirwan Institute for the Study of Race and Ethnicity at The Ohio State University. A major theme of our conference was to understand and identify the relationship between the growing foreclosures we were seeing in communities of color and global finance. In short, we wanted to understand how bad loans and vacant homes in poor urban communities like Cleveland, Ohio were caused by, and related to, changes within our financial system. More importantly, how does this relationship provide insight on helping these communities who were beginning to face significant challenges?

Despite our best efforts to understand this emerging issue, it was very challenging to identify research which made this connection visible. It was also difficult to garner much interest in a topic which was so complex and abstract. But, those last weeks in September 2008 changed everything as a dramatic series of events triggered a global economic crisis and further destabilized the housing market. On September 7, Fannie Mae and Freddie Mac (and the $5 trillion in debt securities backed by them) were placed under government conservatorship.[1] By September 15, Lehman Brothers had declared bankruptcy and Merrill Lynch was sold to Bank of America. Two days later, the US Federal Reserve had to lend $85 billion to avoid bankruptcy by AIG (American International Group). By the end of September, Wachovia and Washington Mutual were bought off by Citigroup and JP Morgan Chase, and the stock market dropped $1.2 trillion in value on September 29.[2] One day after closing our conference, on October 3, President Bush signed TARP, effectively bailing out major Wall Street financial institutions with more than $700 billion in federal funds.[3]

The culmination of events in 2008 represent a critical point in the history of fair housing and fair credit in the United States. Unfair lending practices and unsustainable loans have released a torrent of foreclosures across the nation, harming our neighborhoods, crippling our national housing market and weakening both the national and international economy.[4] Unequal access to fair housing, and more importantly fair credit, sits at the core of our current global economic crisis.[5] We not only have a dual housing market but also a dual credit market.[6] As we begin to pull back the layers of complexity around the housing and credit crisis, we see that the history of racial discrimination, redlining, a new global market with inadequate oversight and poor enforcement of existing housing laws all contributed to our current crisis. What is often not addressed in our evaluation of this crisis is why the overrepresentation of subprime or predatory loans (and foreclosures) occurred in black and Latino communities. When this is discussed, the popular yet inaccurate narrative is that those people took out loans they knew they could not afford, and banks were forced to loan to them because of the Community Reinvestment Act.[7] This inaccurate but popular narrative suggests that efforts to loan to these communities of color lie at the heart of our global crisis. This story or narrative is not just incomplete but is factually wrong; in fact, this narrative can lead to dangerous assumptions, which could undermine fair housing. The lesson likely learned from this story is not only to avoid making loans or investments in historically redlined communities, but to lock them out of the credit market more tightly.[8] These communities that were historically left out of the exploding new housing and credit market in the '40s, '50s and '60s may once again lose ground to the white community in terms of both home ownership and wealth, and be locked out of the housing market again as we recover from this recent crisis.

The tremendous damage inflicted on communities of color from this challenge represents a true crisis facing these communities and our nation. It also demonstrates the deep interconnection between these marginalized communities and our entire global system. But crisis represents more than just peril—it also represents a turning point, or "an unstable or crucial time or state of affairs in which a decisive change is impending."[9] The current housing crisis has already spurred perilous conditions and uncertainty, but also new actions and possibilities. In order to benefit from the opportunity, we must have an approach that understands the foreclosure issue as a credit issue and as a global economic issue.

The systemic relationship between global finance and fair housing concerns in communities of color revealed itself in a powerful way, as growing foreclosures eroded confidence in mortgage-backed securities and the financial entities holding these securities produced chaos on Wall Street and economic anxiety across our nation and abroad. The once elusive relationship between our financial industry and the proliferation of predatory subprime loans and foreclosures made in marginalized communities was suddenly very visible. What was once seen as a marginal issue by the media and in our national discourse was suddenly paramount, providing a vivid illustration of the systemic connectivity between predatory and unsustainable lending in communities of color, Wall Street, our national economy and the global economy. In light of the unraveling of the US economy and our housing sector, this transformative moment became a departure point for our work, kick-starting a long commitment by the Kirwan Institute to understand how credit and communities relate and how we can help those communities and families undermined by bad loans, sinking home values and foreclosures.

More than two years later we look back at the aftermath of the subprime crisis to review the lessons we have learned from this experience, and to look forward to the principles which should drive our policy, planning and civil rights or fair housing advocacy into the future. The rest of this chapter provides an assessment of the current housing and credit crisis through a racial-justice lens. The chapter explores how race was interwoven into the current crisis, and demonstrates the racialized impacts of the housing and credit crisis. We also explore some of the current challenges facing fair housing in our society, presenting concepts and models of reform to promote true integration with opportunity. Two years later, we are still struggling to both understand the subprime crisis and to effectively respond, especially in meeting the needs of our most vulnerable and marginalized communities caught up in the crisis. Although some progress has been made and Wall Street is stabilized and profitable again, the aftermath of this crisis is still resonating throughout America, from the vacant homes that pockmark entire neighborhoods to *underwater* homeowners struggling to maintain their prime mortgage in the aftermath of the recession. Despite progress, much work is to be done, and our policies, institutions and structural arrangements must still be remade to remedy this crisis and to assure solutions, which provide sustainable credit, sustainable housing and healthy communities.

FROM THE INNER CITY TO WALL STREET AND BEYOND: THE CREDIT CRISIS AND GLOBAL SYSTEMS OF MARGINALIZATION

The housing and credit crisis presents a difficult racial equity challenge for the traditional advocacy community to tackle. In our global economy, advocates are directly confronted by a true systemic global challenge, which produces disparate local outcomes. The media often represents this challenge as a case of Wall Street v. Main Street.[10] In reality, the global scope of this crisis stretches beyond Wall Street, touching financial centers and nations across the globe, from Europe to Asia.[11] The crisis does not represent just one or two bad actors, but a system that is poorly structured and inadequately regulated.[12] Our failure to understand this crisis as a systems breakdown, and not just an individual moral breakdown, is critical to understanding the challenges in existing policy reforms to stem the crisis. Do we assign blame to people or the system? Do we redesign policies to make people behave differently, or do we restructure the system to produce better outcomes?[13] Unfortunately, many efforts to understand and respond to this crisis ignore this global aspect of the challenge. We must not view this crisis as singular, but understand that in our ever more interconnected world and global economy, these systemic global challenges will continue to arise as societies and economies around the world become more tightly interwoven.

Securitization, Deregulation and the Credit Crisis

The origins of the housing and credit crisis extend well beyond the behavior of borrowers and lenders. The introduction of credit securitization (and an associated deregulation of financial services) was critical to the growth of the subprime industry and are at the root of the current credit crisis.[14] As described in Chapter 3 by Chris Peterson at the University of Utah Law School, securitization was critical to the development of modern capital markets:

> In recent years, Wall Street financiers opened up a new frontier of home mortgage lending to Americans of relatively modest means with minimal down payments and through exotic, untested financial products. Capital markets largely funded this new breed of aggressive subprime mortgage finance through "securitization"—the process of bundling assets, such as mortgage loans, into large pools and then reselling those assets as securities to investors. Financiers justified this new private "subprime" home mortgage market to leaders and to the American people with a promise of new opportunities for home ownership. Today, the course of events has proven this promise to be, at least for the time being, empty.[15]

The first use of securitization by Ginnie Mae and Freddie Mac provided a model which the private sector found enticing, with Bank of America and Salomon Brothers initiating the first mortgage backed securities in the late 1970s.[16] Additional congressional acts, such as the Secondary Mortgage Market Enhancement Act of 1984, encouraged the growth of the securitization by reducing legal barriers to mortgage securitization.[17] The Depository

Institutions Deregulation and Monetary Control Act of 1980 and Alternative Mortgage Transaction Parity Act helped set the stage for the growth of the subprime industry by easing restrictions on mortgage interest rates and preempting state regulations on non-traditional mortgages.[18] The growth of private sector mortgage securitization spread financial risk and created a new pool for global investment, further fueling the availability of subprime mortgages.[19]

With the expansion of the global economy and a growing pool of global investment capital, mortgage securities became a popular investment: private mortgage securities doubled between 1994 and 1998.[20] But the financial industry needed new markets to invest in and needed continued mortgage loan growth to support the global demand for mortgage securities.[21] Subprime loans and other non-traditional mortgages extended loans under unusual terms to many new borrowers, who may not have qualified for traditional mortgages. As the subprime market flourished, lenders and brokers became less risk adverse and reckless, with more and more borrowers directed toward subprime products.[22] They were also able to shift more risk to the borrower.[23] Because many of these loans were held for short periods of time, lenders were less concerned about their worthiness. Brokers were incentivized to generate as many loans as possible as their commission was dependent on the number of loans they originated and not long-term loan performance. As a result of these complex changes in the regulatory environment and global financial markets, the mortgage industry changed. Lenders were bundling and selling loans and were not as concerned with the long-term sustainability of the loan. As explained by Kevin Phillips:

> They (mortgage backed securities) were sectoral growth hormones as well as profit makers. Instead of being kept on firm ledgers, mortgage loans could be stripped of risk by derivative contract, or in most circumstances sold off in a mortgage backed security or structured CDO (Collateralized Debt Obligation). The money received could be used for another loan or mortgage, then again— and again. Lending limitations became non-limitations. However, as volume swelled, loan and mortgage making standards dropped. Enticements to sign up marginal borrowers—through the 'exotic' forms of mortgages little used before—took on an ever larger role.[24]

With risk spread throughout various mortgage securities, unsustainable loan originations became a powerful profit-generating mechanism in the industry.[25] Brokers responded to the "yield spread premium" they were awarded for issuing subprime loans, further incentivizing the growth of the subprime market.[26] Unfortunately, regulatory systems did not necessarily adjust to the changing marketplace. But as the amount of credit in the world grew, it continued to search out new markets. The most undeveloped housing markets in the United States were in the black and Latino communities, markets that were still experiencing the effects of redlining—reverberations from policies in place decades before.[27] The securitization of the mortgage market created a constant desire for new loan originations, pushing bankers and brokers to make more loans and originate loans faster.[28] The subprime and Alt-A market became the ideal product targeted to untapped lending markets.[29] The subprime market grew from $150 billion in 1998 to more than $625 billion by 2005.[30] Similar growth was seen in the Alt-A loan market, which grew by 660% in five years, from $60 billion in 2001 to $400 billion in 2006.[31]

Many communities of color provided the untapped markets for these subprime loans.[32] Lender behavior grew more reckless, with a surge in hybrid option ARM subprime loans making up 80% of the subprime market in 2005 and 2006.[33] There was an assumption that housing prices could continue to rise.[34] Even if an individual could not pay, the underlying value of the property would protect the investor and the investment pool. This was not just an assumption by lenders; it was also shared by Alan Greenspan.[35] As new institutions and brokers got into the housing credit market, there were few regulations in these uncharted waters.[36] There were a number of wrong assumptions. One was that the market would regulate itself.[37] Another was that there would not be a housing bubble nationwide.[38] We were using the equity and growth in housing, in part, to make up for the stagnant wage structure that existed since 1973.[39] Inevitably, risky loans began to go into default. Foreclosure growth choked the housing market, suppressed home values, devalued securities and set off shock waves throughout the national and global economies.[40] The systemic and reinforcing nature of this widening crisis was described by the think tank Demos in their report, *Beyond the Mortgage Meltdown*:

> As prices fall, household wealth erodes, consumers spend less, businesses cut back, jobs disappear, and still more people have trouble making mortgage payments. These are the pathways that led from last year's mortgage crisis to this year's looming recession. They could be carrying us toward something bigger than a recession: a mutually reinforcing downward spiral in the housing market and broader economy.[41]

Their 2008 prediction was proven correct, and in the fall of that year there was an escalating spiral of economic disruption.[42] The foreclosure crisis decimated the perceived wealth in the market's mortgage backed securities, exposing the financial risk and poor health of some of our major financial institutions. Trillions in wealth evaporated on Wall Street and some of the oldest and largest corporations in the world have faced bankruptcy (or currently teeter on insolvency).[43] As the economic consequences of this phenomenon grows, diminished home prices and job losses will encourage more foreclosures, fueling and feeding the systemic crisis already underway.[44]

This crisis clearly exposes the delicate and interconnected systems that dominate our twenty-first century global society: systems that, for better or for worse, link the fate of all communities, nations and people. Analyzing these systemic connections can help us understand how poor lending practices in places like East Cleveland can be fueled by the behavior of financial titans on Wall Street and conversely, where escalating foreclosures in the inner city can wreak havoc on the entire US and global economies. We live in a new age, which requires a new way of thinking, a new paradigm for understanding that we impact the rest of the world and the world impacts us.

Global Systems of Marginalization and an Advocacy Response

When systems fail, marginalized communities bear the brunt of this failure. Often, as global systems change or are reordered, marginalized communities bear the burden of this change, while the benefits accrue to the elite.[45] As global commerce has expanded and systems around the globe have changed, inequality has grown, primarily in nations with poor social safety nets, poor social norms and policies that do not support full societal membership.[46] Just as the globalization of industry has spurred the growth of sweatshops in the Global South, the growth of the credit and financial crisis disproportionately burdened our marginalized communities in the United States. Larger systemic challenges facing our society are often first evident in marginalized communities or among marginalized populations. This phenomenon is described in the *Miner's Canary* by Lani Guiner and Gerald Torrez.[47] If we would only address these systemic challenges early, we would prevent them from expanding to our friends and neighbors. True fair housing, integration with opportunity and sustainable and fair credit practices would have helped us avoid much of the global consequences of the housing and credit crisis. In responding to these systemic challenges, we must focus our energies on these communities most impacted by the crisis, the communities that are disproportionately burdened by systemic discrimination or "structural racialization."[48]

The current housing and credit crisis presents a powerful case study of how systems can produce disparate outcomes for marginalized communities. Fair housing advocates are at the forefront of dealing with this crisis, but many are at a loss when attempting to understand how to intervene in the complex global dynamics that created the crisis. Actions in Congress, on Wall Street and in global financial centers around the globe resulted in discriminatory lending behaviors, vacant properties and community distress in our backyards. Although this systemic crisis presents an unusual challenge for traditional fair housing advocates, we must not shrink away from the challenge just because of its systemic complexity and global reach.

Our communities are part of the global system and vulnerable to a new set of challenges that are dynamic and interactive. We argue that these systemic challenges will become more frequent in the future, especially as our global world becomes more interconnected. The broader social justice community must be prepared to learn how to effectively intervene into these new global systemic challenges. Be it foreclosures created by the credit crisis, job losses due to globalization or another challenge like climate change, advocates must assure that marginalized communities are actively involved in designing solutions to these challenges. In the case of the housing and credit crisis, as fair housing advocates we must not only be at the table, but at the forefront as we redesign critical housing and credit systems and institutions (such as Fannie Mae and Freddie Mac).

THE RACIAL FOOTPRINT OF THE CREDIT CRISIS

There is clear and irrefutable evidence that in the case of the housing and credit crisis, communities of color were disproportionately burdened by the crisis. Race is a critical and salient lens to understand the current credit crisis, and the current crisis is a significant lens to view the overall state of fair housing for communities of color. What is less clear is *why*. Conservatives might argue that it is because the Community Reinvestment Act (CRA) caused banks to make bad loans to irresponsible people.[49] While there certainly were many bad loans, they were not caused by the CRA, but more the result of the new global credit market and the lending frenzy it was creating. Liberals are more likely to see discrimination against communities of color as the reason for the high foreclosure race in these communities.[50] While this may have been a factor, in some cases there was a less nefarious goal of lenders trying to tap an undercapitalized market.[51] This desire to extend credit to these undercapitalized markets was not only an appropriate goal then—it continues to be an appropriate goal *now*. What was missing in this extension of credit was an evaluation of the terms. Credit needs to be extended to these historically credit-maligned communities, but the terms of credit need to be sustainable and fair. Instead of offering sustainable and fair credit, the pricing structure for dealing with risk in underserved communities was to create exploitative credit terms that set the borrower up for failure.

Race and the Credit Crisis: What the Evidence Finds

Across the nation, communities of color were heavily burdened by both discriminatory lending and foreclosures.[52] While some people should not have received a loan, many got the wrong type of loan and unsustainable terms. Nationally, estimates found that people of color were more than three times as likely to receive a subprime loan, and that approximately half of loans given to people of color were subprime.[53] Research by the Center for Responsible Lending found that 52% of home loans for African American families were subprime; these figures were 40% for Latino families and 22% for white families.[54] In 2005, Federal Reserve data found 55% of blacks who took out mortgages received subprime products, compared to 17% of whites and Asians.[55] Even after factoring out for financial differences between white and non-white borrowers, people of color were more than 30% more likely to receive a subprime loan.[56]

The footprint of these loans was not only racially disparate but also geographically disparate, with communities of color victim to significant concentrations of subprime and other non-traditional or predatory loan products.[57] Research by the US Federal Reserve from 2004 to 2006 found that communities with significant minority populations received large concentrations of subprime loans.[58] With a strong link between subprime or predatory loans and foreclosure, people of color and communities of color are being devastated by the rise in foreclosures.[59] Early in the foreclosure crisis, approximately one in ten black and Latino borrowers were affected by foreclosure, compared to less than one in twenty white borrowers.[60] Race and the credit crisis are tightly interwoven, with communities of color and people of color explicitly targeted by poor lending practices and most burdened by the escalating crisis.

Race and the Crisis: The Residual Impact of History and The Ghost of Redlining

Why were people of color and communities of color so disproportionately impacted by the crisis? To answer this question, we must look at both the current challenges facing communities of color and the residual impact of historical patterns of disinvestment and discrimination in these communities. Historically, communities of color were systematically denied credit through public and private policies.[61] The notorious FHA "redlining" maps of the 1930's illustrated government-sanctioned policy to rank racially mixed or segregated communities of color as hazardous investments and discourage financing for these communities. This publicly sanctioned disinvestment was followed by widespread private disinvestment and discrimination in these communities, producing a long-term era of undercapitalization for our nation's communities of color. This era of undercapitalization was followed by a period of capitalization through discriminatory lending products.[62] Jesus Hernandez, at the University of California-Davis, identifies three eras of undercapitalization inflicted on communities of color.[63] First, from 1930 to 1950, publicly sanctioned redlining and restrictive covenants undercapitalized communities of color and reinforced segregation.[64] In the second era, from 1950 to 1980, public policies such as urban renewal and the federal highway program drove white flight, decimating assets in communities of color.[65] Finally, in the post-1980 "reverse redlining" era, a string of discriminatory lending products were targeted into these historically undercapitalized and segregated communities.[66] Hernandez found a concentration of subprime and other high-cost loans in the traditionally redlined communities in California.[67] In the age of reverse redlining, credit discrimination shifted from outright denial to the emergence of a dual credit system.[68] This dual credit system offered products for the majority at prime rates, but provided credit to marginalized borrowers at excessively high interest rates and cost.[69]

After being starved of credit and investment for nearly half a century, predatory actors infiltrated these communities with a number of predatory services, from payday lenders to furniture rental stores, from "buy here, pay here" auto dealers to subprime loans. Residents of these segregated communities were more likely to be lower income or economically marginalized, placing them in a precarious financial position, extremely sensitive to sudden losses in income or unexpected expenses. Homeowners of color in these communities provided great targets for mortgage brokers.[70] These homeowners had some limited home equity but were lower-income; so lenders who aggressively marketed and promised cash back via refinancing provided an enticing offer for those concerned with other financial troubles. This phenomenon may help explain why half of all subprime loans were actually refinance loans.[71] Due to relatively low home ownership rates and little experience with mortgage lending, borrowers in these communities were less aware that they were being given unusual or high-cost loan terms.[72]

Given financial incentives for pushing lucrative subprime products, brokers exploited these vulnerabilities, using aggressive marketing in these communities to lure in new borrowers and then steer inexperienced borrowers into high-cost loan products. By the late years of the subprime loan era, lenders were steering nearly half of borrowers who qualified for prime credit into subprime products.[73] Historical undercapitalization created communities ripe for exploitation by unfair lending practices; subprime loans are just a more recent and extreme manifestation of discriminatory credit concentrated in vulnerable communities.[74]

In the end, a perfect storm of systemic barriers to opportunity produced widespread vulnerability in communities of color.[75] As lenders looked to expand the pool of borrowers to fuel the securitization fire that was overtaking Wall Street, these communities provided perfect targets for non-traditional and predatory lending products.[76] As a result, communities of color became both the most exploited population in respect to this crisis—the root of escalating foreclosures that eventually ensnared our entire housing market and economy.[77]

Why Is This Crisis so Damaging to Communities of Color?

Before the current housing and credit crisis, a number of fair housing challenges degraded access to opportunity for people of color.[78] The damage inflicted upon communities of color as a result of the credit and housing crisis will significantly frustrate fair housing goals and exacerbate many of these existing conditions. As we look toward the future of fair housing, we must not only take stock of the ongoing fair housing challenges that burdened communities of color prior to the crisis, but also assess the direct impacts of today's crisis on the fair housing challenges facing these communities in the future.

FAIR HOUSING CHALLENGES PRE-CREDIT CRISIS:

Heightened attention has been focused on the fair housing implications of credit, lending and foreclosure in light of the credit and housing crisis.[79] This additional energy and attention is needed, but fair housing scholars and advocates must continue to focus on the preexisting fair housing challenges plaguing communities of color. Broadly speaking, although there have been some victories and progress in the forty years after the enactment of the Fair Housing Act, our nation has still fallen far short of meeting the goal of true fair housing and integration with opportunity for people of color.[80] Minority suburbanization and the slow growth of minority homeownership rates must be placed in the context of persistent racial segregation, extremely racialized concentrated poverty, excessive housing cost burdens for people of color and increasing rates of school segregation.[81]

Consider that in 2000, nearly one in ten blacks living in the 100 largest metropolitan areas were living in high poverty neighborhoods.[82] Three out of four of the three million people living in concentrated poverty in 2000 were black or Latino.[83] The fact that more minorities can be found in the suburbs than the inner city has not lessened these numbers; in fact our suburbs are now home to more people in poverty than our central cities.[84] Research indicates that minorities who leave for the suburbs are more likely to be re-concentrated in distressed suburban communities.[85] Integration has become more challenging as our metropolitan areas are becoming more polarized, with middle-income neighborhoods on the decline.[86] Residential rates of segregation remain high, with dissimilarity index results for our nation's metropolitan areas remaining at .65, indicating that nearly two out of three white or black residents would need to relocate to produce integrated neighborhoods.[87] White dissimilarity rates have dropped faster in smaller, less diverse metropolitan areas; in our larger diverse metropolitan regions the decline has been at half the rate found in smaller less diverse areas.[88] Despite changes in our metropolitan landscape in the forty years since the enactment of the Fair Housing Act, residential segregation—most notably for African Americans—remains persistent, and true integration into communities of opportunity for most people of color remains an elusive goal.

A complex web of factors contributes to persistent denial of fair housing and integration with opportunity for communities of color. These dynamic, persistent and reinforcing challenges existed before the current credit and housing crisis and will continue to persist after the crisis. First, we must remember that the housing market serves people of color poorly; our market rarely builds and provides housing at prices that meet the income conditions found in the black and Latino community. Even before addressing the policy and personal contributors to denial of housing opportunity, we must be clear that our current housing system is failing most people of color.

Personal and institutional discrimination in the housing market continues.[89] Steering and "editorializing" by realtors reinforces patterns of residential segregation, while outright discrimination in the market has declined, but is still problematic.[90] But public policy with respect to housing, land use, zoning, development and education plays a profound role in upholding residential segregation and denial of housing opportunity for people of color.[91]

Although the days of explicitly sanctioned government housing discrimination are gone, a number of facially race neutral factors produce clear racially disparate and discriminatory outcomes for people of color.[92] Localism and exclusionary zoning (and similar land use policies) produce severe obstacles to the development of affordable and rental housing, which denies access to opportunity-rich communities for most people of color.[93]

In addition, land use policies and infrastructure policies that encourage suburban sprawl have heightened the opportunity divide facing inner city communities of color.[94] Court decisions that have limited the possibility of interregional school desegregation (focusing only on intercity desegregation) have contributed to the racial segregation in our metropolitan regions and encouraged white flight.[95]

Finally, subsidized housing (which in metropolitan areas disproportionately serves people of color) is largely concentrated in distressed and segregated neighborhoods.[96] Although the era of traditional public housing towers is ending, much of our nation's subsidized housing inventory in metropolitan areas is found in our central cities, usually in more segregated and higher poverty neighborhoods. In 2000, 75% of federally subsidized housing and

59% of Low Income Housing Tax Credit (LIHTC) units were located in central cities, while only 37% of the nation's population resides in central cities.[97] In 2000, the average metropolitan neighborhood had a poverty rate of 13%, while the average neighborhood with LIHTC units had a poverty rate of approximately 20%. For the average neighborhood with other types of subsidized housing, the poverty rate was 29%.[98]

NEW CHALLENGES POST-CREDIT CRISIS

The foreclosure crisis is expanding housing pressure on families of color, creating widespread financial hardship for homeowners of color and decimating many communities of color. Families immediately impacted by foreclosures face great economic hardship and dislocation, and must seek new housing in a tightening rental market.[99] Renters are also being unexpectedly displaced as inner city property investors are allowing properties to go into default.[100] The social fabric of neighborhoods is ripped apart when homeowners and renters are displaced and children are forced to relocate to new schools. Communities of color, many of which had faced a number of challenges already, such as high poverty, disinvestment or vacant properties prior to the foreclosure epidemic, are now facing extreme conditions. The foreclosure crisis is producing widespread vacant properties, which act like a toxin in the urban environment, poisoning the health of the entire community.[101] The growth in vacant properties is further dragging down property values, creating extensive blight and safety risks in communities of color, and in some cases spiraling stable neighborhoods into a permanent state of distress, as well as undermining entire cities.[102] For people of color and others living segregated in these neighborhoods, the crisis is creating widespread burdens, ensnaring all residents, even those who are not facing foreclosure.[103] The impact of living in one of these neighborhoods is cumulative and not adequately captured by just focusing on the number of homes in foreclosure; residents face a variety of challenges outside of housing, including education, economic health and public health.

Research also finds the crisis will have significant impacts on the racial wealth gap in the United States. In 2000, US Census Bureau studies found the disparity between assets held by white households and black households to exceed 900%, thus for every $1 held in assets for blacks, whites held $9 in assets.[104] Home equity is the primary source of assets and wealth for American households, therefore disparity in home equity is a significant contributor to the wealth gap.[105] Wealth is critical to advancement and stability in our society and a far more important indicator of financial well-being than income.[106]

Due to assets lost directly from foreclosure and the home equity losses from surrounding foreclosures, the wealth impacts of the crisis on people of color are predicted to be tremendous.[107] United for a Fair Economy's 2008 study on the wealth impacts of the crisis projected a net loss of nearly a quarter trillion dollars in assets for black and Latino homeowners.[108] In addition, research indicates that black and Latino borrowers are also draining their existing non-home-based assets (e.g. savings and retirement accounts) to avoid foreclosure.[109] This phenomenon, described as "asset stripping" is depleting the other assets held by borrowers of color, just before they lose their home equity via foreclosure.[110]

The foreclosure crisis also could bring about a new wave of redlining or substantially restricted credit for borrowers and communities of color.[111] As financial institutions attempt to stabilize and stem their exposure to future loss, credit will be more difficult to obtain.[112] People of color who have been directly impacted by foreclosure will find their credit permanently marred for years.[113] Their neighborhoods will continue to be locked in a credit system that does not serve them well and does not lead to effective participation in the larger credit market. Borrowers who have not been foreclosed upon will still face a restrictive lending environment. Borrowers of color seeking to refinance are also more likely to be impacted by declining home values and will be more prone to denial for refinance loans.[114] An increasingly tight and restrictive credit market will only further expand the denial of prime credit to borrowers and communities of color and create further impediments to fair housing.

MOVING FROM CRISIS TO OPPORTUNITY: LOOKING FORWARD

The dire fair housing challenges described in this book presents a serious problem for social justice advocates and for our nation. Housing and fair credit provide more than just shelter and resources in our society; housing and credit are transformational vehicles which can be critical pathways or bridges to opportunity. Fair housing provides the best mechanism to produce true integration into communities of opportunity. Access to good schools, stable and safe neighborhoods, productive employment opportunities and strong professional and social networks is dependent on living in or near neighborhoods that contain these assets. Therefore, civil rights advocates have rightly focused great attention on fair housing, the "last plank" of the civil rights movement as the "structural linchpin" of inequality, the critical intervention point to produce a more just and racially equitable society.[115]

Sustainable credit also is a transformative intervention, opening a number of opportunities such as wealth building or allowing investments in education or training. Sustainable credit can allow families to survive economic dislocation and provide a bridge to new opportunities, like a college education or a home in an opportunity-rich neighborhood. Because of the significance of both fair housing and sustainable credit, we must continue to push for the implementation of a true transformative vision of fair housing for our nation. We must not be discouraged by the new challenges created by the current housing and credit crisis; we must instead utilize this window of opportunity to advocate and implement a transformative vision of fair housing.

From Linear to Systems Oriented Solutions

In designing fair housing initiatives and policies, we must use new principles to guide our thinking. A new era of systemic social justice challenges requires a new approach and response, a new paradigm and way of thinking about our challenges. The root of the housing and credit crisis is a systemic challenge that requires a new method of analysis and calls for different types of solutions. Our traditional "Newtonian" perspective on causation, utilized a simple linear model of determining causes and identifying solutions.[116]

A systemic approach to understanding causation moves away from this linear approach, recognizing that causation is impacted by multiple factors or represents a system of interactions between various factors. Causation is reciprocal, mutual and cumulative. In understanding the fair housing problems created by the housing and credit crisis, these dynamics become quite clear. The elements that contributed to the crisis in communities of color were not just the result of one factor but also the result of multiple factors, involving borrowers, neighborhoods, lenders, the financial markets and others. These factors reinforced each other and worked together to produce disparate outcomes in communities of color. As Jeffrey Sachs notes in *The End of Poverty*, "economies are complex systems." Sachs calls systems thinking "clinical economics."[117]

To adequately intervene in these complex systems, we must fully understand them and design our responses with clear recognition of the systems' complex interactions. Our solutions should both provide comprehensive relief while looking for strategic intervention points within the system that would have the greatest impact. In the case of the foreclosure crisis, too many responses have not taken this "clinical" or systemic approach. For example, extensive efforts have been made to prevent foreclosure through mediation or "work outs," but these strategies will only be effective in a broad way if other factors in the system cooperate. So, if servicers are not coerced or mandated to be more involved in work outs or are non-responsive to homeowners seeking help, then public policy efforts to encourage work outs among borrowers will not be an effective transformative strategy to end the crisis.

Tailoring Solutions to be Sensitive to Situational Constraints

All communities and people are influenced by a set of situational constraints. For marginalized communities and populations, these situational constraints can be severe and create a tremendous impediment to opportunity. For example, borrowers in communities of color were far more vulnerable to subprime mortgage brokers than the general population; they had a number of situational constraints which enhanced their vulnerability to predatory lenders. Factors such as reduced financial literacy, heightened economic insecurity and community conditions created different vulnerabilities for these populations. Meanwhile, the lending system changed with rapid growth in new types of predatory loans and actors due to changes in the financial industry.

Our current protections to assure fair lending did not take all of these situational constraints or dynamic changes in the mortgage market into account. Policies which may have protected the majority population were very insufficient to protect marginalized communities who are situated differently and more vulnerable. As stated by Katz in *Our Lot*:

> In hindsight, the scheme was mind-blowingly naïve—a vestige of a more innocent time not long ago when it was possible to believe that the fixed income managers of Lehman Brothers and cashiers who couldn't even save for a down payment would both profit by doing business together—on terms set by one side, infinitely wealthier and more powerful than its partner.[118]

Our policies and initiatives to promote fair housing and fair credit must accept and be designed by these situational constraints. Fair housing solutions and norms must be sensitive to the hyper vulnerability of marginalized communities of color. The critical insight is this: treating people who are situated differently as if they were equally able to access the benefits of "universal" policies can in fact lead to greater inequities.

Being Goal-Oriented and Inclusive in Process

Systems are inherently dynamic and subject to change. For this reason, we cannot allow our fair housing efforts to be dominated by process. Instead, they should be goal-focused. In the case of the foreclosure crisis, we cannot allow ourselves the luxury of expecting the dynamics that produced the crisis to remain stagnant and unchanging. Housing in particular is a very dynamic system; housing prices, interest rates, credit and the economy all interact to influence the environment of the housing market. This has direct implication to fair housing. When market conditions are hot, policies such as inclusionary zoning would be a very successful strategy for expanding affordable housing opportunities in opportunity-rich areas, but when the housing market cools, builders are not building as much new housing, and inclusionary zoning suddenly becomes a less successful strategy. If we were goal-oriented in this scenario, we would alter our policy approach to focus on other means of providing affordable housing in those communities, such as targeting Section VIII vouchers.

Similar unexpected dynamic changes have already occurred as a result of this crisis. The tightened credit market has diminished the market value of the tax credit and has substantially limited the effectiveness of using Low Income Housing Tax Credits to build affordable housing.[119] The LIHTC program is the primary affordable housing production program in our nation. As production falls due to market dynamics, we must adjust our strategies or we will face an even greater shortage of affordable housing in the future.

In the case of the foreclosure crisis, we must be prepared to change course if system dynamics alter the factors causing foreclosure. For example, traditional assumptions are that unjust loan terms are the principal cause of foreclosure. As a result, many of our policy solutions are targeting modifying loan terms to resolve the crisis. But, given the housing and credit crisis' impact on economy and the recession, job losses or loss of income may become the primary factor causing foreclosure in the near future. In this scenario, policies and initiatives set up to alter loan terms would be insufficient to keep borrowers in their homes if most are entering foreclosure due to income loss via joblessness. Thus, we must remain flexible to change our strategies and approaches as the complexities of the system change. By maintaining a goal-oriented approach to fair housing and staying away from a process orientation, we can remain flexible enough to adapt to these changing conditions.

Inclusive Design Solutions for the Housing and Credit Markets

Finally, as we design new approaches to housing, credit and fair housing in the aftermath of this crisis, we must assure that marginalized communities, in particular communities of color that are most impacted by the crisis, are at the table and included in this redesign. We recommend creating a public/private commission that would look at what it would take to affirmatively address both the housing and credit needs of historically marginal communities. The goal should be not just to stem foreclosures or even end intentional discrimination, but to eliminate the dual housing and credit market and its negative effects.

As we remake the market and credit systems, we should be deliberate not to continue the previous models that used the majority population as a model to frame and design policies. Marginalized communities are differently situated and require more accessible, available, and inclusive credit instruments to be sustainable. We must embrace an approach and process that is inclusive at all stages, where marginalized people and communities have a direct voice in designing responses to fair housing challenges. In addition, there is a great need to develop, extend, and connect local community development capacity.

In short, everyone should have an opportunity to give voice to the future of their communities. This includes supporting efforts to improve the participation of marginalized groups in policy design, and improving data collection, monitoring and evaluation of local, state and federal programs. Also, this means identifying and lifting up—or bringing to scale—programs that are working to produce fair housing and credit options in marginalized communities. We cannot design systemic reforms that will produce fair credit, fair housing and a just society without deliberately projecting the voice of marginalized communities made vulnerable by the current institutional arrangements.

CONCLUSIONS

This turning point in our history will eventually yield new opportunities to address our nation's fair housing and credit challenges and our potential for advancing racial equity. For better or worse, our housing and credit system in the United States will be permanently altered and transformed. As housing advocates, scholars and researchers, we must ask if these changes will promote or suppress fair housing, racial justice and true integration with opportunity. The larger housing community must be at the forefront of these changes, affirmatively pushing to assure that the restructuring of housing finance and credit options benefits those communities of color most marginalized by our current structural and institutional arrangements.

The world, our credit market and our society continue to be dynamic and grow increasingly more interconnected every day. A number of complex global systems have emerged in the new global economy. These complex systems require a new framework to understand our fair housing challenges and to reach fair housing goals. This systemic era requires new ways of thinking, a new paradigm to identify the causes and solutions to inequity in our society. We must understand how systems (like the global credit market) can produce disparate impacts in our neighborhoods and communities. We must also understand how to identify systematic reforms to address problems and seek critical intervention points to produce transformative change.

As we look toward the future of fair housing, we should orient our work around two clear goals. First, we must end the dual credit system, which has further exploited and marginalized communities of color. This provision also means assuring that our response to ending the dual credit system does not exacerbate existing challenges by instituting another era of redlining for marginalized communities. We must assure that in the future, communities of color are brought into and have full (and equal) participation in the credit market. We must implement policies, credit products and tools that assure that communities of color are provided sustainable credit options. Second, we must continue to work to create a society where fair housing produces affordable housing in communities of opportunity. This opportunity-based approach to fair housing must be the fundamental premise guiding all of our fair housing and community development efforts. To have a just and sustainable nation and society, we must assure that fair housing opportunity is available to all.

NOTES

1. Duhigg, Charles, "Loan-Agency Woes Swell From a Trickle to a Torrent", the *New York Times*, Friday, July 11, 2008.

2. Twin, Alexandra, "Stocks Crushed: Approximately $1.2 trillion in market value is gone after the House rejects the $700 billion bank bailout plan. CnnMoney.com. September 29, 2008.

3. Bush signs $700 billion bailout bill, National Public Radio, October 3, 2008.4. *See* Chris Peterson, The Kirwan Inst. for the Study of Race and Ethnicity, Subprime Lending, Foreclosure and Race: An Introduction to the Role of Securitization in Residential Mortgage Finance 1 (2008), http://4909e99d35cada63e7f757471b7243be73e53e14.gripelements.com/pdfs/Peterson_Securitization_Primer.pdf.

5. Juliana Babassa, *Report: Minorities Hit by Foreclosures*, USA Today, Mar. 6, 2008, http://www.usatoday.com/money/economy/housing/2008–03–06–minority-foreclose_N.htm.

6. *See* Christy Rogers, The Kirwan Inst. for the Study of Race and Ethnicity, Subprime Loans, Foreclosure and the Credit Crisis: What Happened and Why?— A Primer 4 (2008), http://4909e99d35cada63e7f757471b7243be73e53e14.gripelements.com/publications/foreclosure_and_race_primer_dec_2008.pdf.

7. The Community Reinvestment Act of 1977, 12 U.S.C. § 2901 (2005), intended to meet the depository needs of the communities, including low and moderate income communities, in which they operated. The Federal Reserve Board, Community Reinvestment Act, http://www.federalreserve.gov/dcca/cra/ (last visited March 27, 2009).

8. Redlining is defined as "credit discrimination by a financial institution that refuses to make loans on properties in allegedly bad neighborhoods." Black's Law Dictionary 1283 (7th ed. 1999).

9. Merriam-Webster Online Dictionary, http://www.merriam-webster.com/dictionary/crisis (last visited Mar. 11, 2009).

10. *See* Nina Easton, *Main Street turns against Wall Street*, Fortune, Sept. 28, 2008, http://money.cnn.com/2008/09/26/news/economy/easton_backlash.fortune/index.htm; Mark Trumbull, *Credit crisis has Main Street watching Wall Street*, *Christian Science Monitor*, Aug. 13, 2007, http://www.csmonitor.com/2007/0813/p01s01–usec.html.

11. Beth Ann Bovino, *The Global Economy: Strong Headwinds for Europe and Asia, BusinessWeek*, Mar. 11, 2009, http://www.businessweek.com/investor/content/mar2009/pi20090310_612593.htm?campaign_id=rss_null.

12. Treisa Martin & Caitlin Watt, The Kirwan Inst. for the Study of Race & Ethnicity, Subprime Crisis: A Comprehensive Analysis from a Systems Thinking Perspective (2008), http://4909e99d35cada63e7f757471b7243be73e53e14.gripelements.com/publications/Subprime_Crisis_Analysis_From_Systems_Thinking_Perspective_Aug2008.pdf.

13. We are not asserting a mutually exclusive binary between people's moral behavior and the functioning of systems. But our popular narrative overly focuses on "bad actors"—either in minority communities or on Wall Street. This is a simplistic narrative that leads to a gross misunderstanding of the problem and solution. We have incentive structures that help shape action on the part of investors, but our current laws and regulations are designed for an antiquated two party system in the changing global credit market. We also have our discussion that action around the credit market is largely sealed off from a discussion of foreclosure and the needs of minority communities in the United States. These non-connected and individualistic policy responses will not be an effective approach to remedy a housing and credit system that is structured poorly.

14. *See* Christy Rogers, The Kirwan Inst. for the Study of Race and Ethnicity, Subprime Loans, Foreclosure and the Credit Crisis: What Happened and Why?—A Primer 4 (2008), http://4909e99d35cada63e7f757471b7243be73e53e14.gripelements.com/publications/foreclosure_and_race_primer_dec_2008.pdf.

15. Chris Peterson. *Subprime Lending, Foreclosure and Race: An Introduction to the Role of Securitization in Residential Mortgage Finance.* Paper Commissioned for the Kirwan Institute for the Study of Race & Ethnicity National Convening on Subprime Lending, Foreclosure and Race. (September 2008). Page 1. Available on-line at: http://4909e99d35cada63e7f757471b7243be73e53e14.gripelements.com/pdfs/Peterson_Securitization_Primer.pdf

16. Chris Peterson. *Subprime Lending, Foreclosure and Race: An Introduction to the Role of Securitization in Residential Mortgage Finance.* Paper Commissioned for the Kirwan Institute for the Study of Race & Ethnicity National Convening on Subprime Lending, Foreclosure and Race. (September 2008). Page 7. Available on-line at: http://4909e99d35cada63e7f757471b7243be73e53e14.gripelements.com/pdfs/Peterson_Securitization_Primer.pdf

17. Chris Peterson. *Subprime Lending, Foreclosure and Race: An Introduction to the Role of Securitization in Residential Mortgage Finance.* Paper Commissioned for the Kirwan Institute for the Study of Race & Ethnicity National Convening on Subprime Lending, Foreclosure and Race. (September 2008). Available on-line at: http://4909e99d35cada63e7f757471b7243be73e53e14.gripelements.com/pdfs/Peterson_Securitization_Primer.pdf

18. Treisa Martin and Caitlin Watt. *Subprime Crisis. A Comprehensive Analysis From a Systems Thinking Perspective.* The Kirwan Institute for the Study of Race & Ethnicity. The Ohio State University. August 2008. Available on-line at: htt p://4909e99d35cada63e7f757471b7243be73e53e14.gripelements.com/publications/ Subprime_Crisis_Analysis_From_Systems_Thinking_Perspective_Aug2008.pdf

19. Christy Rogers. *Subprime Loans, Foreclosure and the Credit Crisis: What Happened and Why? A Primer.* The Kirwan Institute for the Study of Race and Ethnicity. The Ohio State University. December 2008. Available on-line at: http://490 9e99d35cada63e7f757471b7243be73e53e14.gripelements.com/publications/foreclo sure_and_race_primer_dec_2008.pdf

20. Chris Peterson. *Subprime Lending, Foreclosure and Race: An Introduction to the Role of Securitization in Residential Mortgage Finance.* Paper Commissioned for the Kirwan Institute for the Study of Race & Ethnicity National Convening on Subprime Lending, Foreclosure and Race. (September 2008). Available on-line at: ht tp://4909e99d35cada63e7f757471b7243be73e53e14.gripelements.com/pdfs/Peterson_ Securitization_Primer.pdf

21. *See* Richard A. Oppel, Jr. & Patrick McGeehan, *Lenders Try to Fend Off Laws on Subprime Loans, N.Y. Times,* Apr. 4, 2001, at C1.

22. *See* Max Fraser, *The Housing Folds: The Housing Market and Irrational Exuberance,* The Nation, Nov. 25, 2008, http://www.thenation.com/doc/20081215/fraser; Associated Press, *Brokers, bankers play subprime blame game,* MSNBC, May 22, 2007, http://www.msnbc.msn.com/id/18804054/.

23. *See* Max Fraser, *The Housing Folds: The Housing Market and Irrational Exuberance, The Nation,* Nov. 25, 2008, http://www.thenation.com/doc/20081215/fraser; Associated Press, *Brokers, bankers play subprime blame game,* MSNBC, May 22, 2007, http://www.msnbc.msn.com/id/18804054/.

24. Kevin Phillips, Bad Money: Reckless, Finance, Failed Politics, and the Global Crisis of American Capitalism 104 (2008).

25. *See* David Olinger & Aldo Svaldi, *Examining the subprime-lending crisis,* the *Denver Post,* Dec. 2, 2007, http://www.denverpost.com/business/ci_7612850 ("182 billion or more in profit was shared by brokers, lenders and investment banks.").

26. James Lardner, Beyond the Mortgage Meltdown: Addressing the Current Crisis and Avoiding a Future Catastrophe 9 (2008), http:// www.demos.org/pubs/ housingpaper_6_24_08.pdf.

27. James Lardner, Beyond the Mortgage Meltdown: Addressing the Current Crisis and Avoiding a Future Catastrophe 9 (2008), http:// www.demos.org/pubs/housing paper_6_24_08.pdf.

28. *Id.* at 20.

29. Basically, Alt-A loans are considered riskier than A-paper, or "prime", and less risky than "subprime," the riskiest category.

30. Ira Goldstein & Dan Urevick-Ackelsberg, The Kirwan Inst. for the Study of Race and Ethnicity, Subprime Lending, Mortgage Foreclosures and Race: How Far Have we come and How Far Have we to go? 5 (2008), http://4909e99d35cada63e7f7 57471b7243be73e53e14.gripelements.com/pdfs/goldstein_trf_paper.pdf.

31. Ira Goldstein & Dan Urevick-Ackelsberg, The Kirwan Inst. for the Study of Race and Ethnicity, Subprime Lending, Mortgage Foreclosures and Race: How Far Have we come and How Far Have we to go? 5 (2008), http://4909e99d35cada63e7f7 57471b7243be73e53e14.gripelements.com/pdfs/goldstein_trf_paper.pdf.

32. Amaad Rivera et al., United for a Fair Economy, Foreclosed: State of the Dream 2008 (2008), http://www.faireconomy.org/files/StateOfDream_01_16_08_Web.pdf.

33. James Lardner, Beyond the Mortgage Meltdown: Addressing the Current Crisis and Avoiding a Future Catastrophe 9 (2008), http:// www.demos.org/pubs/housing paper_6_24_08.pdf.

34. *See* Bruce Bartlett, *Who Saw the Housing Bubble Coming?*, *Forbes*, Jan. 2, 2009, http://www.forbes.com/2008/12/31/housing-bubble-crash-oped-cx_bb_0102bartlett .html.

35. *See* Bruce Bartlett, *Who Saw the Housing Bubble Coming?*, *Forbes*, Jan. 2, 2009, http://www.forbes.com/2008/12/31/housing-bubble-crash-oped-cx_bb_0102bartlett .html.

36. *See* Anthony Faiola et al., *What Went Wrong*, the *Washington Post*, Oct. 15, 2008, http:// www.washingtonpost.com/wp-dyn/content/article/2008/10/14/AR2008101403343_ pf.html.

37. *See* Anthony Faiola et al., *What Went Wrong*, the *Washington Post*, Oct. 15, 2008, http://www.washingtonpost.com/wp-dyn/content/article/2008/10/14/ AR2008101403343_pf.html.

38. *See* Krishna Guha, *Greenspan alert on US house prices*, *Financial Times*, Sept. 16, 2007, http://www.ft.com/cms/s/0/31207860–647f-11dc-90ea-0000779fd2ac .html?nclick_check=1.

39. Jared Bernstein & Lawrence Mishel, Economic Policy Institute, Economy's Gains Fail to Reach Most Workers' Paychecks (2007), http://www.epi.org/publications/entry/bp195/. Real wage trends, after adjusting for inflation, have remained largely stagnant for low and high wage workers between 1973 and 2007; whereas the real wage trends for high wage workers during the same time has increased. *Id.*

40. Roger Altman, *The Great Crash, 2008: A Geopolitical Setback for the West*, *Foreign Affairs*, Jan./Feb. 2009, http://www.foreignaffairs.org/20090101faessay88101/ roger-c-altman/the-great-crash-2008.html.

41. Demos: A Network for Ideas and Action. *Beyond the Mortgage Meltdown: Addressing the Current Crisis and Avoiding a Future Catastrophe.* 2008. Page 3.

42. Alexandra Twin, *Another huge Dow loss,* CNNMoney.com, Oct. 15, 2008, http:// money.cnn.com/2008/10/15/markets/markets_newyork/index.htm; Les Christie, *U.S. homes lose $2 trillion in value in '08,* CNNMoney.com, Dec. 16, 2008, http://money. cnn.com/2008/12/15/real_e state/underwater_borrowers_near_12million/ index.htm.

43. Jonathan D. Glater, *Advantages of Corporate Bankruptcy is Dwindling*, *N.Y. Times*, Nov. 18, 2008, at B1; Jessica Dickler, *Personal Bankruptcies on the rise*, CNNMoney.com, http://money.cnn.com/2008/10/24/pf/bankruptcy_filings/ index. htm; Andrew Ross Sorkin, *Lehman Files for Bankruptcy, Merrill Is Sold*, N.Y. Times, Sept. 14, 2008, at A1; Katie Merx, *GM Grapples to avoid filing bankruptcy as cash vanishes*, Detroit Free Press, November 8, 2008 (West).

44. Pallavi Gogoi et al., *Bailout Plan: Foreclosure issue still a major hurdle*, USA *Today*, Feb. 2, 2009, http://www.usatoday.com/money/economy/2009-02-10-bailout-details_N.htm.

45. john a. powell & S.P. Udayakumar, Race, Poverty and Globalization, Poverty and Race, Poverty and Race Research Action Council (2000).

46. Paul Krugman, The Conscience of a Liberal 129 (2007); Paul Krugman, Op-Ed, *For Richer, N.Y. Times*, Oct. 20, 2002, § 6, at 62; Christopher Jencks, *Why Do So Many Jobs Pay So Badly?*, *in* Inequality Matters: The Growing Economic Divide in America and its Poisonous Consequences 129–131 (James Lardner & David A. Smith eds., 2005).

47. Lani Guinier & Gerald Torres, The Miner's Canary: Enlisting Race, Resisting Power, Transforming Democracy 12 (2003).

48. Structural racialization refers to the ways in which the joint operations of institutions produce racialized outcomes. john a. powell, Structural Racialization and Implicit Social Cognition (2008), http://74.125.95.132/search?q=cache:vL406C 8yV5cJ:4909e99d35cada63e7f757471b7243be73e53e14.gripelements.com/presenta-tions/2008_6_19_NLADA_Plenary_SR_and_IB.ppt+structural+racialization&cd=2 &hl=en&ct=clnk&gl=us&client=firefox-a.

49. *See* Ben S. Bernanke, Chairman, Federal Reserve System, The Community Reinvestment Act: Its Evolution and New Challenges, Speech at the Washington D.C. Community Affairs Research Conference (March 30, 2007).

50. Posting of Jeff Tone to The Liberal Curmudgeon Blog, Republicans Played Active Role in Subprime Loan Mess, http://www.theliberalcurmudgeon.com/2008/10/republicans-played-active-role-in.html (Oct. 12, 2008, 15:30 EST).

51. Amaad Rivera et. Al. *Foreclosed: State of the Dream 2008.* United for a Fair Economy. January 15, 2008. http://www.faireconomy.org/files/StateOf-Dream_01_16_08_Web.pdf

52. *See* James H. Carr, National Community Reinvestment Coalition, Responding to the Foreclosure Crisis, 18 Housing Policy Debate (2007).

53. Amaad Rivera et. Al. *Foreclosed: State of the Dream 2008.* United for a Fair Economy. January 15, 2008. http://www.faireconomy.org/files/StateOf-Dream_01_16_08_Web.pdf

54. Center for Responsible Lending, A Snapshot of the Subprime Market 2 (2007), http://www.responsiblelending.org/pdfs/snapshot-of-the-subprime-market.pdf.

55. Sue Kirchoff & Judy Keen, *Minorities hit hard by rising cost of subprime loans*, USA *Today*, Apr. 25, 2007, http://www.usatoday.com/money/economy/hous-ing/2007–04–25–subprime-minorities-usat_N.htm.

56. Debbie Gruenstein Bocian, Keith S. Ernst & Wei Li, Center for Responsible Lending, Unfair Lending: The Effect of Race and Ethnicity on the Price of Subprime Mortgages 3 (2006), http://www.responsiblelending.org/pdfs/rr011–Unfair_Lend-ing-0506.pdf.

57. Rick Cohen, The Kirwan Instit. For the Study of Race and Ethnicity, Nat'l Convening on Subprime Lending, Foreclosure and Race, A Structural Racism Lens on Subprime Foreclosures and Vacant Properties 4 (2008).

58. Ira Goldstein and Dan Urevick-Ackelsberg, *Subprime Lending, Mortgage Foreclosures and Race: How Far Have we come and How Far Have we to go?* The Reinvestment Fund, Paper Commissioned for the Kirwan Institute for the Study of

Race & Ethnicity National Convening on Subprime Lending, Foreclosure and Race. (September 2008).

59. Demos: A Network for Ideas and Action. *Beyond the Mortgage Meltdown: Addressing the Current Crisis and Avoiding a Future Catastrophe.* 2008.

60. Ellen Schloemer et al., Ctr. For Responsible Lending, Losing Ground: Foreclosures in the Subprime Market and Their Cost to Homeowners 23 (2006), http://www.responsiblelending.org/pdfs/foreclosure-paper-report-2–17.pdf.

61. Gregory D. Squires, Capital and Communities in Black and White: The Intersection of Race, Class, and Uneven Development 52 (1994).

62. Gregory D. Squires, Capital and Communities in Black and White: The Intersection of Race, Class, and Uneven Development 52 (1994).

63. Jesus Hernandez, Written Testimony Submitted to the National Commission on Fair Housing and Equal Opportunity Connecting Segregation to Contemporary Housing Credit Practices and Foreclosures: A Case Study of Sacramento 4 (2008), http://www.prrac.org/projects/fair_housing_commission/los_angeles/hernandez.pdf.

64. Jesus Hernandez, Written Testimony Submitted to the National Commission on Fair Housing and Equal Opportunity Connecting Segregation to Contemporary Housing Credit Practices and Foreclosures: A Case Study of Sacramento 4 (2008), http://www.prrac.org/projects/fair_housing_commission/los_angeles/hernandez.pdf.

65. Jesus Hernandez, Written Testimony Submitted to the National Commission on Fair Housing and Equal Opportunity Connecting Segregation to Contemporary Housing Credit Practices and Foreclosures: A Case Study of Sacramento 4 (2008), http://www.prrac.org/projects/fair_housing_commission/los_angeles/hernandez.pdf.

66. *See id.* at 10–11; *see also* Gregory D. Squires, *Predatory Lending: Redlining in Reverse*, 139 Shelterforce Online, Jan./Feb. 2005, http://www.nhi.org/online/issues/139/redlining.html.

67. Jesus Hernandez, Written Testimony Submitted to the National Commission on Fair Housing and Equal Opportunity Connecting Segregation to Contemporary Housing Credit Practices and Foreclosures: A Case Study of Sacramento 4 (2008), http://www.prrac.org/projects/fair_housing_commission/los_angeles/hernandez.pdf.

68. Goliath.com, California Banks Continue to Fail African American and Latino Borrowers; Mortgage Lending Study Reveals Dual Credit System, http://goliath.ecnext.com/coms2/gi_0199–3339538/California-Banks-Continue-to-Fail.html#readmore (last visited April 6, 2009).

69. Goliath.com, California Banks Continue to Fail African American and Latino Borrowers; Mortgage Lending Study Reveals Dual Credit System, http://goliath.ecnext.com/coms2/gi_0199–3339538/California-Banks-Continue-to-Fail.html#readmore (last visited April 6, 2009).

70. Ira Goldstein and Dan Urevick-Ackelsberg, *Subprime Lending, Mortgage Foreclosures and Race: How Far Have we come and How Far Have we to go?* The Reinvestment Fund, Paper Commissioned for the Kirwan Institute for the Study of Race & Ethnicity National Convening on Subprime Lending, Foreclosure and Race. (September 2008).

71. Center for Responsible Lending, 14 Subprime Lending: A Net Drain on Homeownership (2007), http://www.responsiblelending.org/pdfs/Net-Drain-in-Home-Ownership.pdf.

72. Debbie Gruenstein Bocian, Keith S. Ernst & Wei Li, Center for Responsible Lending, Steered Wrong: Brokers, Borrowers, and Subprime Loans (2008), http://www.responsiblelending.org/pdfs/steered-wrong-brokers-borrowers-and-subprime-loans.pdf; *see also* Lardner, *supra* note 37.

73. Rick Brooks & Ruth Simon, *Subprime Debacle Traps Even Very Credit-Worthy*, *Wall Street Journal*, Dec. 3, 2007, at A1.

74. Richard Williams et al., *The Changing Face of Inequality in Home Mortgage Lending*, *in* 52 Social Problems 181–208 (2005).

75. Rick Brooks & Ruth Simon, *Subprime Debacle Traps Even Very Credit-Worthy*, *Wall Street Journal*, Dec. 3, 2007, at A1.

76. Richard Williams et al., *The Changing Face of Inequality in Home Mortgage Lending*, *in* 52 Social Problems 181–208 (2005).

77. Richard Williams et al., *The Changing Face of Inequality in Home Mortgage Lending*, *in* 52 Social Problems 181–208 (2005

78. *See* Jonathan Brown & Charles Bennington, Racial Redlining: A Study of Racial Discrimination by Banks and Mortgage Companies in the United States, GIS for Equitable and Sustainable Communities (1993), http://public-gis.org/reports/redindex.html.

79. john a. powell, *Reflections on the Past, Looking to the Future: The Fair Housing Act at 40*, 41 Ind.L. Rev.605 (2008).

80. john a. powell, *Reflections on the Past, Looking to the Future: The Fair Housing Act at 40*, 41 Ind.L. Rev.605 (2008).

81. john a. powell, *Race, Place and Opportunity*, 19 *Am. Prospect*, A21–23 (2008).

82. U.S. Census Bureau, Census 2000 Special Reports, *Areas with Concentrated Poverty: 1999* (July 2005),, www.census.gov/prod/2005pubs/censr-16.pdf (last visited Mar. 9, 2009).

83. Paul Jargowsky, *Studding Progress, Hidden Problems: The Dramatic Decline of Concentrated Poverty in the 1990's*, The Brookings Institution, (2003), http://www.brookings.edu/es/urban/publications/jargowskypoverty.htm.

84. Haya El Nasser, *Minorities Reshape Suburbs*, *USA Today*, Jul. 9, 2001,http://www.usatoday.com/news/nation/census/2001-07-09-burbs.htm.

85. Samantha Friedman & Emily Rosenbaum, *Does Suburban Residence Mean Better Neighborhood Conditions for All Households? Assessing the Influence of Nativity Status and Race/Ethnicity*, 36 Social Science Research 22–24 (2007); Myron Orfield & Thomas Luce, *Minority Suburbanization and Racial Change: Stable Integration, Neighborhood Transition, and the Need for Regional Approaches*, Report of Institute on Race and Poverty (presentation at the *Race and Regionalism Conference*, MN May 6–7, 2005); Monifa Thomas, *Suburbs no guarantee of opportunity: Affluent blacks leaving the city tend to cluster in just a few communities, but many offer limited economic benefits or access to good schools, jobs*, *Chicago Sun-Times*, Nov. 15, 2005, at 6.

86. George Galster, et al., *Where Did They Go? The Decline of Middle Income Neighborhoods in Metropolitan America*, The Brookings Institution.(2006), www. brookings.edu/reports/2006/06poverty-booza.aspx.

87. E. Glaeser & J. Vigdor, *Racial Segregation in the 2000 Census*, The Brookings Institution (2001), http://www.brookings.edu/dybdocroot/es/urban/census/glaeser.pdf.

88. John Logan, *Ethnic Diversity Grows: Neighborhood Integration Lags Behind*, Lewis Mumford Center for Comparative Urban and Regional Analysis (2001), http://mumford1.dyndns.org/cen2000/report.html.

89. *See* John Yinger, *Housing Discrimination Is Still Worth Worrying About,* 9 Housing Policy Debate 893–927 (1998); *see also* *The Crisis of Segregation: 2007 Fair Housing Trends Report*, National Fair Housing Alliance, Apr. 30, 2007, www. nationalfairhousing.org.

90. George Galster & Erin Godfrey, *By Words and Deeds: Racial Steering by Real Estate Agents in the US in 2000*, 71 J, Am. Planning Ass'n 251, 253 (2005).

91. *See* john a. powell, *Sprawl, Fragmentation, and the Persistence of Racial Inequality: Limiting Civil Rights by Fragmenting Space*, *in* Urban Sprawl: Causes, Consequences, and Policy Responses (Gegory Squires ed. 2002); john a. powell, *2002 Report of the Citizens' Commission on Civil Rights: Rights at Risk, Equality in an Age of Terrorism*, *in* Urban Fragmentation as a Barrier to Equal Opportunity (2002); George Galster, *Residential segregation in American cities: A contrary review*, 7 Population Research and Policy Review 93–112 (1988).

92. Menendian et al., *A Report to the U.N. Committee for the Elimination of Racial Discrimination on the occasion of its review of the Periodic Report of the United States of America* (Feb. 2008), http://www2.ohchr.org/english/bodies/cerd/docs/ngos/usa/USHRN2.doc.

93. *See* Pendall, Rolf, *Local Land Use Regulation and the Chain of Exclusion*, 66 J. Am. Planning Ass'n 125–42 (2000); *powell, 2002 Report of the Citizens' Commission on Civil Rights, supra* note 64.

94. john a. powell, *Achieving Racial Justice: What's Sprawl Got to Do with It?*, Poverty & Race Sept.-Oct. 1999, http://www.prrac.org/full_text.php?text_id=292&item_id=1841&newsletter_id=46&header=Search%20Results.

95. *See* Milliken v. Bradley, 418 U.S. 717 (1974).

96. *See* Florence W. Roisman, *Long Overdue: Desegregation Litigation and Next Steps to End Discrimination and Segregation in the Public Housing and Section 8 Existing Housing Programs*, Cityscape, 1999, http://www.huduser.org/periodicals/cityscape.html.

97. Lance Freeman, *Siting Affordable Housing: Location and Neighborhood Trends of Low Income Housing Tax Credit Developments in the 1990s*, The Brookings Institution (2004), http://www.brookings.edu/urban/pubs/20040405_Freeman.pdf.

98. Lance Freeman, *Siting Affordable Housing: Location and Neighborhood Trends of Low Income Housing Tax Credit Developments in the 1990s*, The Brookings Institution (2004), http://www.brookings.edu/urban/pubs/20040405_Freeman.pdf.

99. David Rothstein, *Collateral Damage: Renters in the Foreclosure Crisis*, Policy Matters Ohio,June 2008, http://www.policymattersohio.org/Collateral-Damage2008.htm; Danilo Pelletiere & Keith Wardip, *Renters and the Housing*

Credit Crisis, Poverty & Race July/Aug. 2008, https://www2398.ssldomain.com/nlihc/doc/Pelletiere-Wardrip-7–8–08PRRAC.pdf; Danilo Pelletiere, Renters in Foreclosure: Defining the Problem, Identifying Solutions, National Low Income Housing Coalition (2009), https://www2398.ssldomain.com/nlihc/doc/renters-in-foreclosure.pdf.

100. David Rothstein, *Collateral Damage: Renters in the Foreclosure Crisis*, Policy Matters Ohio,June 2008, http://www.policymattersohio.org/CollateralDamage2008.htm;

101. *See* David Kraut, *Hanging Out the No Vacancy Sign: Eliminating the Blight of Vacant Buildings from Urban Areas*, 74 N.Y.U. L. Rev. 1139 (1999).

102. *See* Scott Simon, *In Cleveland, Foreclosures Decimate Neighborhoods*, National Public Radio (May 24, 2008), http://www.npr.org/templates/story/story.php?storyId=90745303; Robert Gavin, *As Foreclosures Widen, a Neighborhood Erodes, Crisis Tests Many in North Lawrence*, The Boston Globe, Oct. 7, 2007, http://www.boston.com/realestate/news/articles/2007/10/07/as_foreclosures_widen_a_neighborhood_erodes/; Kraut, *supra* note 130; William Spelman, *Abandoned Buildings: Magnets for Crime?*, 21 J. Crim. Just. 481 (1993); R. Taylor & A. Harrell, Physical Environment and Crime, National Institute of Justice Research Report, Jan. 1996, http://www.ncjrs.gov/pdffiles/physenv.pdf.

103. David Kraut, *Hanging Out the No Vacancy Sign: Eliminating the Blight of Vacant Buildings from Urban Areas*, 74 N.Y.U. L. Rev. 1139 (1999).

104. U.S. Census Bureau, Household Economic Studes, Net Worth and Asset Ownership 1998–2000, http://www.censusbureau.biz/prod/2003pubs/p70–88.pdf (last visited Apr. 7, 2009).

105. U.S. Census Bureau, Household Economic Studes, Net Worth and Asset Ownership 1998–2000, http://www.censusbureau.biz/prod/2003pubs/p70–88.pdf (last visited Apr. 7, 2009).

106. *See* Dalton Conley, Being Black, Living in the Red: Race, Wealth, and Social Policy in America (Univ. of Cal. Press 1999); *see also* Melvin L. Oliver & Thomas M. Shapiro, Black Wealth/White Wealth : A New Perspective on Racial Inequality (Routledge 1995).

107. Ed Cutlip, *Subprime Crisis Causing Historic Wealth Loss for People of Color*, Media Mouse, Feb. 5, 2008, http://www.mediamouse.org/news/2008/02/subprime-crisis.php.

108. Amaad Rivera et. Al. *Foreclosed: State of the Dream 2008.* United for a Fair Economy. January 15, 2008. http://www.faireconomy.org/files/StateOf-Dream_01_16_08_Web.pdf

109. *See* Hannah Thomas, Brandeis University, Panel Presentation at the Kirwan Institute for the Study of Race and Ethnicity National Convening on Subprime Lending, Foreclosure and Race (Oct. 2, 2008) (transcript *available at* http://kirwaninstitute.org/events/archive/subprime-convening/agenda.php).

110. Hannah Thomas, Brandeis University, Panel Presentation at the Kirwan Institute for the Study of Race and Ethnicity National Convening on Subprime Lending, Foreclosure and Race (Oct. 2, 2008) (transcript *available at* http://kirwaninstitute.org/events/archive/subprime-convening/agenda.php).

111. To live in a marginal neighborhood segregated from opportunity negatively impacts all people including Whites living in such neighborhoods. The impact of this creates a negative incentive to live in such neighborhoods.

112. Valeria Fernandez, *Communities Foreclosed*, ColorLines, Jan./Feb. 2009, http://colorlines.com/article.php?ID=475.

113. *See* Vikas Bajaj & Ron Nixon, *For Minorities, Signs of Trouble in Foreclosures*, the *New York Times*, Feb. 22, 2006, http://query.nytimes.com/gst/fullpage.htm l?res=9505E7DD1E3EF931A15751C0A9609C8B63&sec=&spon=&pagewanted=all.

114. *See* Vikas Bajaj & Ron Nixon, *For Minorities, Signs of Trouble in Foreclosures*, the *New York Times*, Feb. 22, 2006, http://query.nytimes.com/gst/fullpage.htm l?res=9505E7DD1E3EF931A15751C0A9609C8B63&sec=&spon=&pagewanted=all.

115. Oliver & Shapiro, *supra* note 136; (referring to Lawrence Bobo, *Keeping the Linchpin in Place: Testing the Multiple Sources of Opposition to Residential Integration*, 2 Revue Internationale De Psychologie Sociale 305, 307 (1989)); Sheryl D. Cashin, The Failures of Integration: How Race and Class Are Undermining the American Dream 3 (2004) ("Housing was the last plank in the civil rights revolution, and it is the realm in which we have experienced the fewest integration gains.").

116. D.A. Freedman, Linear Statistical Models for Causation: A Critical Review 2 (2005), http://www.wiley.com/legacy/wileychi/eosbs/pdfs/bsa598.pdf.

117. Jeffrey Sachs, *Development Economics as Clinical Economics*, The Globalist, July 5, 2005, http://www.theglobalist.com/StoryId.aspx?StoryId=4602.

118. Katz, Allyssa. "Our Lot: How Real Estate Came to Own Us." Bloomsbury, USA. NY, NY. Page 213.

119. The Low-Income Housing Tax Credit (LIHTC) program is run by the IRS and allows companies to invest in low-income housing, while receiving ten years of tax credits. A. Siudzinski, *Field Guide to Low-Income Housing Tax Credits*, Realtor. org, http://www.realtor.org/library/library/fg720.

Reprinted with permission of *Cleveland State Law Review*, where an original version of this article appeared in 2009: john powell and Jason Reece, *The Future of Fair Housing and Fair Credit: From Crisis to Opportunity,"* Cleveland State Law Review, Volume 57, Number 2. (2009)

Index

Aames Home Loan, *171*

AARP (American Association of
  Retired Persons), 107

ABN AMRO Bank, *169, 172*

Accredited Home Lenders, *170, 171*

ACORN (Association of Community
  Organizations for Reform Now),
  330, 332

ADC (Anti-Discrimination Center),
  220

adjustable-rate mortgages (ARMs): lack
  of information and counseling about,
  100; likelihood of foreclosure, 208;
  liquidity risk, 30; as percentage of
  subprime market, 345

Administrative Procedure Act (APA) of
  1946, 270, 293n15

Aegis, *171*

affirmatively furthering fair housing
  (AFFH): Fannie and Freddie and,
  231, 235, 238–44, 270; importance
  of, 236–38; litigation regarding, 220;
  Neighborhood Stabilization Program
  and, 223, 225–27

Affordable Housing Trust Fund, 259

African Americans: first case where
  pattern or practice of racial
  discrimination in lending was
  charged, 119–20; foreclosures in

Baltimore, 133; foreclosures in
  Boston, *207, 215*; foreclosures in
  Massachusetts, 207; foreclosures in
  North Minneapolis, 168; foreclosures
  in Philadelphia, 129–30; foreclosures
  on households with children, 12;
  high-cost lending rates in Cleveland
  and Cuyahoga County, 151–52,
  152–54; home ownership versus that
  of whites, 241; HUD foreclosure
  and vacancy risk scores, 224, *224*;
  income and wealth inequality,
  352–53; interest rates, 99–100;
  likelihood of receiving higher rate
  subprime loans, 34–35, 99, 100, 122,
  179, 321, *322*, 348; loan rejection,
  120; loan rejection in Cleveland
  and Cuyahoga County, 148–51,
  149–50; loan rejection in North
  Minneapolis, 179; loan underwriting
  by Fannie and Freddie, 272–74,
  294n27; loss of ground in home
  ownership, 213; as payday lender
  customers, 11, 36; population decline
  in Cleveland, 141, *141*; poverty, 350;
  refinancing, 107, 122; segregation
  in Cleveland, *141–43*; subprime and
  manufactured housing loans to, 34,
  99–100; subprime loan delinquency

369

About the Authors

Vanessa Carter, Data Analyst, Program for Environmental and Regional Equity, University of Southern California, Los Angeles, California

Gail C. Christopher, DN, Vice President—Program Strategy, W.K. Kellogg Foundation, Battle Creek, Michigan

Rick Cohen, Freelance Writer; former Executive Director of the National Committee for Responsive Philanthropy, Washington DC

Deyanira Del Rio, Associate Director, Neighborhood Economic Development Advocacy Project, New York, New York

Jeffrey D. Dillman, Co-Director, Fair Housing Project, Legal Aid of North Carolina, Raleigh, North Carolina

Gary A. Dymski, Professor of Economics, University of California, Riverside, California

Ira Goldstein, Director, Policy Solutions, The Reinvestment Fund, Philadelphia, Pennsylvania

Kennen Gross, Senior Policy Analyst, Policy Solutions, The Reinvestment Fund, Philadelphia, Pennsylvania

Mark Ireland, Supervising Attorney, Foreclosure Relief Law Project, Saint Paul, Minnesota

Henry Korman, Co-Counsel, Klein Hornig LLP, Boston, Massachusetts

Jillian Olinger, Research Associate, Kirwan Institute for the Study of Race and Ethnicity, The Ohio State University, Columbus, Ohio

Rhonda Ortiz, Project Manager, Program for Environmental and Regional Equity, University of Southern California, Los Angeles, California

Manuel Pastor, Professor of American Studies and Ethnicity and Director of the Program for Environmental and Regional Equity, University of Southern California, Los Angeles, California

Christopher L. Peterson, Professor of Law, University of Utah, S.J. Quinney College of Law, Salt Lake City, Utah

john a. powell, Executive Director, Kirwan Institute for the Study of Race and Ethnicity; Gregory H. Williams Chair in Civil Rights & Civil Liberties, Moritz College of Law, The Ohio State University, Columbus, Ohio

Jason Reece, Senior Researcher, Kirwan Institute for the Study of Race and Ethnicity, The Ohio State University, Columbus, Ohio

Christy Rogers, Senior Researcher, Kirwan Institute for the Study of Race and Ethnicity, The Ohio State University, Columbus, Ohio

Thomas H. Stanton, Fellow, Center for the Study of American Government, Johns Hopkins University, Washington, DC

Hannah Thomas, Doctoral Candidate, Brandeis University, Waltham, Massachusetts

Dan Urevick-Ackelsberg, Staff Attorney, Community Legal Services of Philadelphia, Philadelphia, Pennsylvania

Mark A. Willis, Fellow, NYU Furman Center for Real Estate and Urban Policy, New York, New York